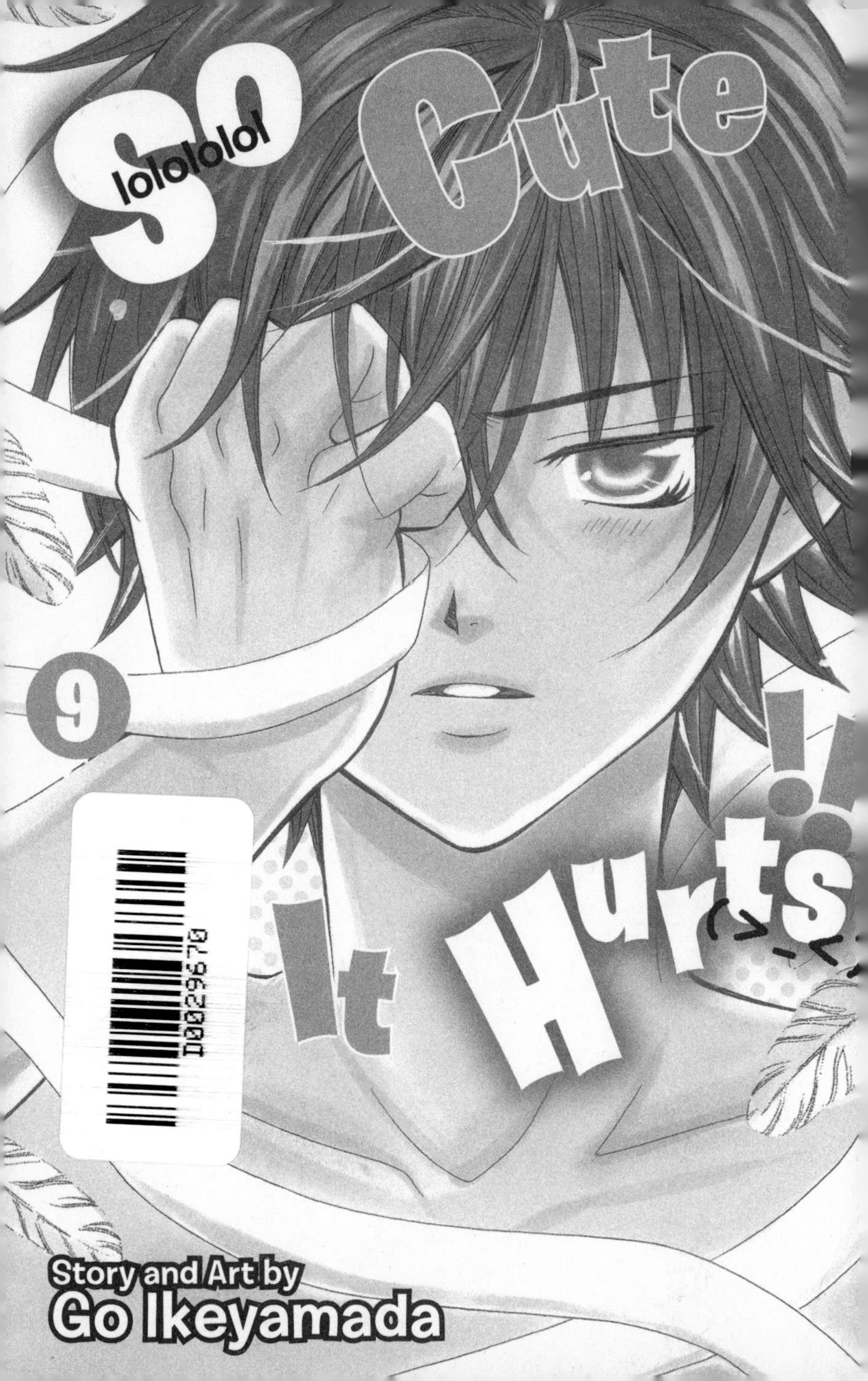

So
lolololol
Cute
It Hurts!!
(>_<)
9
Story and Art by
Go Ikeyamada

CHARACTERS

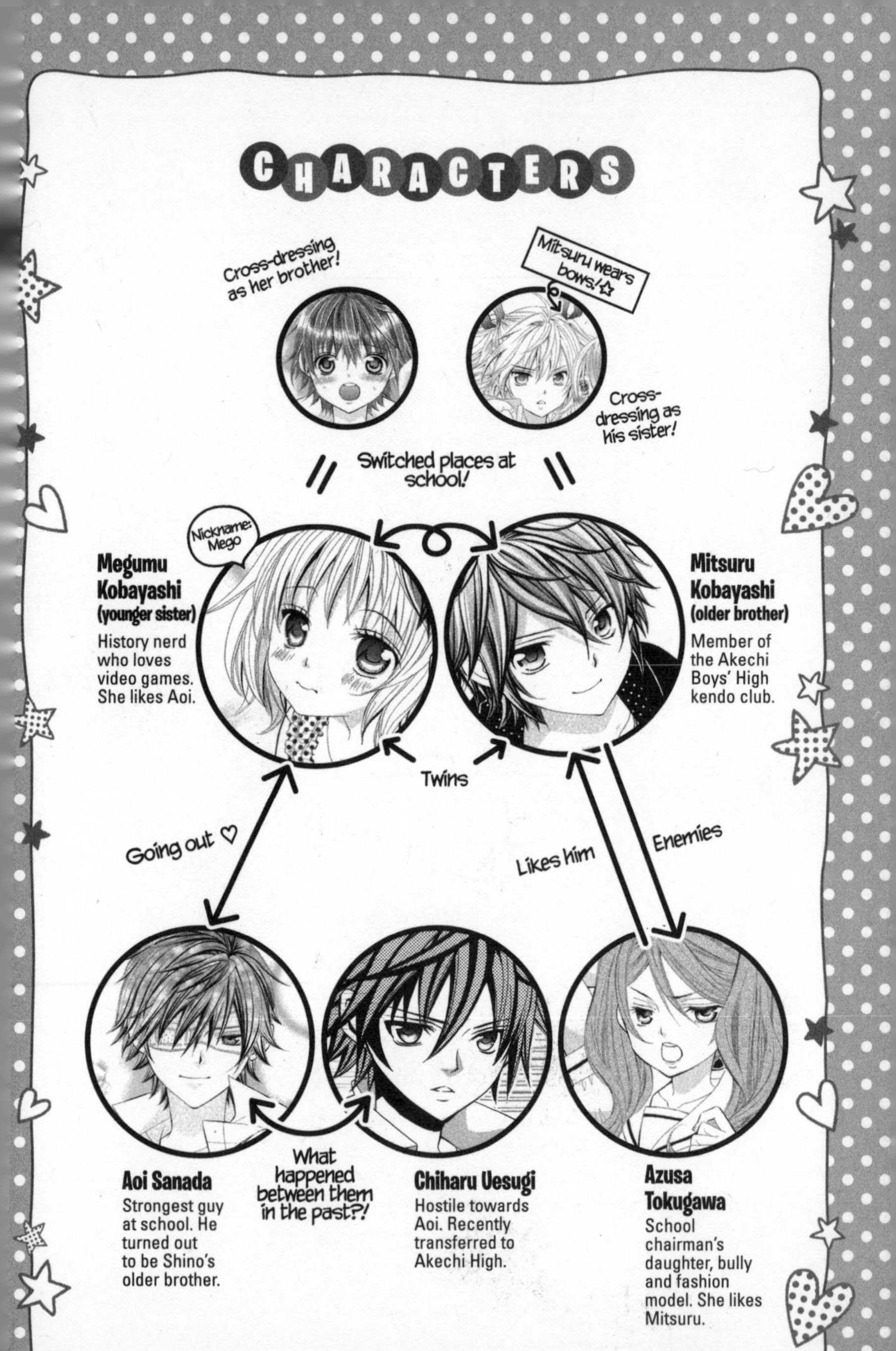
Cross-dressing as her brother!
Mitsuru wears bows!☆
Cross-dressing as his sister!
Switched places at school!
Nickname: Mego
Megumu Kobayashi (younger sister)
History nerd who loves video games. She likes Aoi.
Mitsuru Kobayashi (older brother)
Member of the Akechi Boys' High kendo club.
Twins
Going out ♡
Likes him
Enemies
What happened between them in the past?!
Aoi Sanada
Strongest guy at school. He turned out to be Shino's older brother.
Chiharu Uesugi
Hostile towards Aoi. Recently transferred to Akechi High.
Azusa Tokugawa
School chairman's daughter, bully and fashion model. She likes Mitsuru.

STORY

★ Mitsuru and Megumu are twins. One day they switch places and go to each other's school for a week! That's when Megumu falls in love with Aoi and Mitsuru falls in love with Shino. Azusa and Aoi both discover the twins' ruse but keep quiet for reasons of their own. When the week is over, Megumu declares her love for Aoi, and they start dating. They need to stay two feet apart because of Aoi's extreme discomfort around women, but they plan to work on it. Mitsuru is rejected by Shino, but Azusa starts to have feelings for him.

★ One day Mitsuru rescues Azusa when someone tries to attack her. Worried, Mitsuru swaps places with Megumu again so he can be Azusa's bodyguard. Meanwhile, a mysterious boy named Uesugi, who seems to hate Aoi, has transferred to Akechi High. He initially tries to take advantage of Megumu but ends up admiring her strength and courage.

★ Azusa decides to deal with her stalker by herself, but Mitsuru shows up and they defeat the stalkers together. When Azusa sees Mitsuru going all out for her, she confesses that she really likes him and kisses him!

★ Meanwhile, at Akechi High, Uesugi tells Aoi he's fallen in love with Megumu Kobayashi and that he'll make her his!

CONTENTS

So Cute It Hurts!! (⌐■_■)

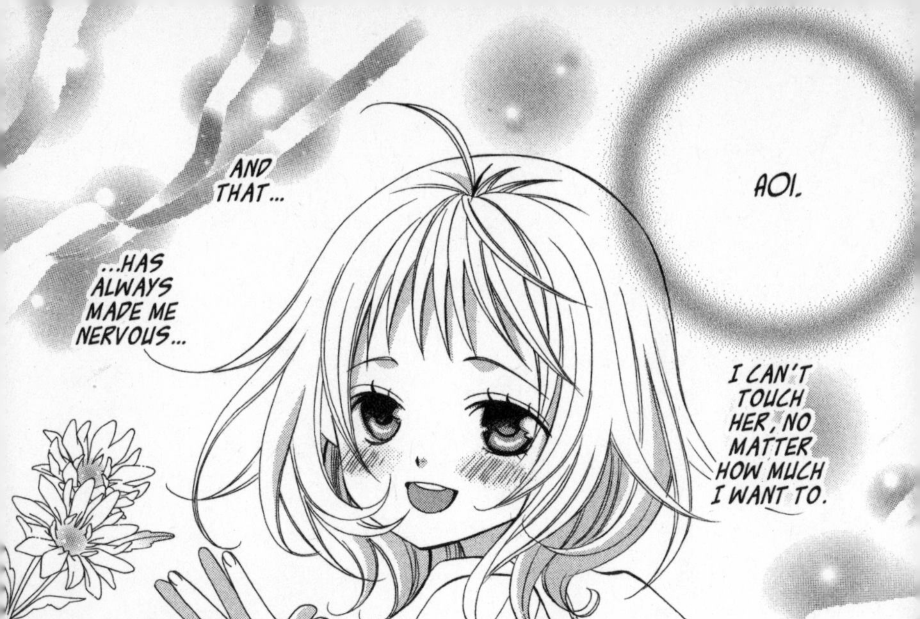
AOI.
I CAN'T TOUCH HER, NO MATTER HOW MUCH I WANT TO.
AND THAT...
...HAS ALWAYS MADE ME NERVOUS...
...BECAUSE I'VE KNOWN...
...A DAY LIKE THIS WOULD COME.
Chapter 41

HELLO. I'M GO IKEYAMADA. THANK YOU FOR PICKING UP MY 52ND BOOK!! THIS IS VOLUME 9 OF *SO CUTE IT HURTS!!* THE SECRET OF AOI'S EYE PATCH IS FINALLY REVEALED...! VOLUMES 9 AND 10 ARE THE CLIMAX OF THE SECOND STORY ARC, AND THE FINAL ARC OF *SO CUTE!* HAS ALREADY STARTED IN *SHO-COMI* MAGAZINE. I WILL DRAW EACH CHAPTER WITH ALL MY HEART. I'LL DO MY ABSOLUTE BEST IN 2015, SO PLEASE KEEP READING. ♡♡

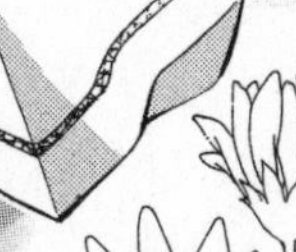
Merry Xmas &
HAPPY NEW YEAR♥

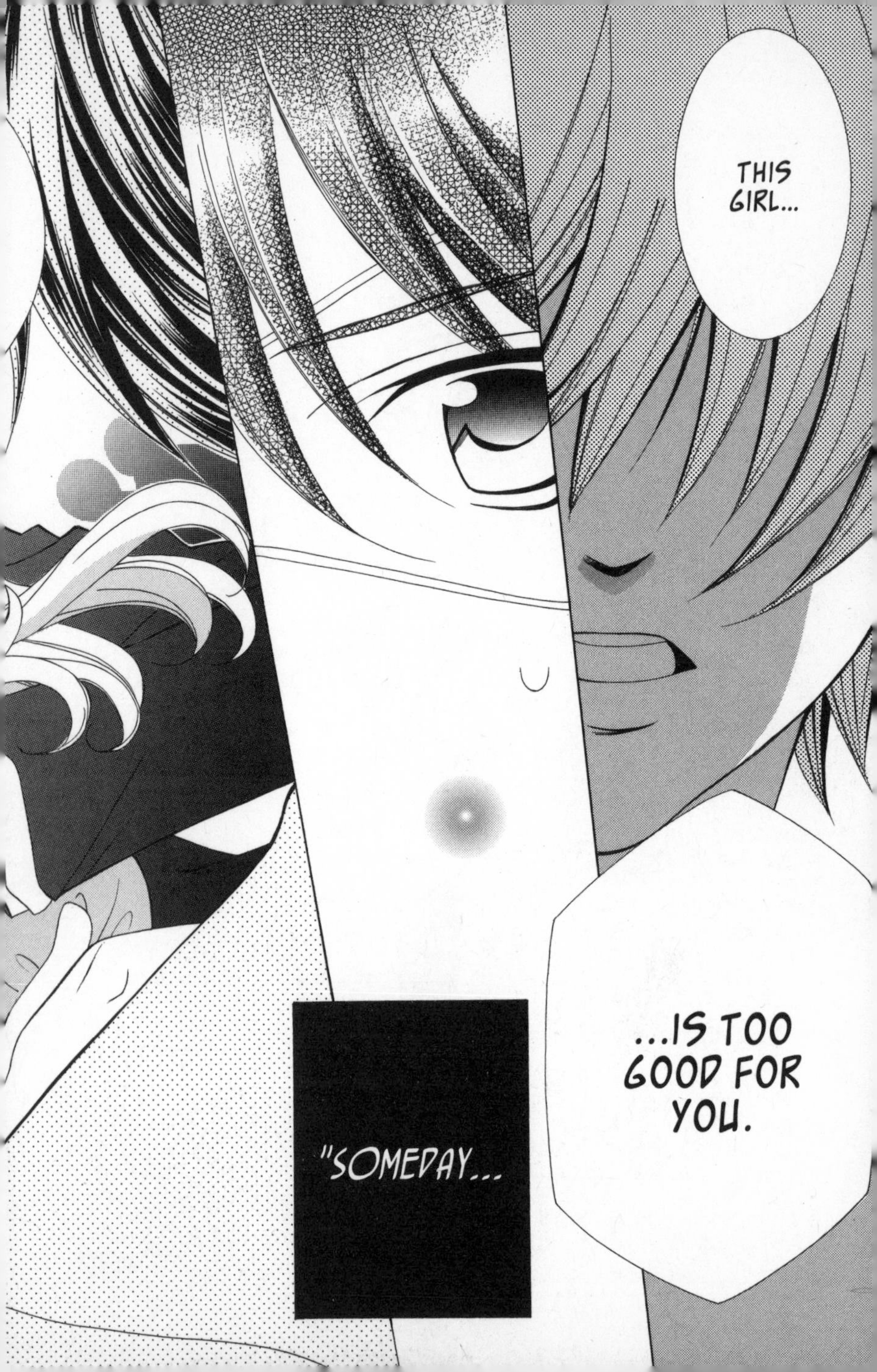
THIS GIRL...
...IS TOO GOOD FOR YOU.
"SOMEDAY...

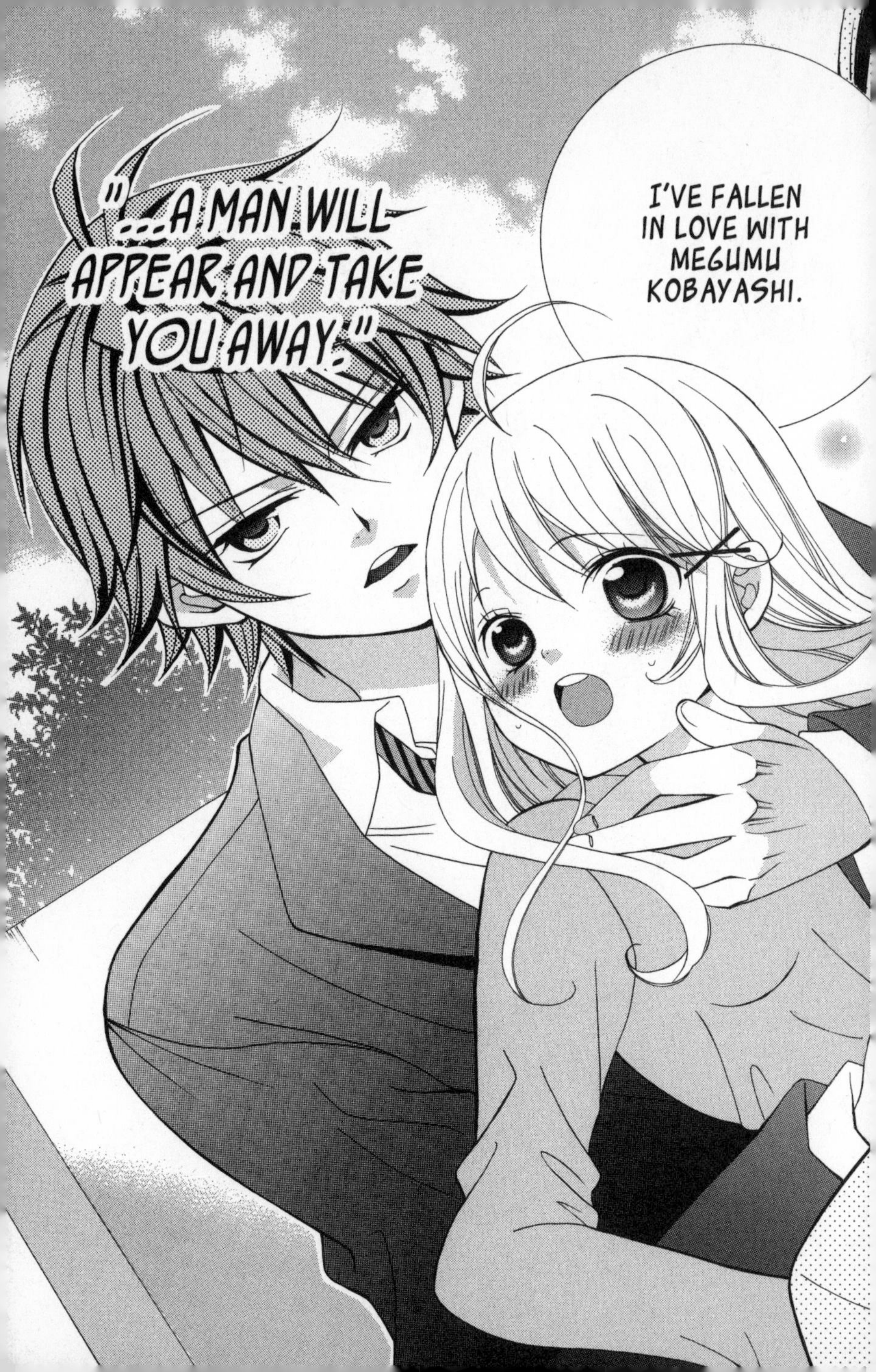
I'VE FALLEN IN LOVE WITH MEGUMU KOBAYASHI.
"...A MAN WILL APPEAR AND TAKE YOU AWAY."

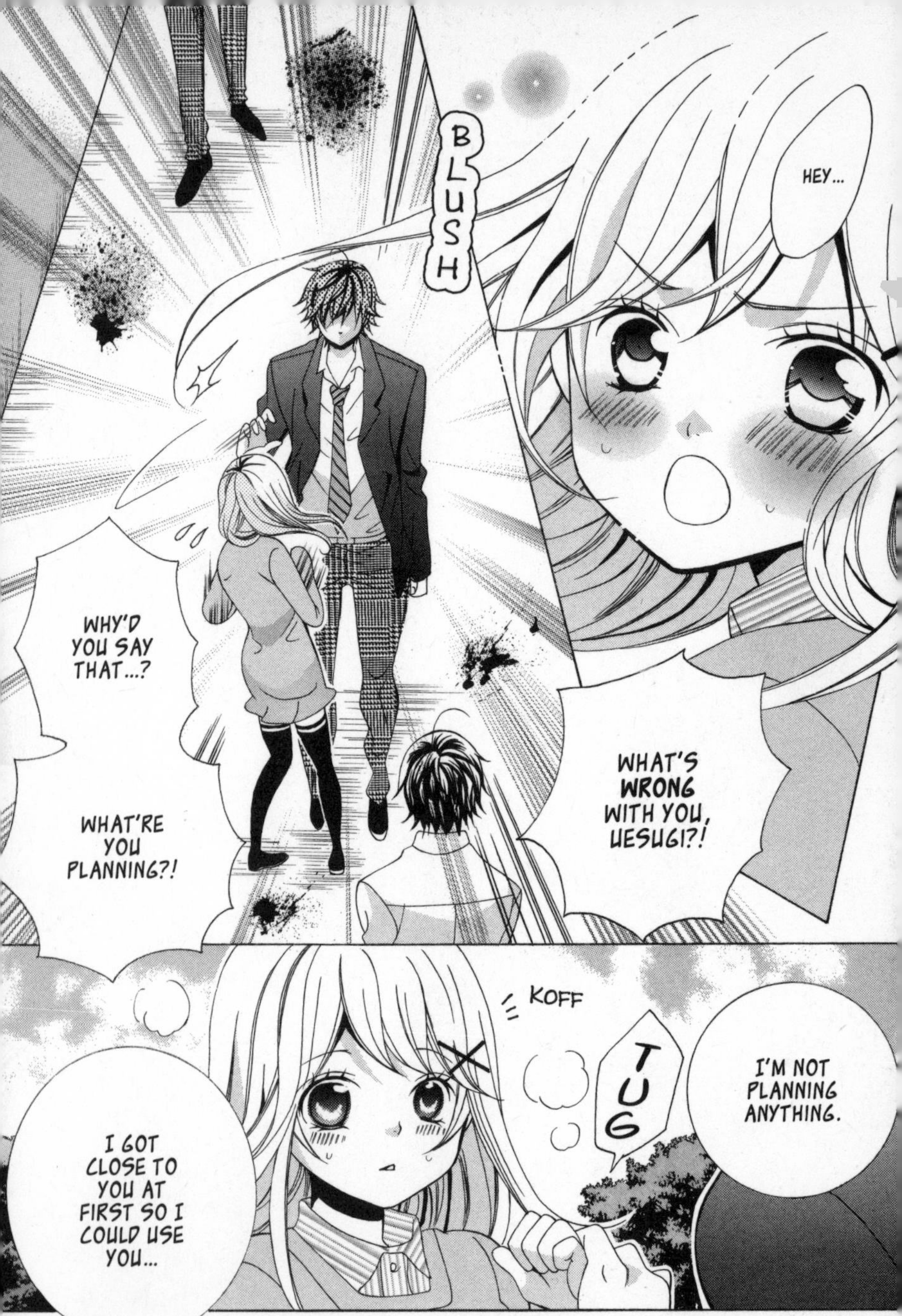
HEY...
WHAT'S WRONG WITH YOU, UESUGI?!
BLUSH
WHY'D YOU SAY THAT...?
WHAT'RE YOU PLANNING?!
I'M NOT PLANNING ANYTHING.
TUG
KOFF
I GOT CLOSE TO YOU AT FIRST SO I COULD USE YOU...

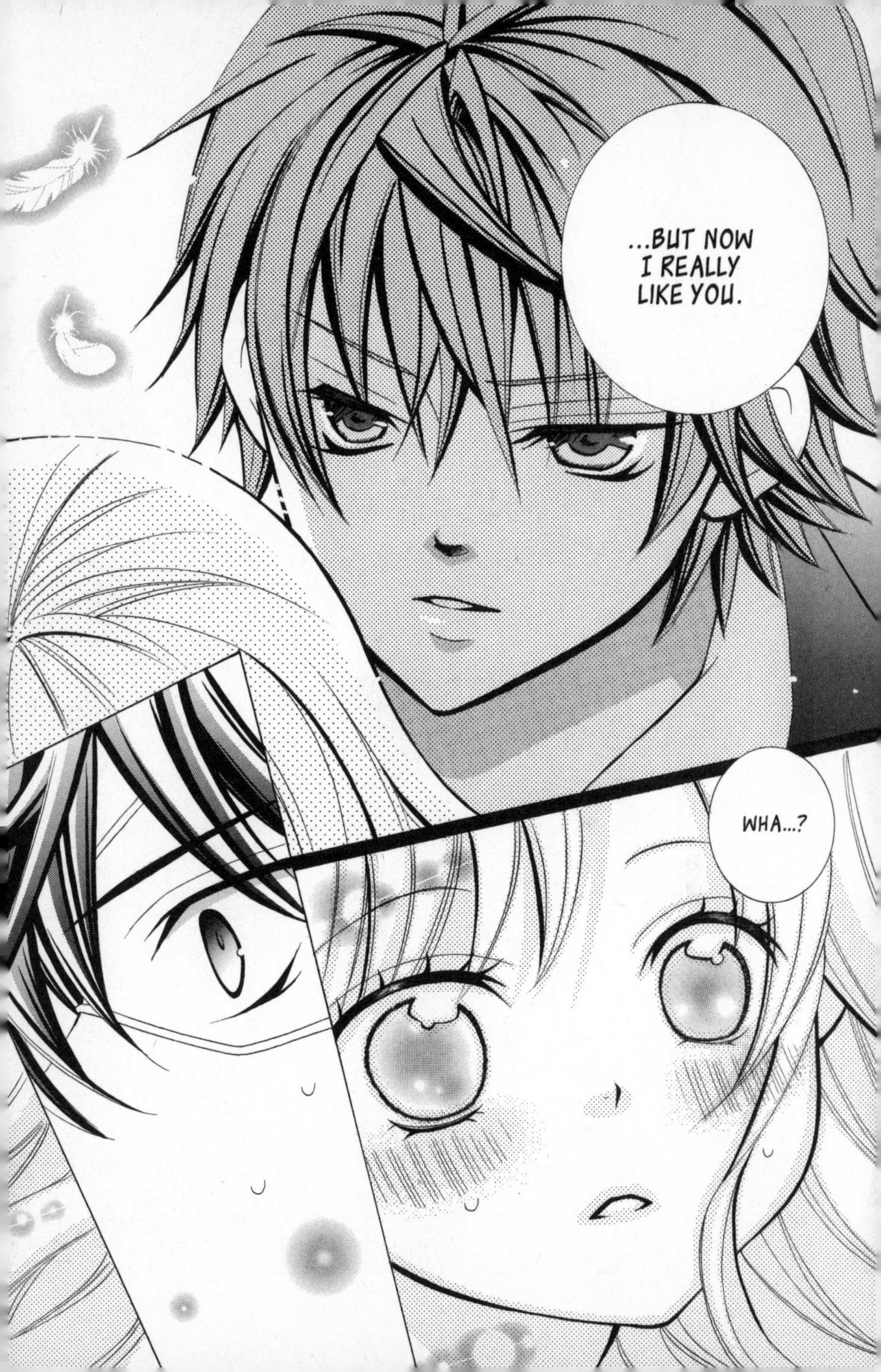
...BUT NOW I REALLY LIKE YOU.
WHA...?

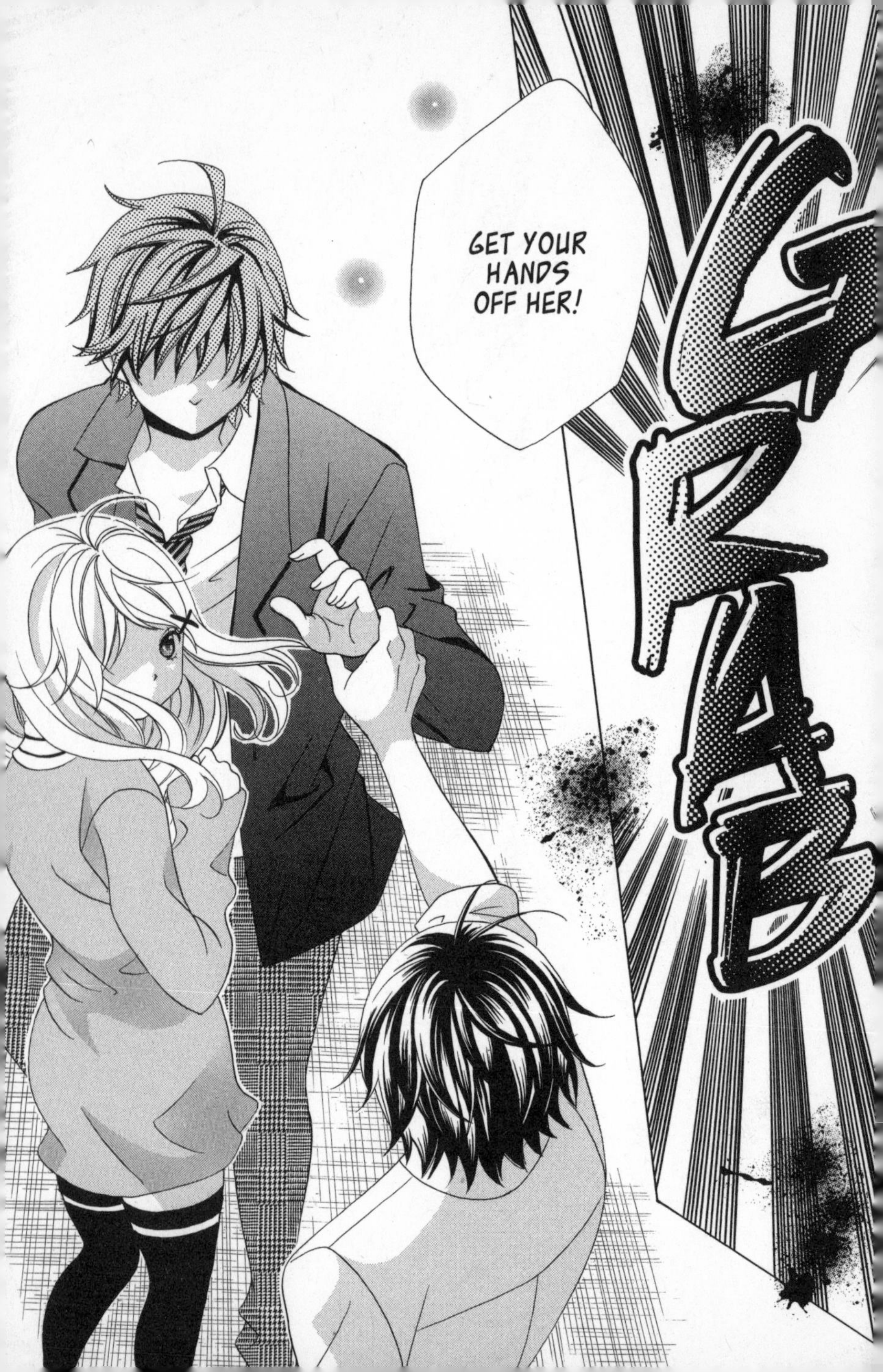
GRAB
GET YOUR HANDS OFF HER!

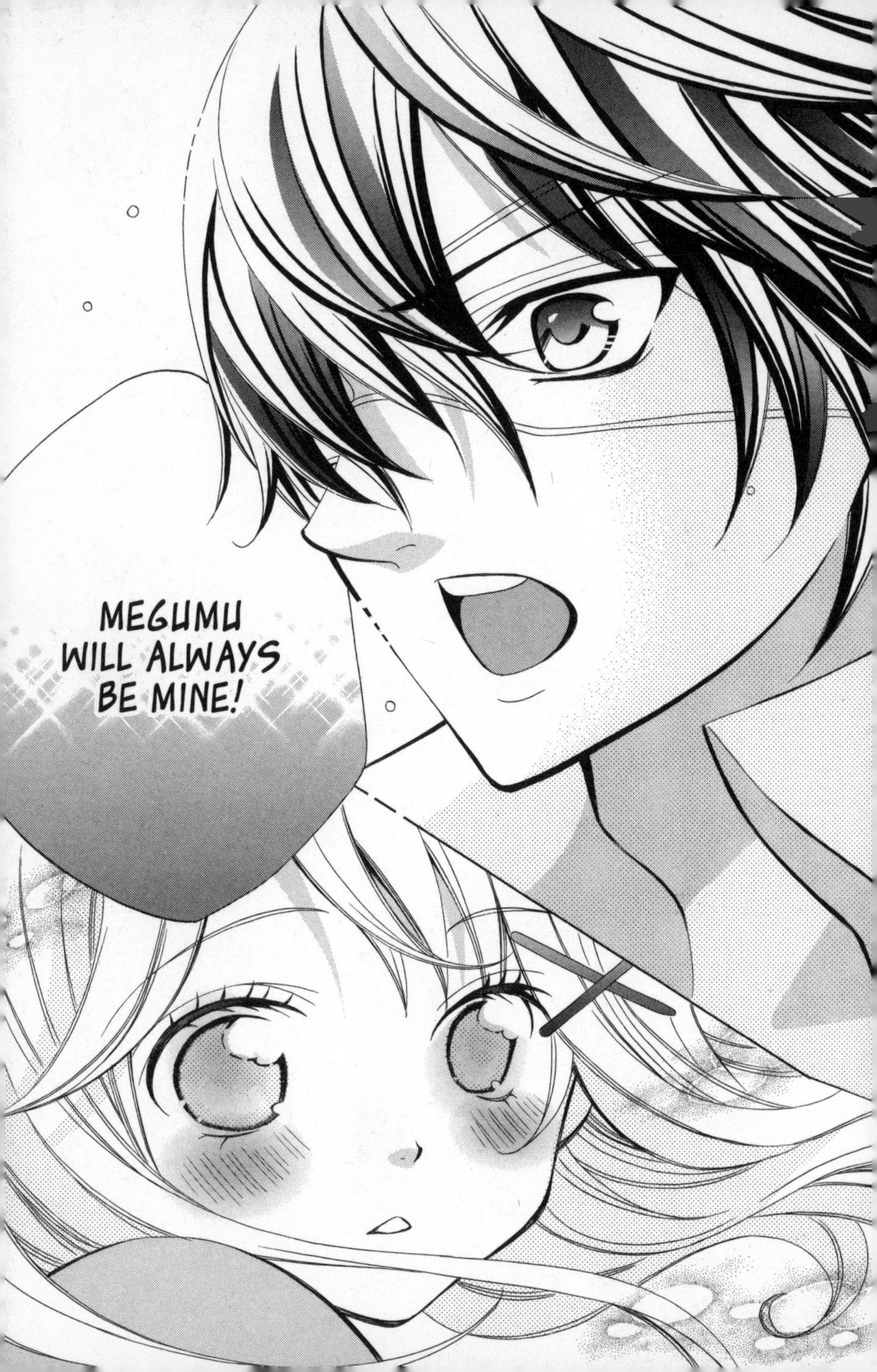
MEGUMU WILL ALWAYS BE MINE!

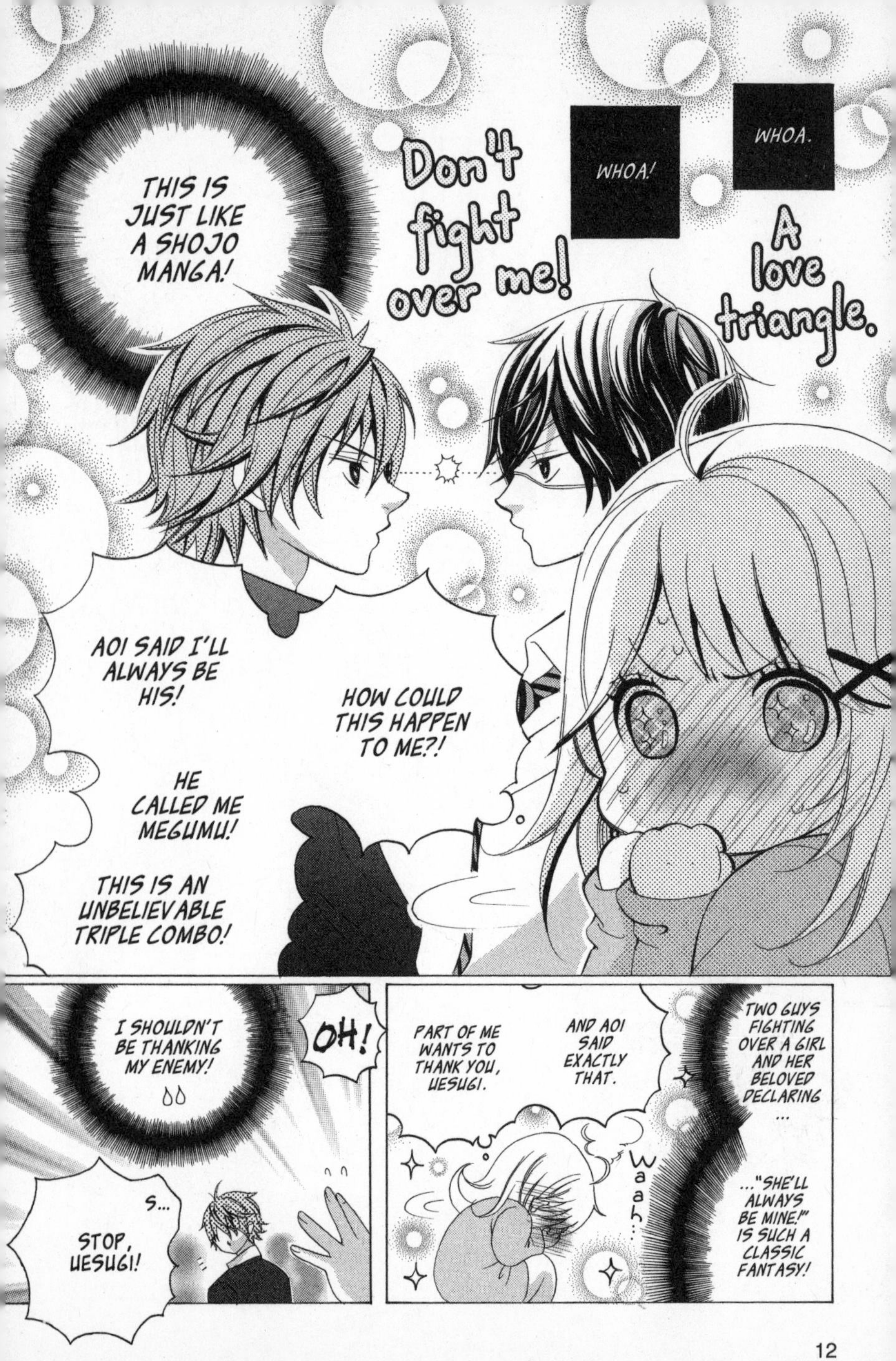
WHOA.
A love triangle.
WHOA!
Don't fight over me!
THIS IS JUST LIKE A SHOJO MANGA!
HOW COULD THIS HAPPEN TO ME?!
AOI SAID I'LL ALWAYS BE HIS!
HE CALLED ME MEGUMU!
THIS IS AN UNBELIEVABLE TRIPLE COMBO!
TWO GUYS FIGHTING OVER A GIRL AND HER BELOVED DECLARING ...
AND AOI SAID EXACTLY THAT.
PART OF ME WANTS TO THANK YOU, UESUGI.
..."SHE'LL ALWAYS BE MINE!" IS SUCH A CLASSIC FANTASY!
Waah...
OH!
I SHOULDN'T BE THANKING MY ENEMY!
S...
STOP, UESUGI!

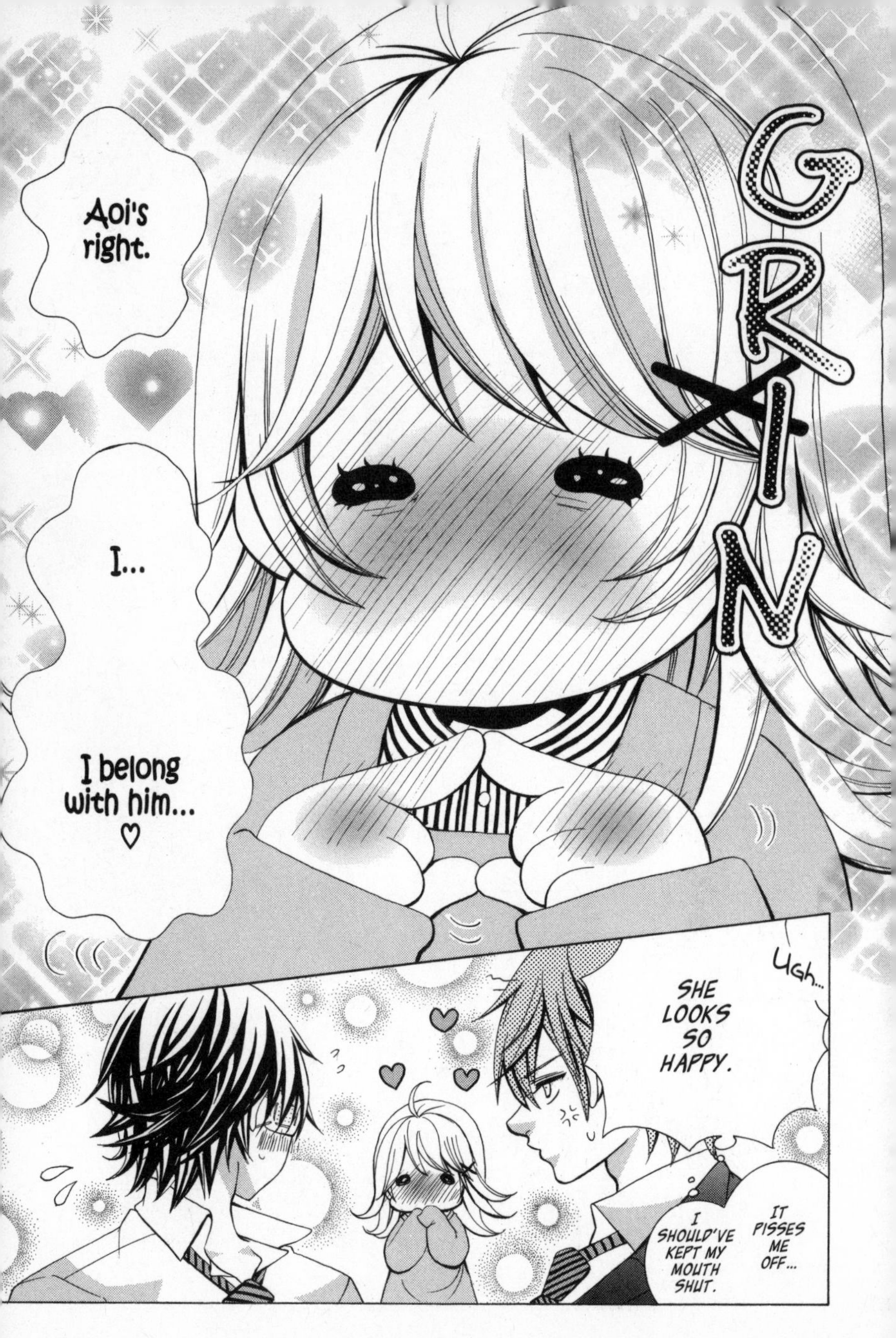
GRIN
Aoi's right.
I...
I belong with him... ♡
Ugh...
SHE LOOKS SO HAPPY.
IT PISSES ME OFF...
I SHOULD'VE KEPT MY MOUTH SHUT.

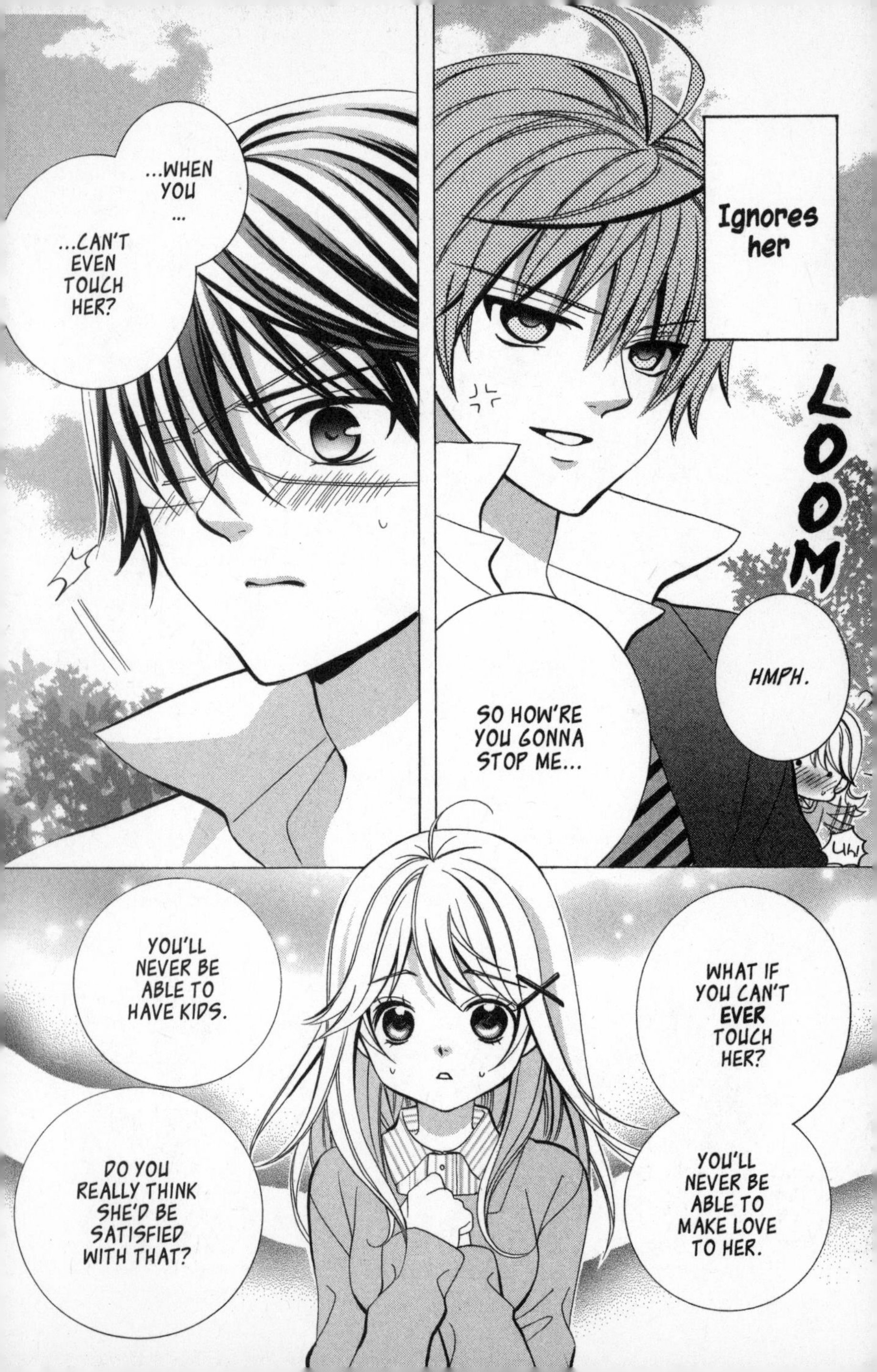
Ignores her
LOOM
HMPH.
UW
SO HOW'RE YOU GONNA STOP ME...
...WHEN YOU ...
...CAN'T EVEN TOUCH HER?
WHAT IF YOU CAN'T EVER TOUCH HER?
YOU'LL NEVER BE ABLE TO MAKE LOVE TO HER.
YOU'LL NEVER BE ABLE TO HAVE KIDS.
DO YOU REALLY THINK SHE'D BE SATISFIED WITH THAT?

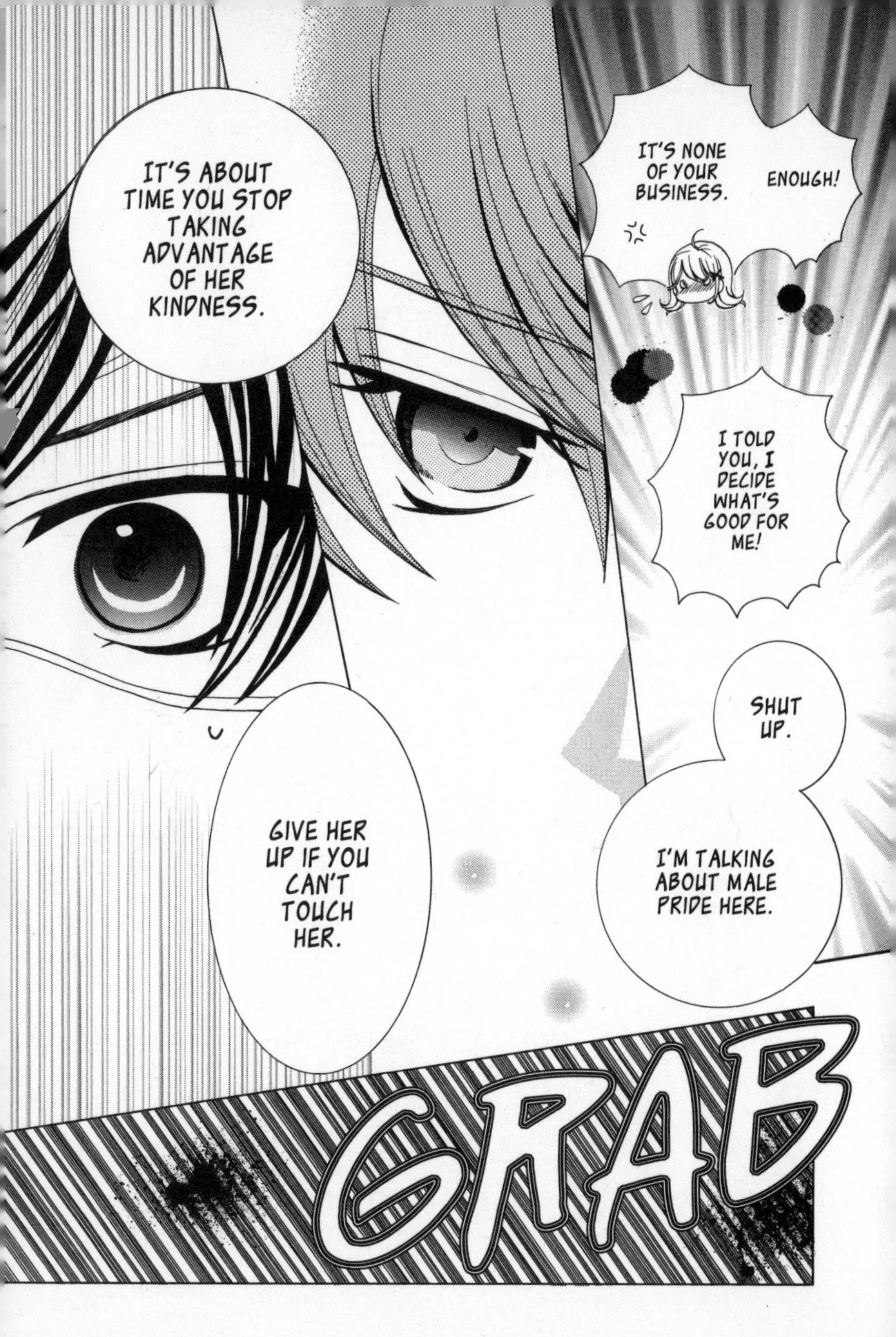
IT'S NONE OF YOUR BUSINESS.
ENOUGH!
I TOLD YOU, I DECIDE WHAT'S GOOD FOR ME!
IT'S ABOUT TIME YOU STOP TAKING ADVANTAGE OF HER KINDNESS.
SHUT UP.
I'M TALKING ABOUT MALE PRIDE HERE.
GIVE HER UP IF YOU CAN'T TOUCH HER.
GRAB

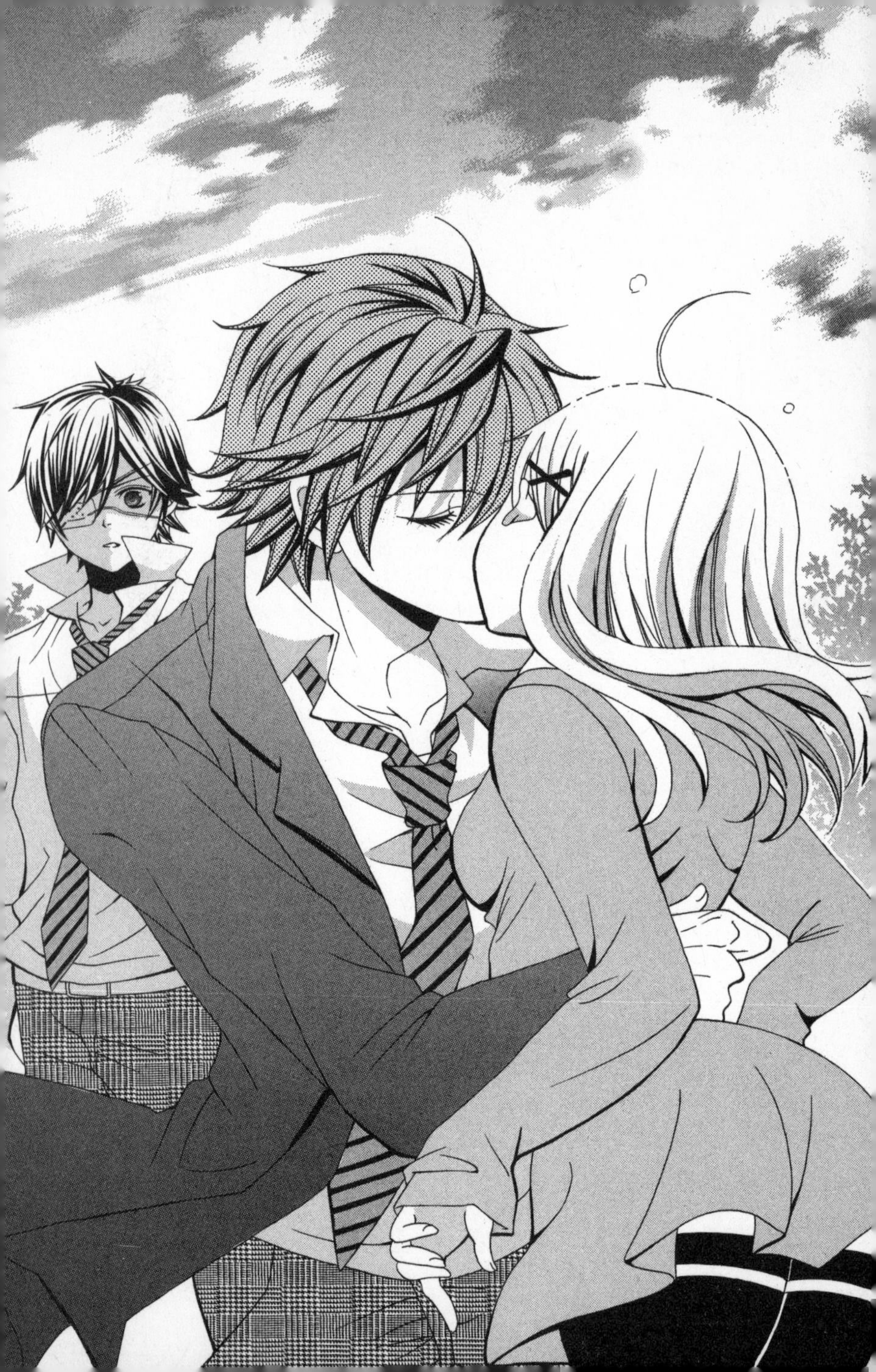

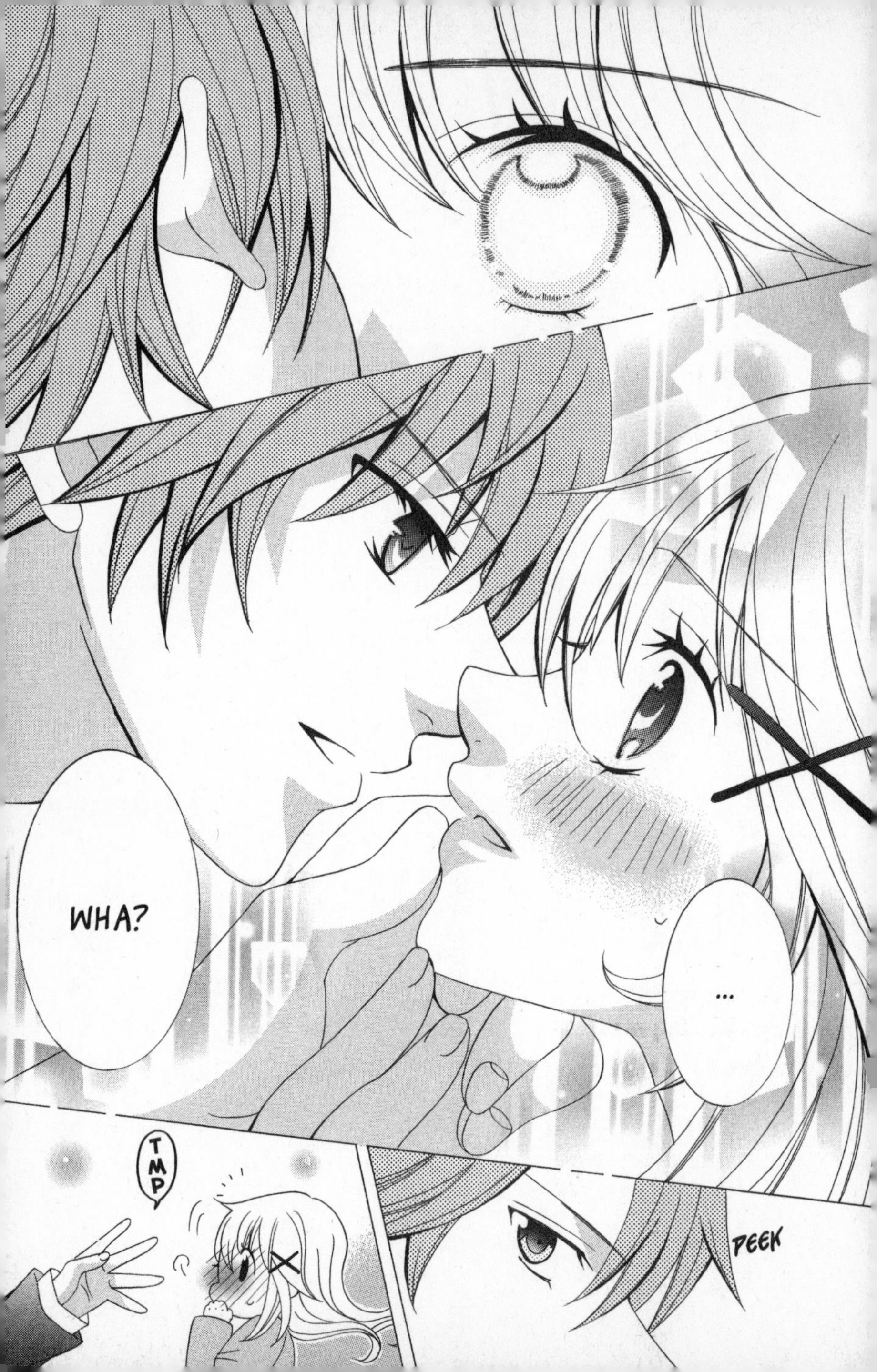
...
WHA?
PEEK
TMP

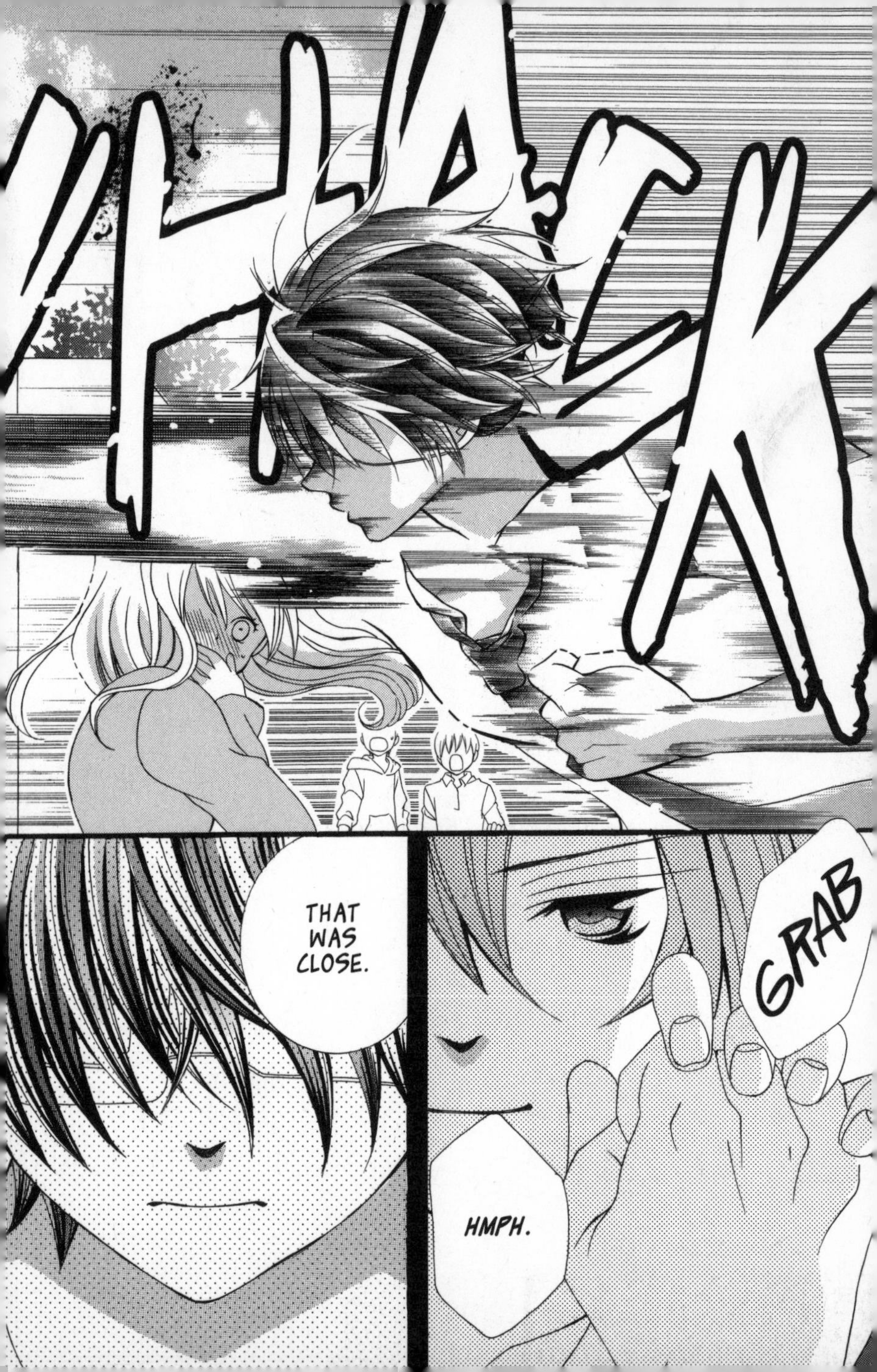
WHACK
GRAB
HMPH.
THAT WAS CLOSE.

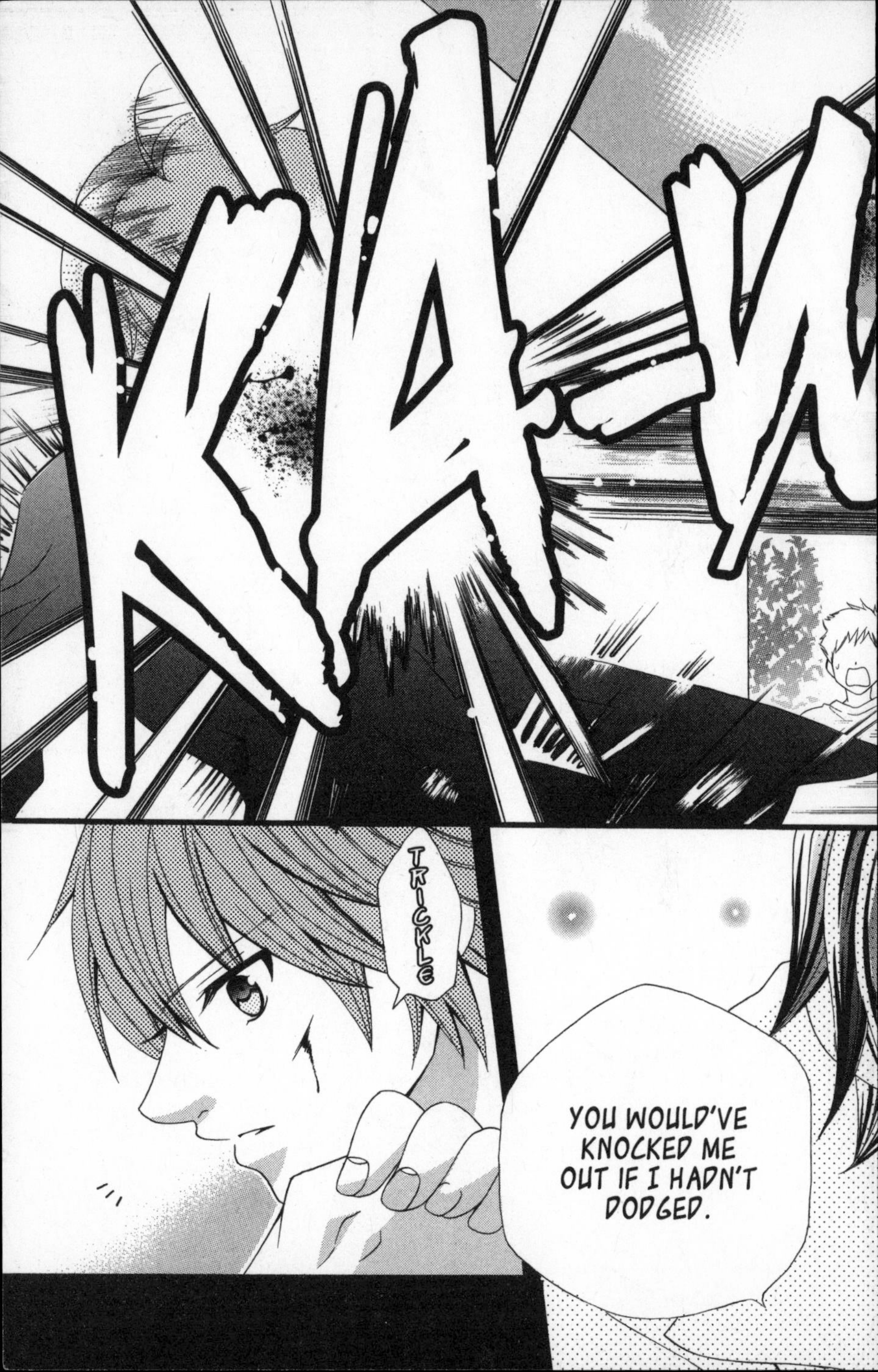
YOU WOULD'VE KNOCKED ME OUT IF I HADN'T DODGED.
TRICKLE

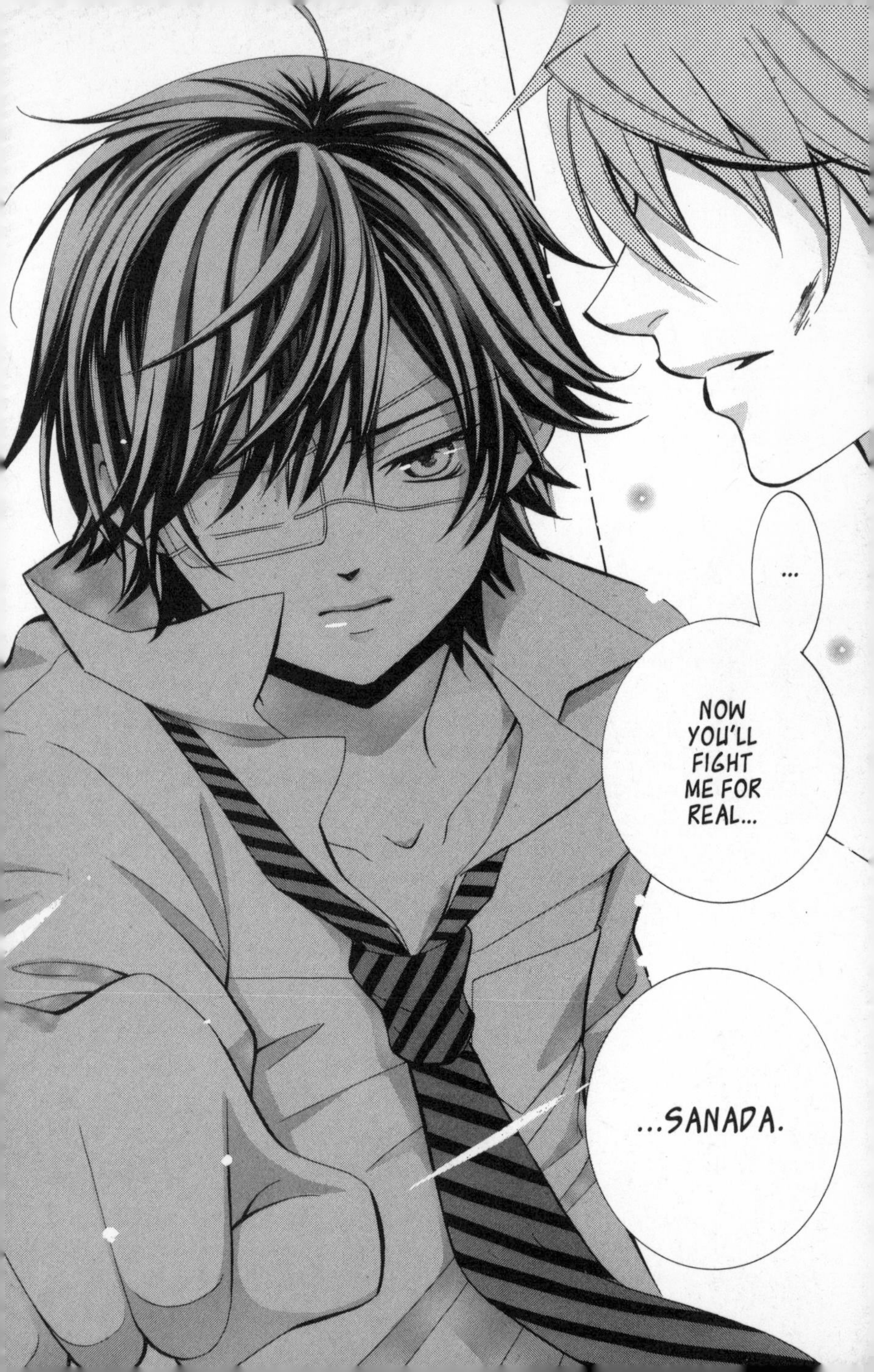
...
NOW YOU'LL FIGHT ME FOR REAL...
...SANADA.

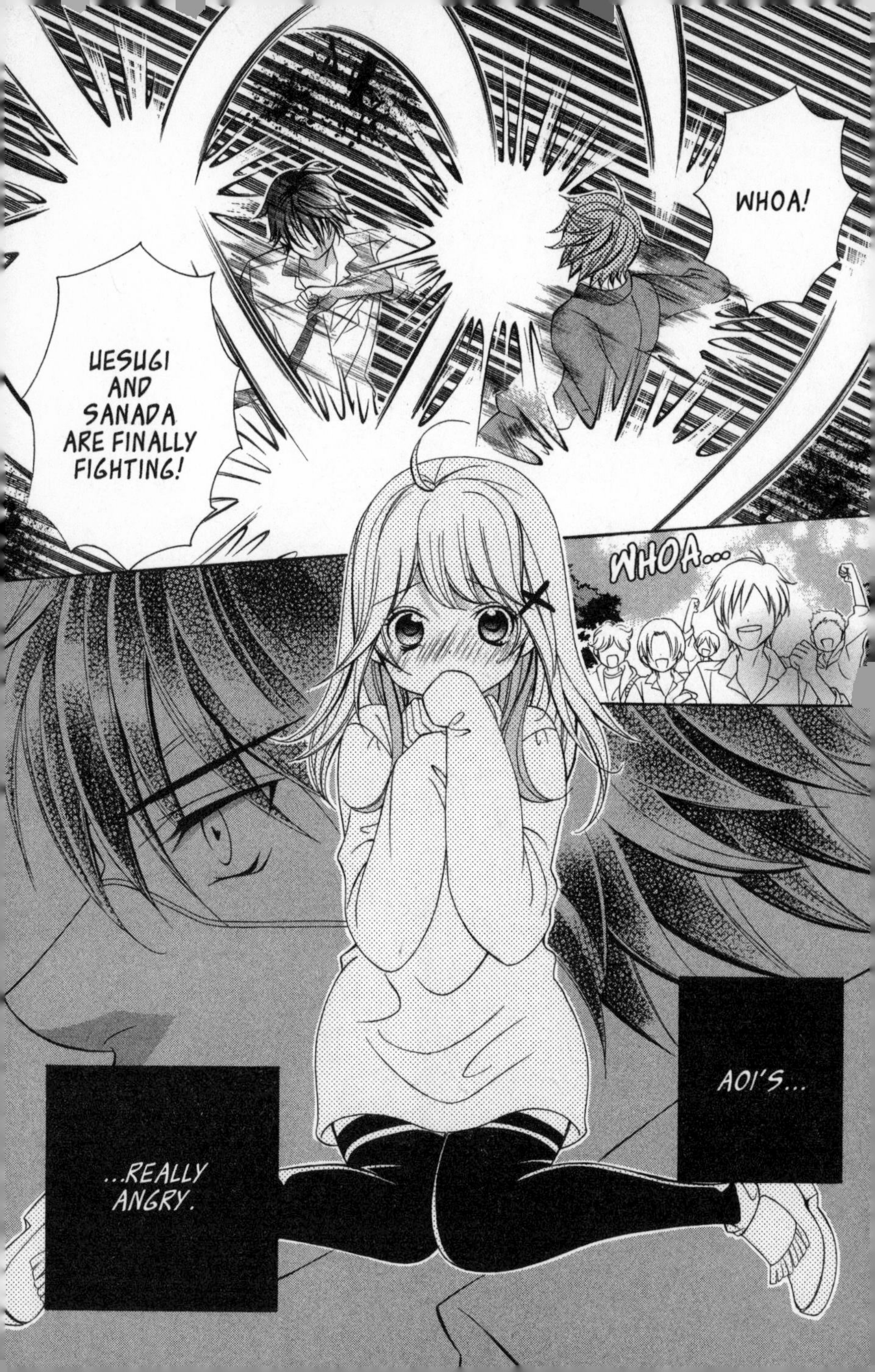
WHOA!
UESUGI AND SANADA ARE FINALLY FIGHTING!
WHOA...
AOI'S...
...REALLY ANGRY.

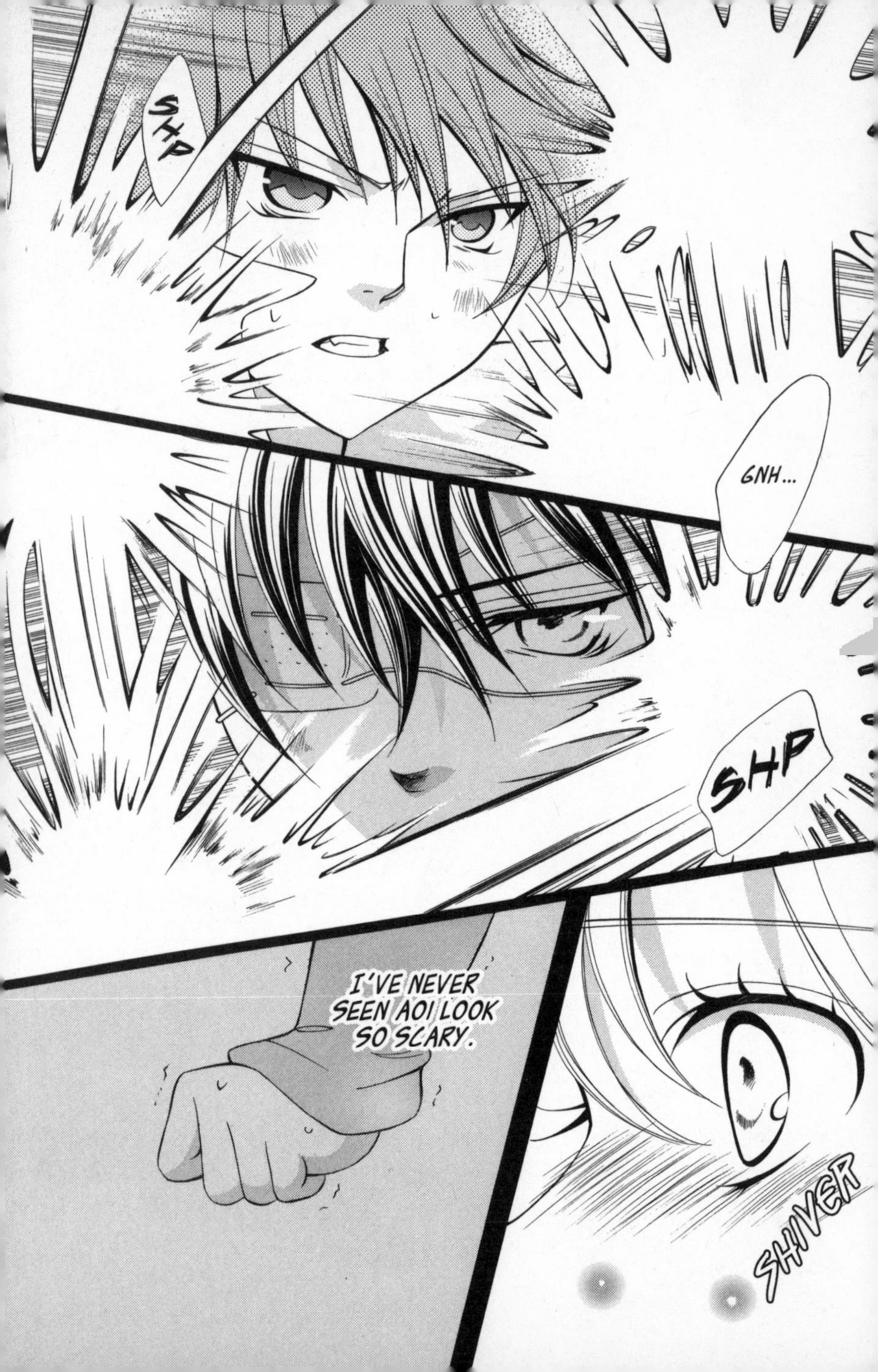
SHP
GNH...
SHP
SHIVER
I'VE NEVER SEEN AOI LOOK SO SCARY.

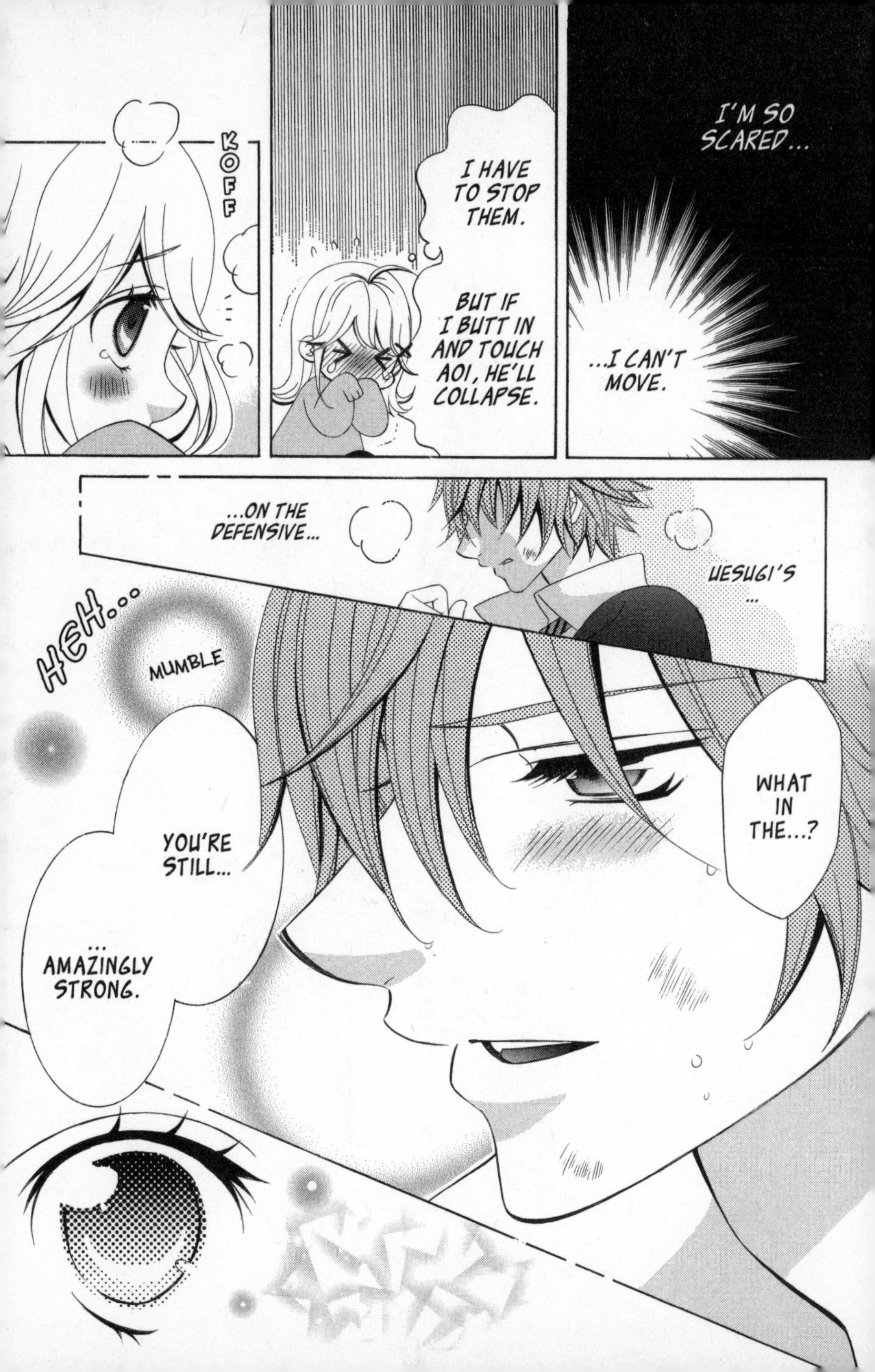
I'M SO SCARED...
...I CAN'T MOVE.
I HAVE TO STOP THEM.
BUT IF I BUTT IN AND TOUCH AOI, HE'LL COLLAPSE.
KOFF
UESUGI'S ...
...ON THE DEFENSIVE...
WHAT IN THE...?
HEH...
MUMBLE
YOU'RE STILL...
... AMAZINGLY STRONG.

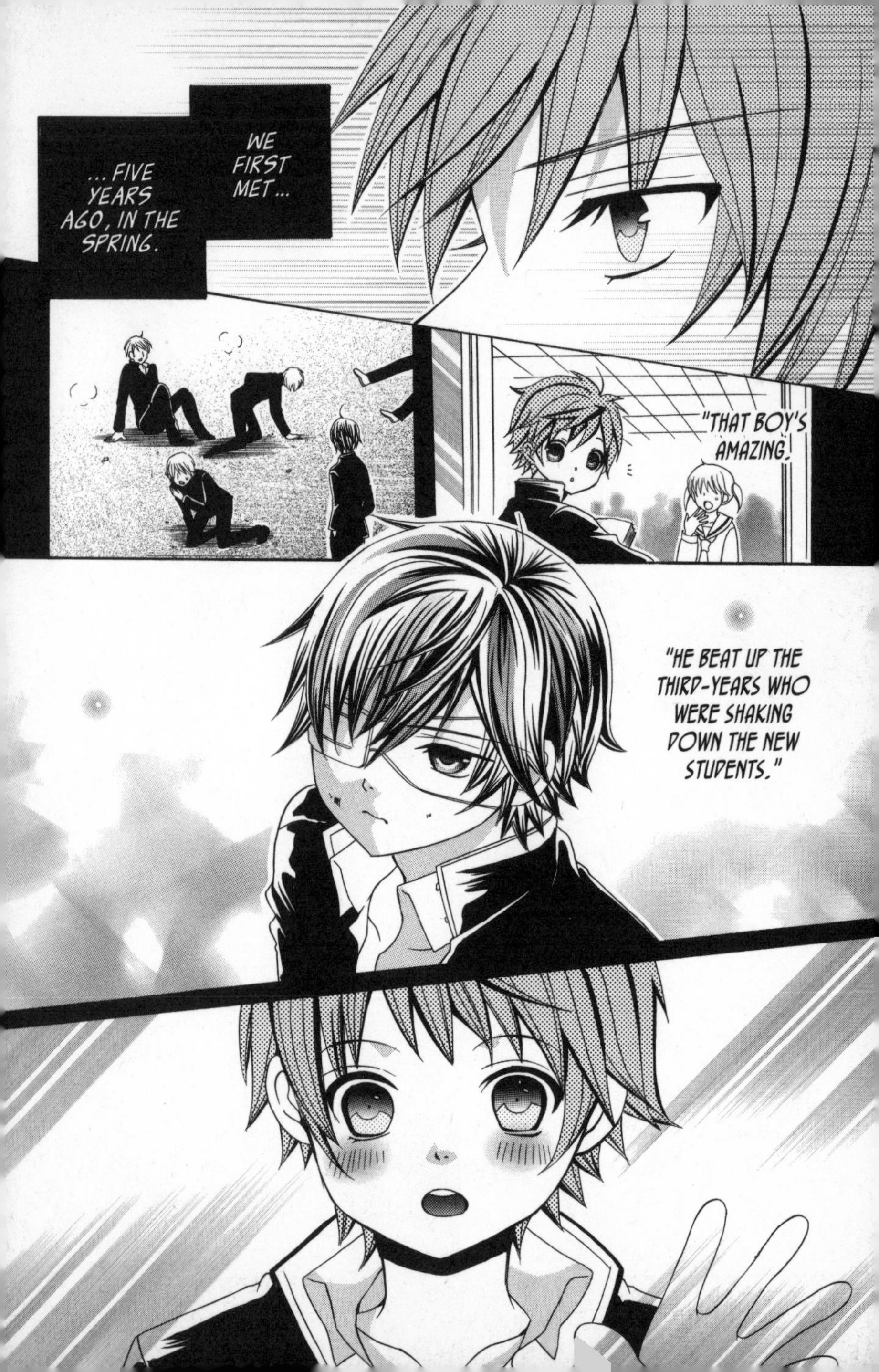
WE FIRST MET...
...FIVE YEARS AGO, IN THE SPRING.
"THAT BOY'S AMAZING!
"HE BEAT UP THE THIRD-YEARS WHO WERE SHAKING DOWN THE NEW STUDENTS."

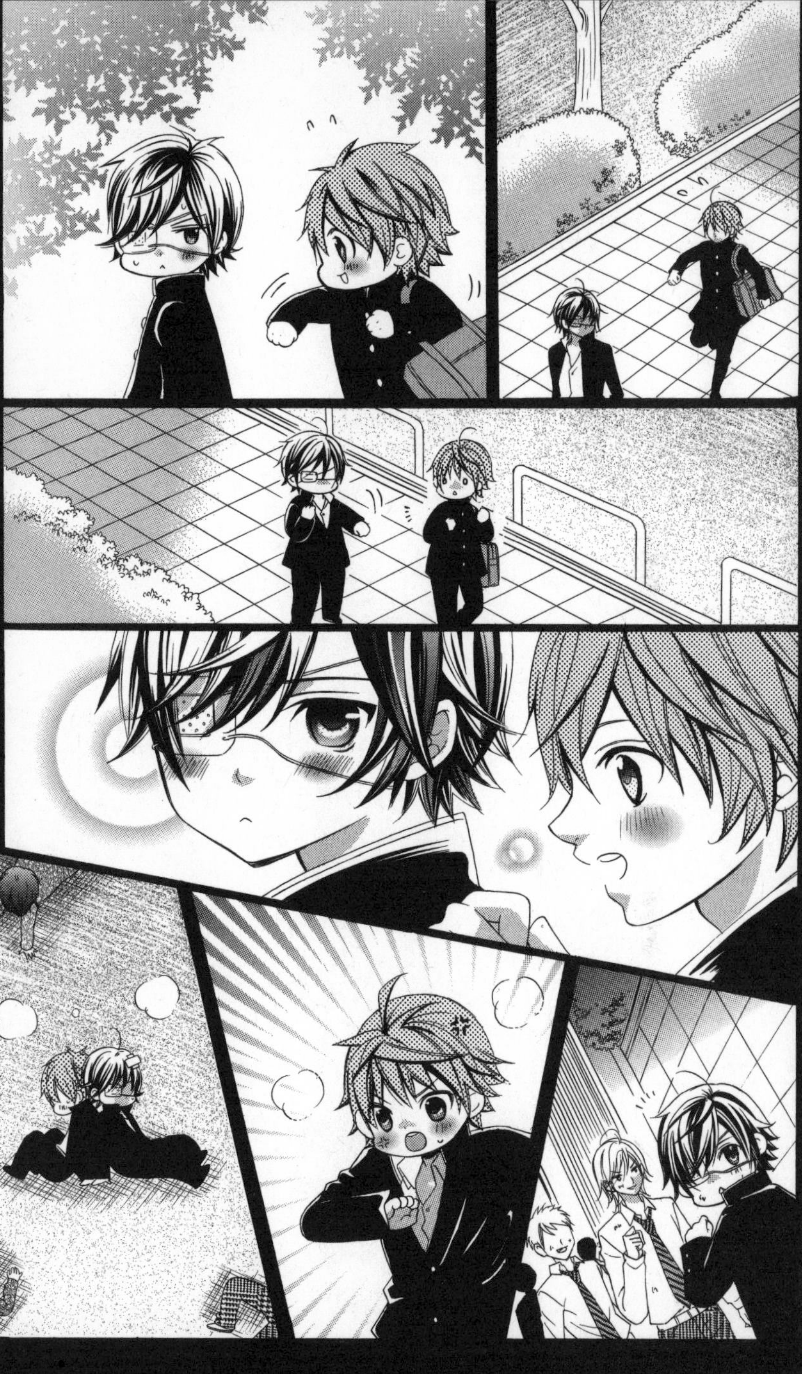

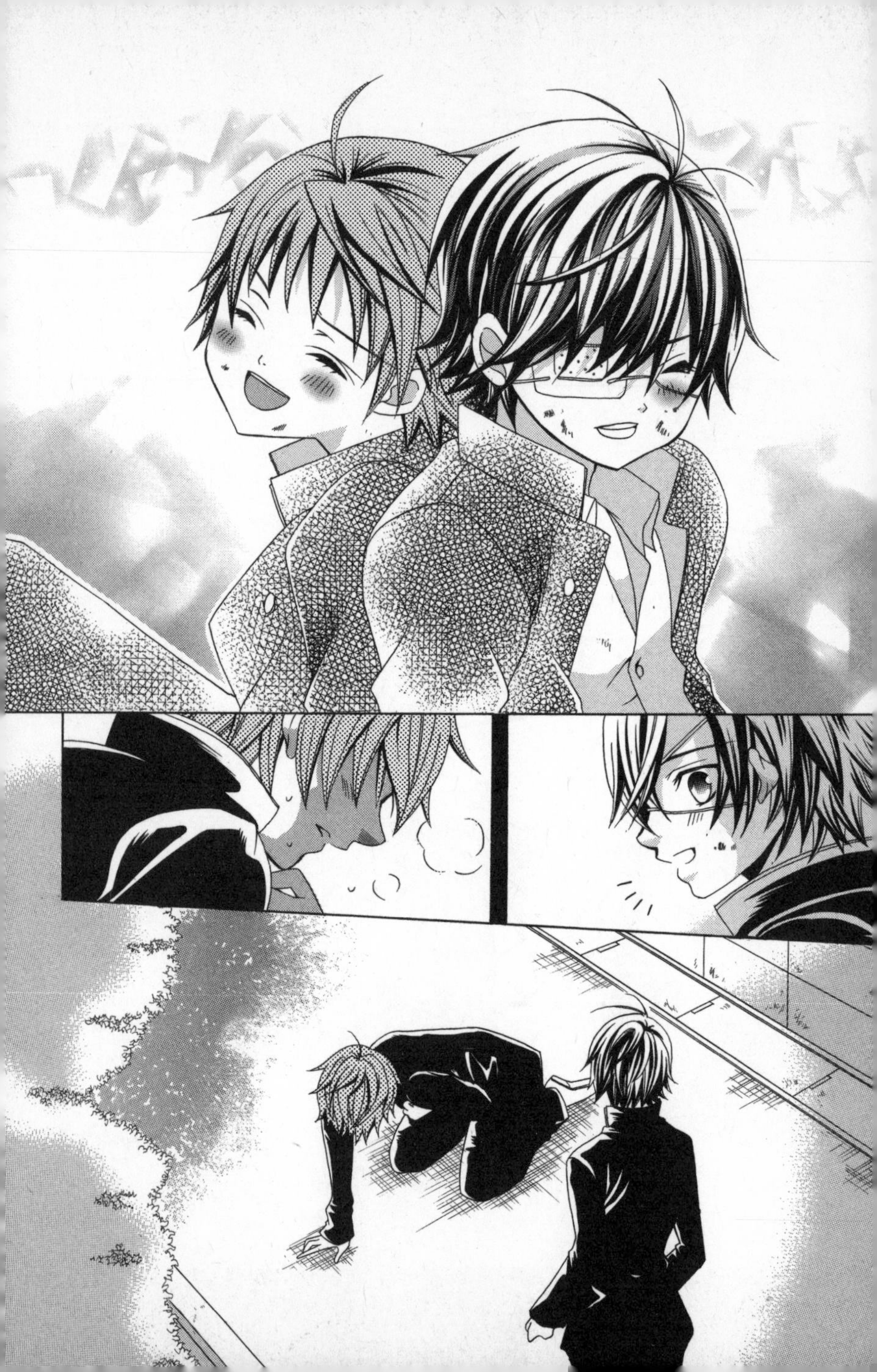

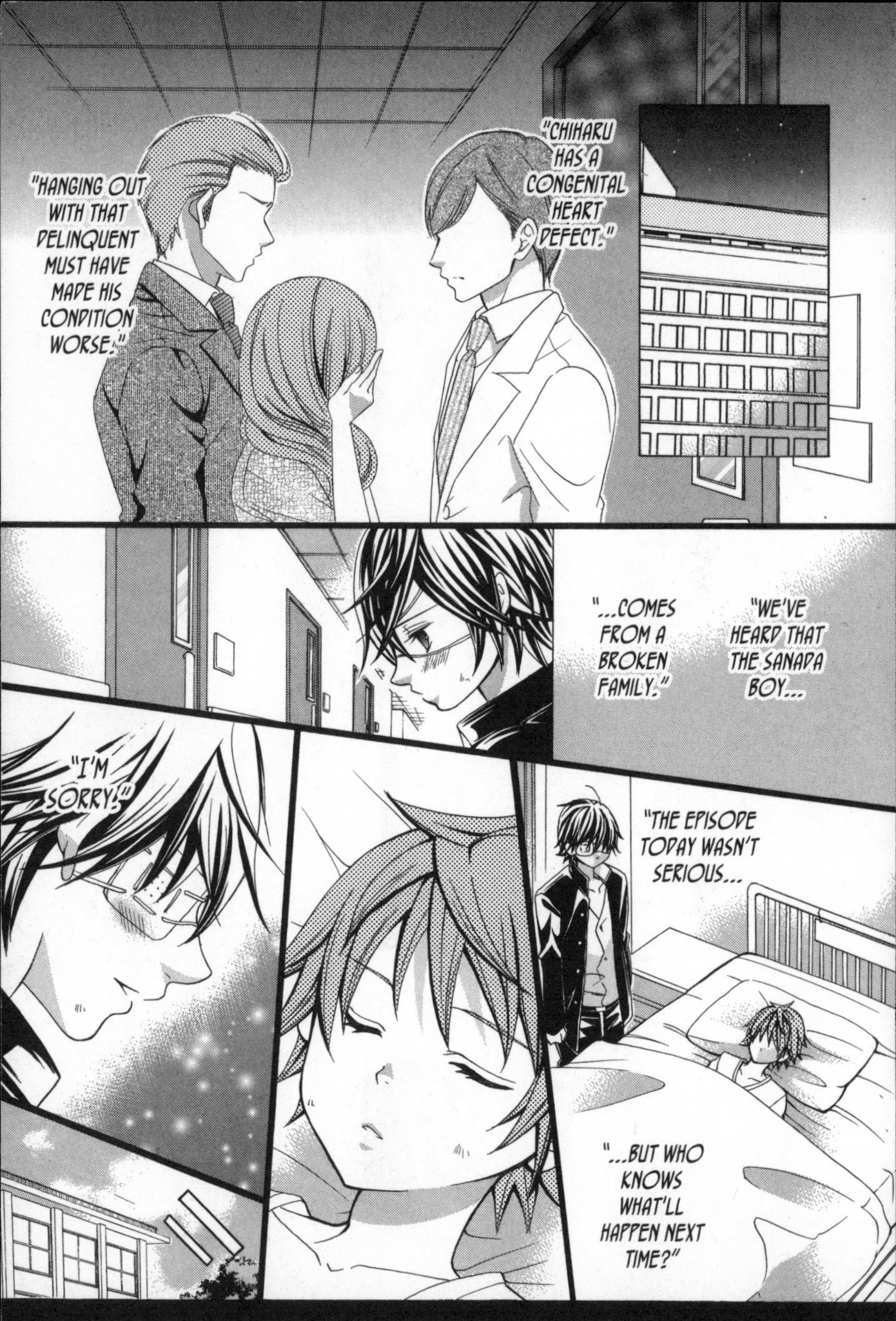
"CHIHARU HAS A CONGENITAL HEART DEFECT."
"HANGING OUT WITH THAT DELINQUENT MUST HAVE MADE HIS CONDITION WORSE."
"WE'VE HEARD THAT THE SANADA BOY...
"...COMES FROM A BROKEN FAMILY."
"THE EPISODE TODAY WASN'T SERIOUS...
"...BUT WHO KNOWS WHAT'LL HAPPEN NEXT TIME?"
"I'M SORRY!"

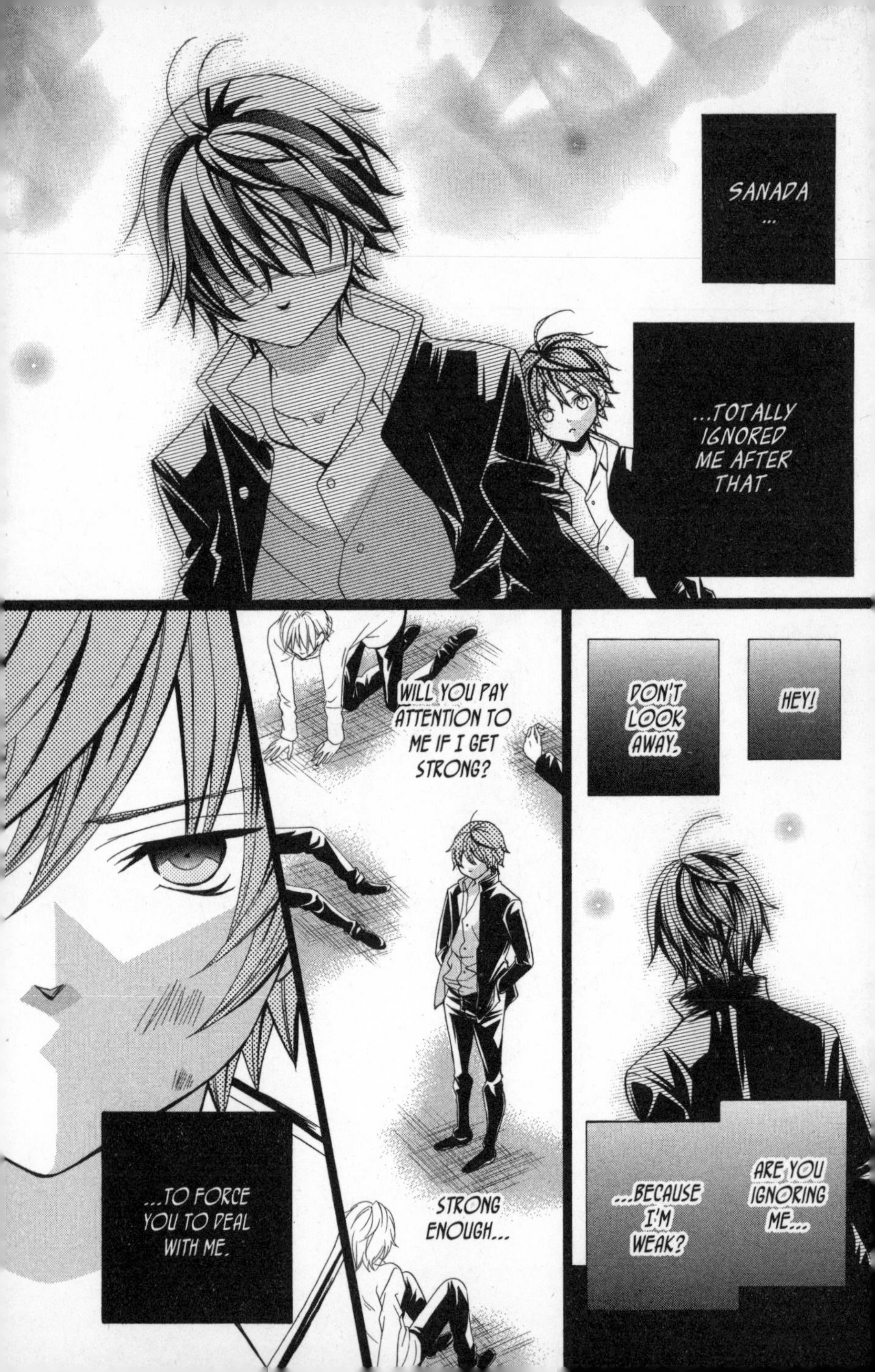
SANADA ...
...TOTALLY IGNORED ME AFTER THAT.
HEY!
DON'T LOOK AWAY.
ARE YOU IGNORING ME...
...BECAUSE I'M WEAK?
WILL YOU PAY ATTENTION TO ME IF I GET STRONG?
STRONG ENOUGH...
...TO FORCE YOU TO DEAL WITH ME.

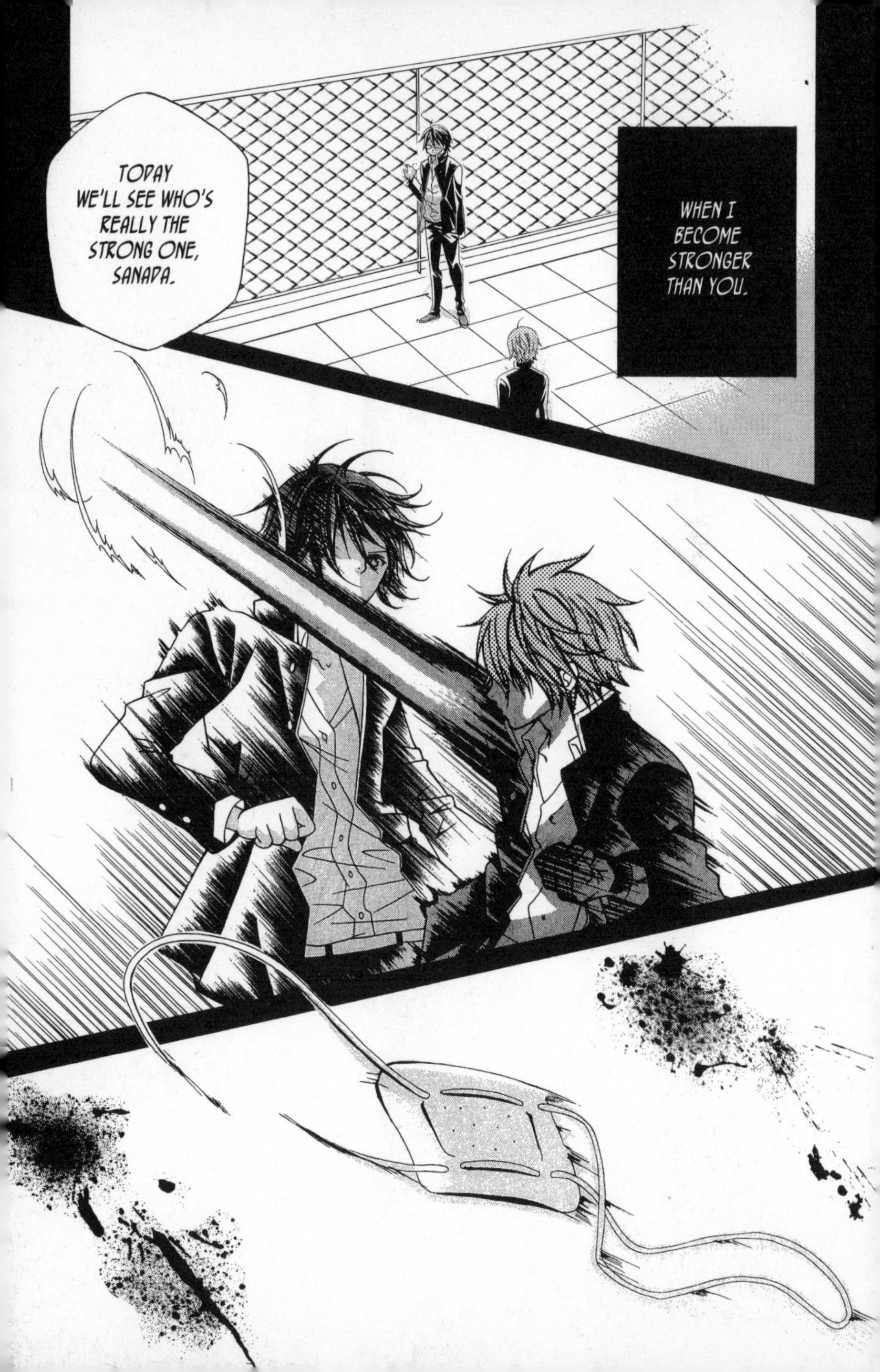
WHEN I BECOME STRONGER THAN YOU.
TODAY WE'LL SEE WHO'S REALLY THE STRONG ONE, SANADA.

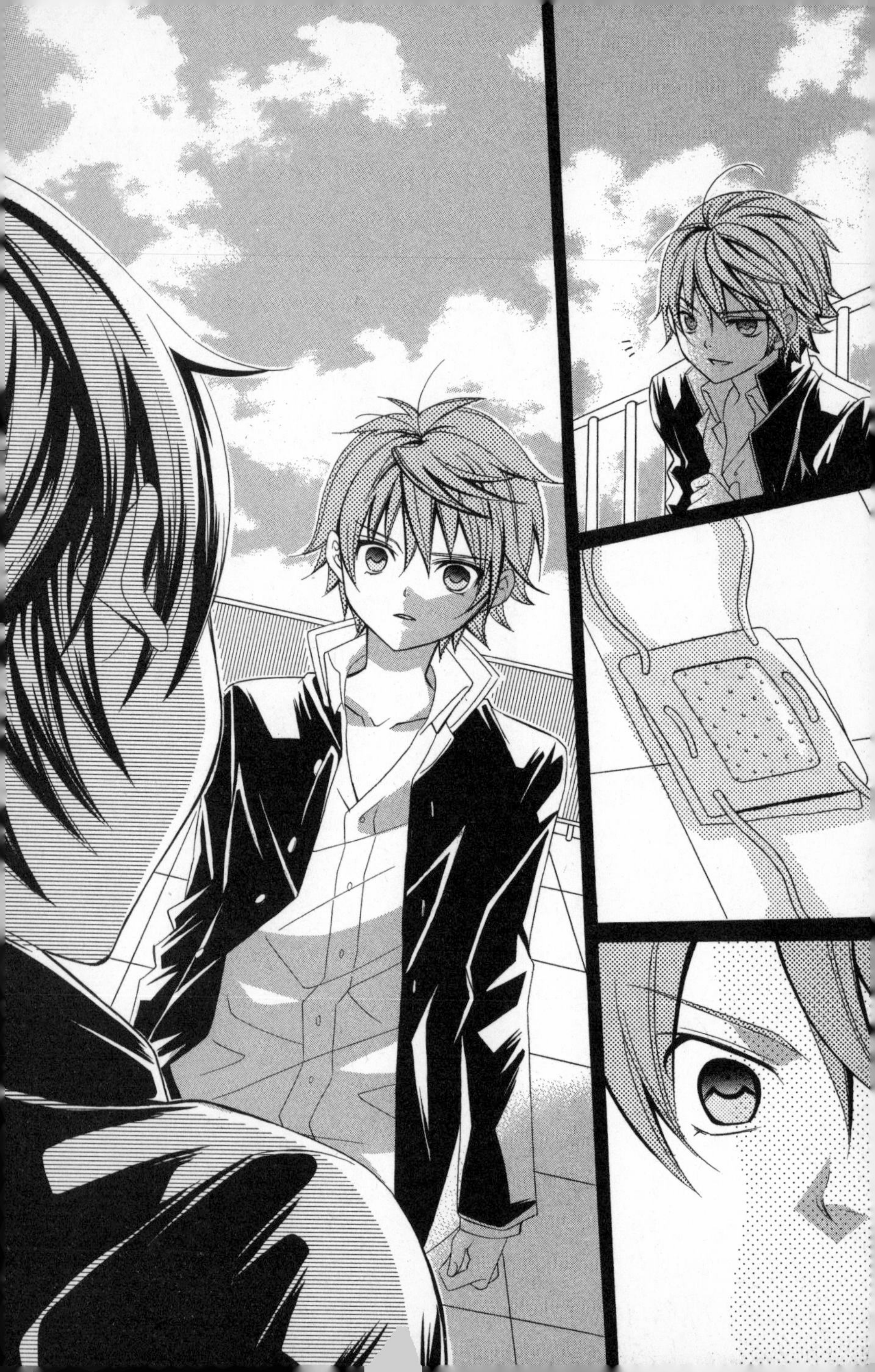

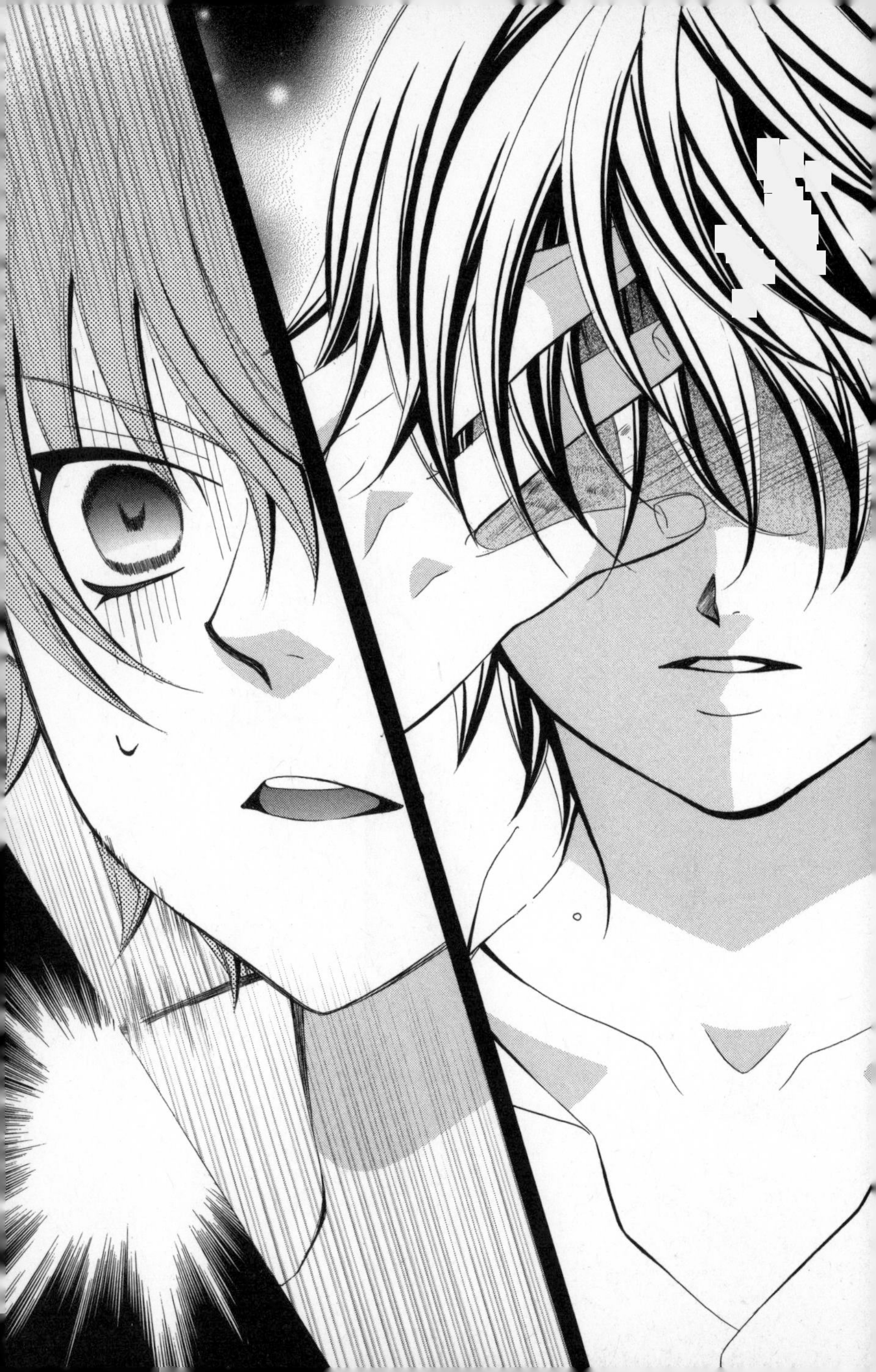

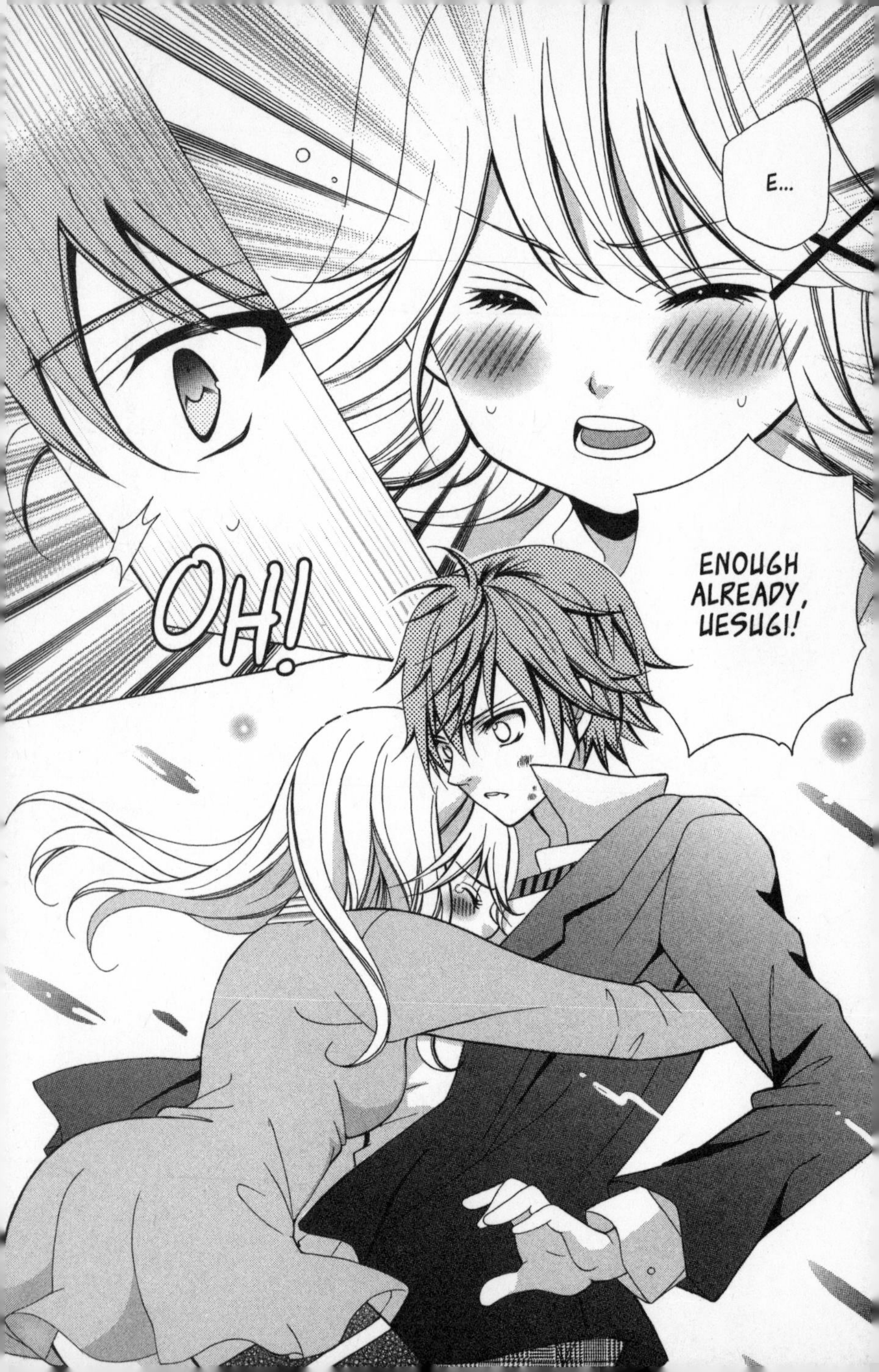
E...
OH!
ENOUGH ALREADY, UESUGI!

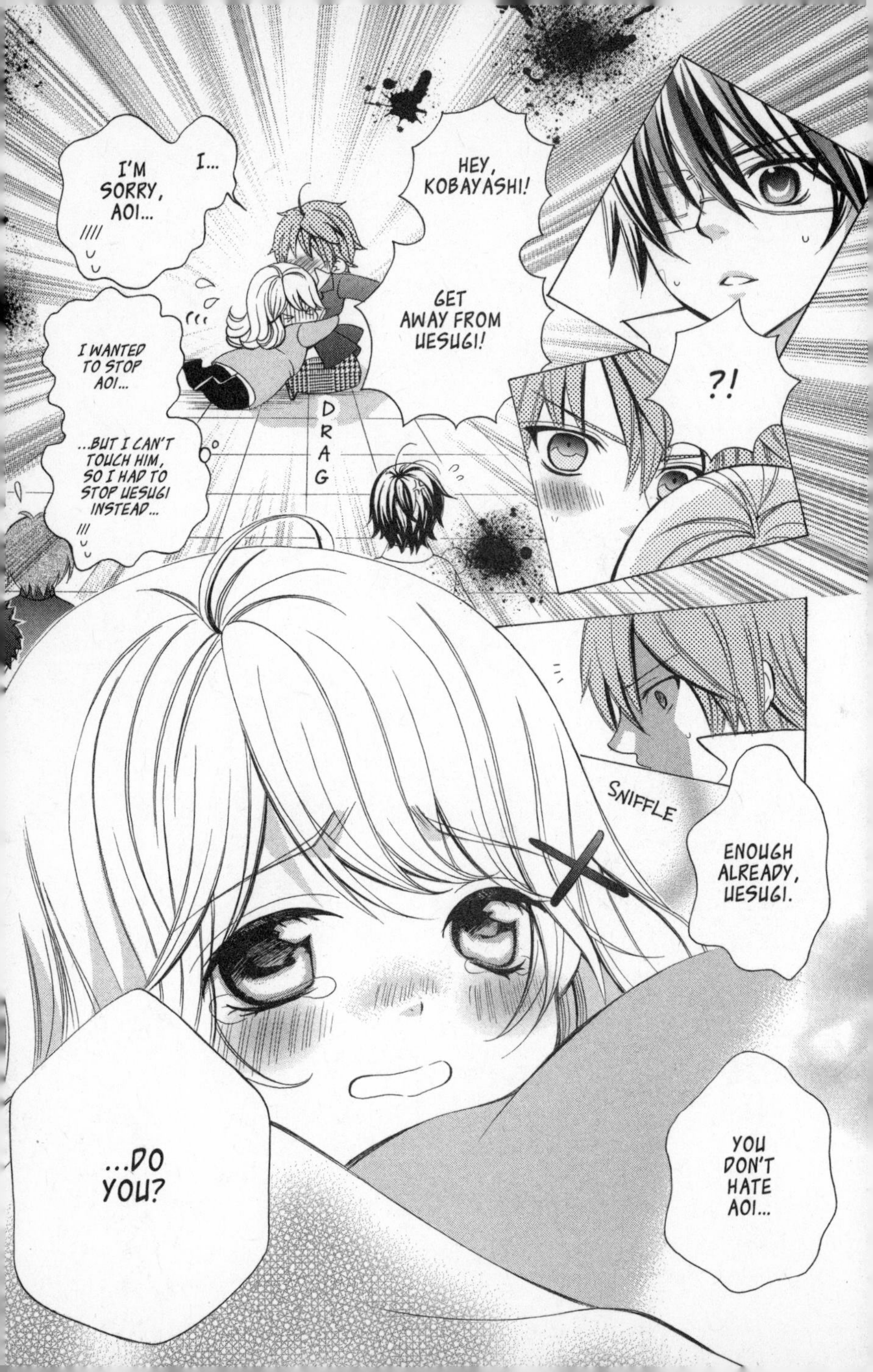
HEY, KOBAYASHI!
GET AWAY FROM UESUGI!
?!
I...
I'M SORRY, AOI...
DRAG
I WANTED TO STOP AOI...
...BUT I CAN'T TOUCH HIM, SO I HAD TO STOP UESUGI INSTEAD...
SNIFFLE
ENOUGH ALREADY, UESUGI.
YOU DON'T HATE AOI...
...DO YOU?

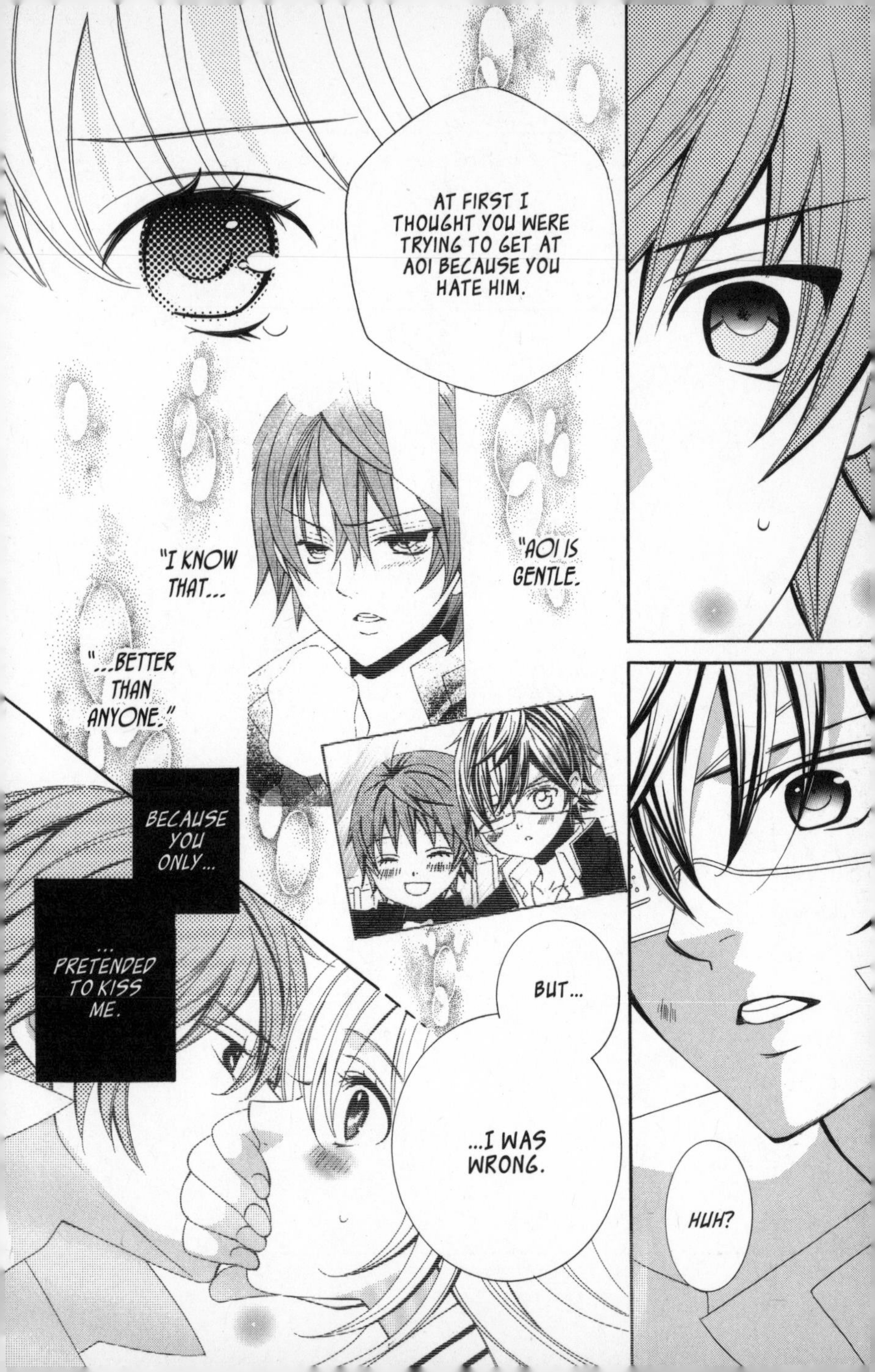
AT FIRST I THOUGHT YOU WERE TRYING TO GET AT AOI BECAUSE YOU HATE HIM.
"AOI IS GENTLE.
"I KNOW THAT...
"...BETTER THAN ANYONE."
BECAUSE YOU ONLY...
...PRETENDED TO KISS ME.
BUT...
...I WAS WRONG.
HUH?

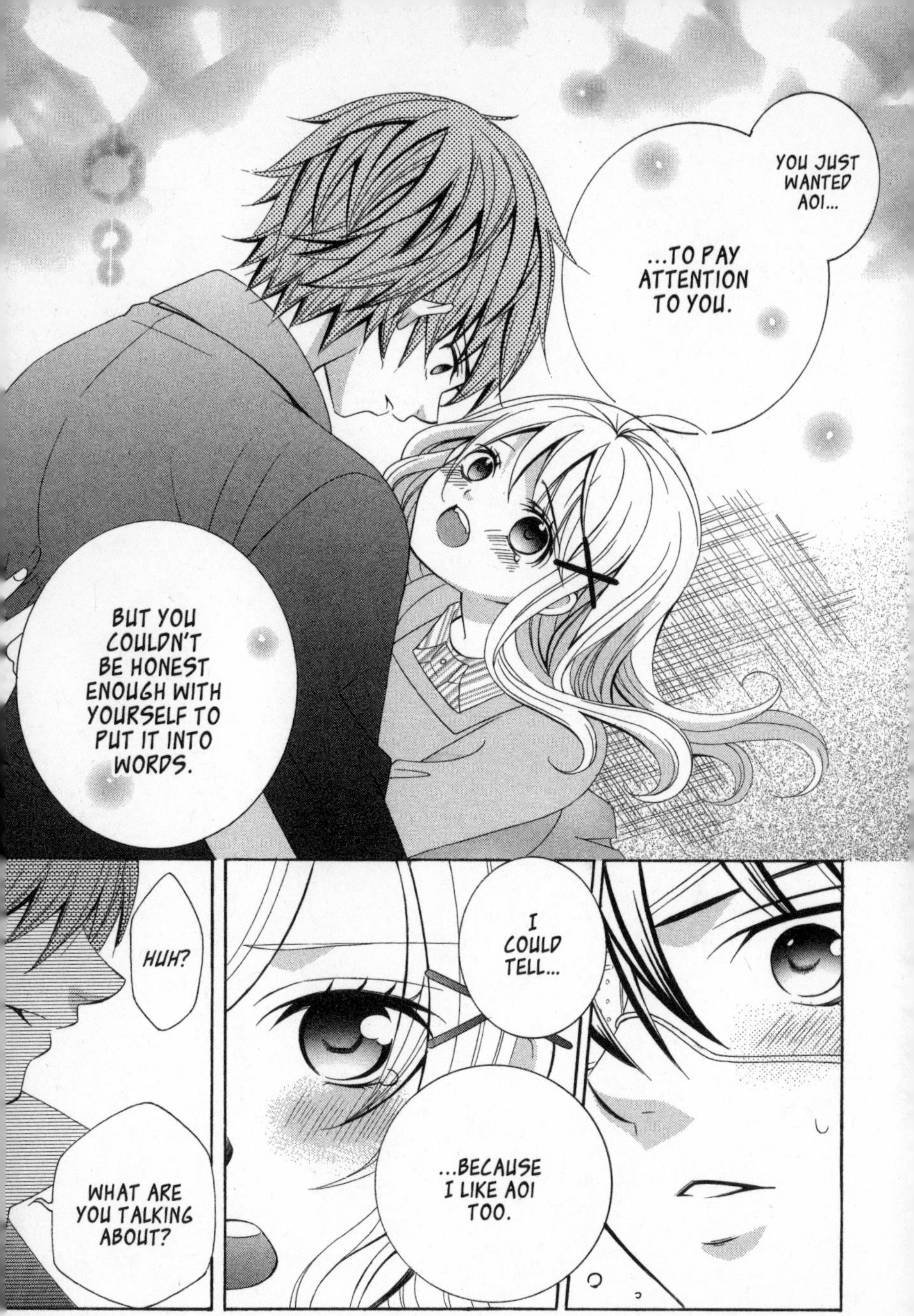
YOU JUST WANTED AOI...
...TO PAY ATTENTION TO YOU.
BUT YOU COULDN'T BE HONEST ENOUGH WITH YOURSELF TO PUT IT INTO WORDS.
I COULD TELL...
...BECAUSE I LIKE AOI TOO.
HUH?
WHAT ARE YOU TALKING ABOUT?

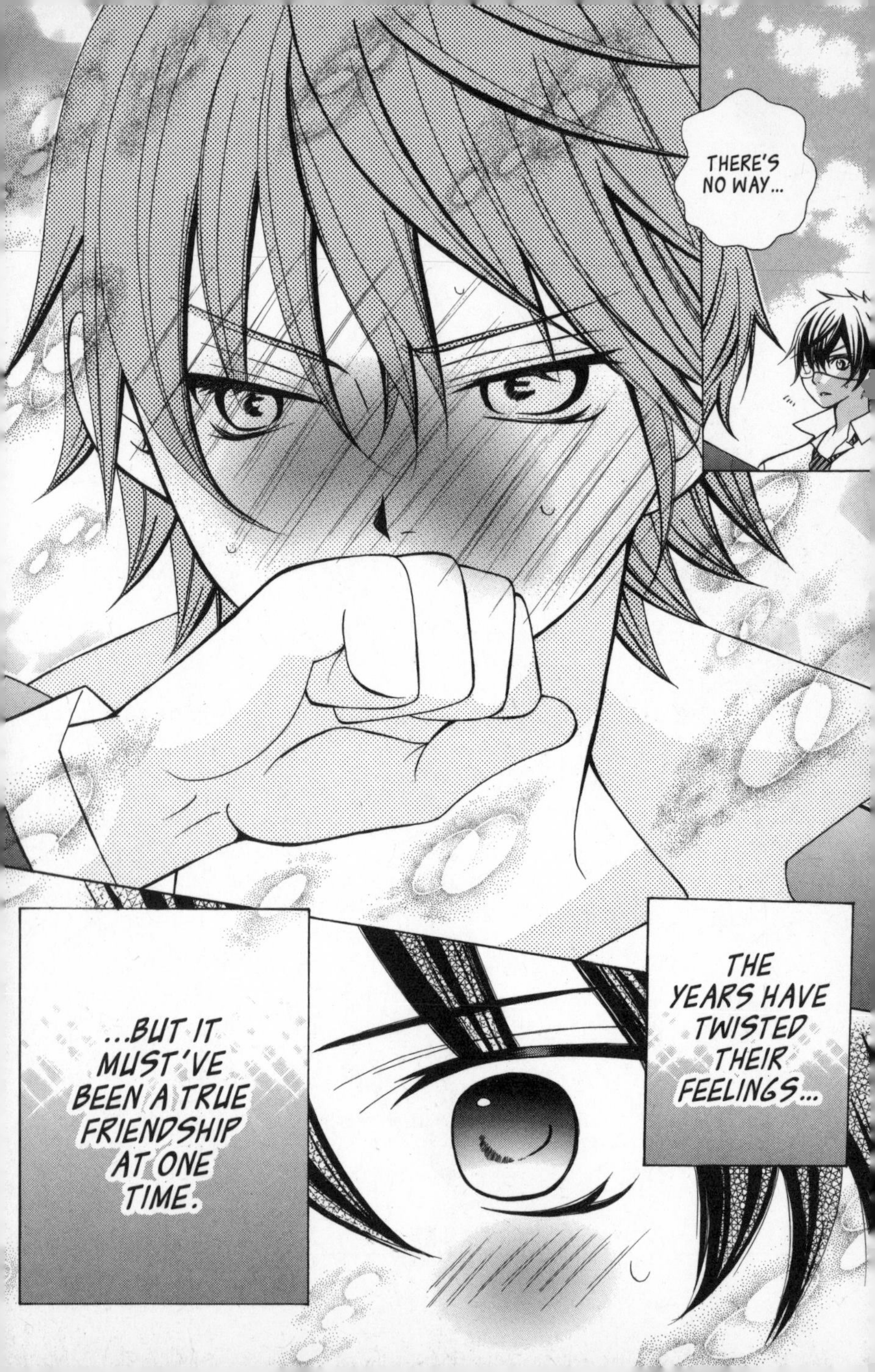
THERE'S NO WAY...
THE YEARS HAVE TWISTED THEIR FEELINGS...
...BUT IT MUST'VE BEEN A TRUE FRIENDSHIP AT ONE TIME.

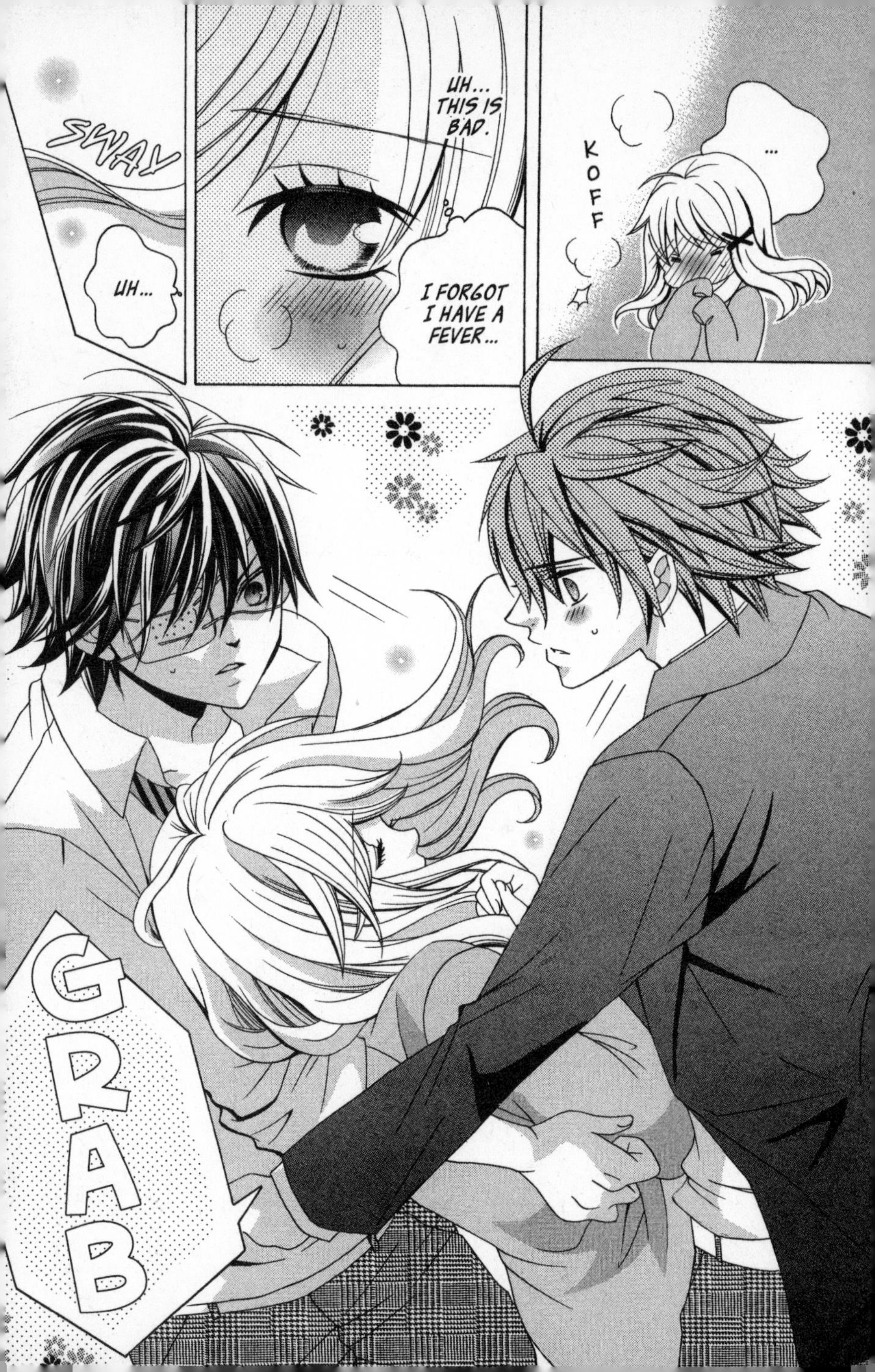
...
KOFF
UH... THIS IS BAD.
I FORGOT I HAVE A FEVER...
SWAY
UH...
GRAB

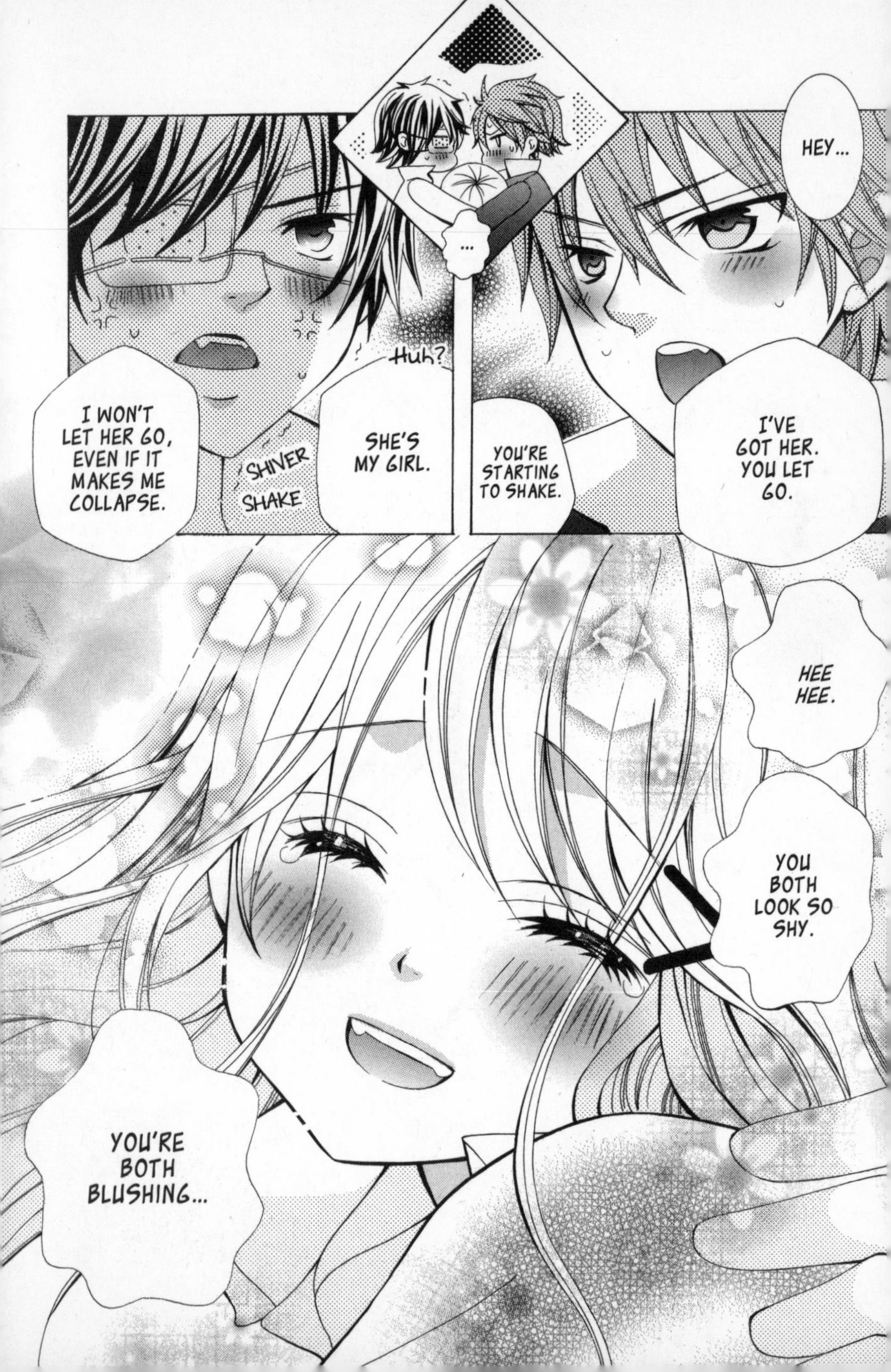
HEY...
I'VE GOT HER. YOU LET GO.
YOU'RE STARTING TO SHAKE.
...
Huh?
SHE'S MY GIRL.
SHIVER
SHAKE
I WON'T LET HER GO, EVEN IF IT MAKES ME COLLAPSE.
HEE HEE.
YOU BOTH LOOK SO SHY.
YOU'RE BOTH BLUSHING...

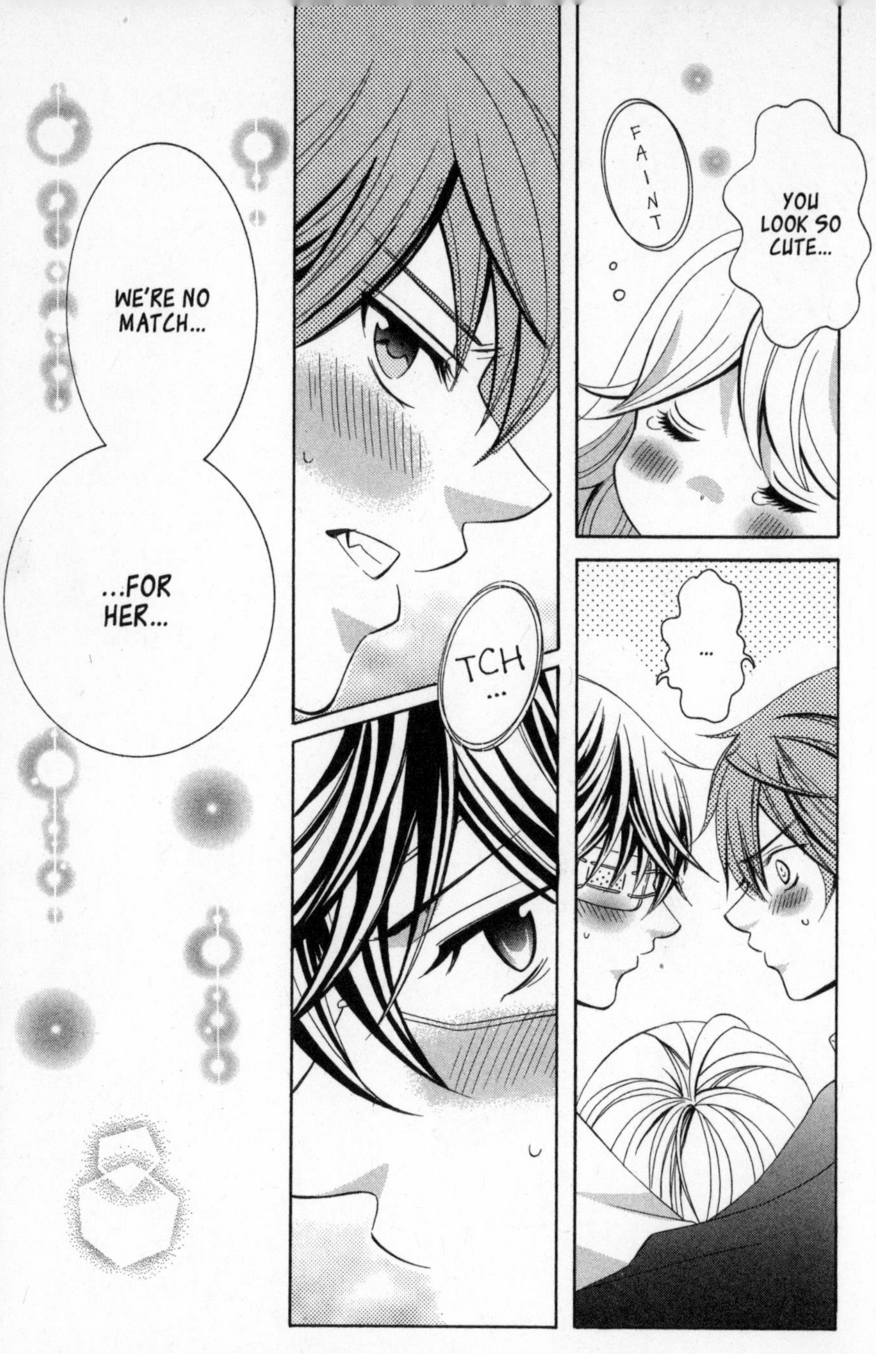
FAINT
YOU LOOK SO CUTE...
...
TCH...
WE'RE NO MATCH... ...FOR HER...

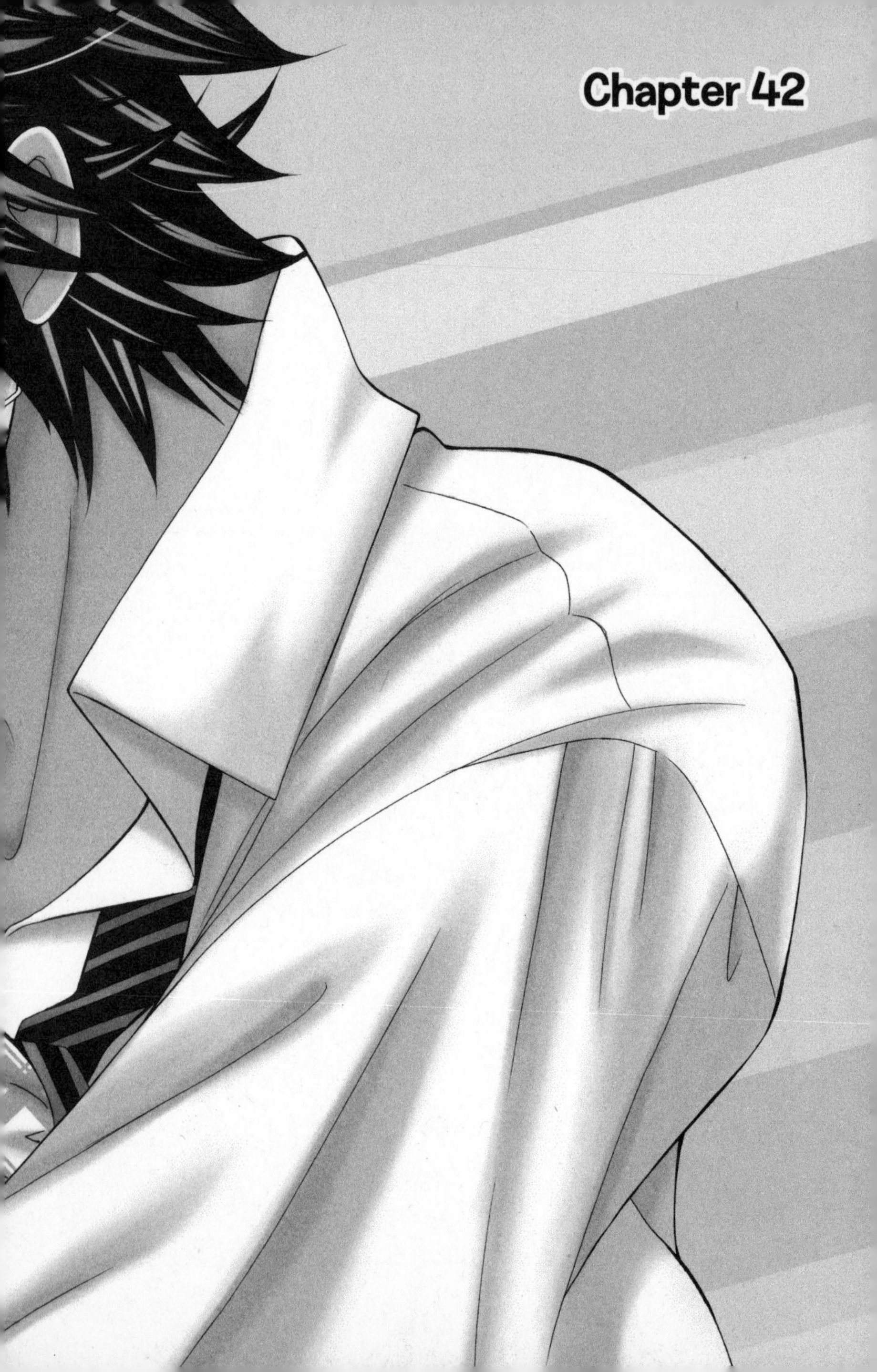
Chapter 42

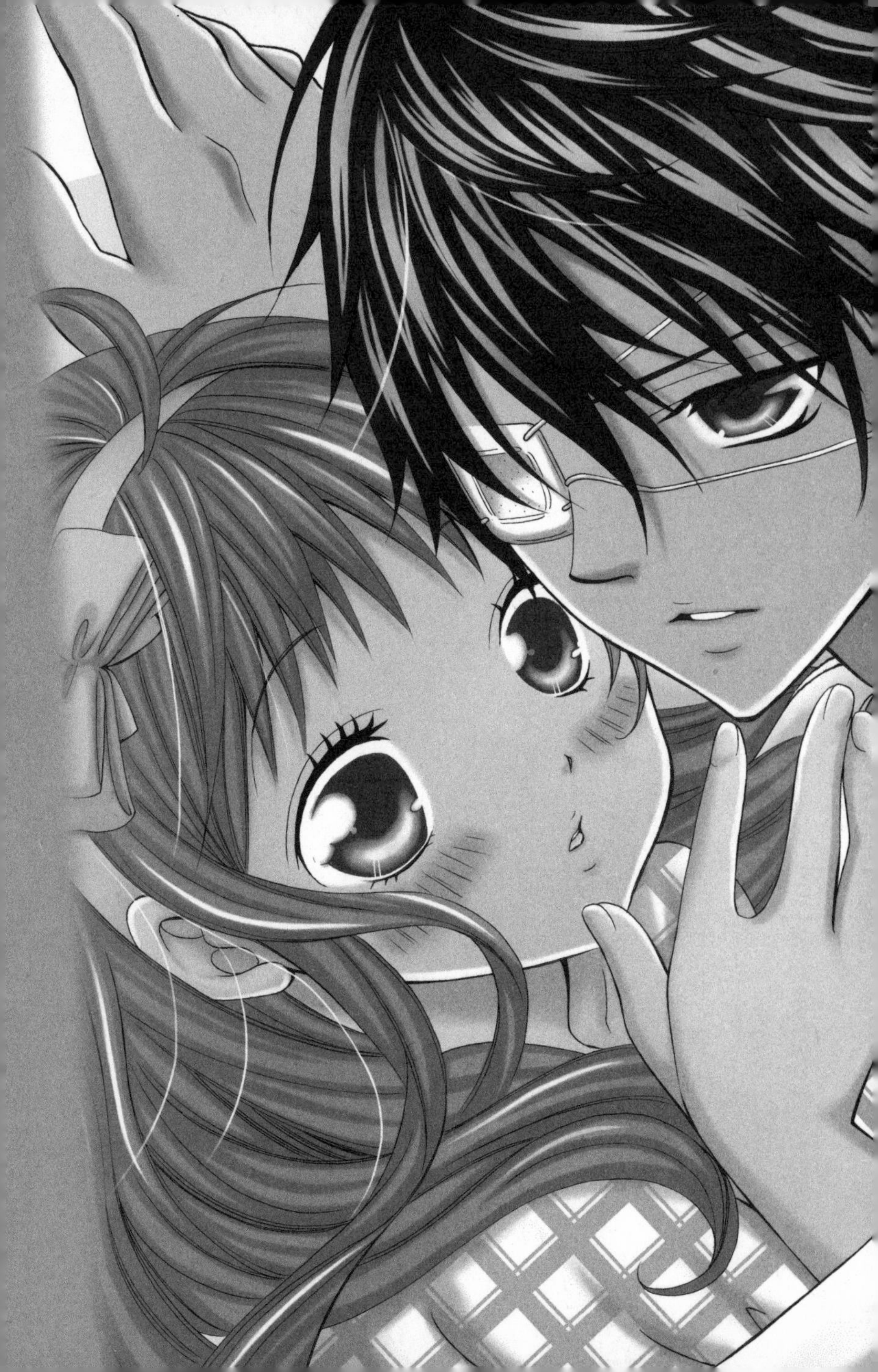

So Cute! Fan Art Feature ♥

EVERYONE'S DRAWINGS ARE SO CUTE, THEY HURT!!

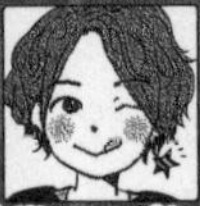

Editor: Shoji

Editor Shoji has commented on each one this time!!

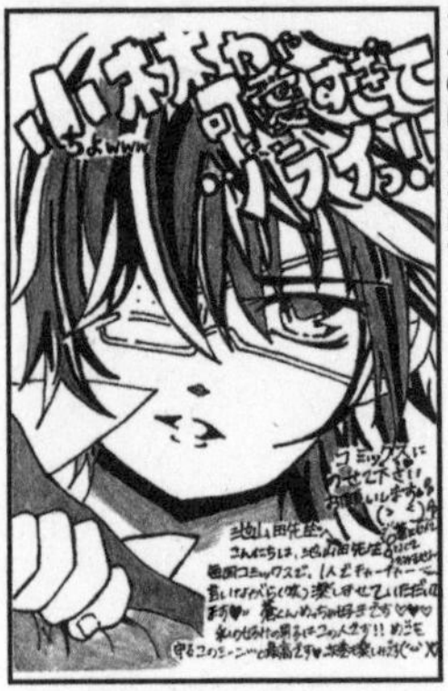

← Seiu (Toyama)
Ed.: This Aoi looks so cool, I'm going to fall in love with him!!

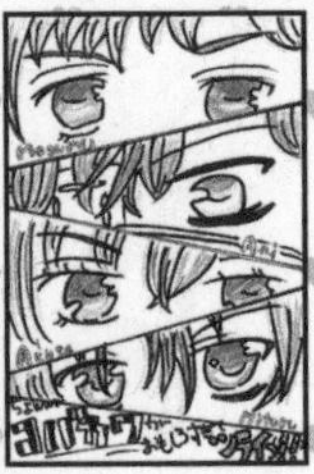

→ Himawari (Yamaguchi)
Ed.: Their eyes knocked me out!

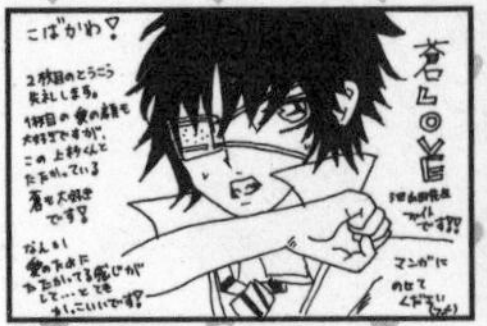

Pokky (Tokyo) ↑
Ed.: My heart flutters at the manly Aoi. ♥

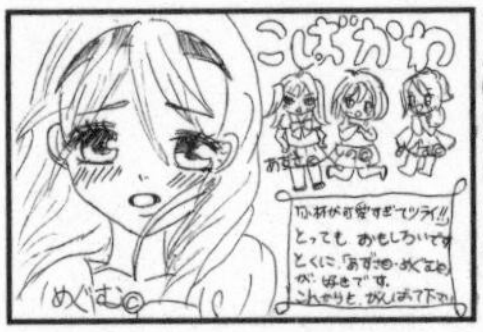

← Aika Sasaki (Saga)
Ed.: I love Mego's slanted eyebrows. ♥

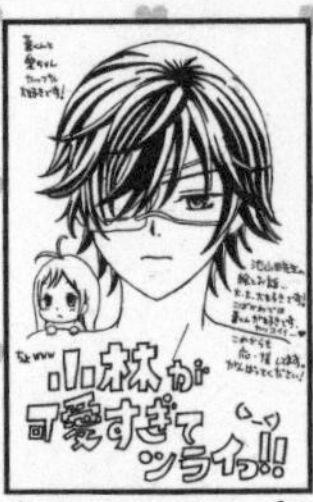

↑ Natsuki Sato (Gifu)
Ed.: I love the way Mego's sitting on Aoi's shoulder.

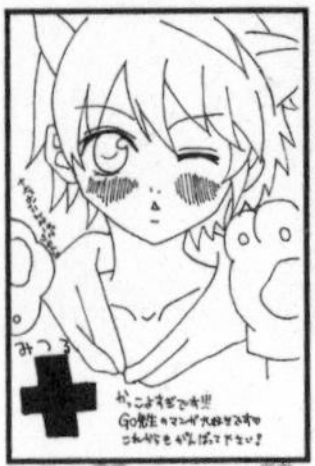

← Kokorin (Hiroshima)
Ed.: Cat ears warning! Mitsuru looks so cute!!

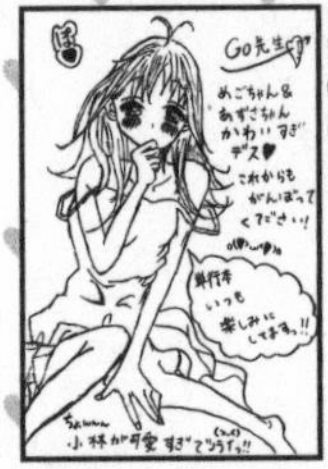

← Ruppy LOL LOL (Nagasaki)
Ed: Mego... looks sexy. ♥

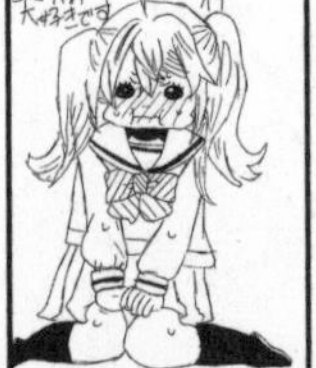

↑ Ami Sakuma (Saitama)
Ed.: I like the pouting Azusa too. ♥

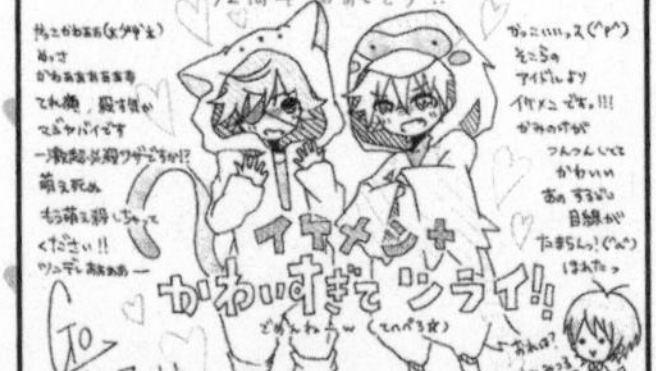

↑ Asuka (Gifu)
Ed.: What's with these cool and cute beings?!

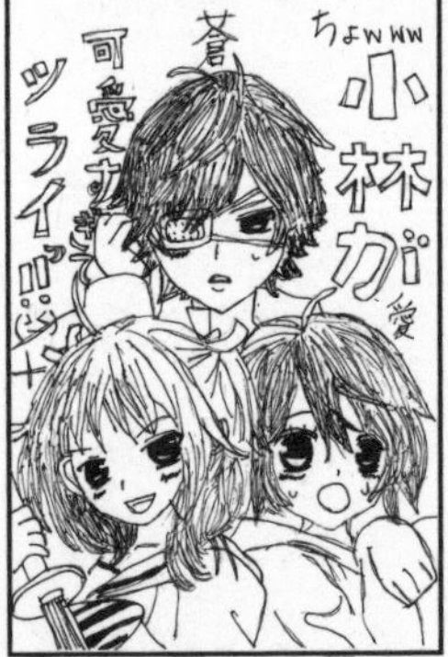

↑ Marin Kubo (Oita)
Ed.: The classic trio!!

YOU'LL BE LATE FOR SCHOOL!

MITSURU!

TIME TO GET UP!

DAZED

THANK YOU FOR ALWAYS SENDING ME LOVELY LETTERS AND DRAWINGS. ♡ ♡
READERS WHO STARTED WITH *SO CUTE!*.
READERS WHO HAVE BEEN SUPPORTING ME SINCE MY DEBUT AND STILL CONTINUE TO WRITE ME LETTERS...
I FIND IT VERY ENCOURAGING THAT SO MANY PEOPLE ARE ROOTING FOR ME.

I HOPE YOU SEND YOUR THOUGHTS AND DRAWINGS AFTER READING VOLUME 9. ♡

GO IKEYAMADA
C/O SHOJO BEAT
VIZ MEDIA, LLC
P.O. BOX 77010
SAN FRANCISCO, CA
94107 (^o^)

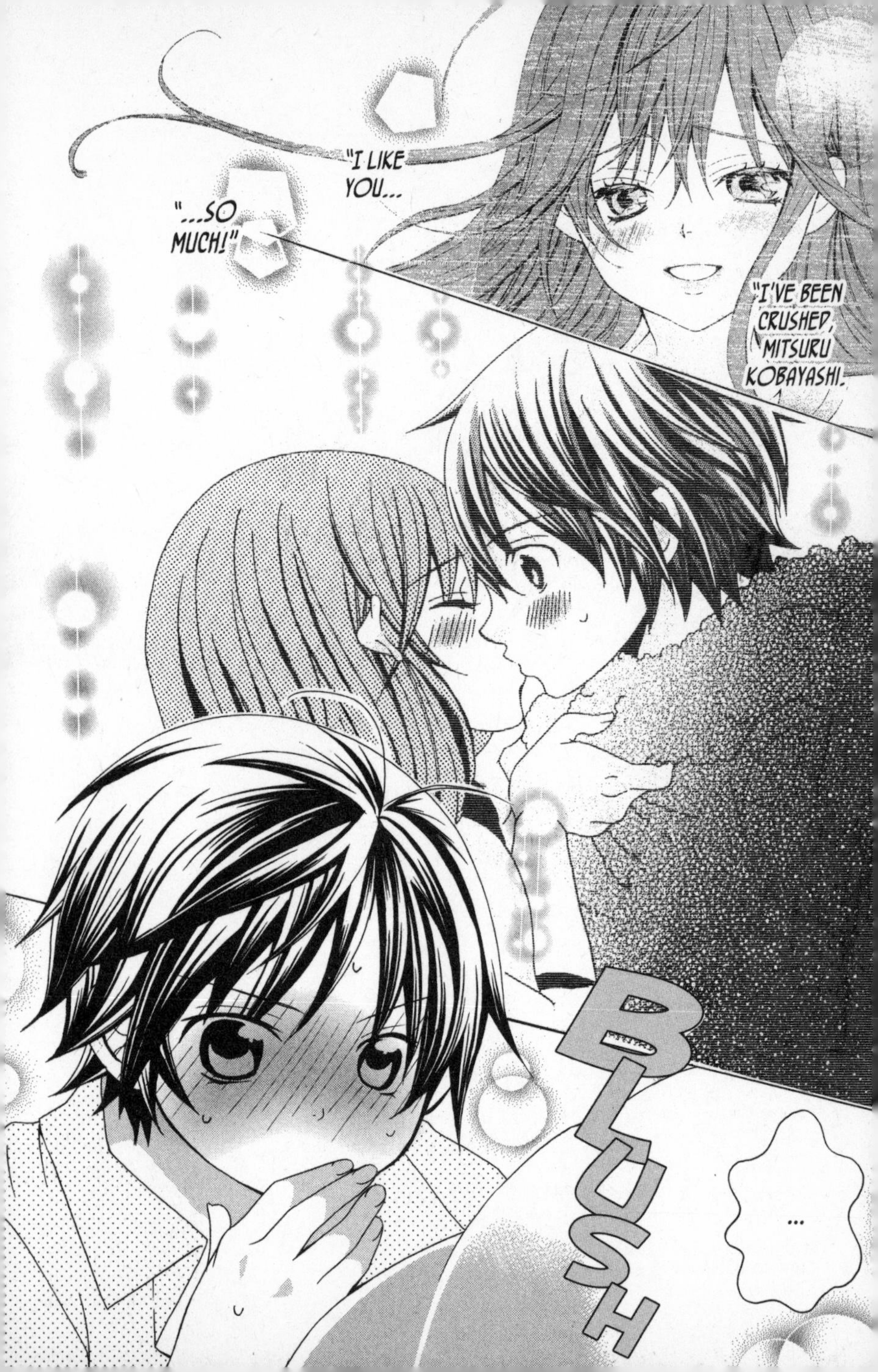
"I'VE BEEN CRUSHED, MITSURU KOBAYASHI."
"I LIKE YOU...
"...SO MUCH!"
...
BLUSH

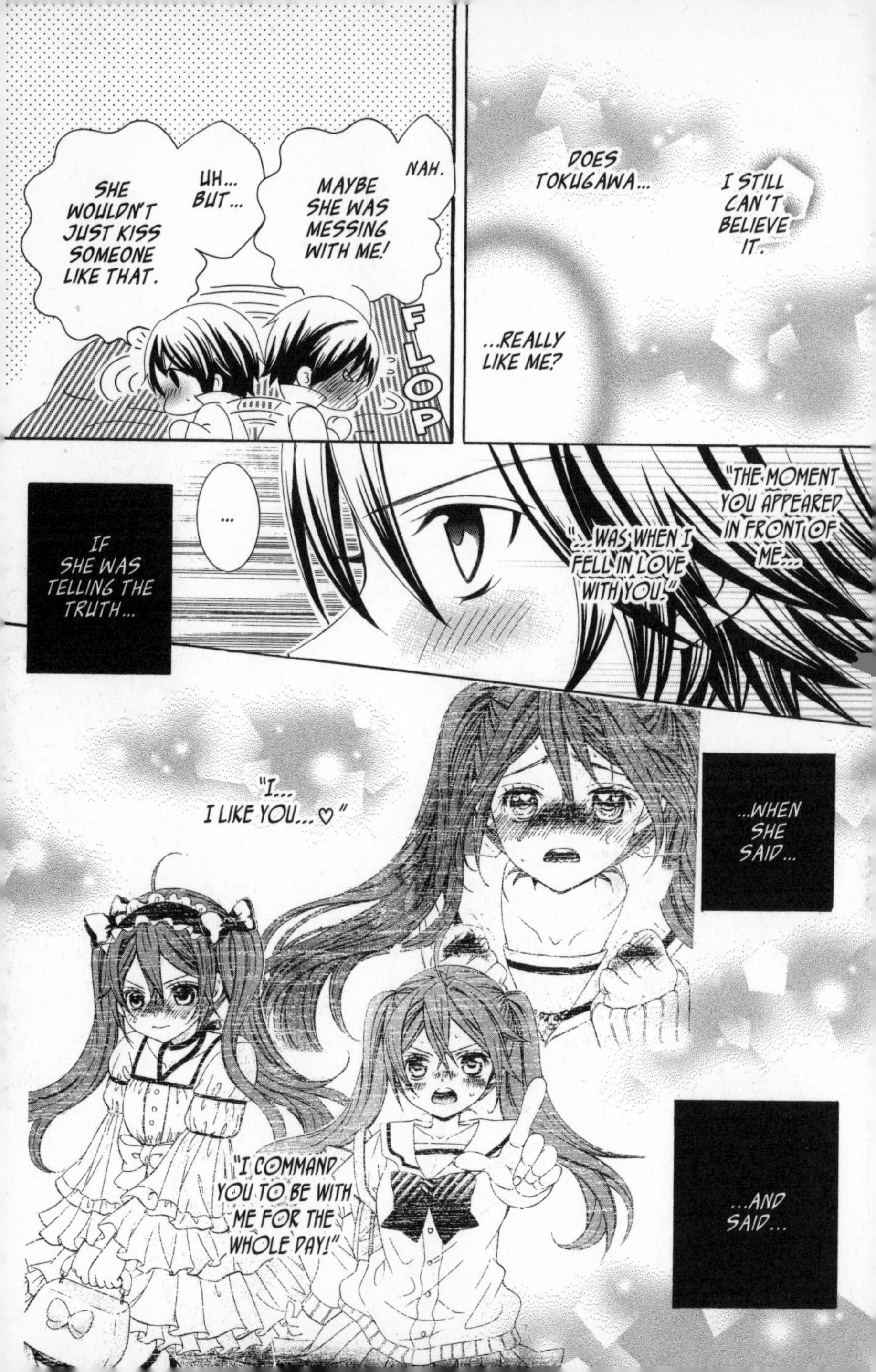
I STILL CAN'T BELIEVE IT.
DOES TOKUGAWA...
...REALLY LIKE ME?
NAH.
MAYBE SHE WAS MESSING WITH ME!
UH... BUT...
SHE WOULDN'T JUST KISS SOMEONE LIKE THAT.
FLOP
"THE MOMENT YOU APPEARED IN FRONT OF ME...
...WAS WHEN I FELL IN LOVE WITH YOU."
...
IF SHE WAS TELLING THE TRUTH...
...WHEN SHE SAID...
"I... I LIKE YOU... ♡"
...AND SAID...
"I COMMAND YOU TO BE WITH ME FOR THE WHOLE DAY!"

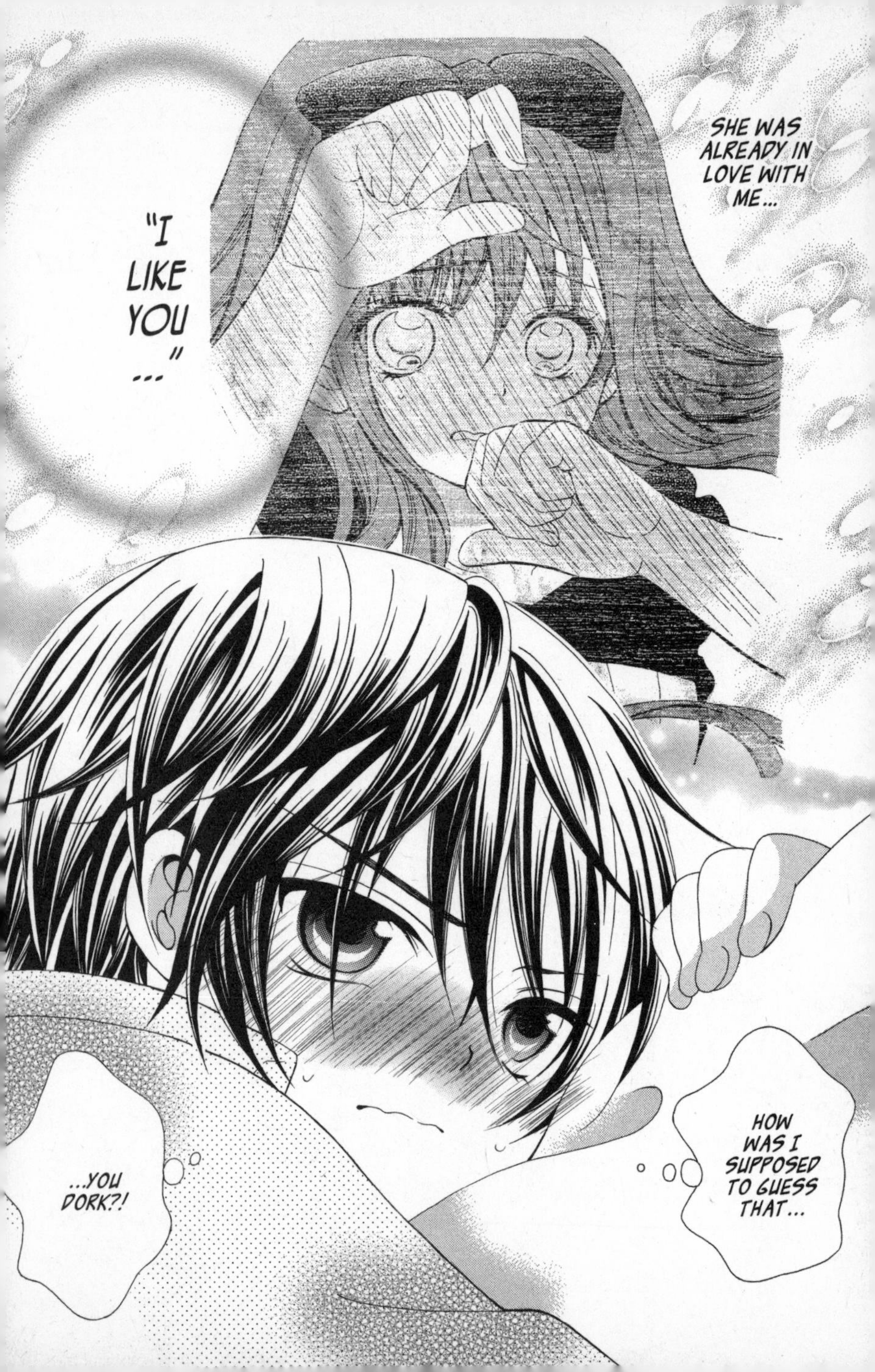
SHE WAS ALREADY IN LOVE WITH ME...
"I LIKE YOU..."
HOW WAS I SUPPOSED TO GUESS THAT...
...YOU DORK?!

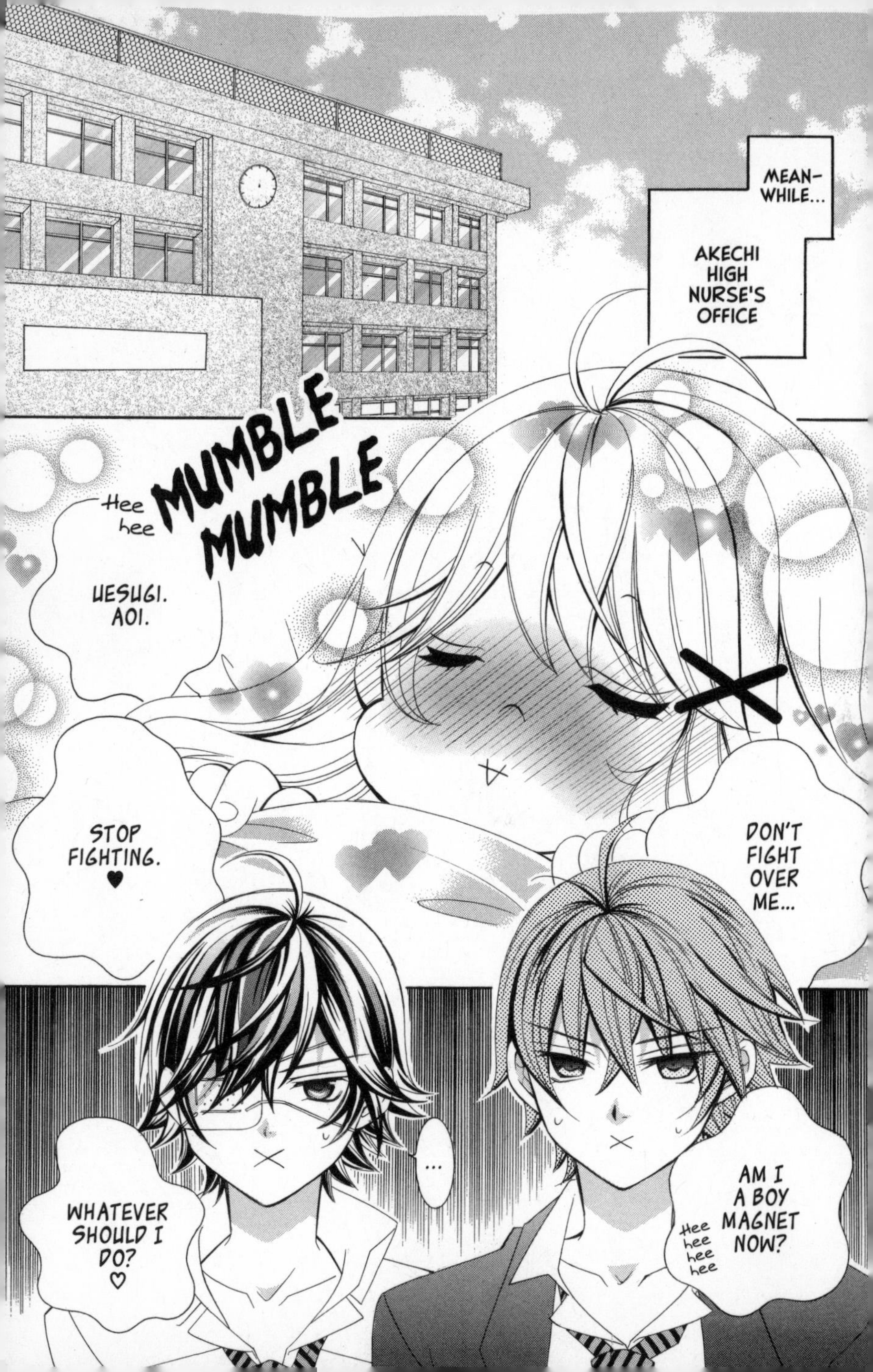
MEAN-WHILE...
AKECHI HIGH NURSE'S OFFICE
MUMBLE MUMBLE
Hee hee
UESUGI. AOI.
DON'T FIGHT OVER ME...
STOP FIGHTING. ♥
AM I A BOY MAGNET NOW?
Hee hee hee hee
...
WHATEVER SHOULD I DO? ♡

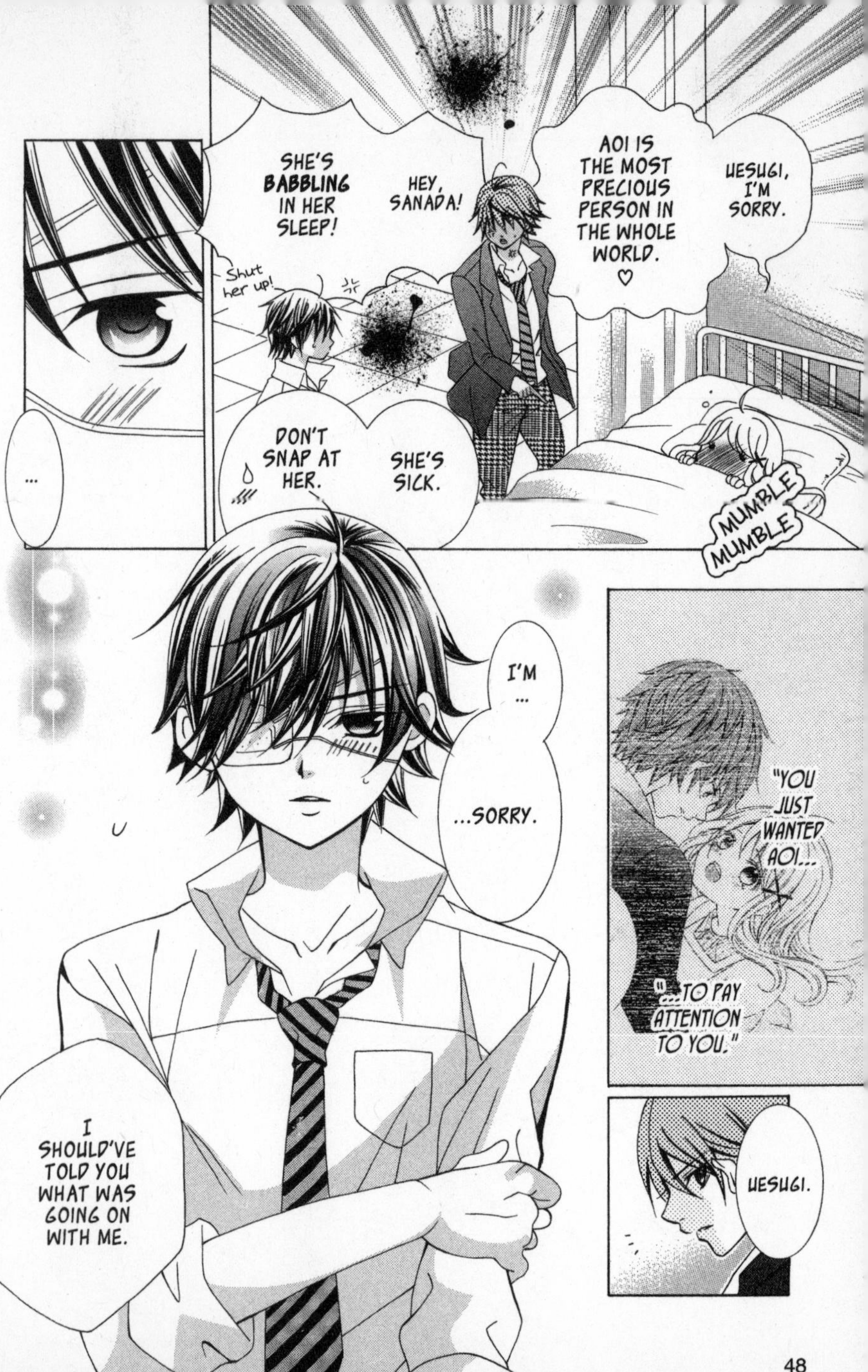
UESUGI, I'M SORRY.
AOI IS THE MOST PRECIOUS PERSON IN THE WHOLE WORLD. ♡
HEY, SANADA!
SHE'S **BABBLING** IN HER SLEEP!
Shut her up!
MUMBLE MUMBLE
SHE'S SICK.
DON'T SNAP AT HER.
...
"YOU JUST WANTED AOI...
"...TO PAY ATTENTION TO YOU."
UESUGI.
I'M ...
...SORRY.
I SHOULD'VE TOLD YOU WHAT WAS GOING ON WITH ME.

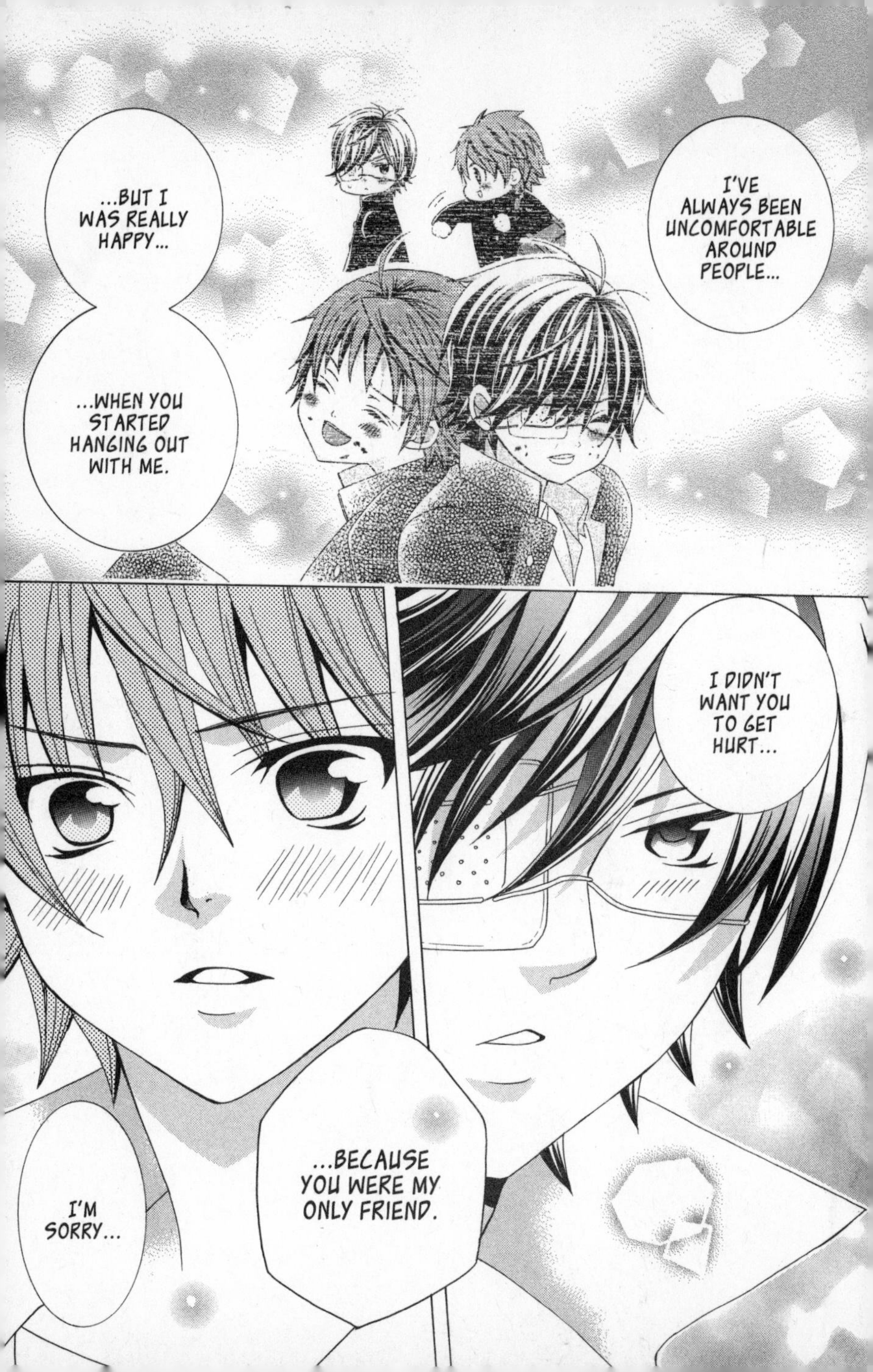
I'VE ALWAYS BEEN UNCOMFORTABLE AROUND PEOPLE...
...BUT I WAS REALLY HAPPY...
...WHEN YOU STARTED HANGING OUT WITH ME.
I DIDN'T WANT YOU TO GET HURT...
...BECAUSE YOU WERE MY ONLY FRIEND.
I'M SORRY...

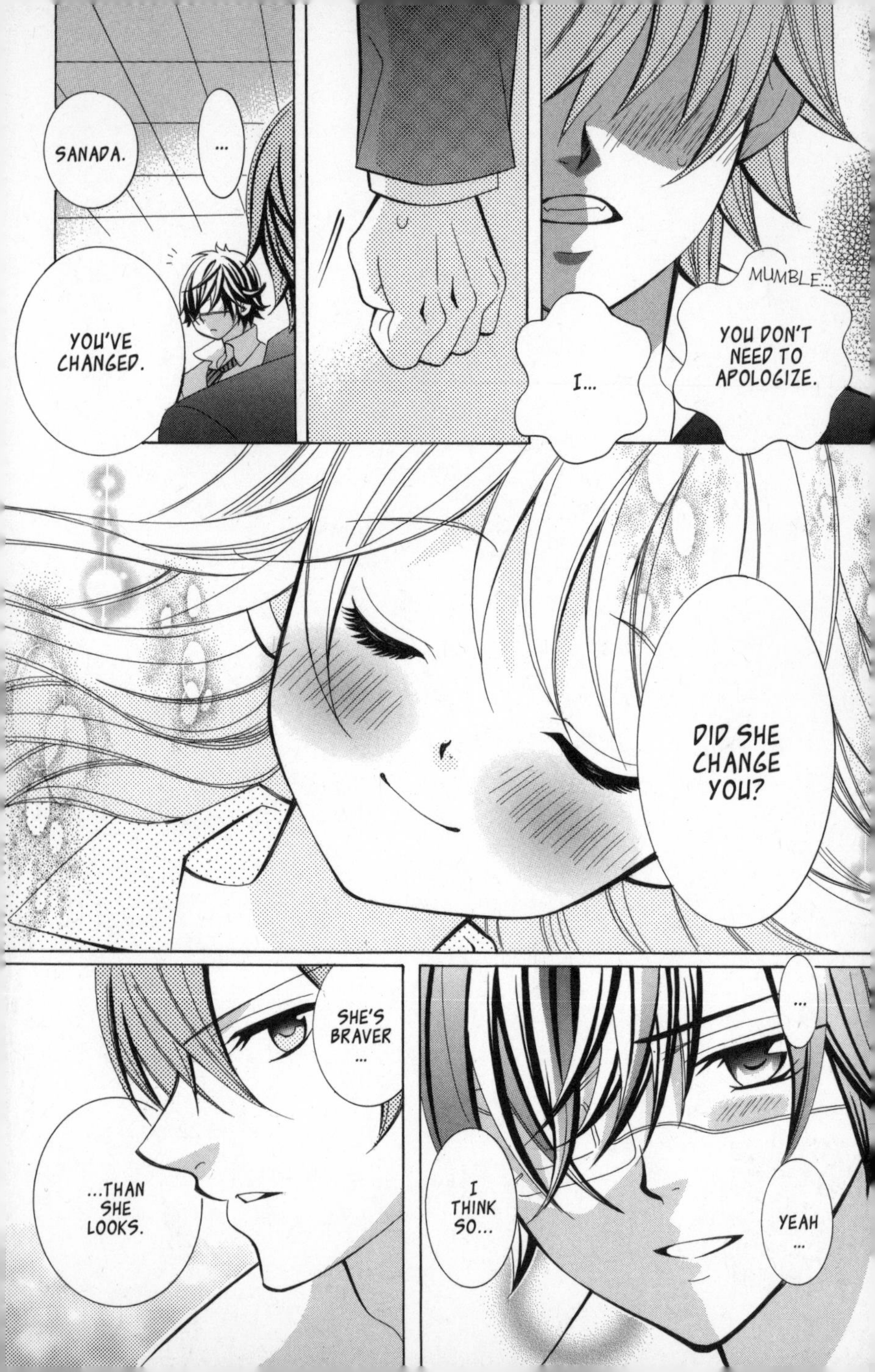
MUMBLE...
YOU DON'T NEED TO APOLOGIZE.
I...
...
SANADA.
YOU'VE CHANGED.
DID SHE CHANGE YOU?
...
YEAH ...
I THINK SO...
SHE'S BRAVER ...
...THAN SHE LOOKS.

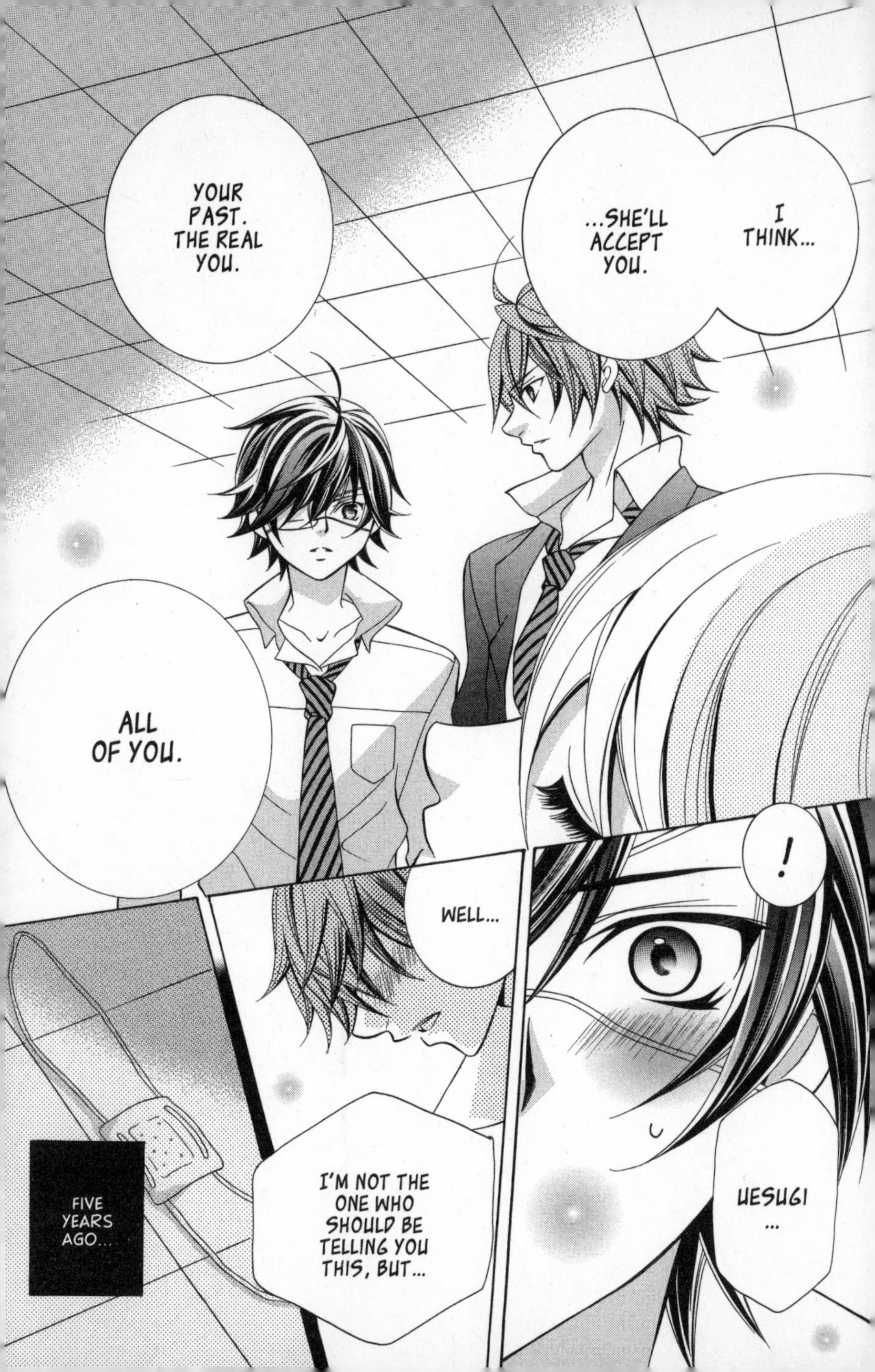
I THINK...
...SHE'LL ACCEPT YOU.
YOUR PAST. THE REAL YOU.
ALL OF YOU.
!
UESUGI...
WELL...
I'M NOT THE ONE WHO SHOULD BE TELLING YOU THIS, BUT...
FIVE YEARS AGO...

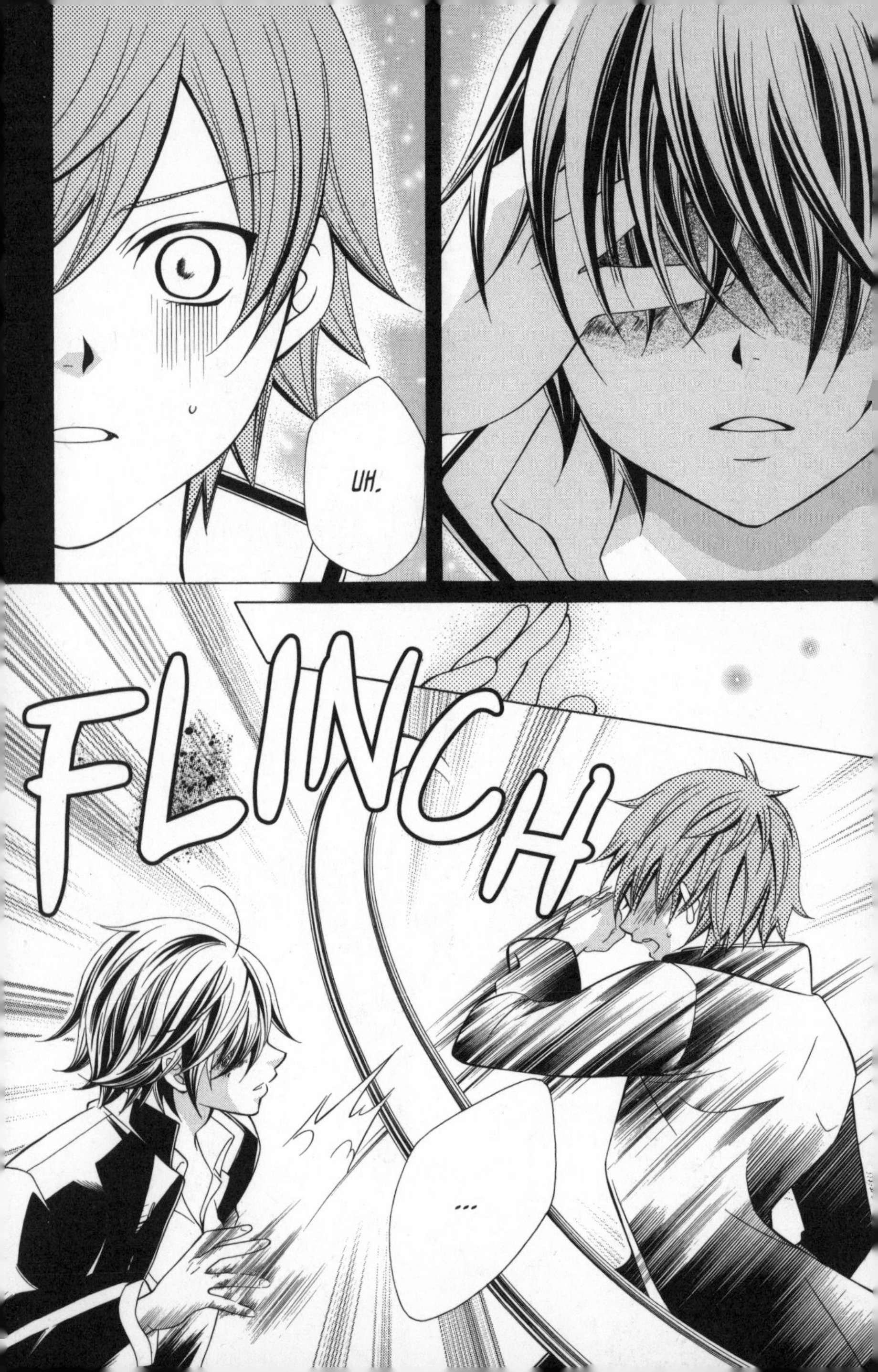
UH.
FLINCH
...

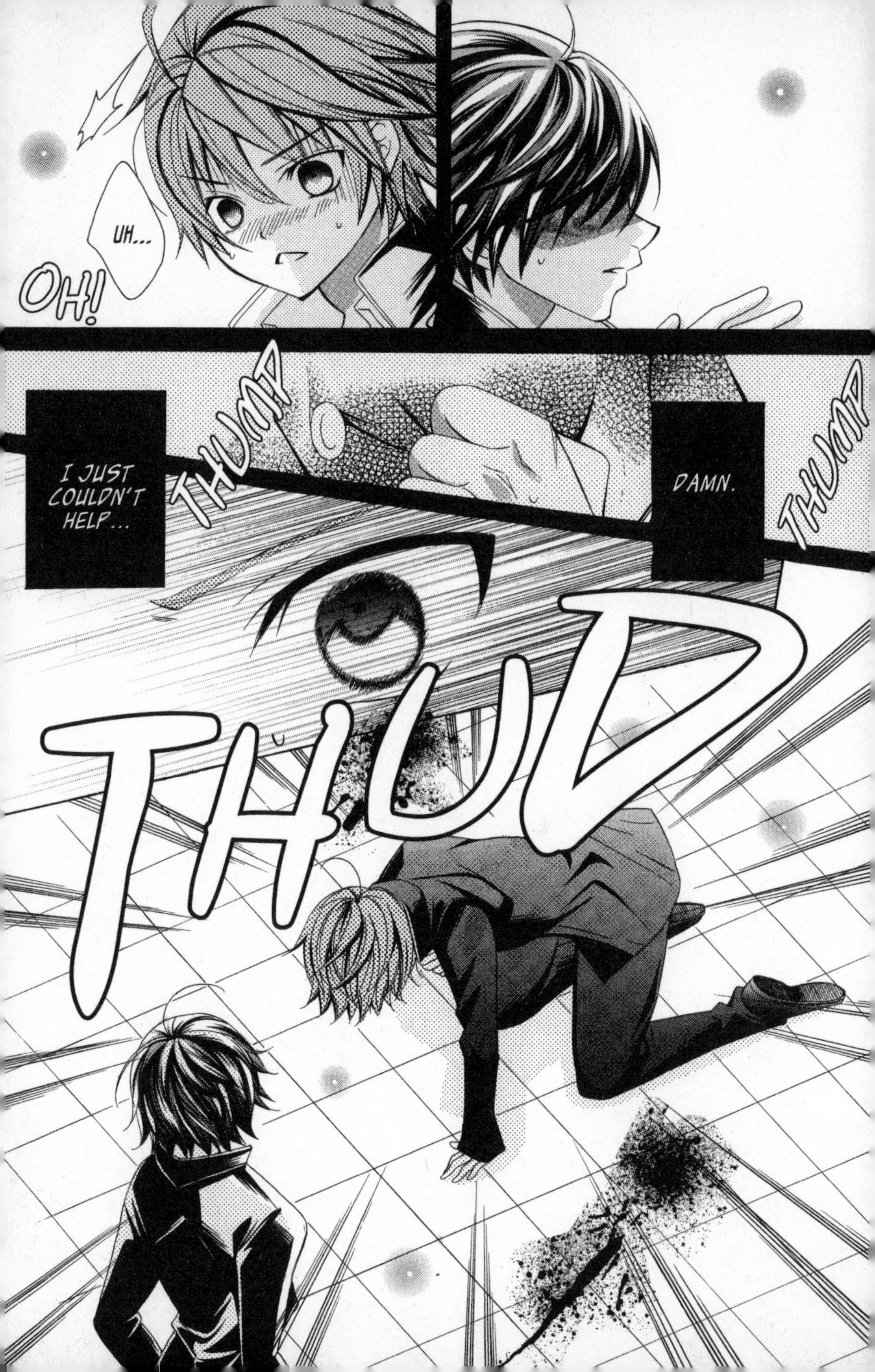
UH...
OH!
THUMP
DAMN.
THUMP
I JUST COULDN'T HELP...
THUD

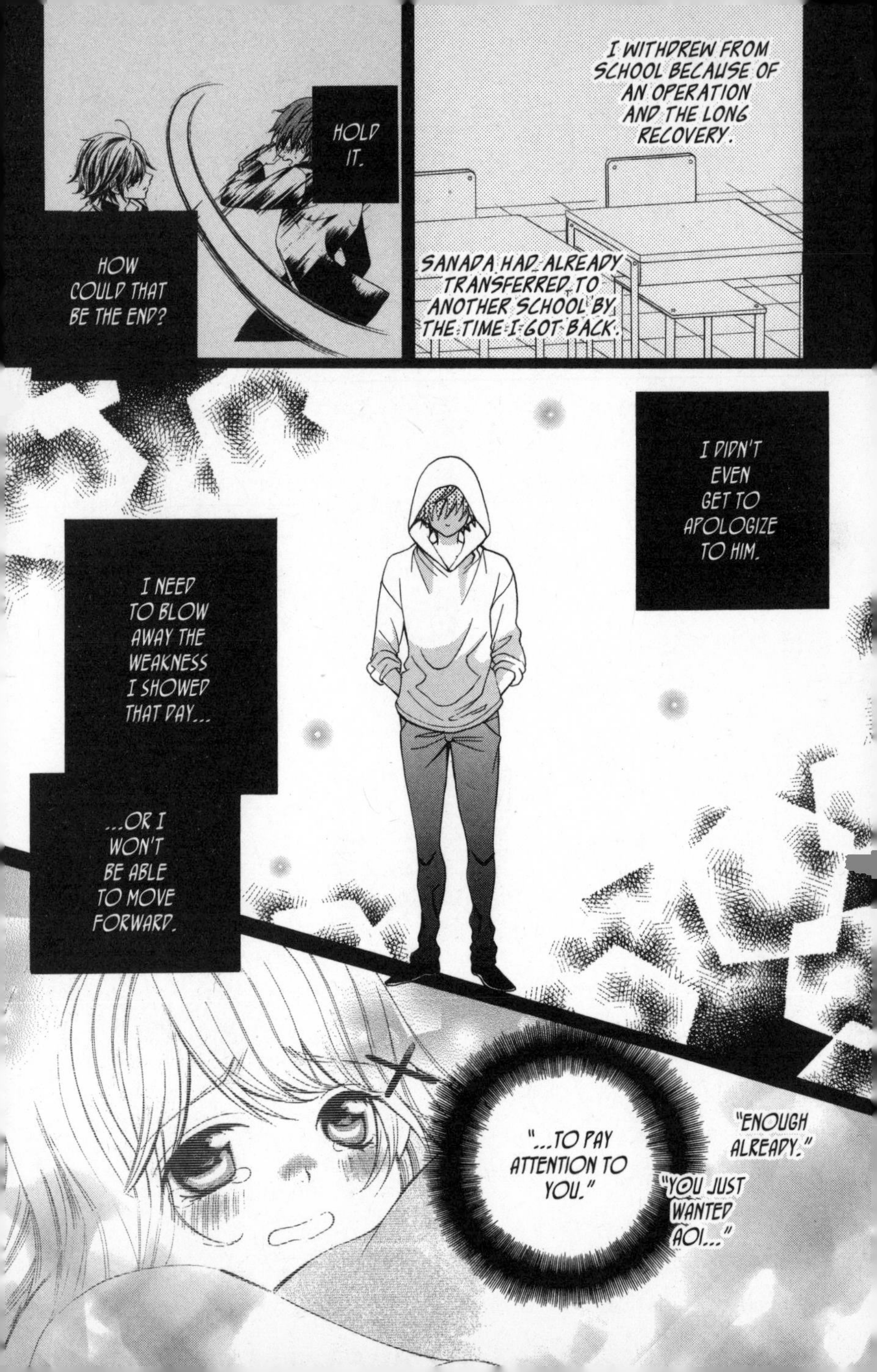
I WITHDREW FROM SCHOOL BECAUSE OF AN OPERATION AND THE LONG RECOVERY.
SANADA HAD ALREADY TRANSFERRED TO ANOTHER SCHOOL BY THE TIME I GOT BACK.
HOLD IT.
HOW COULD THAT BE THE END?
I DIDN'T EVEN GET TO APOLOGIZE TO HIM.
I NEED TO BLOW AWAY THE WEAKNESS I SHOWED THAT DAY...
...OR I WON'T BE ABLE TO MOVE FORWARD.
"ENOUGH ALREADY."
"YOU JUST WANTED AOI..."
"...TO PAY ATTENTION TO YOU."

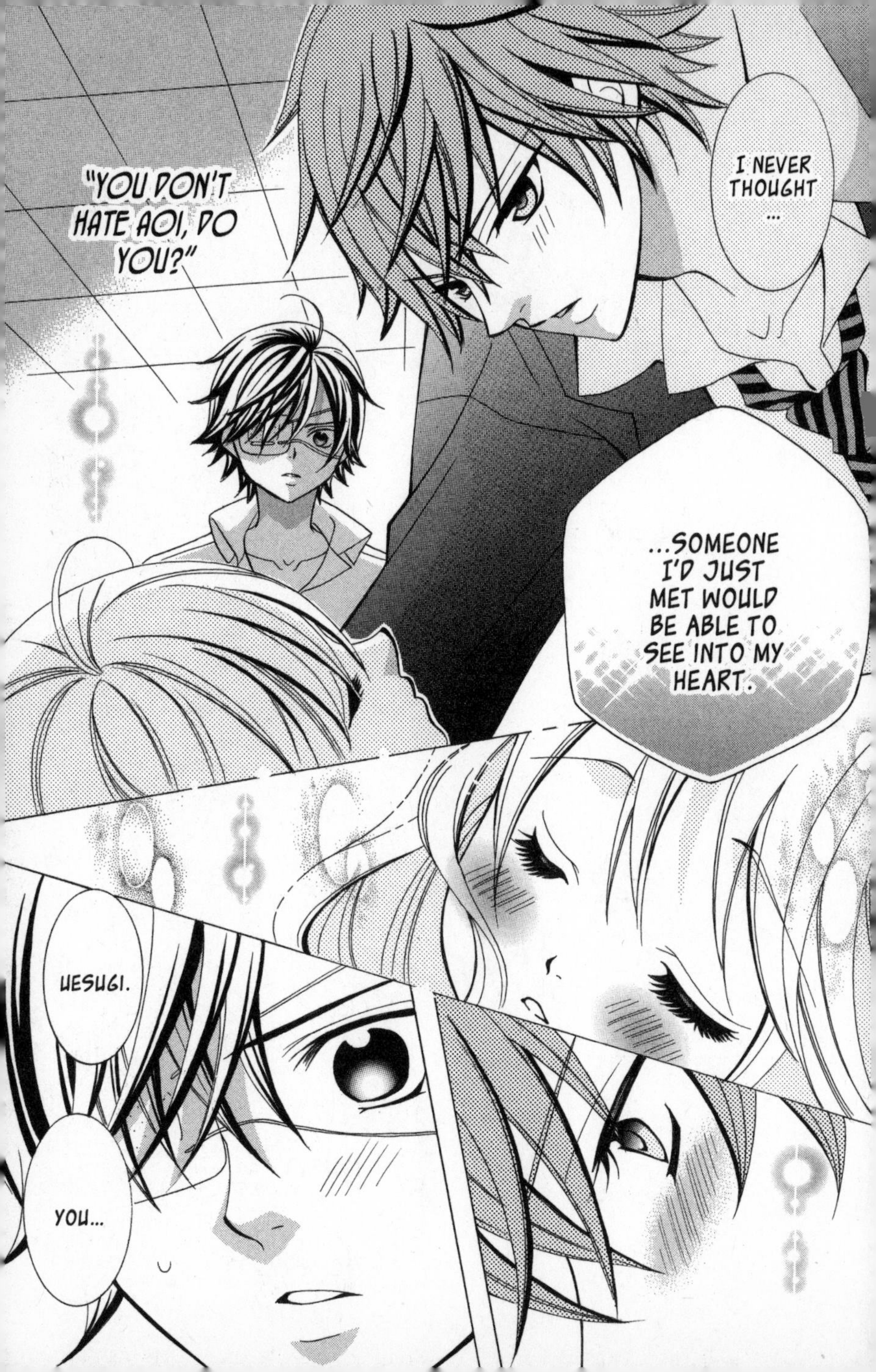
I NEVER THOUGHT ...
"YOU DON'T HATE AOI, DO YOU?"
...SOMEONE I'D JUST MET WOULD BE ABLE TO SEE INTO MY HEART.
UESUGI.
YOU...

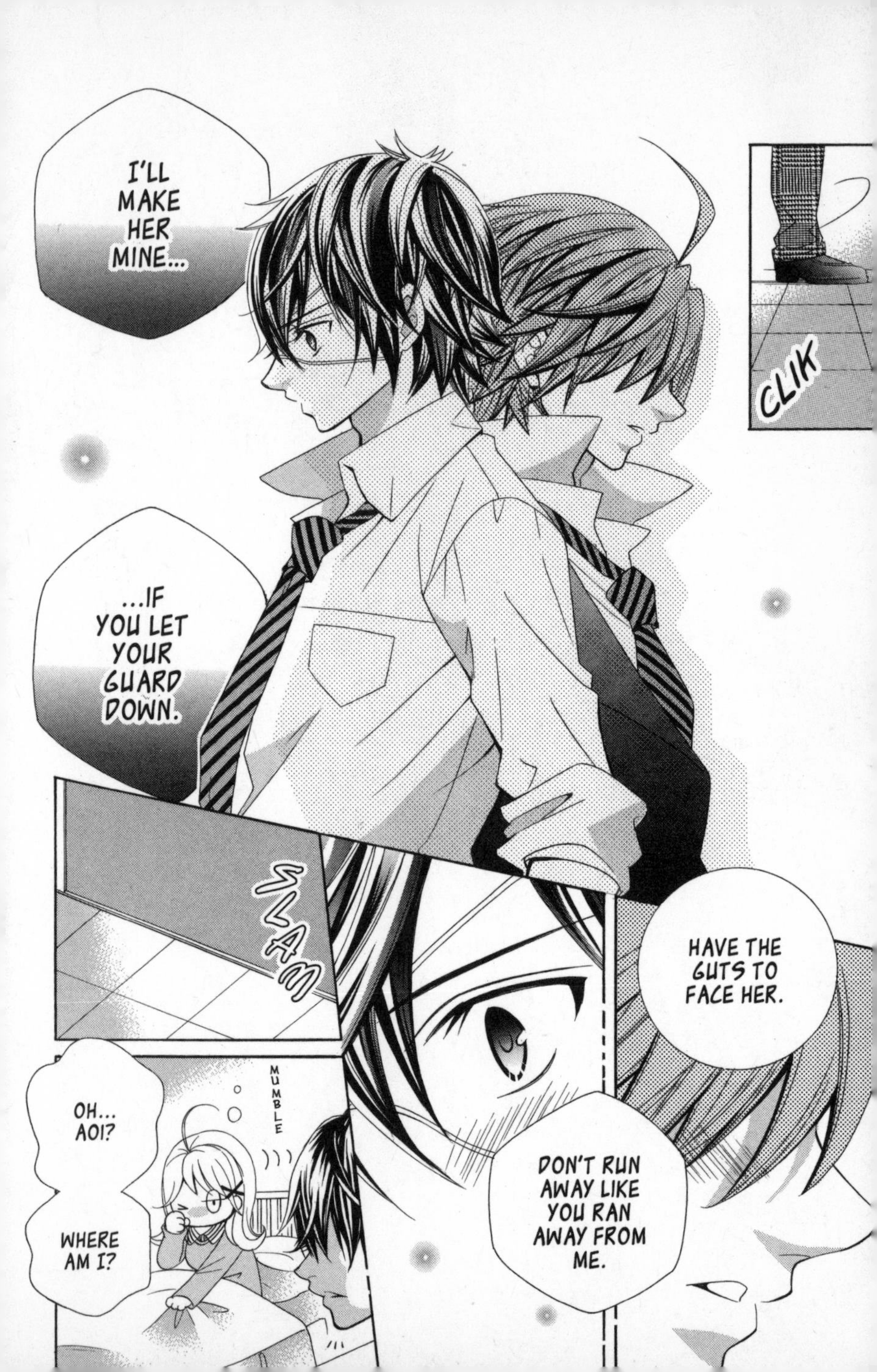
CLIK
I'LL MAKE HER MINE...
...IF YOU LET YOUR GUARD DOWN.
HAVE THE GUTS TO FACE HER.
DON'T RUN AWAY LIKE YOU RAN AWAY FROM ME.
SLAM
OH... AOI?
MUMBLE
WHERE AM I?

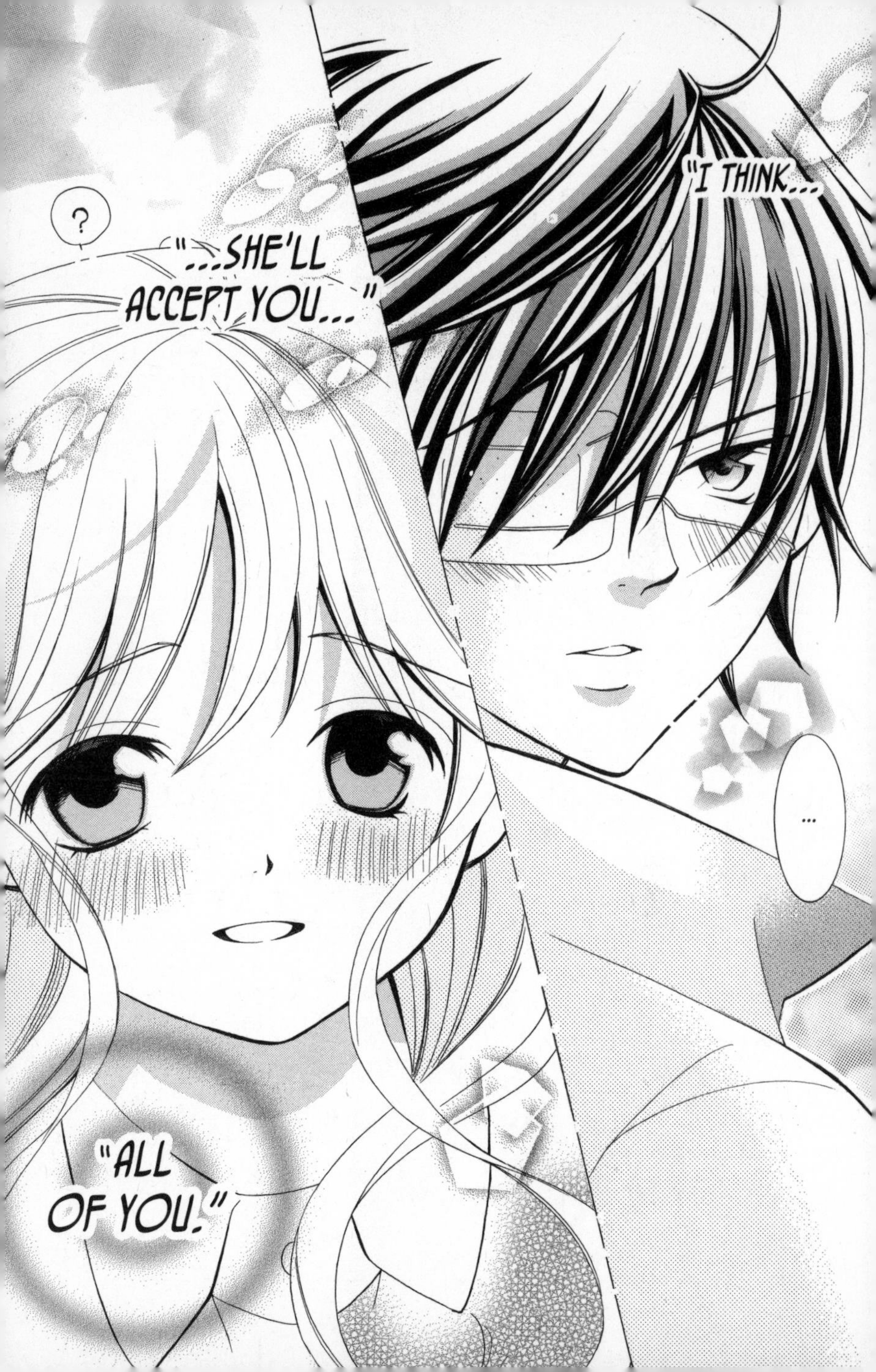
"I THINK...
"...SHE'LL ACCEPT YOU..."
?
...
"ALL OF YOU."

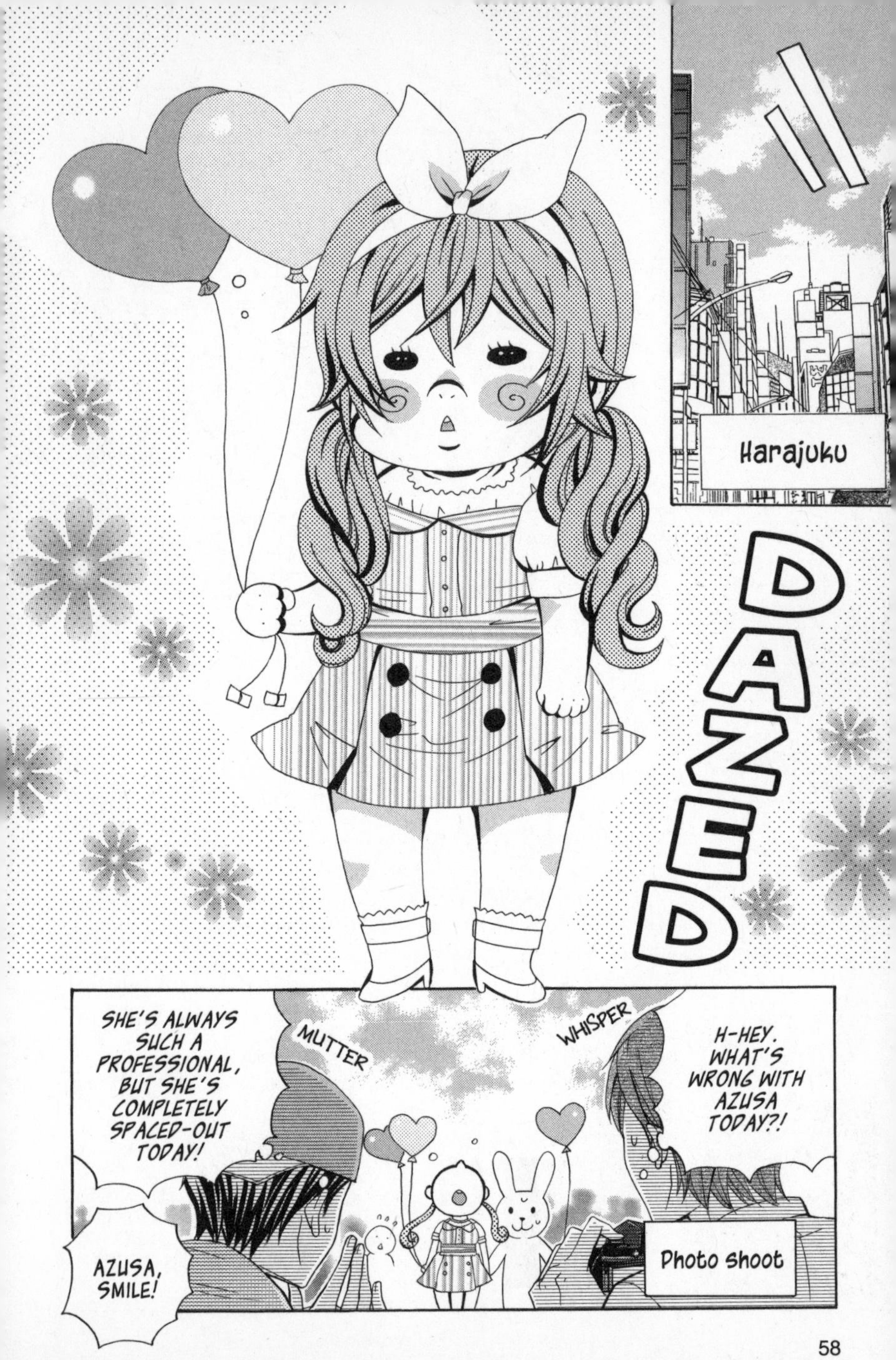
Harajuku
DAZED
H-HEY. WHAT'S WRONG WITH AZUSA TODAY?!
WHISPER
Photo shoot
MUTTER
SHE'S ALWAYS SUCH A PROFESSIONAL, BUT SHE'S COMPLETELY SPACED-OUT TODAY!
AZUSA, SMILE!

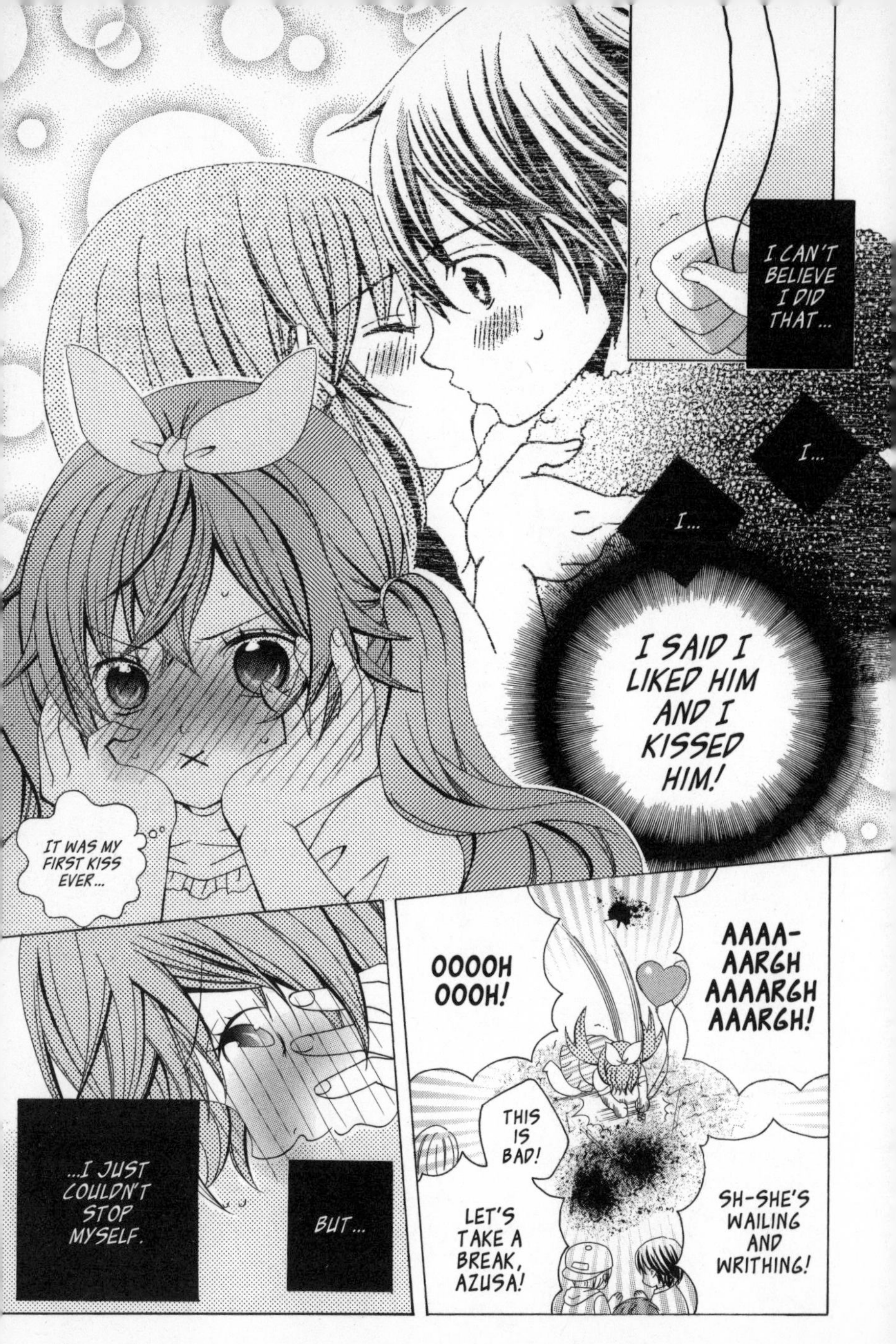
I CAN'T BELIEVE I DID THAT...
I...
I...
I SAID I LIKED HIM AND I KISSED HIM!
IT WAS MY FIRST KISS EVER...
AAAA-AARGH AAAARGH AAARGH!
OOOOH OOOH!
THIS IS BAD!
SH-SHE'S WAILING AND WRITHING!
LET'S TAKE A BREAK, AZUSA!
BUT...
...I JUST COULDN'T STOP MYSELF.

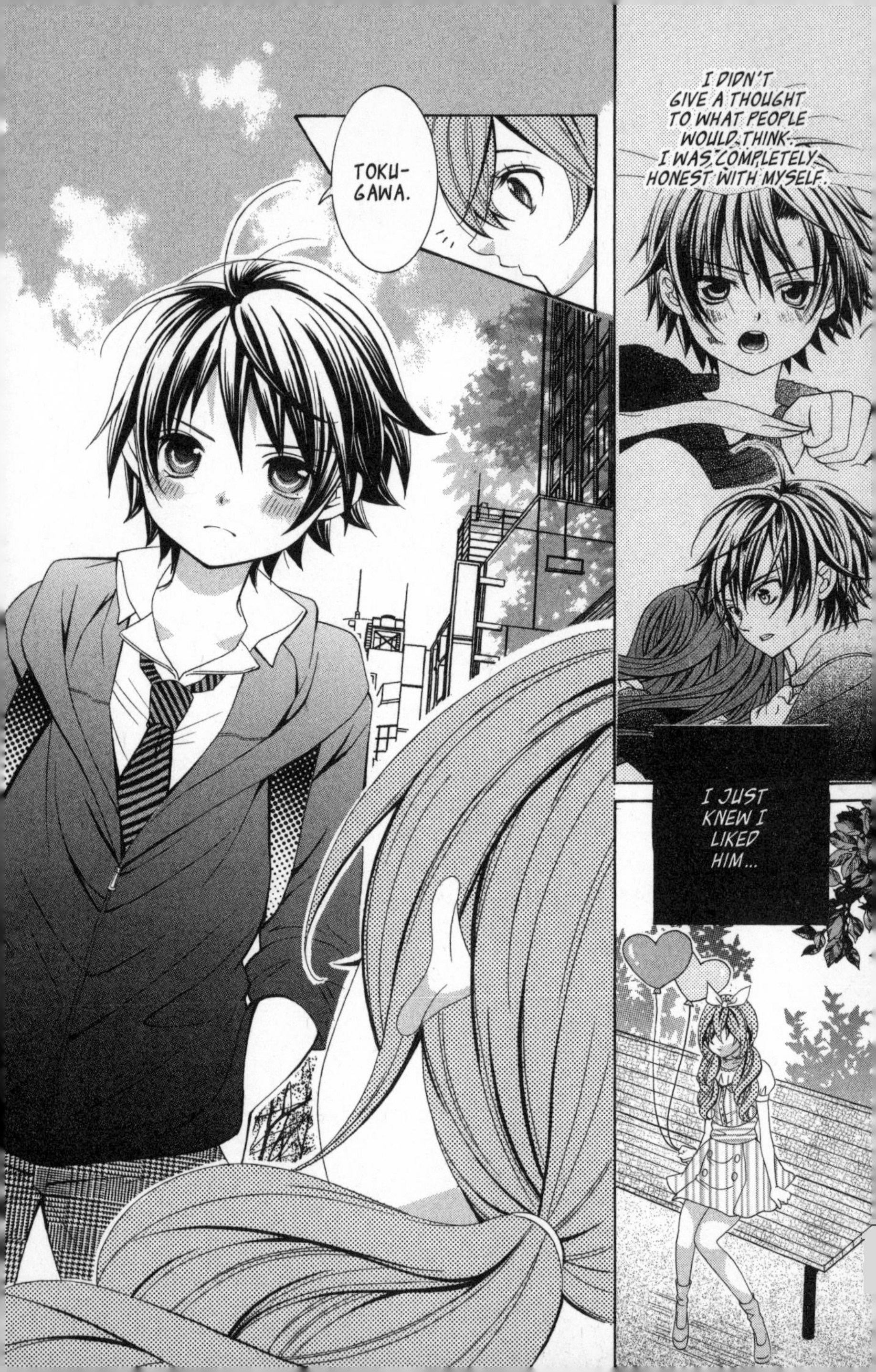
I DIDN'T GIVE A THOUGHT TO WHAT PEOPLE WOULD THINK. I WAS COMPLETELY HONEST WITH MYSELF.
I JUST KNEW I LIKED HIM...
TOKU-GAWA.

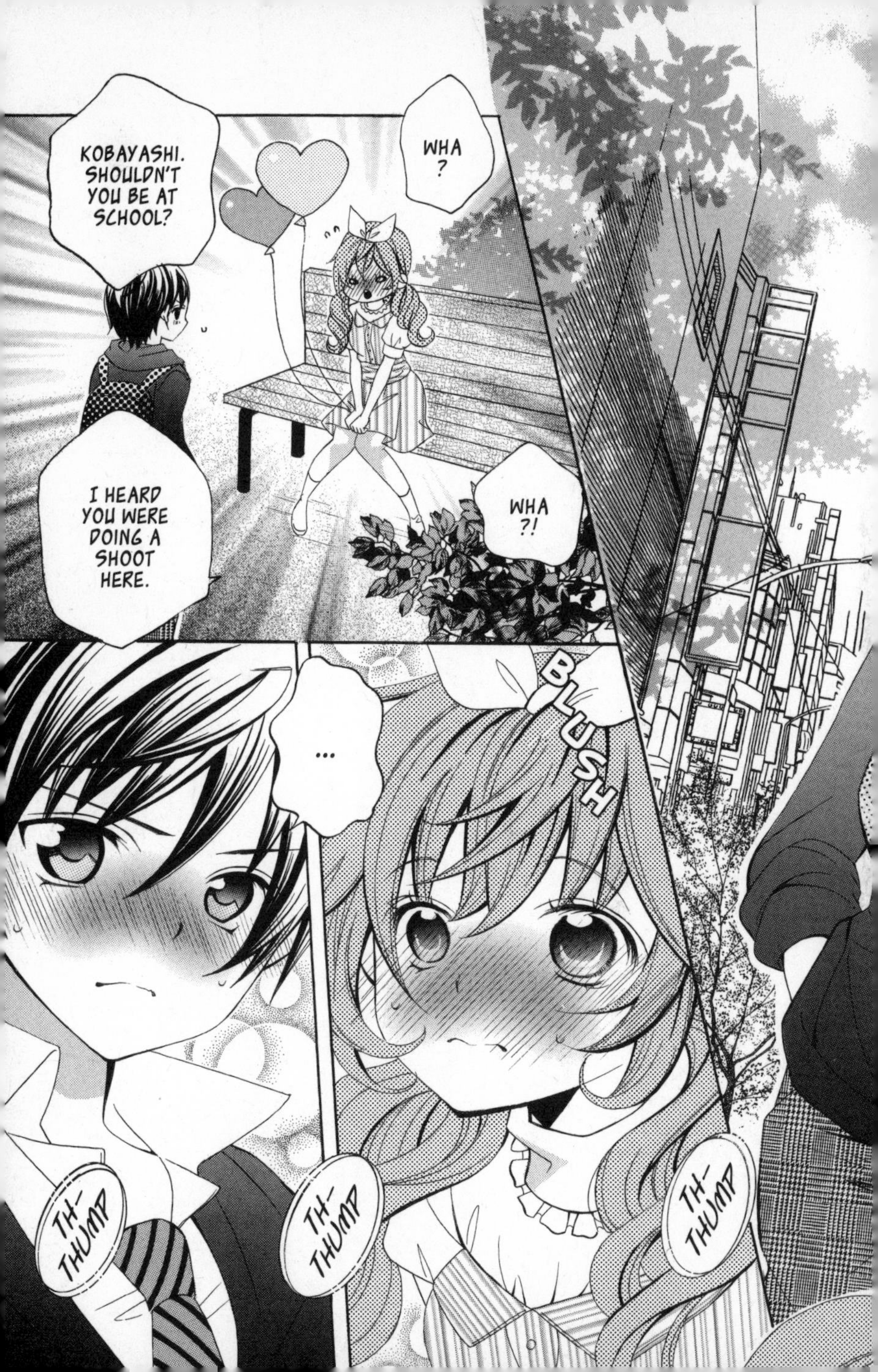
WHA ?
KOBAYASHI. SHOULDN'T YOU BE AT SCHOOL?
WHA ?!
I HEARD YOU WERE DOING A SHOOT HERE.
BLUSH
...
TH-THUMP
TH-THUMP
TH-THUMP

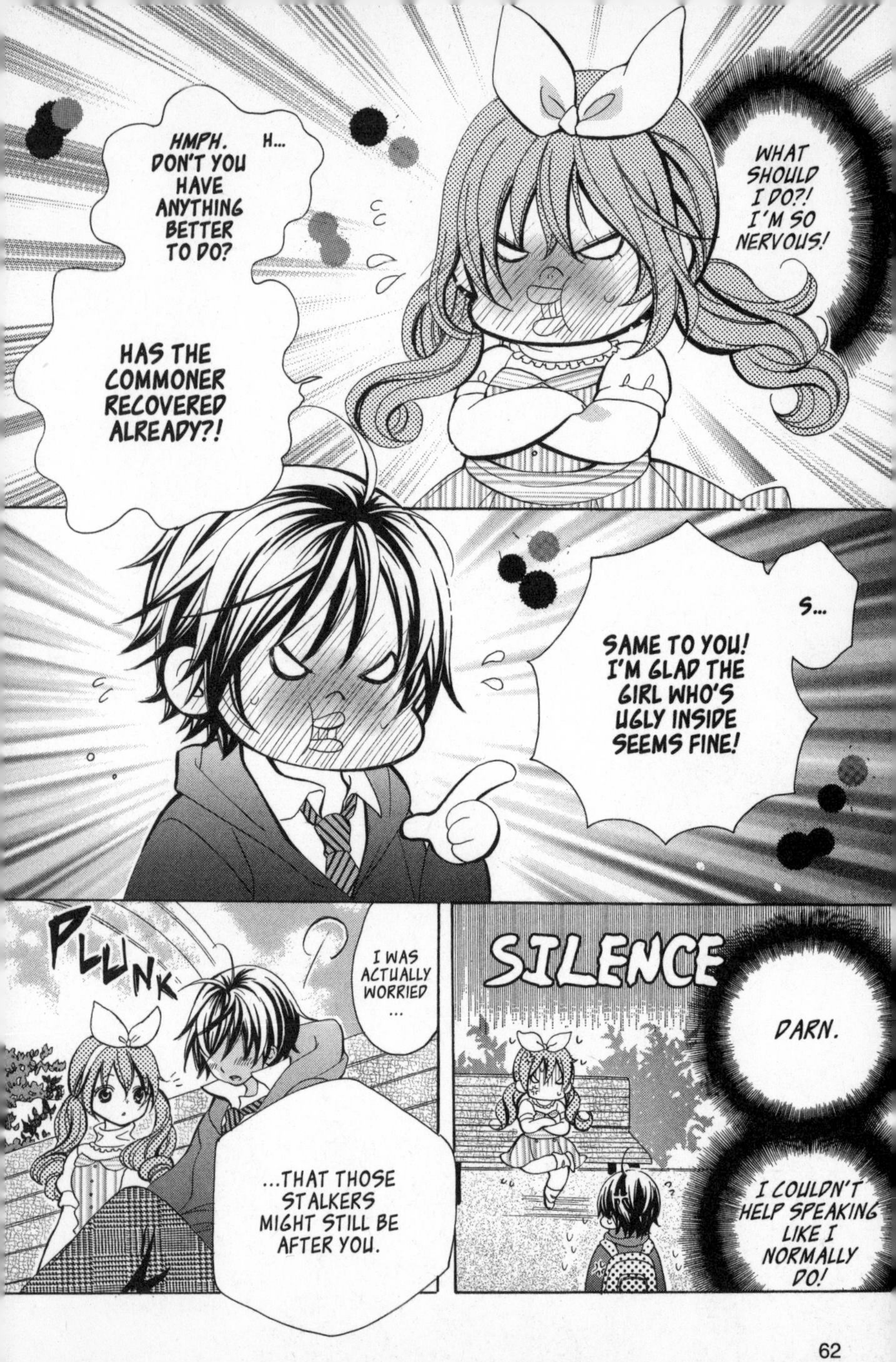
WHAT SHOULD I DO?! I'M SO NERVOUS!
H... HMPH. DON'T YOU HAVE ANYTHING BETTER TO DO?
HAS THE COMMONER RECOVERED ALREADY?!
S...
SAME TO YOU! I'M GLAD THE GIRL WHO'S UGLY INSIDE SEEMS FINE!
SILENCE
DARN.
I COULDN'T HELP SPEAKING LIKE I NORMALLY DO!
PLUNK
I WAS ACTUALLY WORRIED ...
...THAT THOSE STALKERS MIGHT STILL BE AFTER YOU.

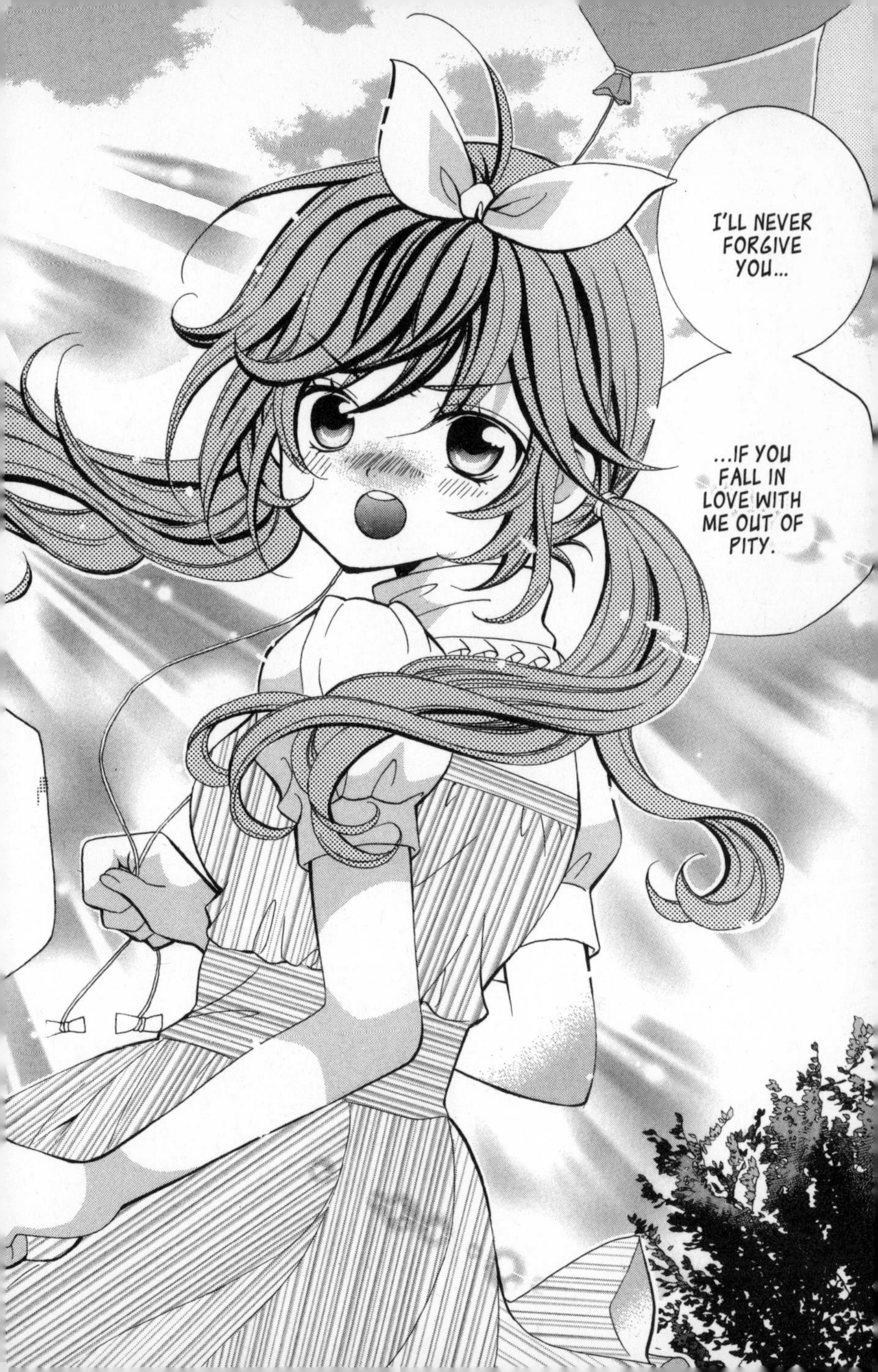
I'LL NEVER FORGIVE YOU...
...IF YOU FALL IN LOVE WITH ME OUT OF PITY.

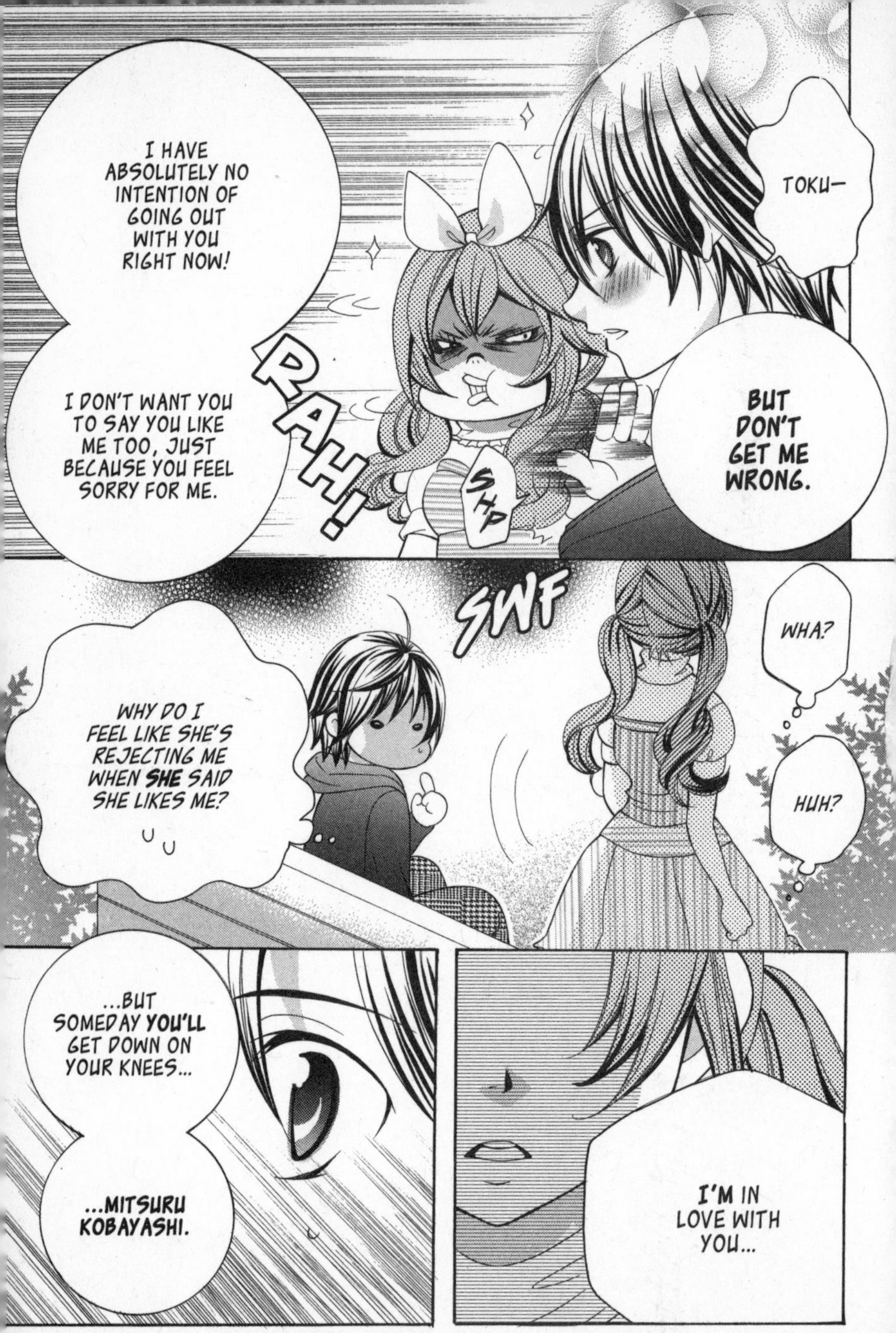
TOKU—
BUT DON'T GET ME WRONG.
I HAVE ABSOLUTELY NO INTENTION OF GOING OUT WITH YOU RIGHT NOW!
RAH!
SHP
I DON'T WANT YOU TO SAY YOU LIKE ME TOO, JUST BECAUSE YOU FEEL SORRY FOR ME.
WHA?
HUH?
SWF
WHY DO I FEEL LIKE SHE'S REJECTING ME WHEN SHE SAID SHE LIKES ME?
I'M IN LOVE WITH YOU...
...BUT SOMEDAY YOU'LL GET DOWN ON YOUR KNEES...
...MITSURU KOBAYASHI.

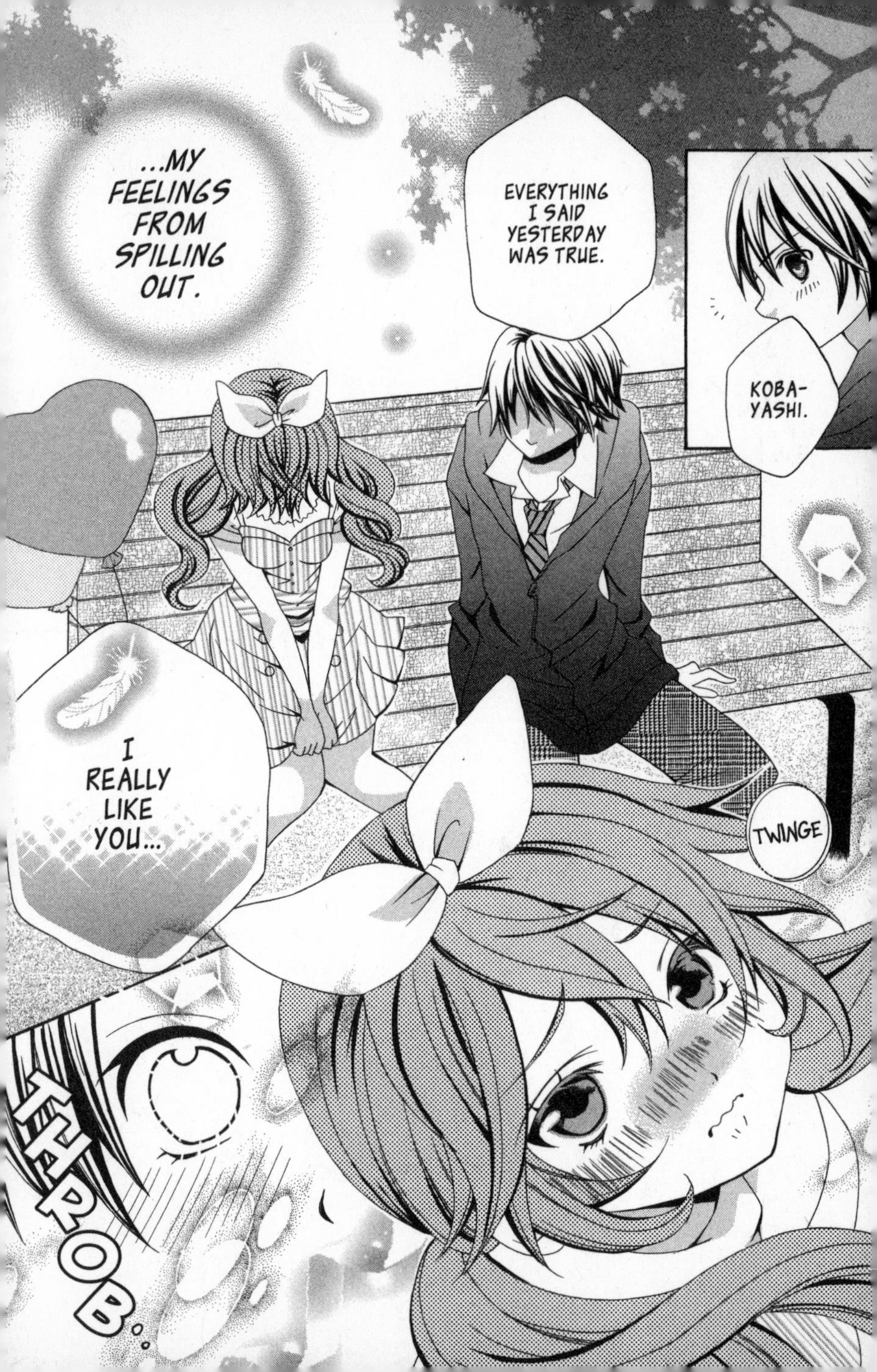
...MY FEELINGS FROM SPILLING OUT.
EVERYTHING I SAID YESTERDAY WAS TRUE.
I REALLY LIKE YOU...
KOBA-YASHI.
TWINGE
THROB

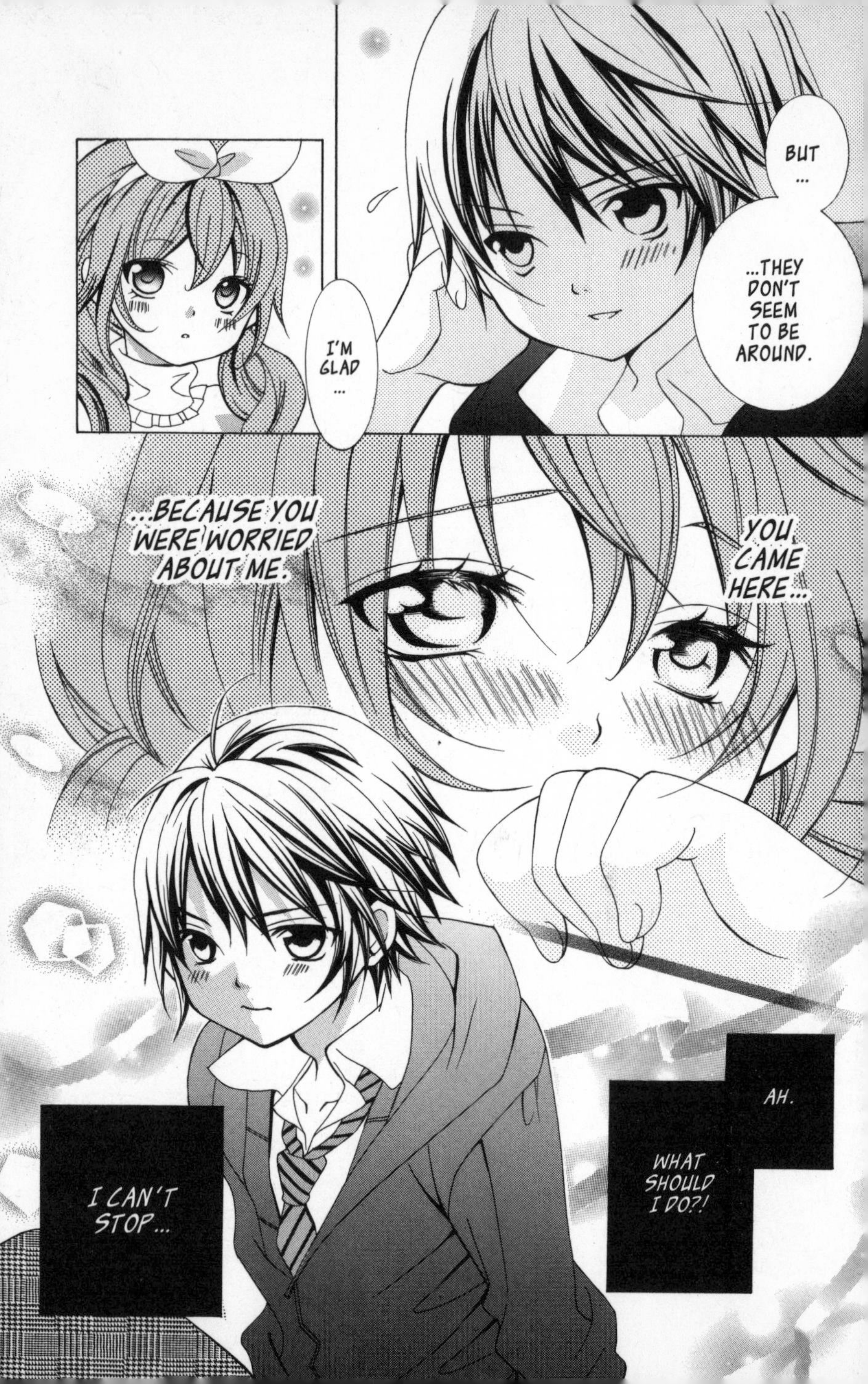
BUT ...
...THEY DON'T SEEM TO BE AROUND.
I'M GLAD ...
YOU CAME HERE...
...BECAUSE YOU WERE WORRIED ABOUT ME.
AH.
WHAT SHOULD I DO?!
I CAN'T STOP...

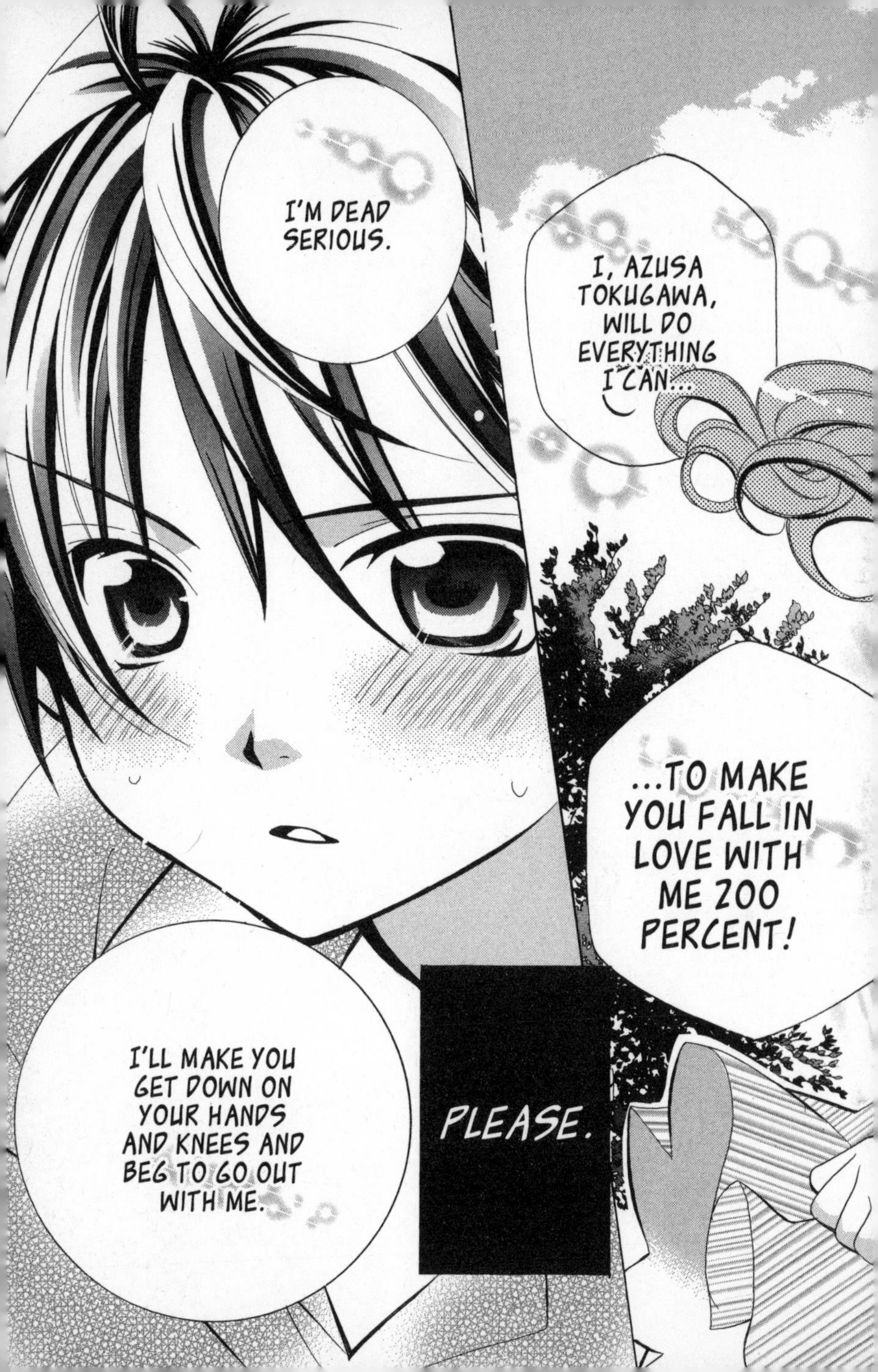
I, AZUSA TOKUGAWA, WILL DO EVERYTHING I CAN...
...TO MAKE YOU FALL IN LOVE WITH ME 200 PERCENT!
I'M DEAD SERIOUS.
PLEASE.
I'LL MAKE YOU GET DOWN ON YOUR HANDS AND KNEES AND BEG TO GO OUT WITH ME.

"LOOK AT ME.
"I WANT TO BE YOUR ONE AND ONLY."
I WANT YOU TO LIKE ME MUCH, MUCH MORE THAN YOU LIKED SHINO...
...AND EVERYONE ELSE YOU'VE EVER GONE OUT WITH!

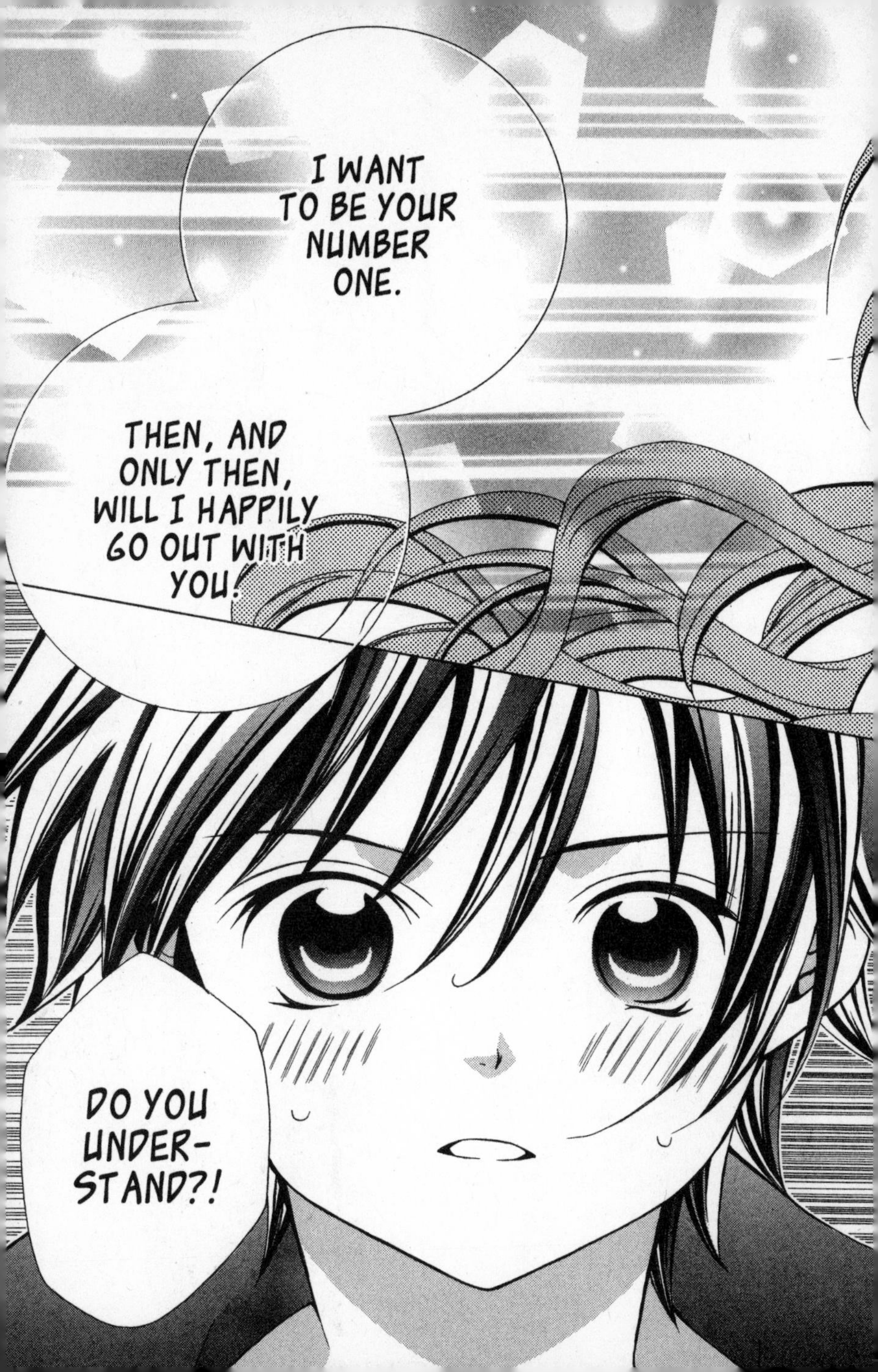
I WANT TO BE YOUR NUMBER ONE.
THEN, AND ONLY THEN, WILL I HAPPILY GO OUT WITH YOU!
DO YOU UNDER-STAND?!

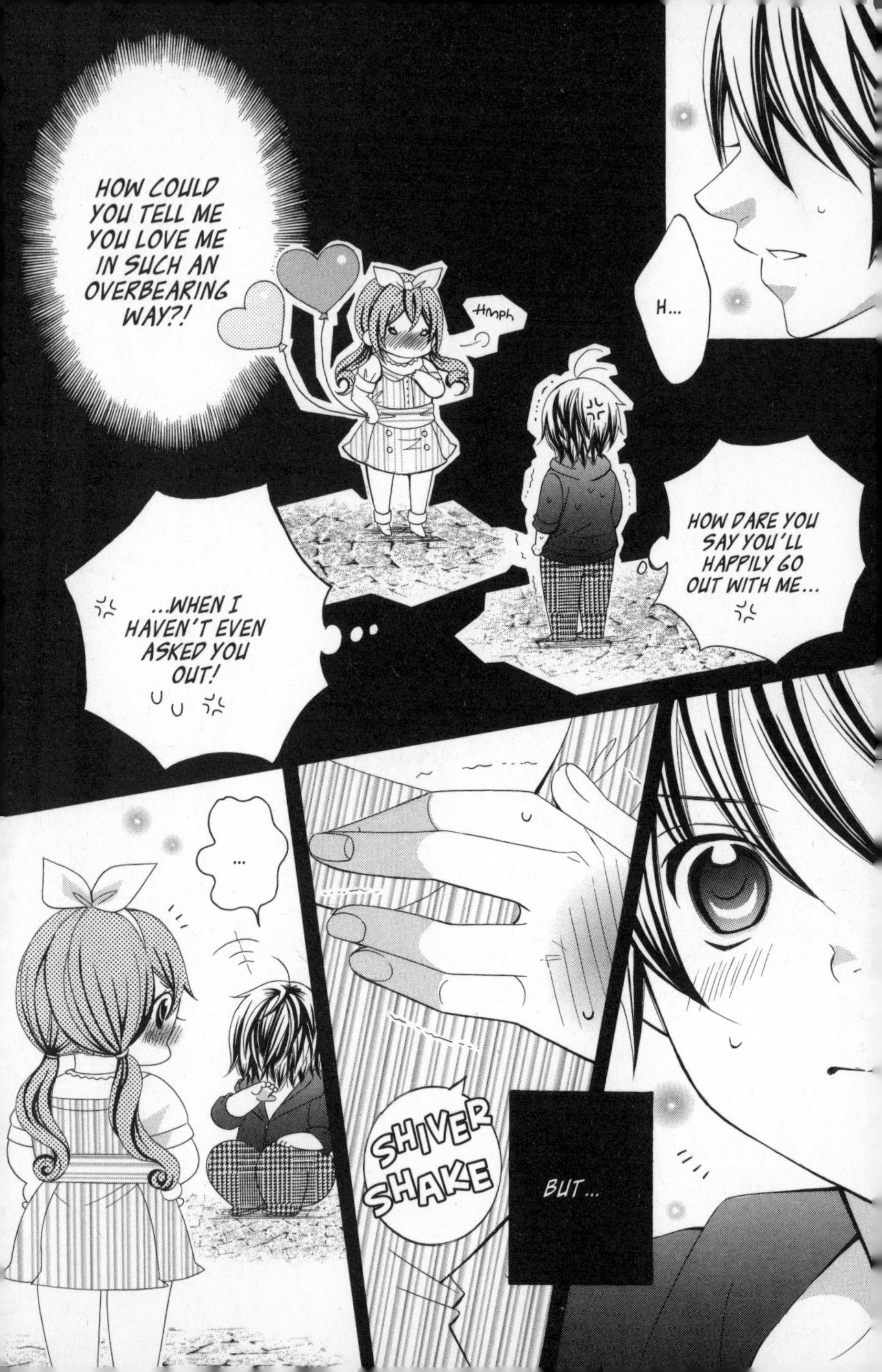
H...
HOW COULD YOU TELL ME YOU LOVE ME IN SUCH AN OVERBEARING WAY?!
Hmph
HOW DARE YOU SAY YOU'LL HAPPILY GO OUT WITH ME...
...WHEN I HAVEN'T EVEN ASKED YOU OUT!
BUT...
SHIVER SHAKE
...

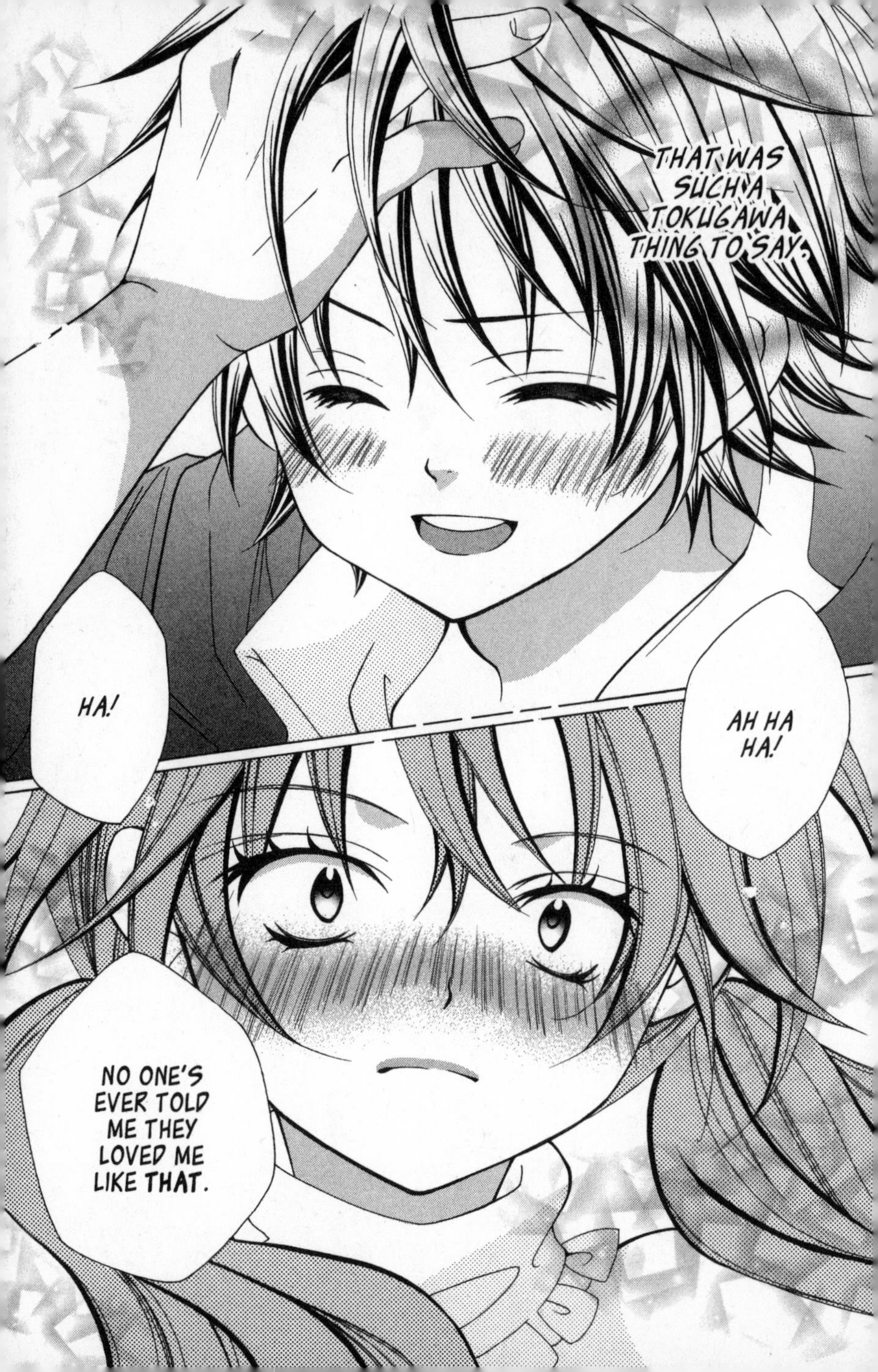
THAT WAS SUCH A TOKUGAWA THING TO SAY.
AH HA HA!
HA!
NO ONE'S EVER TOLD ME THEY LOVED ME LIKE THAT.

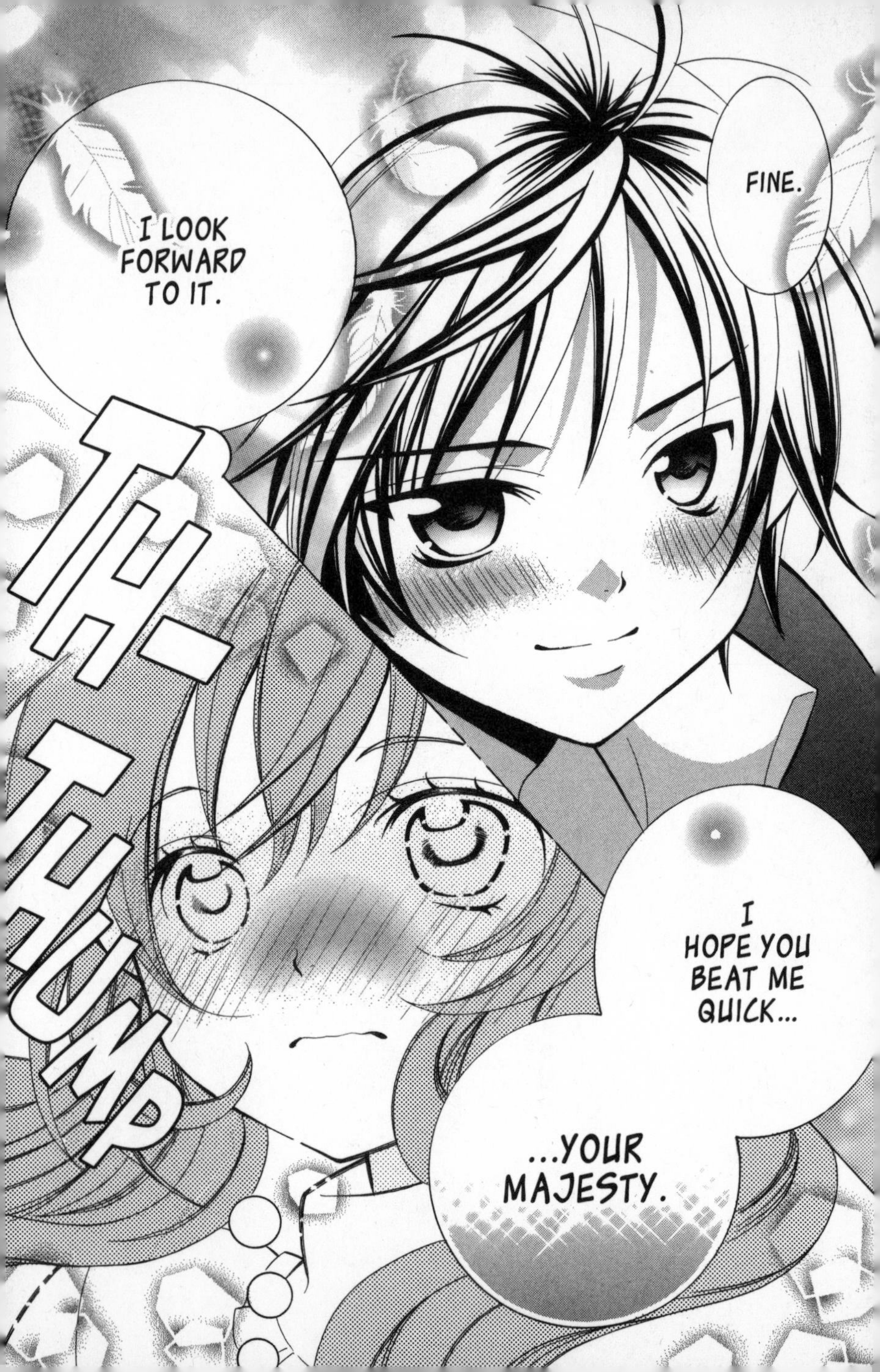
FINE.
I LOOK FORWARD TO IT.
TH-THUMP
I HOPE YOU BEAT ME QUICK...
...YOUR MAJESTY.

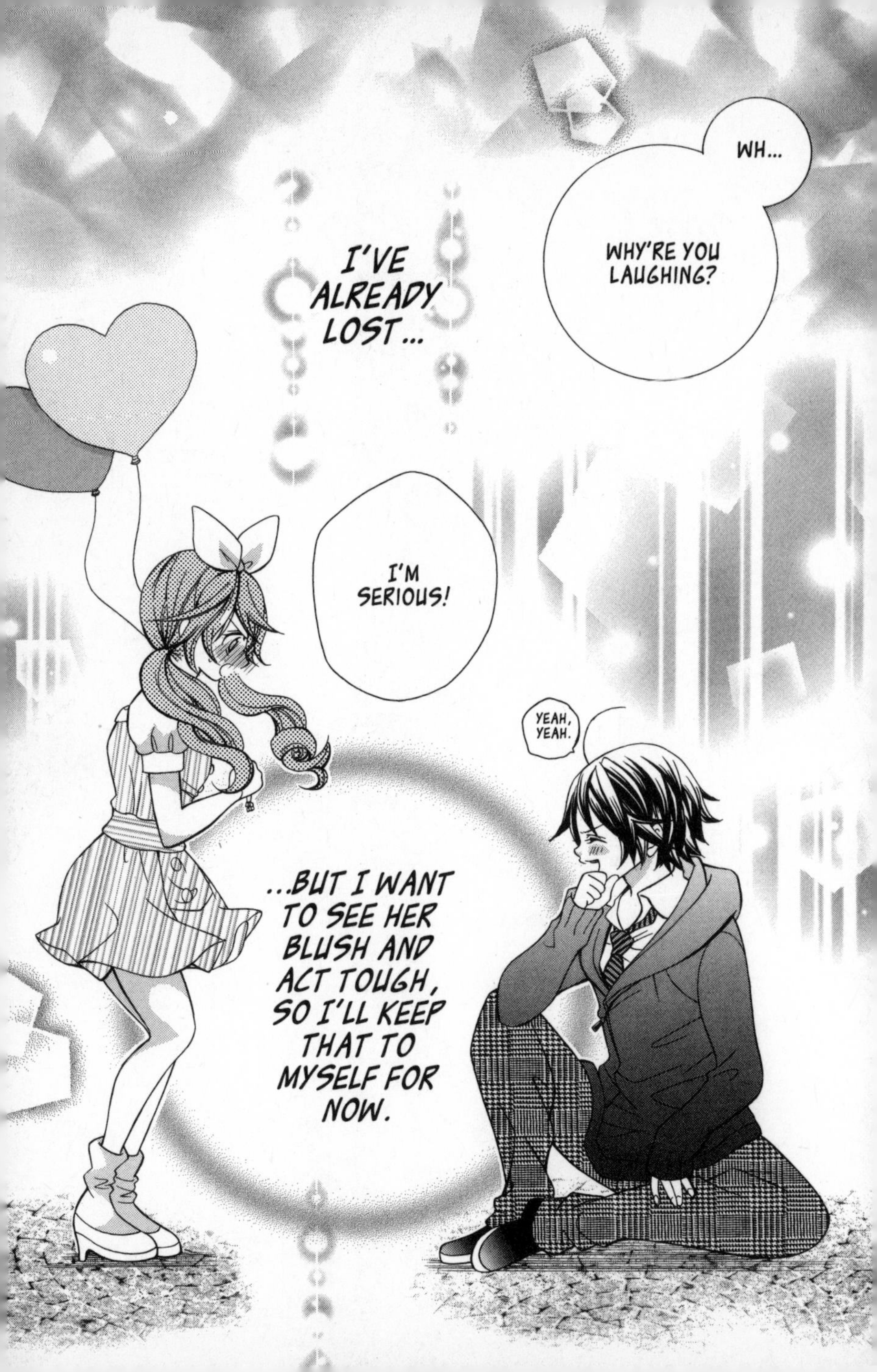
WH...
WHY'RE YOU LAUGHING?
I'VE ALREADY LOST...
I'M SERIOUS!
YEAH, YEAH.
...BUT I WANT TO SEE HER BLUSH AND ACT TOUGH, SO I'LL KEEP THAT TO MYSELF FOR NOW.

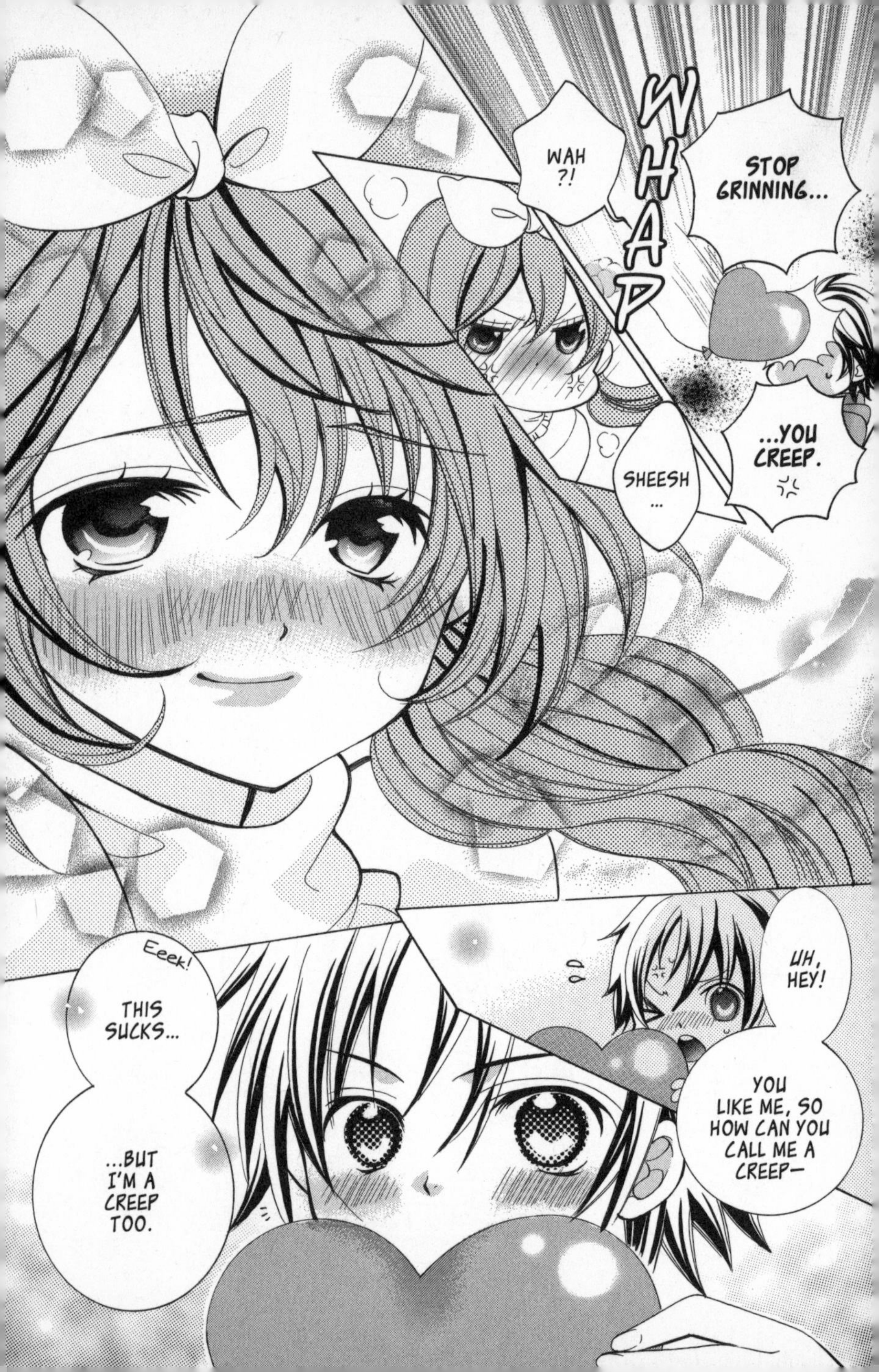
STOP GRINNING...
WHAP
WAH?!
...YOU CREEP.
SHEESH...
UH, HEY!
YOU LIKE ME, SO HOW CAN YOU CALL ME A CREEP—
Eeek!
THIS SUCKS...
...BUT I'M A CREEP TOO.

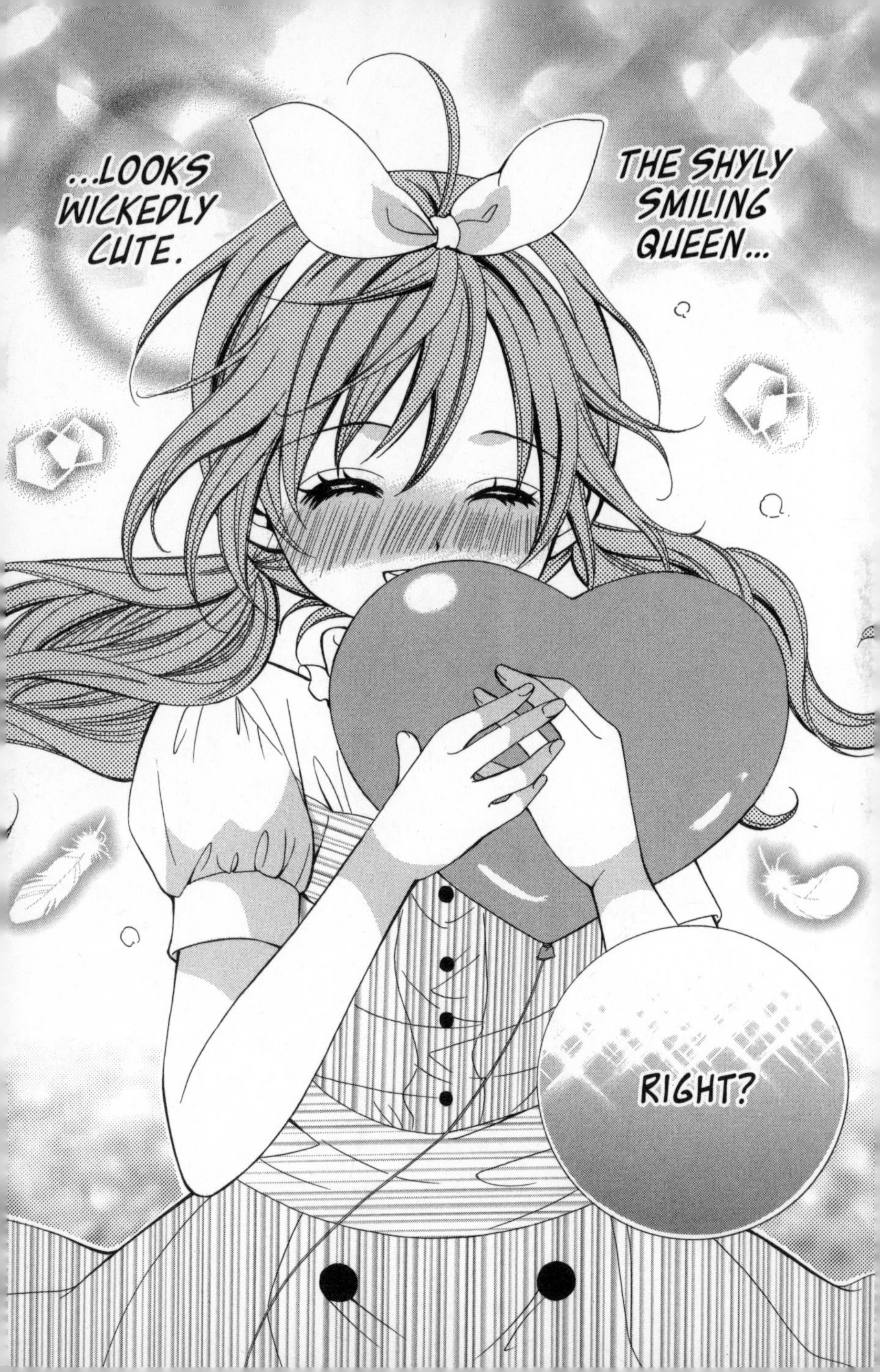
THE SHYLY SMILING QUEEN...
...LOOKS WICKEDLY CUTE.
RIGHT?

Chapter 43

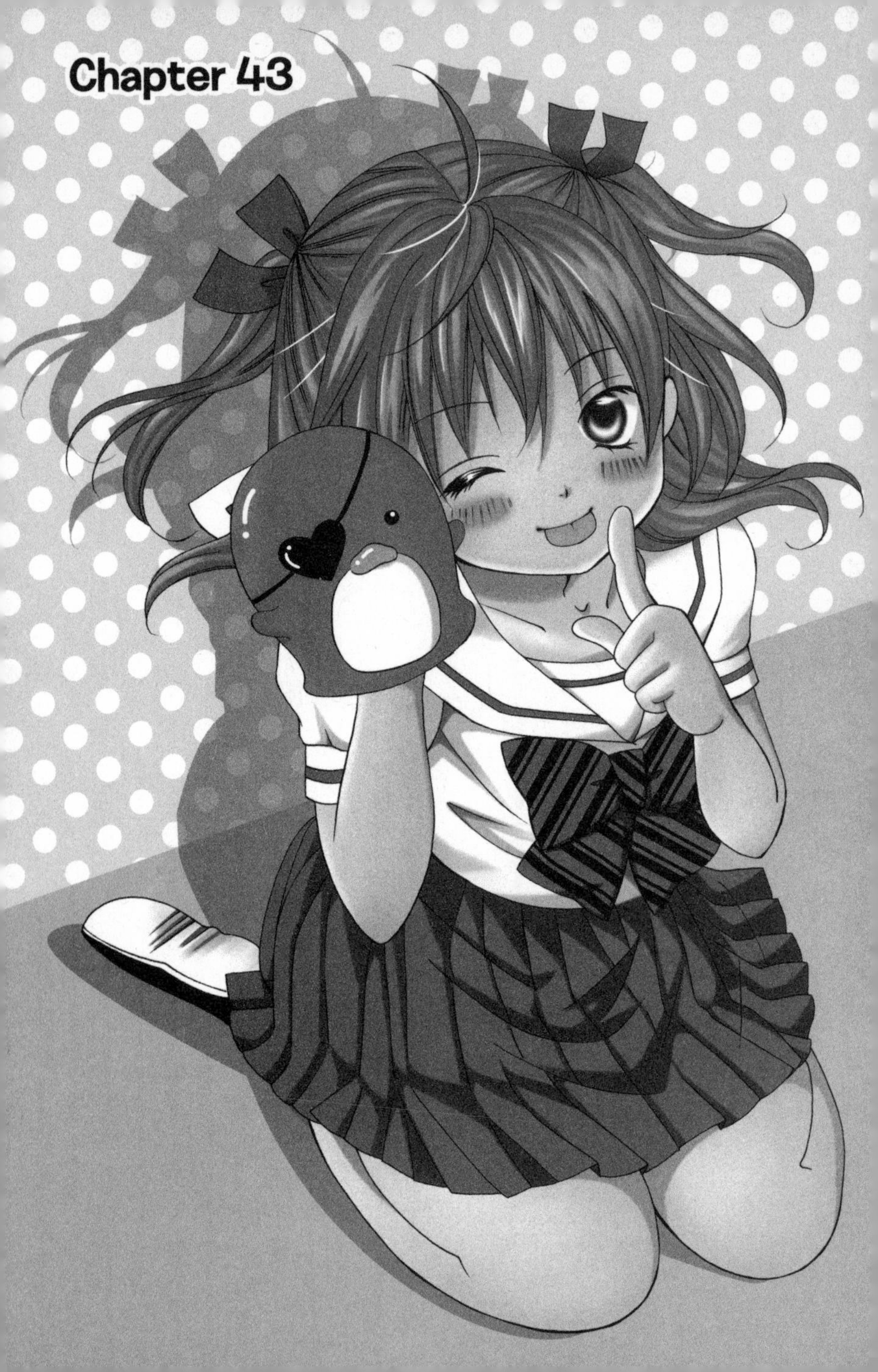

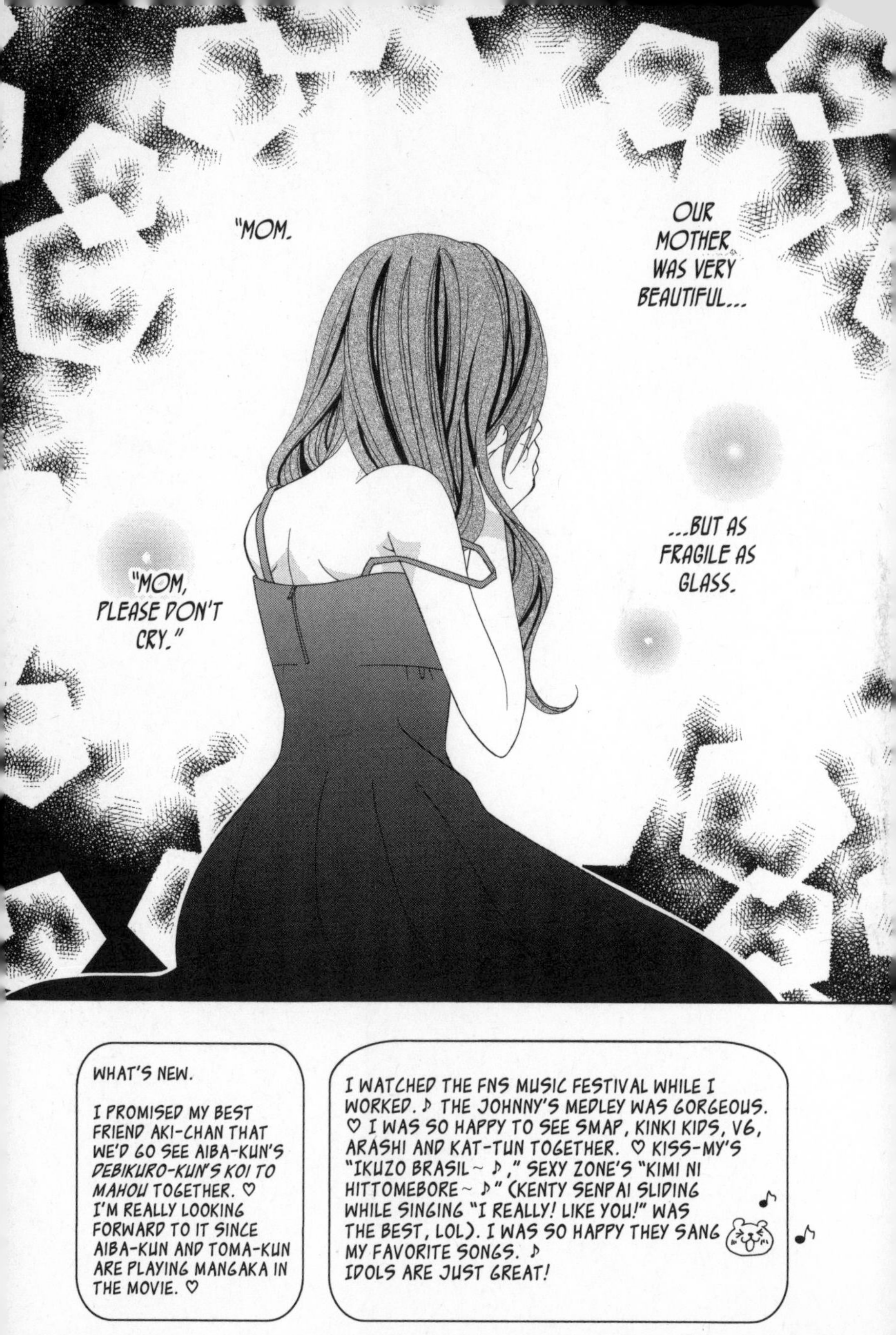
OUR MOTHER WAS VERY BEAUTIFUL...
"MOM.
...BUT AS FRAGILE AS GLASS.
"MOM, PLEASE DON'T CRY."

WHAT'S NEW.

I PROMISED MY BEST FRIEND AKI-CHAN THAT WE'D GO SEE AIBA-KUN'S *DEBIKURO-KUN'S KOI TO MAHOU* TOGETHER. ♡ I'M REALLY LOOKING FORWARD TO IT SINCE AIBA-KUN AND TOMA-KUN ARE PLAYING MANGAKA IN THE MOVIE. ♡

I WATCHED THE FNS MUSIC FESTIVAL WHILE I WORKED. ♪ THE JOHNNY'S MEDLEY WAS GORGEOUS. ♡ I WAS SO HAPPY TO SEE SMAP, KINKI KIDS, V6, ARASHI AND KAT-TUN TOGETHER. ♡ KISS-MY'S "IKUZO BRASIL~ ♪," SEXY ZONE'S "KIMI NI HITTOMEBORE~ ♪" (KENTY SENPAI SLIDING WHILE SINGING "I REALLY! LIKE YOU!" WAS THE BEST, LOL). I WAS SO HAPPY THEY SANG MY FAVORITE SONGS. ♪
IDOLS ARE JUST GREAT!

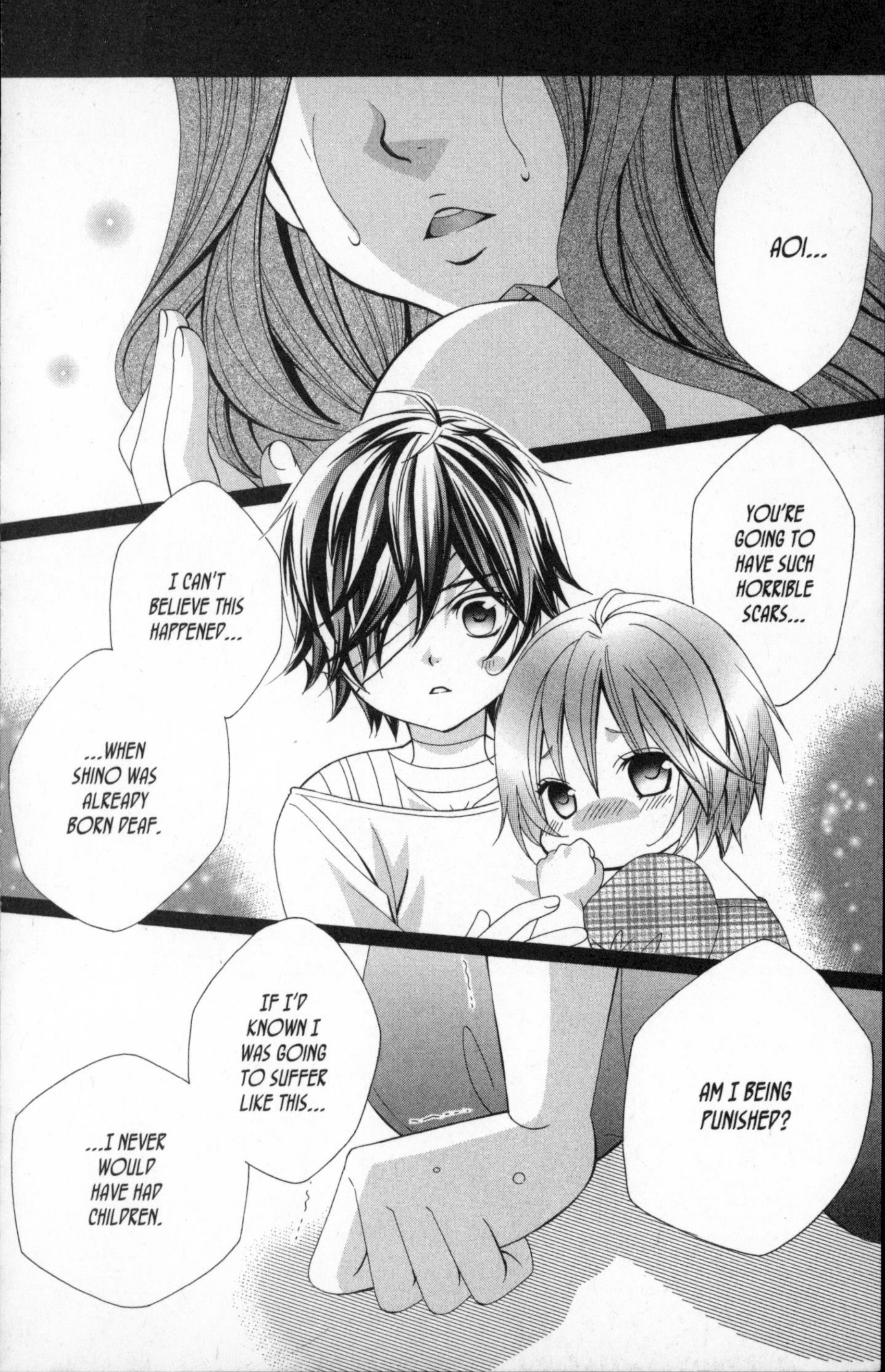
AOI...
YOU'RE GOING TO HAVE SUCH HORRIBLE SCARS...
I CAN'T BELIEVE THIS HAPPENED...
...WHEN SHINO WAS ALREADY BORN DEAF.
AM I BEING PUNISHED?
IF I'D KNOWN I WAS GOING TO SUFFER LIKE THIS...
...I NEVER WOULD HAVE HAD CHILDREN.

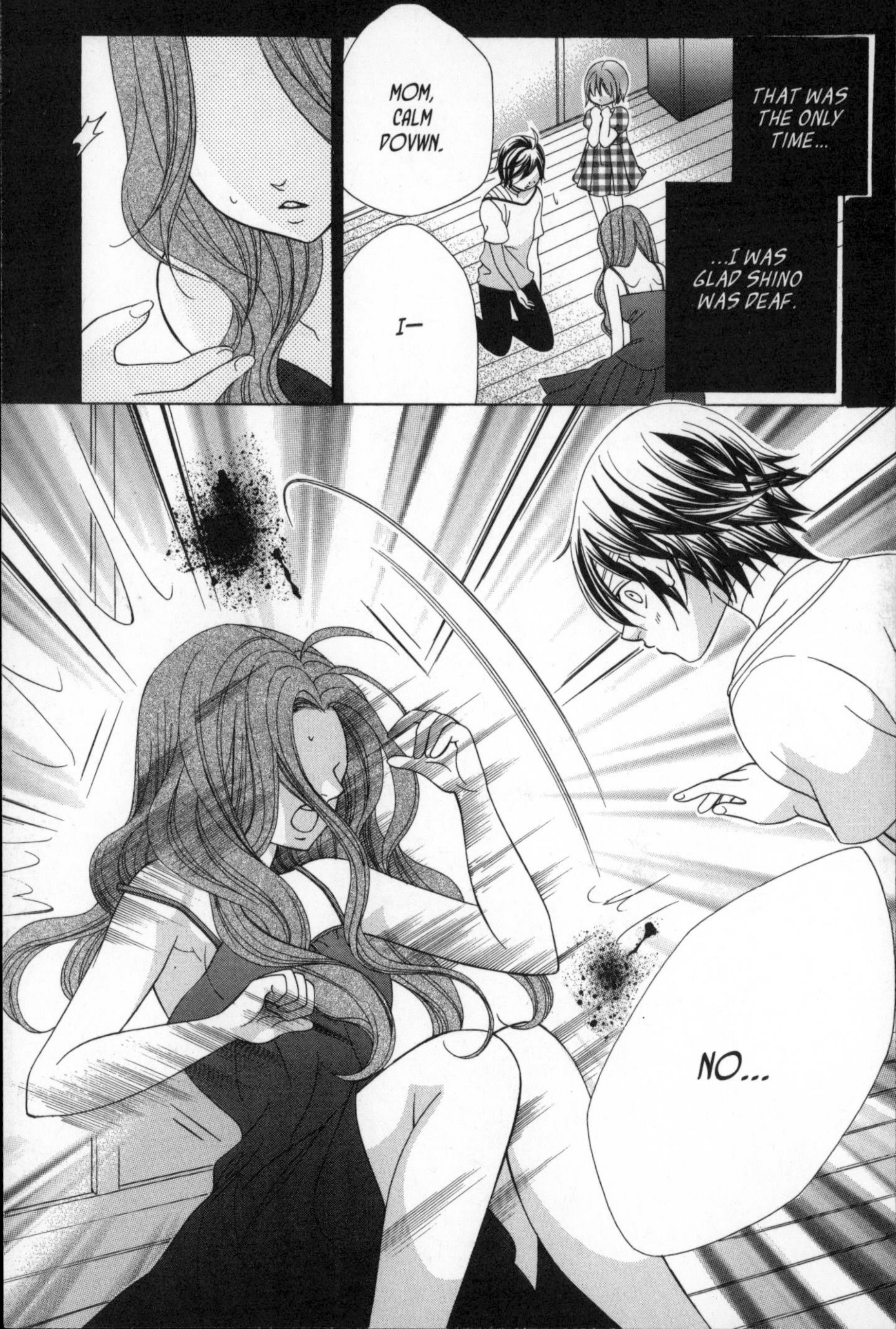
THAT WAS THE ONLY TIME...
...I WAS GLAD SHINO WAS DEAF.
MOM, CALM DOWN.
I—
NO...

NO!
DON'T GET NEAR ME WITH THOSE HIDEOUS SCARS!
SINCE THEN...
...I HAVEN'T BEEN ABLE TO TOUCH WOMEN.

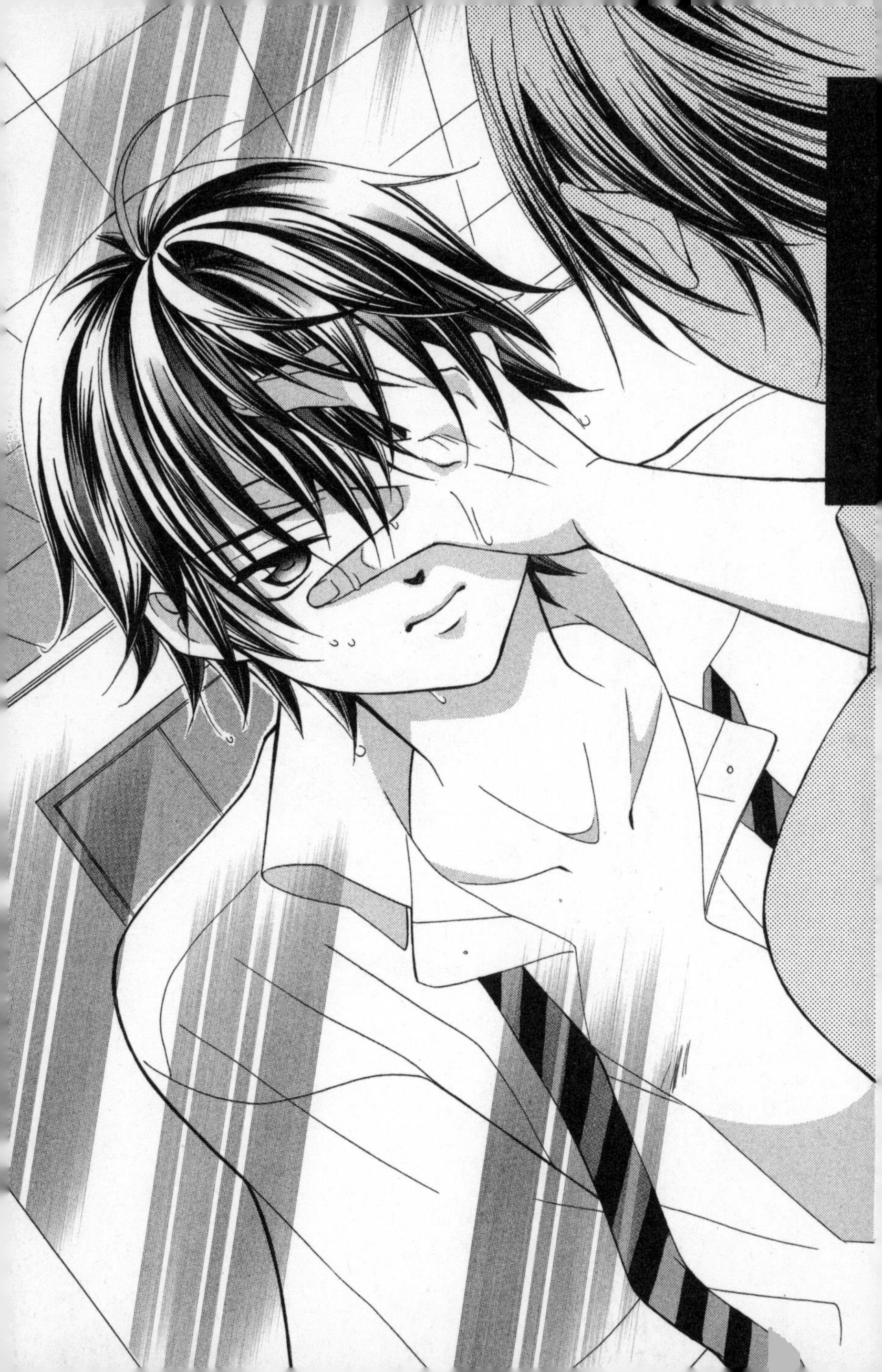

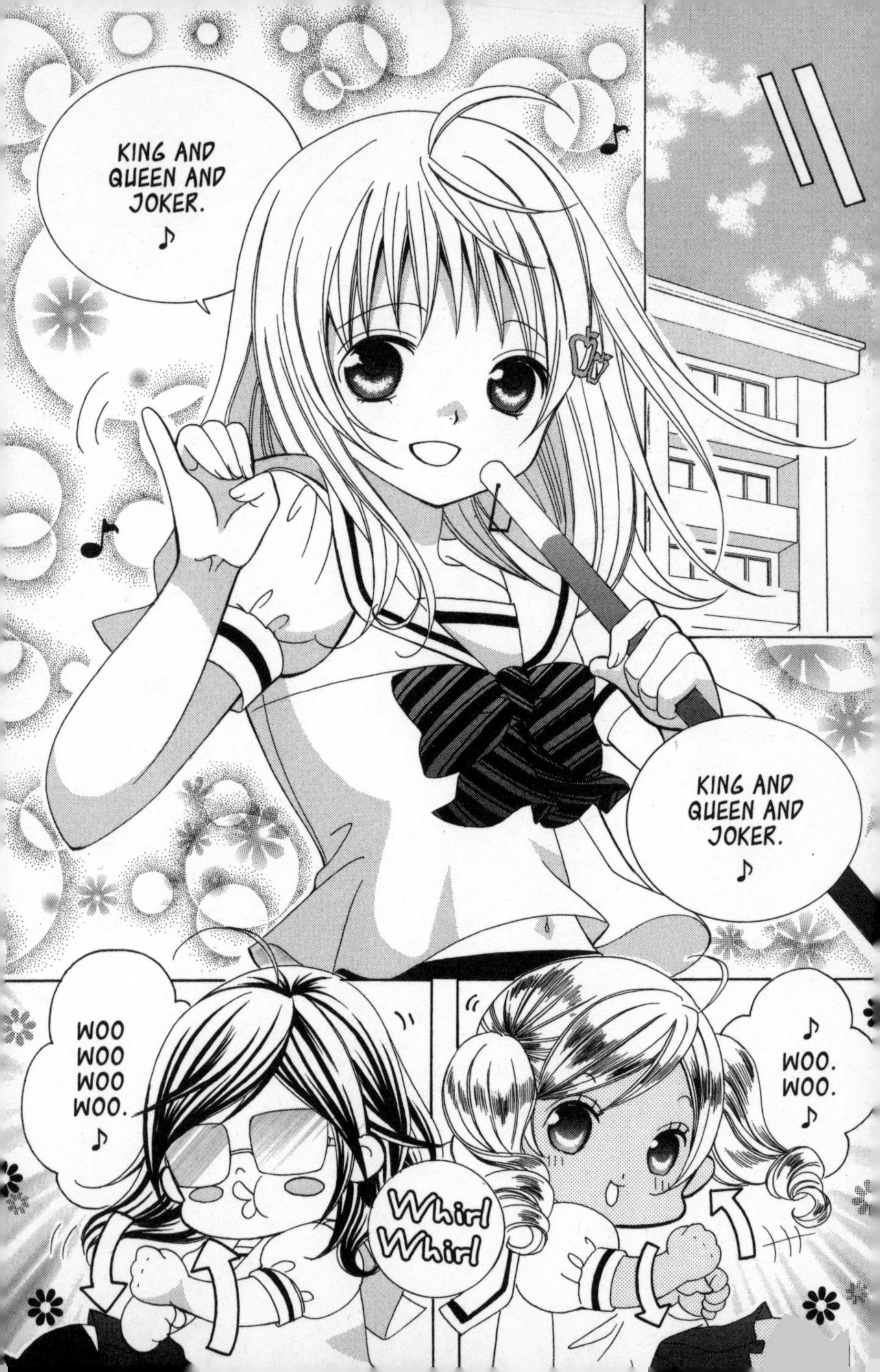
KING AND QUEEN AND JOKER. ♪
KING AND QUEEN AND JOKER. ♪
♪ WOO. WOO. ♪
Whirl Whirl
WOO WOO WOO WOO. ♪

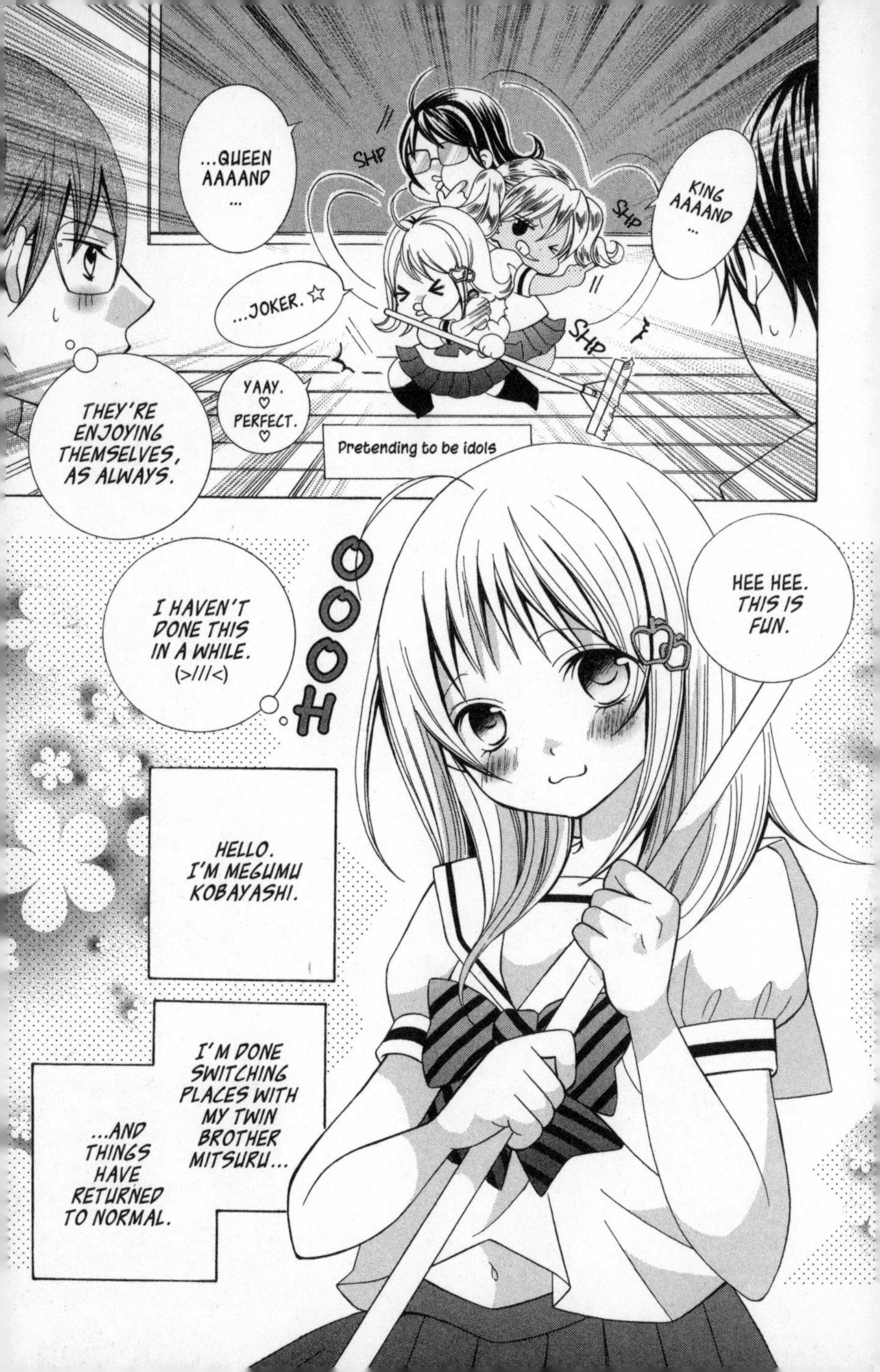
KING AAAAND ...
SHP
...QUEEN AAAAND ...
SHP
...JOKER. ☆
SHP
Pretending to be idols
YAAY. ♡ PERFECT. ♡
THEY'RE ENJOYING THEMSELVES, AS ALWAYS.
HEE HEE. THIS IS FUN.
HOOO
I HAVEN'T DONE THIS IN A WHILE. (>///<)
HELLO. I'M MEGUMU KOBAYASHI.
I'M DONE SWITCHING PLACES WITH MY TWIN BROTHER MITSURU...
...AND THINGS HAVE RETURNED TO NORMAL.

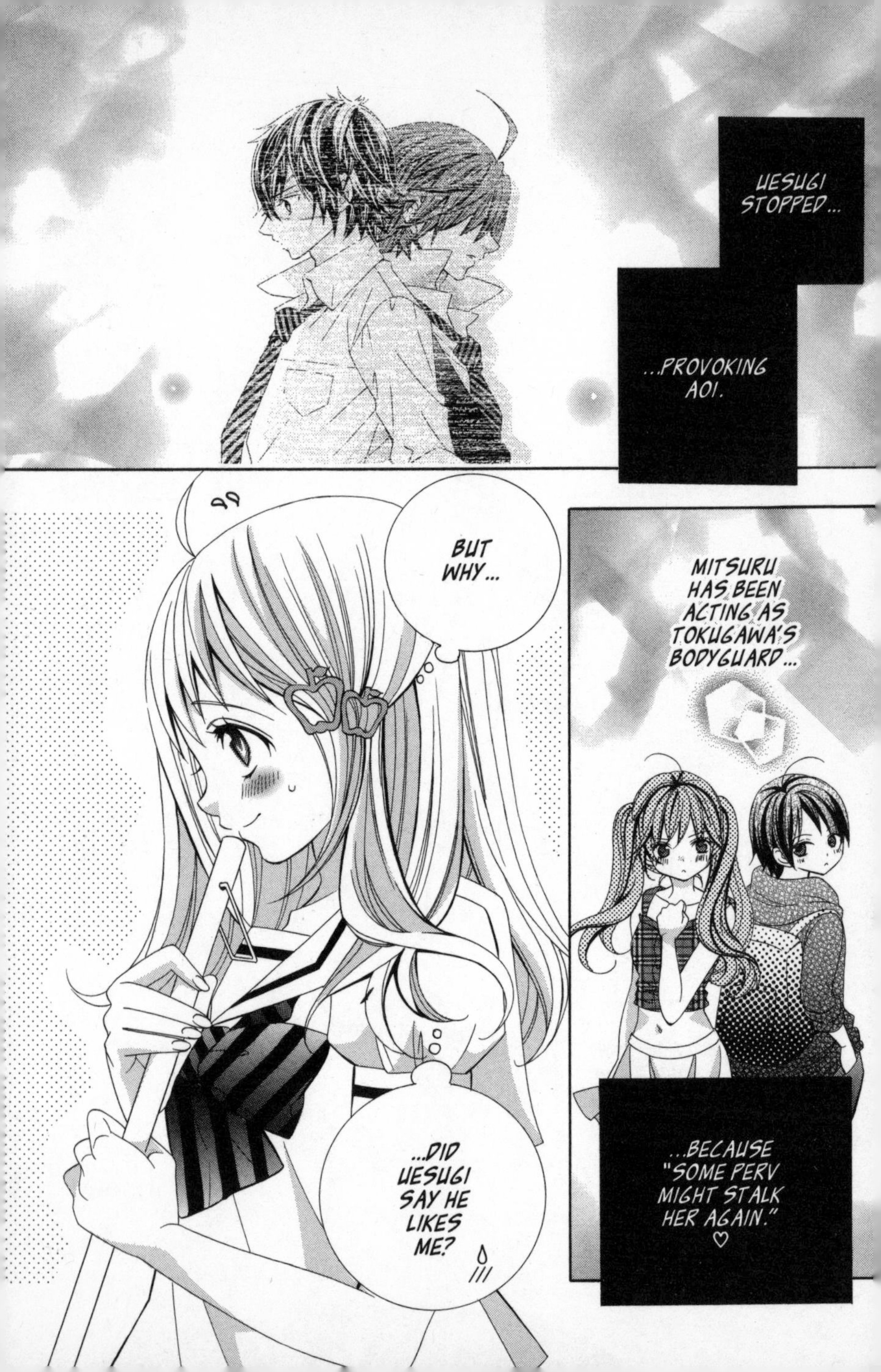
UESUGI STOPPED...
...PROVOKING AOI.
MITSURU HAS BEEN ACTING AS TOKUGAWA'S BODYGUARD...
...BECAUSE "SOME PERV MIGHT STALK HER AGAIN." ♡
BUT WHY...
...DID UESUGI SAY HE LIKES ME?

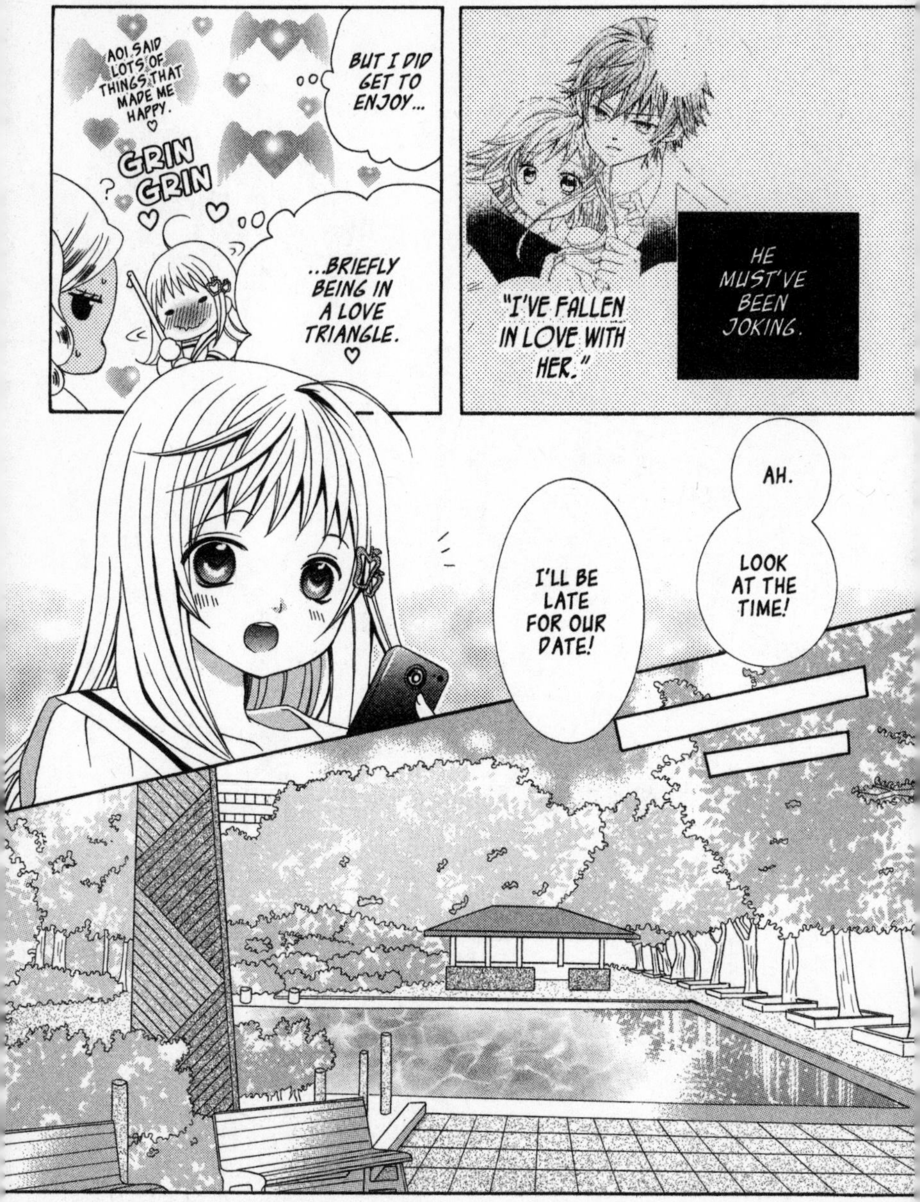
"I'VE FALLEN IN LOVE WITH HER."
HE MUST'VE BEEN JOKING.
BUT I DID GET TO ENJOY...
AOI SAID LOTS OF THINGS THAT MADE ME HAPPY. ♡
...BRIEFLY BEING IN A LOVE TRIANGLE. ♡
GRIN GRIN
AH.
LOOK AT THE TIME!
I'LL BE LATE FOR OUR DATE!

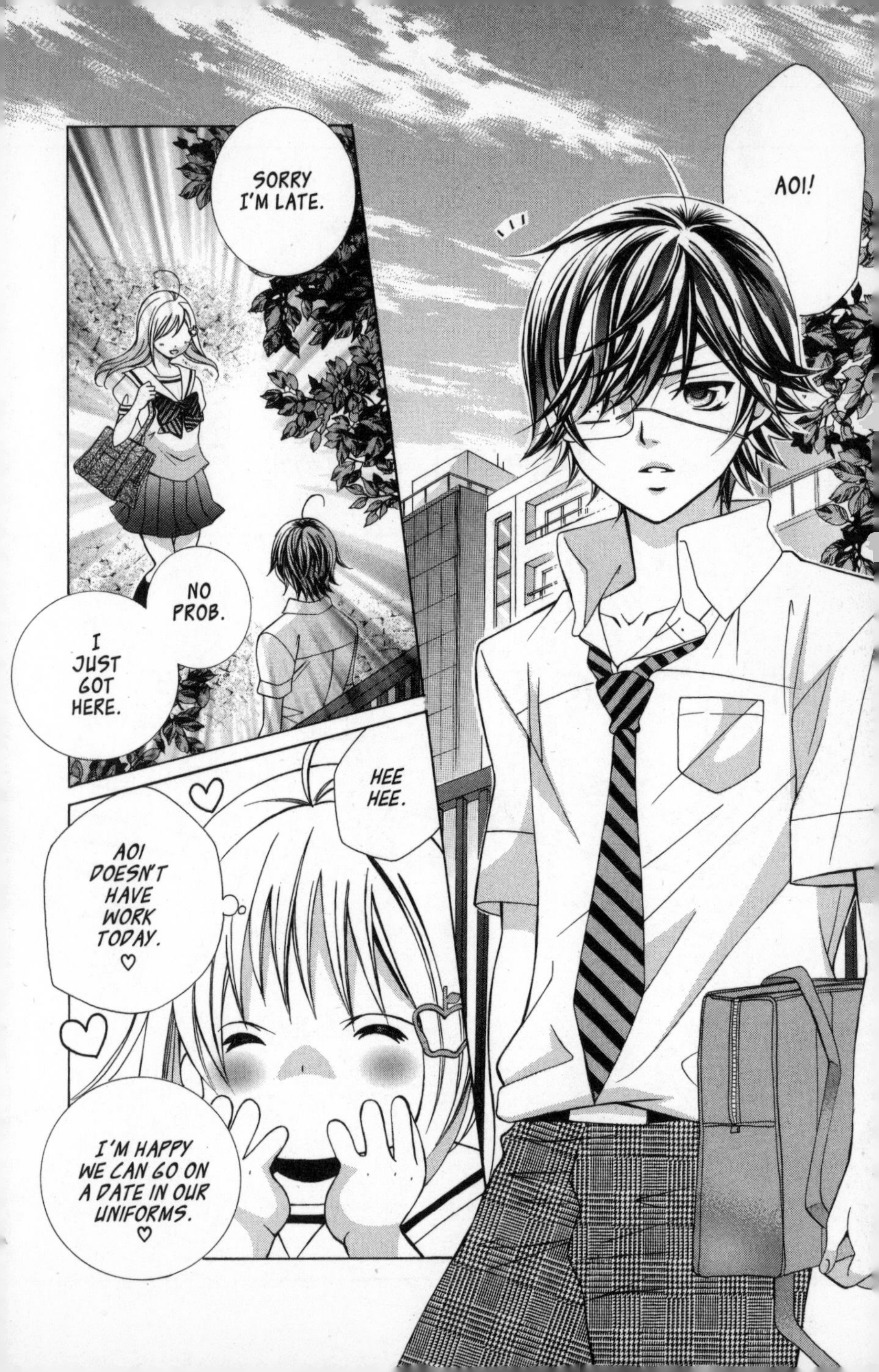
AOI!
SORRY I'M LATE.
NO PROB.
I JUST GOT HERE.
HEE HEE.
AOI DOESN'T HAVE WORK TODAY. ♡
I'M HAPPY WE CAN GO ON A DATE IN OUR UNIFORMS. ♡

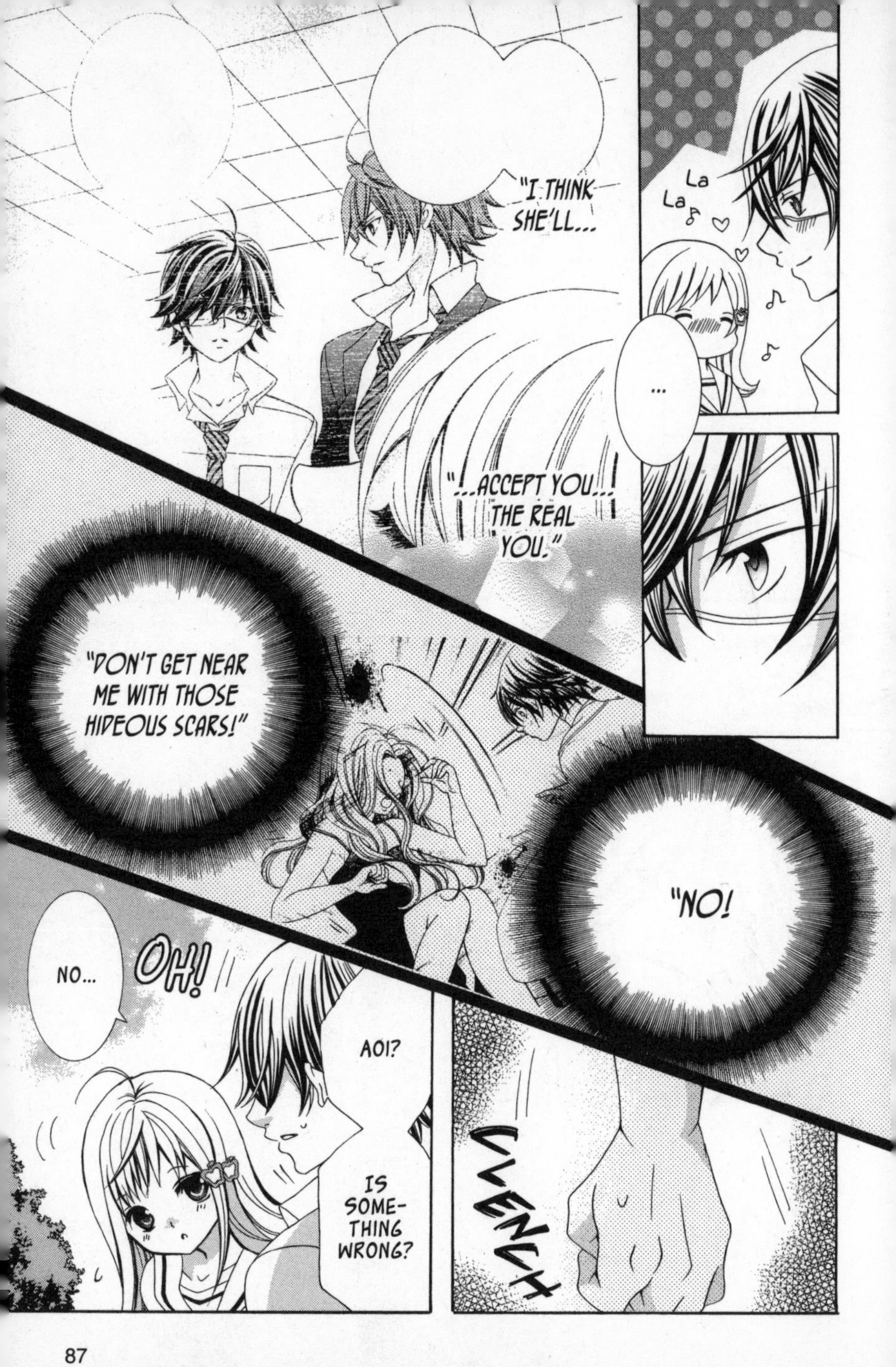

La
La ♪
...
"I THINK SHE'LL...
"...ACCEPT YOU... THE REAL YOU."
"NO!
"DON'T GET NEAR ME WITH THOSE HIDEOUS SCARS!"
CLENCH
AOI?
IS SOME-THING WRONG?
OH!
NO...

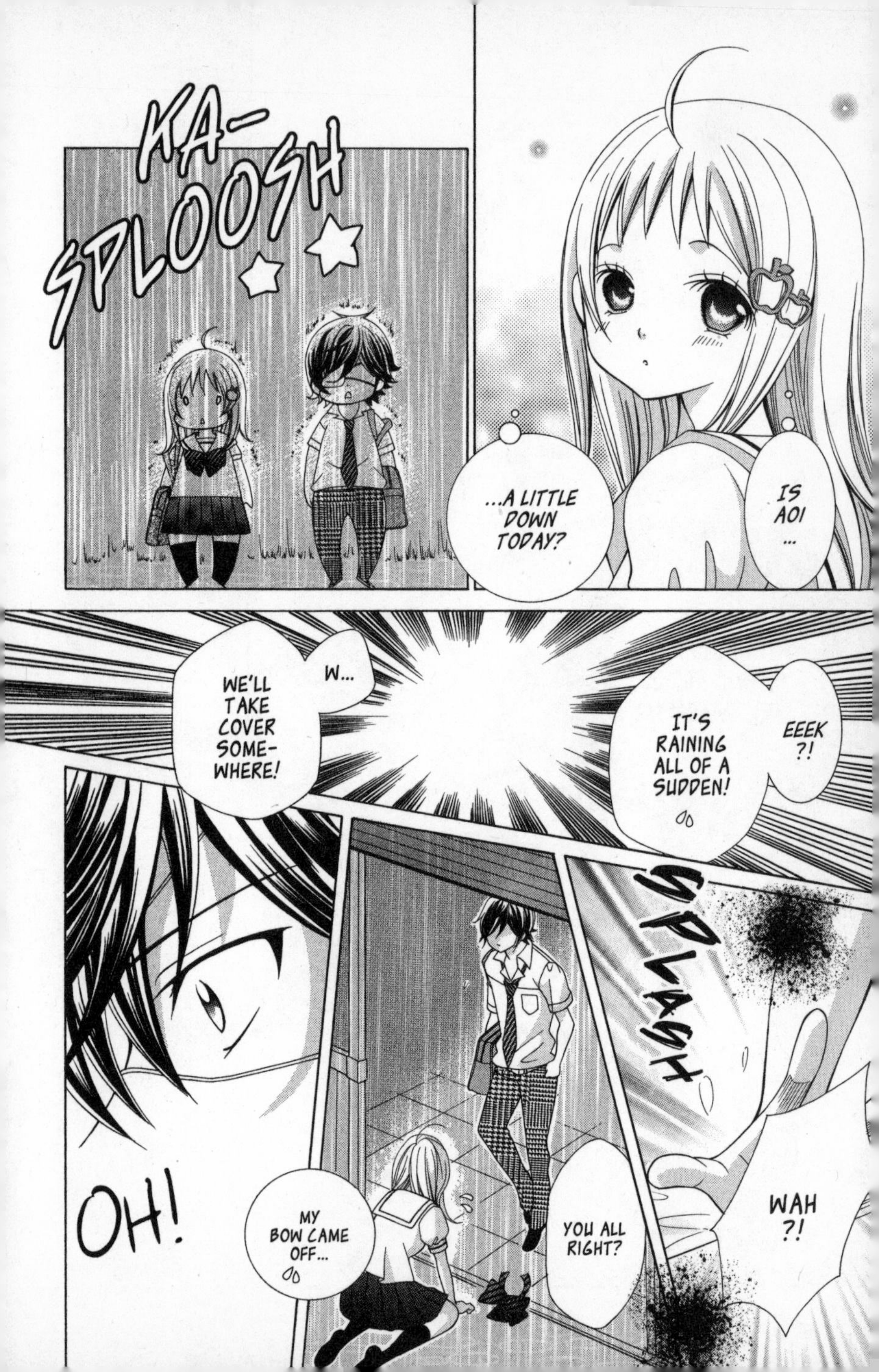
IS AOI ...
...A LITTLE DOWN TODAY?
KA-SPLOOSH
EEEK ?!
IT'S RAINING ALL OF A SUDDEN!
W...
WE'LL TAKE COVER SOME-WHERE!
SPLASH
WAH ?!
YOU ALL RIGHT?
MY BOW CAME OFF...
OH!

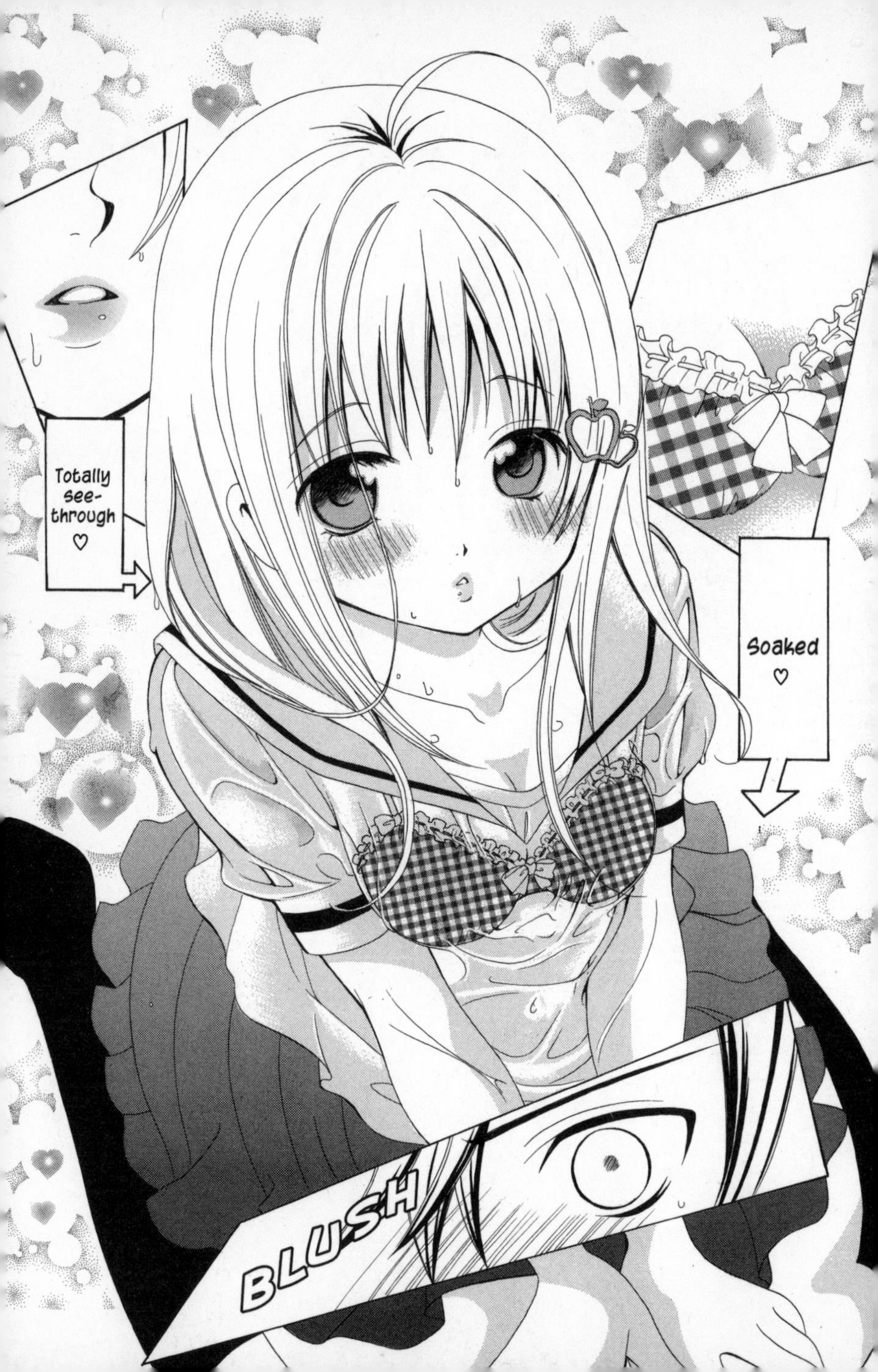
Soaked ♡
Totally see-through ♡
BLUSH

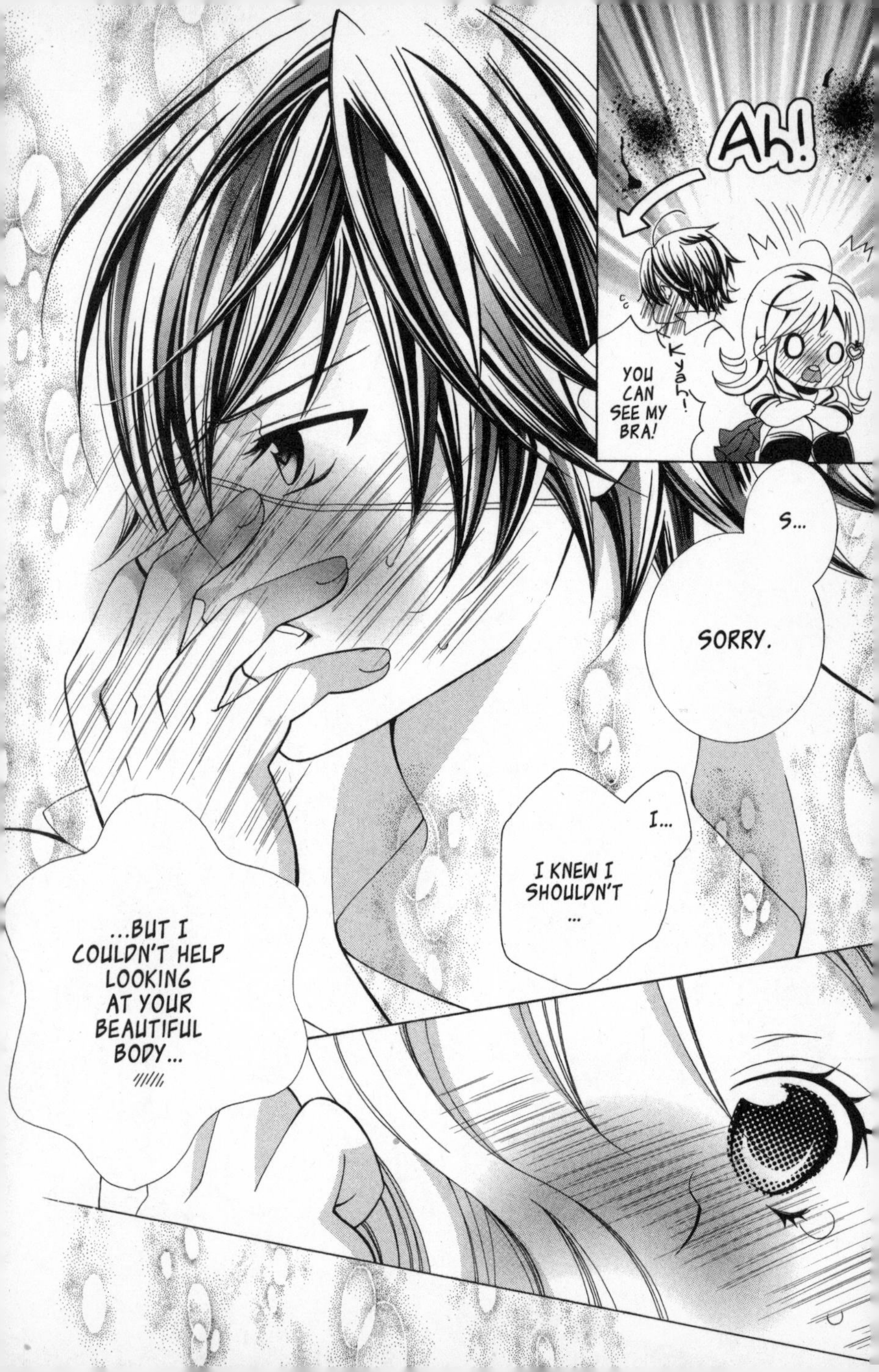
Ah!
Kyah!
YOU CAN SEE MY BRA!
S...
SORRY.
I...
I KNEW I SHOULDN'T ...
...BUT I COULDN'T HELP LOOKING AT YOUR BEAUTIFUL BODY...

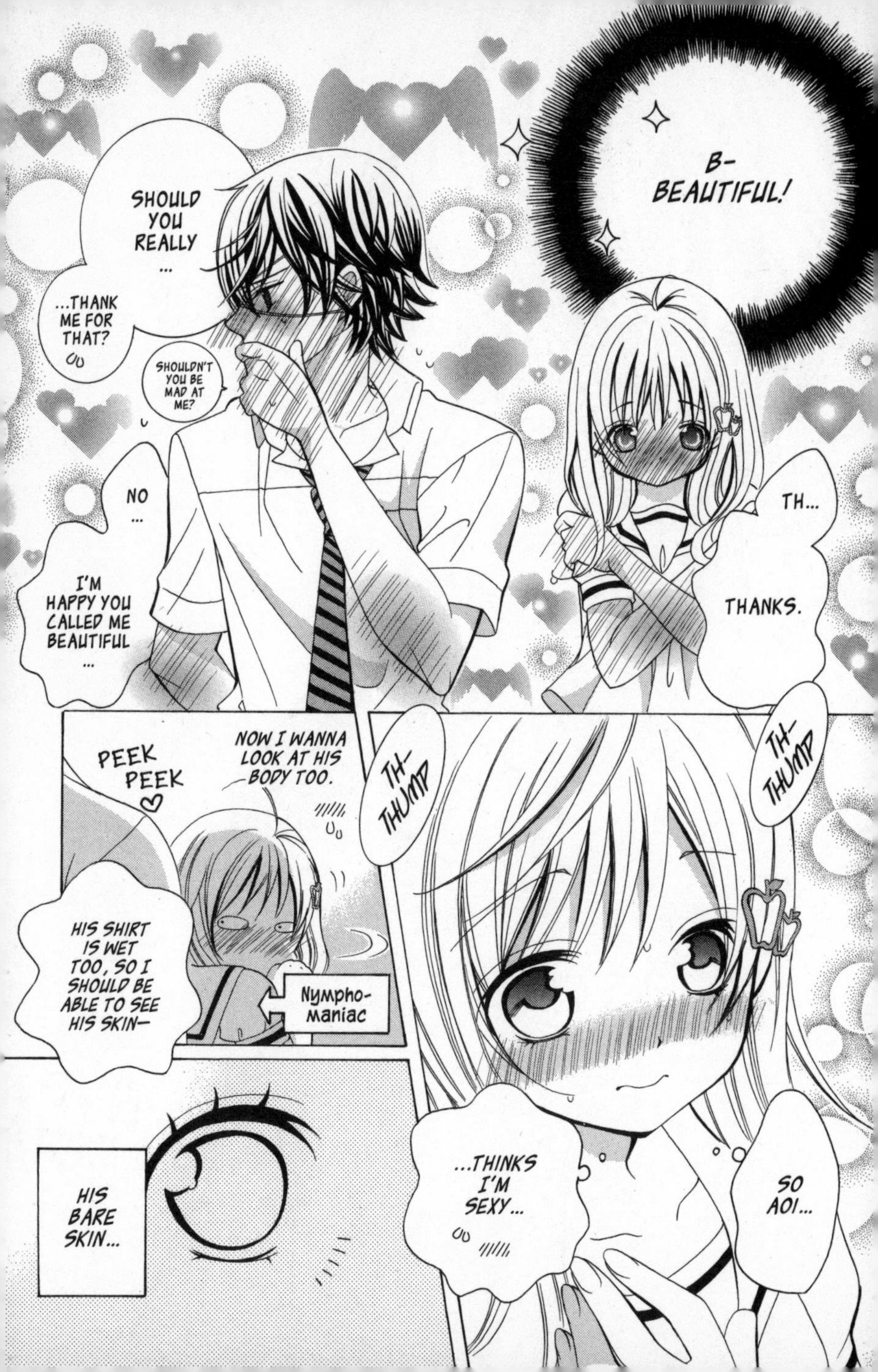
B-BEAUTIFUL!
TH... THANKS.
SHOULD YOU REALLY ...
...THANK ME FOR THAT?
SHOULDN'T YOU BE MAD AT ME?
NO ...
I'M HAPPY YOU CALLED ME BEAUTIFUL ...
TH-THUMP
TH-THUMP
SO AOI...
...THINKS I'M SEXY...
NOW I WANNA LOOK AT HIS BODY TOO.
PEEK PEEK
HIS SHIRT IS WET TOO, SO I SHOULD BE ABLE TO SEE HIS SKIN—
Nympho-maniac
HIS BARE SKIN...

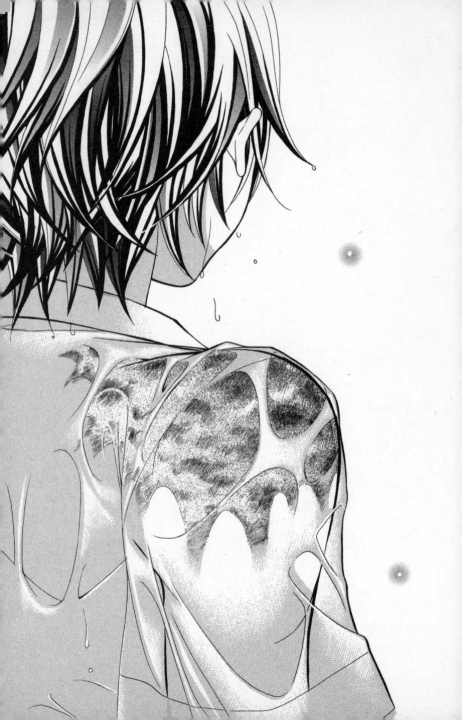

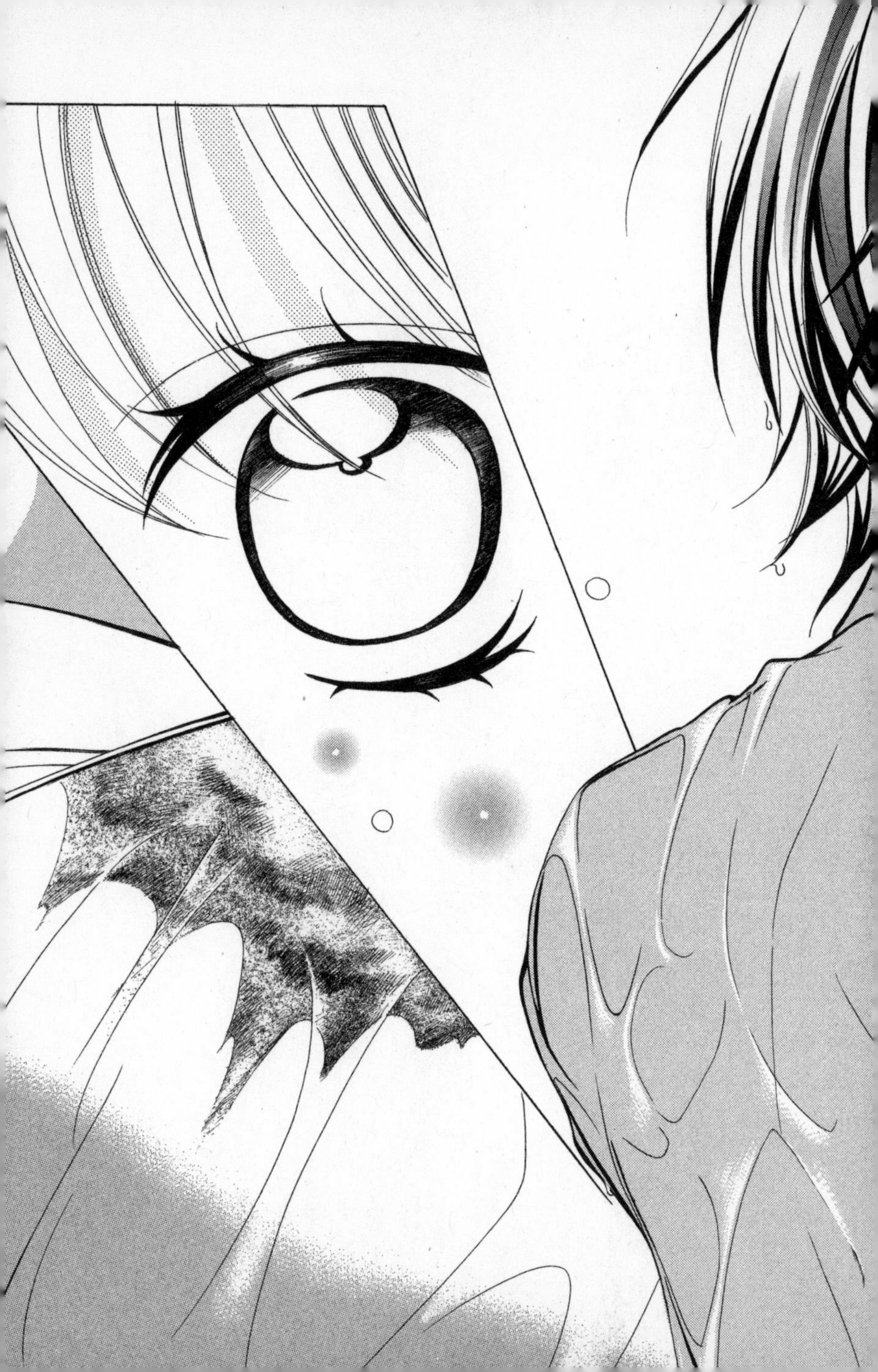

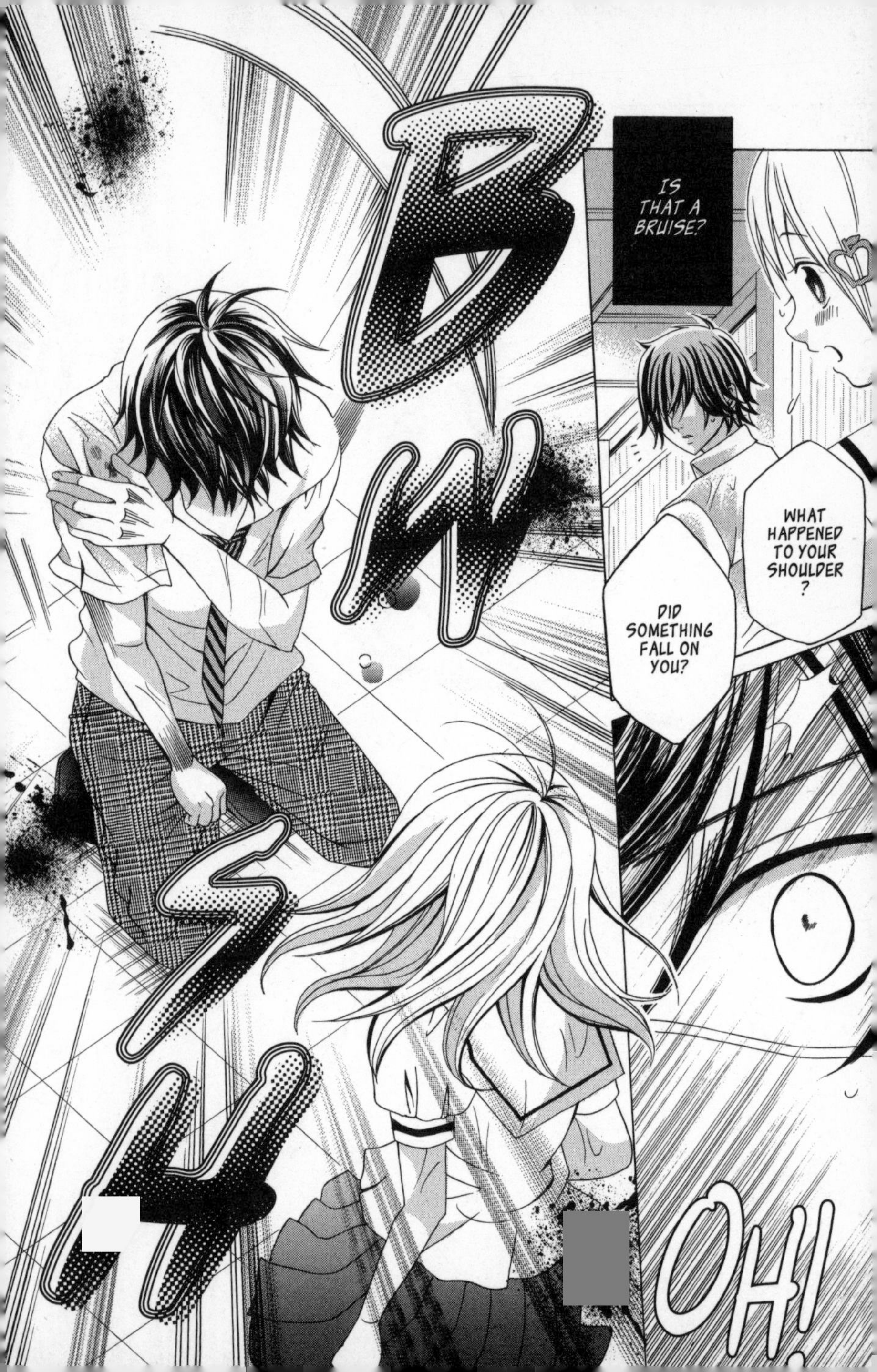
IS THAT A BRUISE?
WHAT HAPPENED TO YOUR SHOULDER?
DID SOMETHING FALL ON YOU?
OH!
BWSH

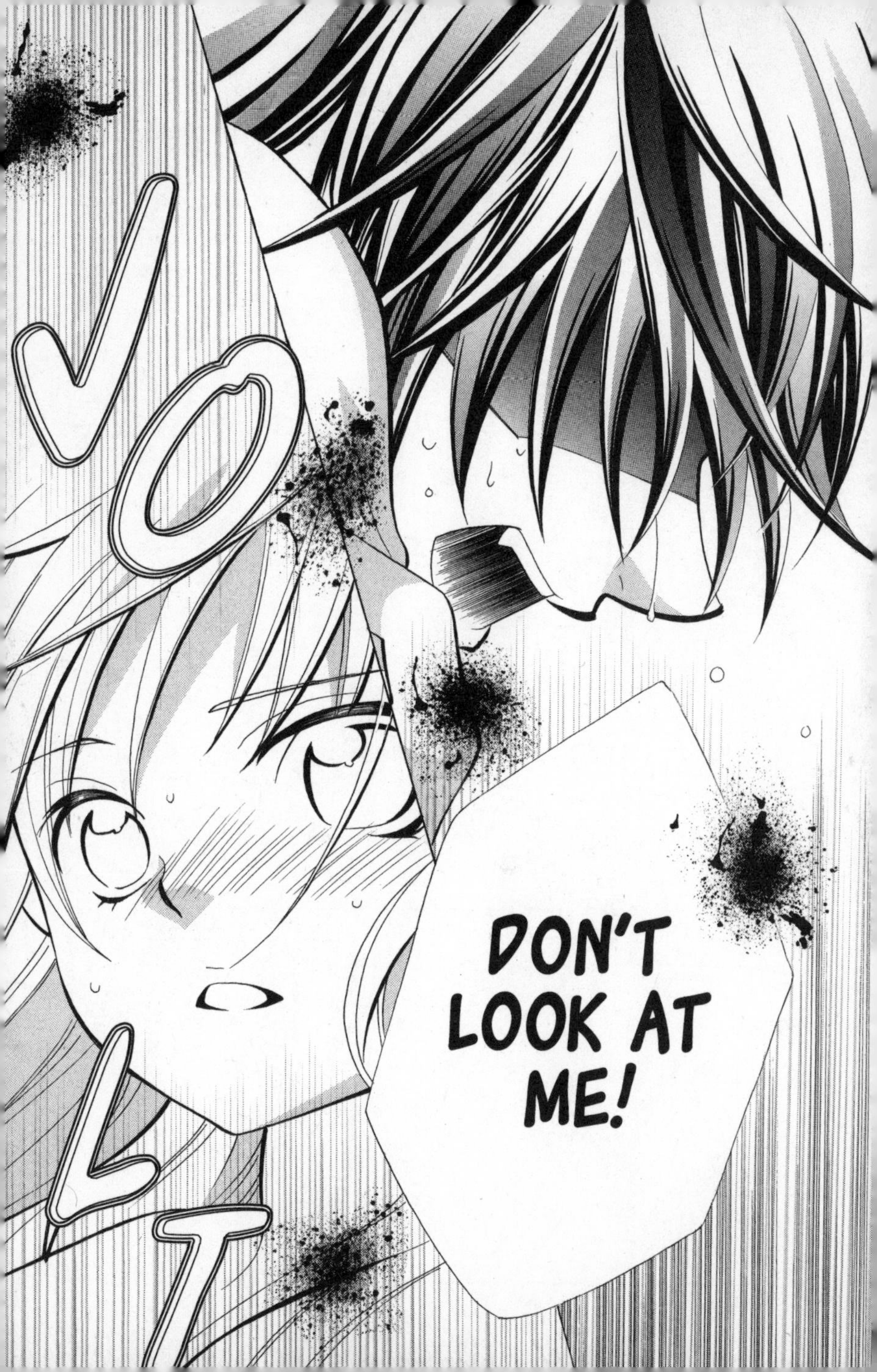
DON'T LOOK AT ME!

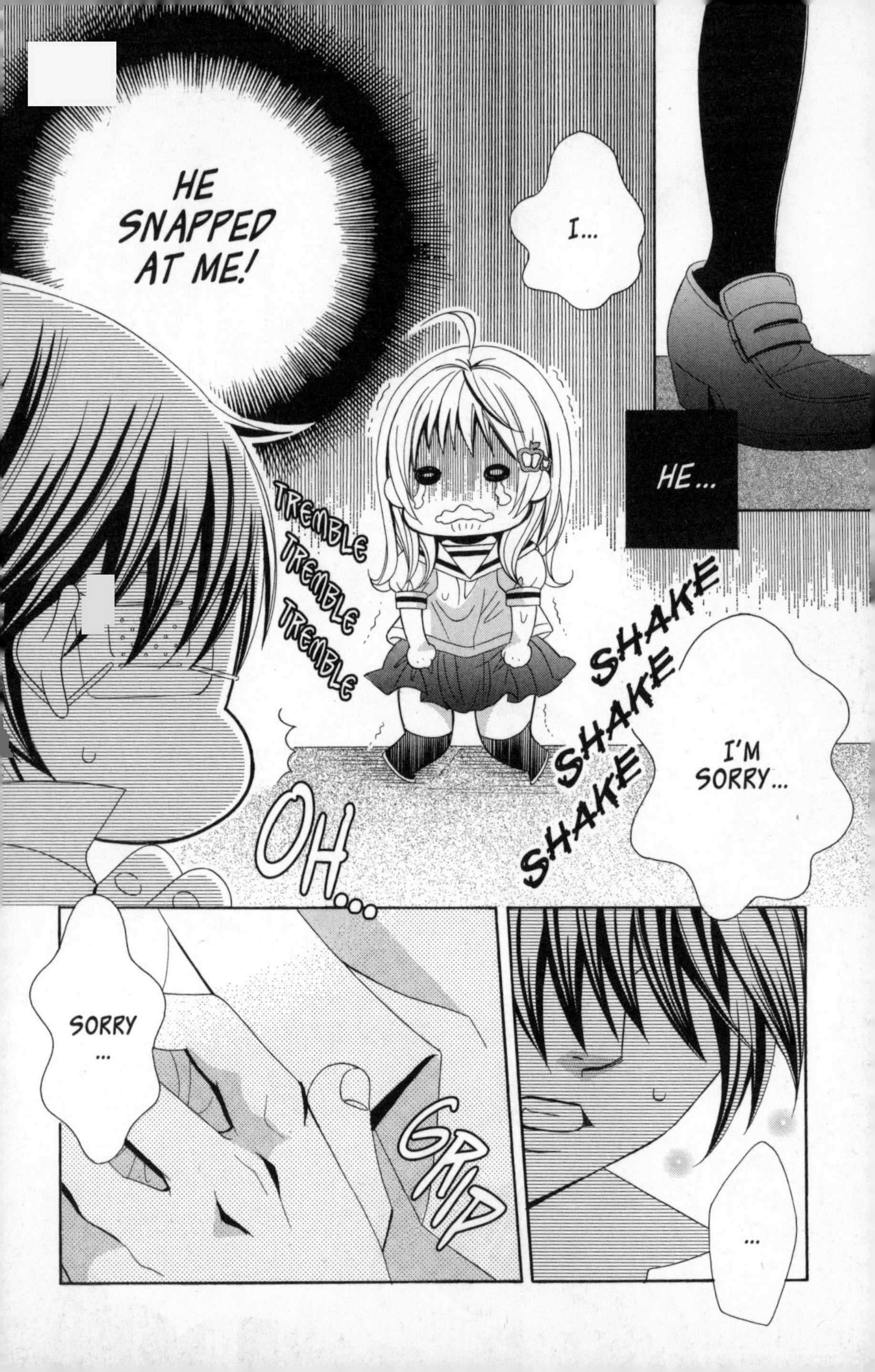
I...
HE...
HE SNAPPED AT ME!
I'M SORRY...
SHAKE SHAKE SHAKE
TREMBLE TREMBLE TREMBLE
OH...
...
SORRY ...
GRIP

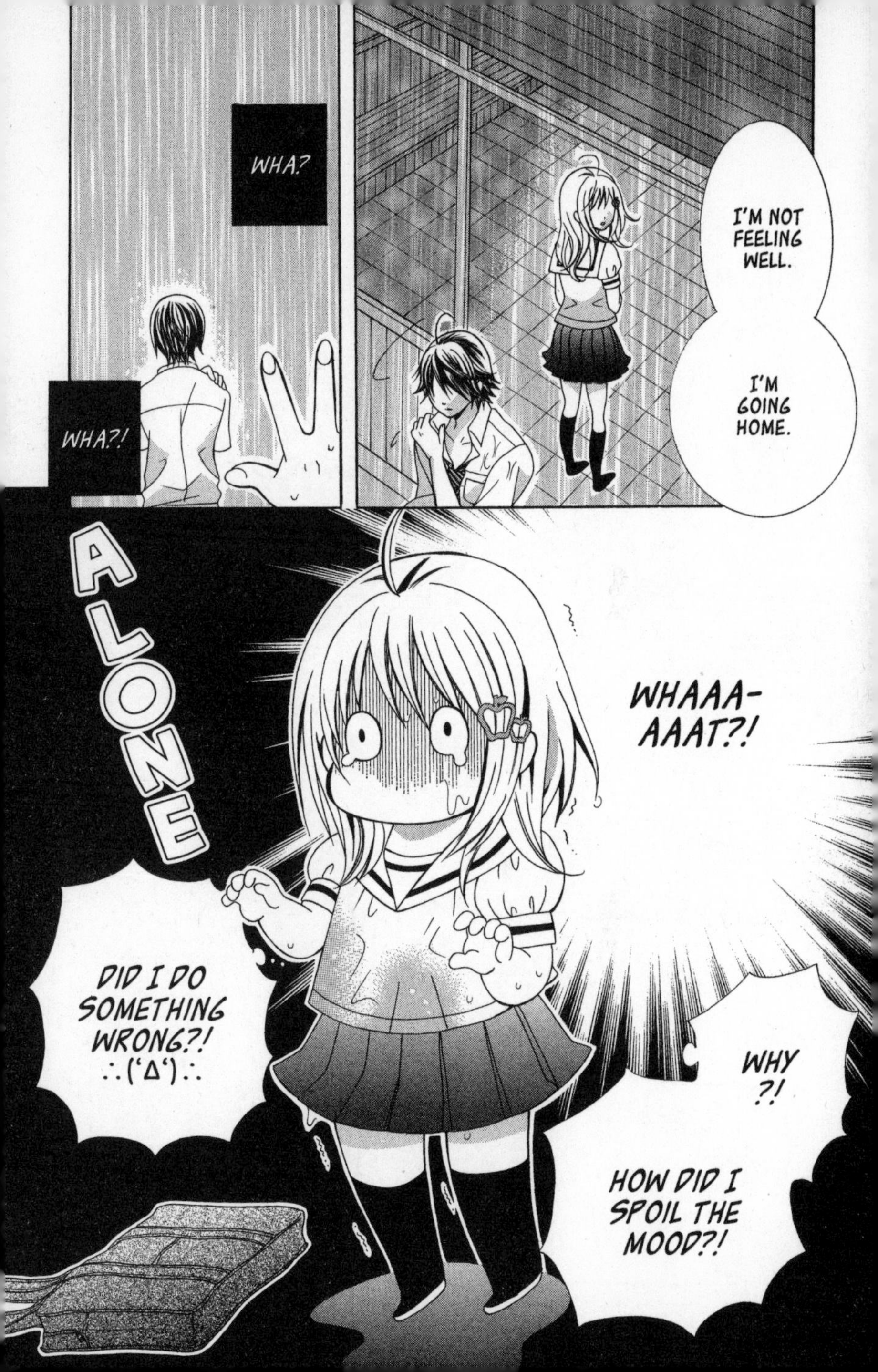

I'M NOT FEELING WELL.
I'M GOING HOME.
WHA?
WHA?!
WHAAA-AAAT?!
ALONE
WHY?!
HOW DID I SPOIL THE MOOD?!
DID I DO SOMETHING WRONG?! ∴(‘Δ‘)∴

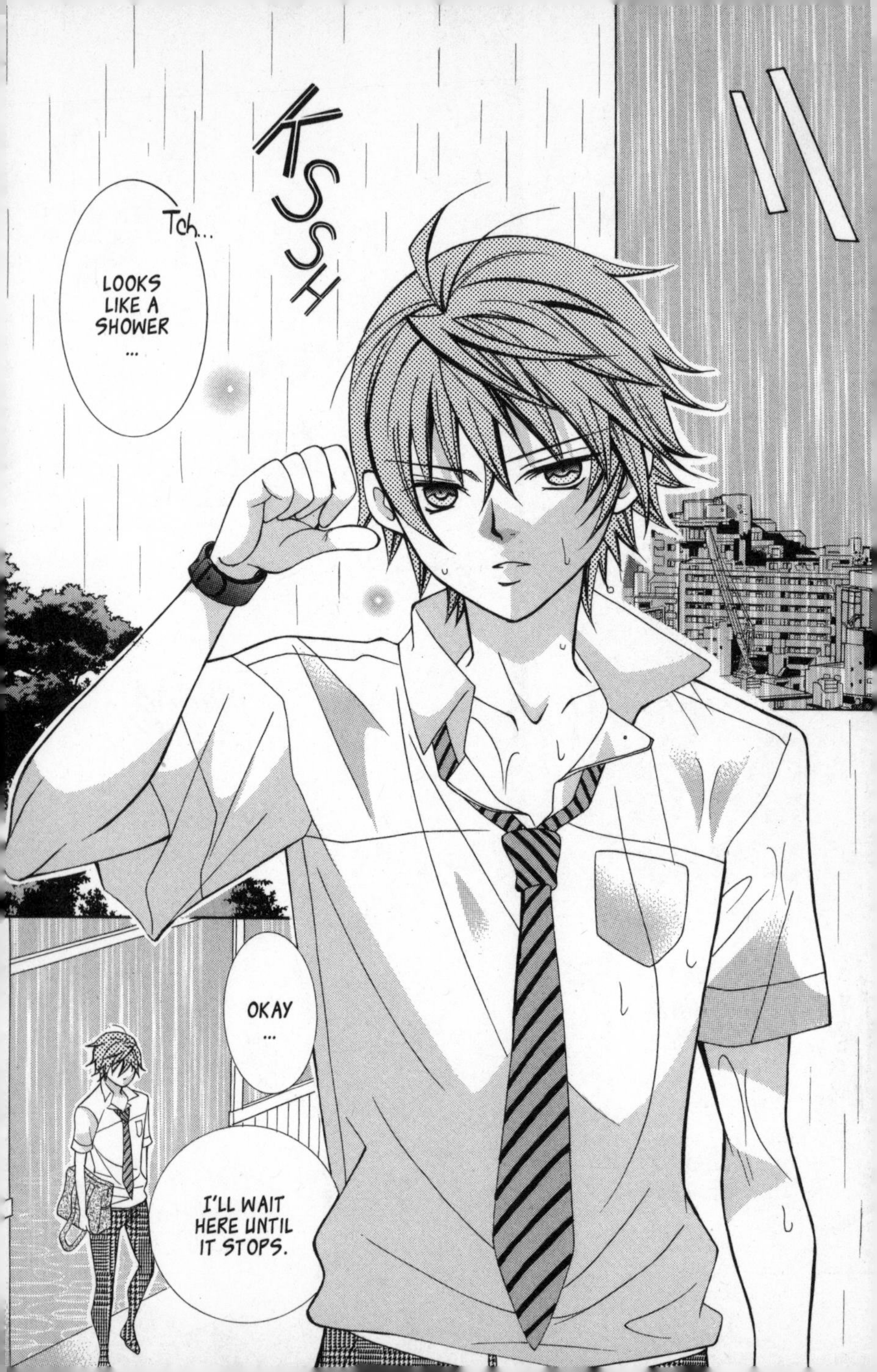
KSSH
Tch... LOOKS LIKE A SHOWER ...
OKAY ...
I'LL WAIT HERE UNTIL IT STOPS.

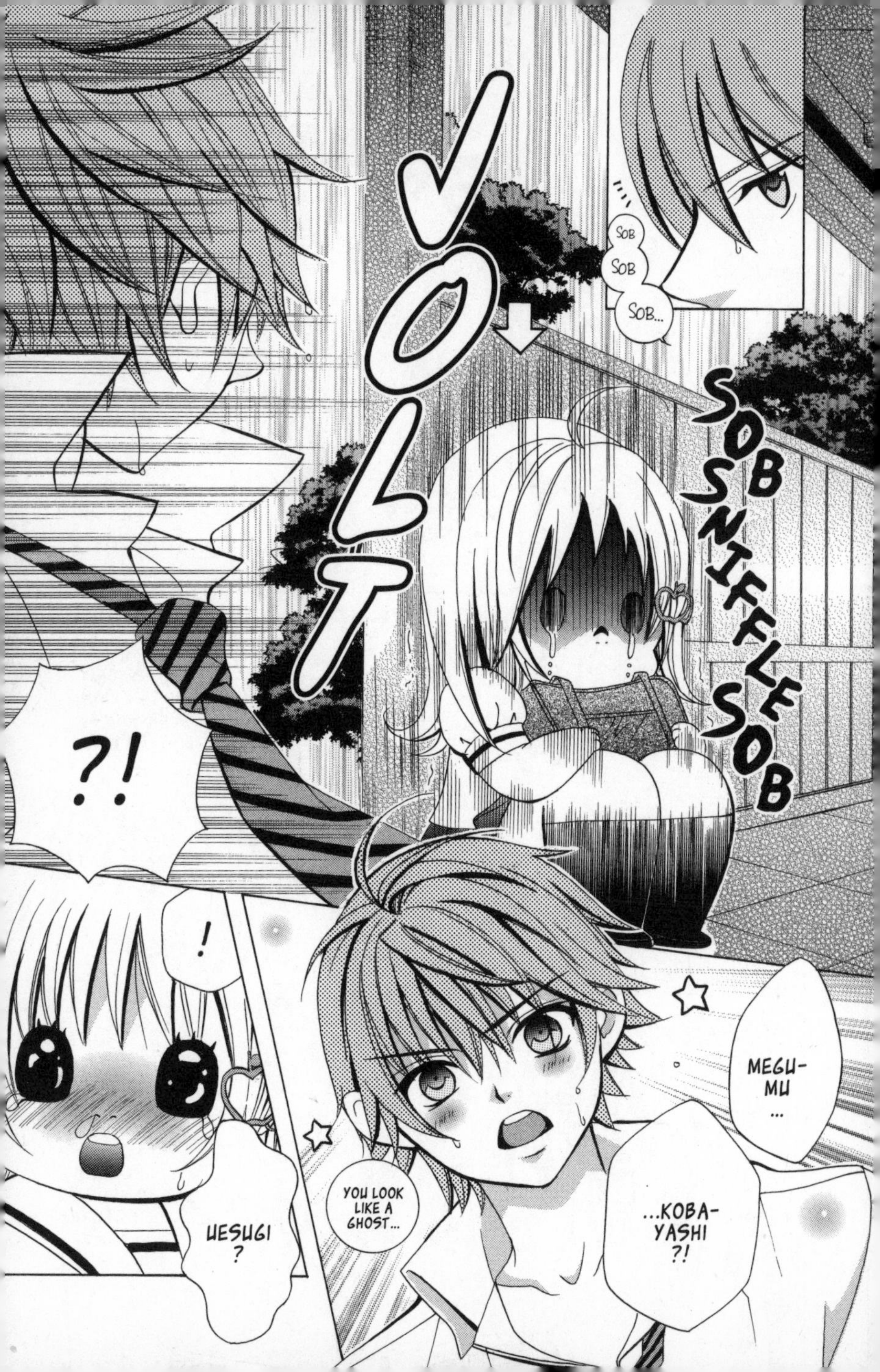
SOB
SOB
SOB...
SOB SNIFFLE SOB
VOLT
?!
MEGU-MU...
...KOBA-YASHI?!
YOU LOOK LIKE A GHOST...
!
UESUGI?

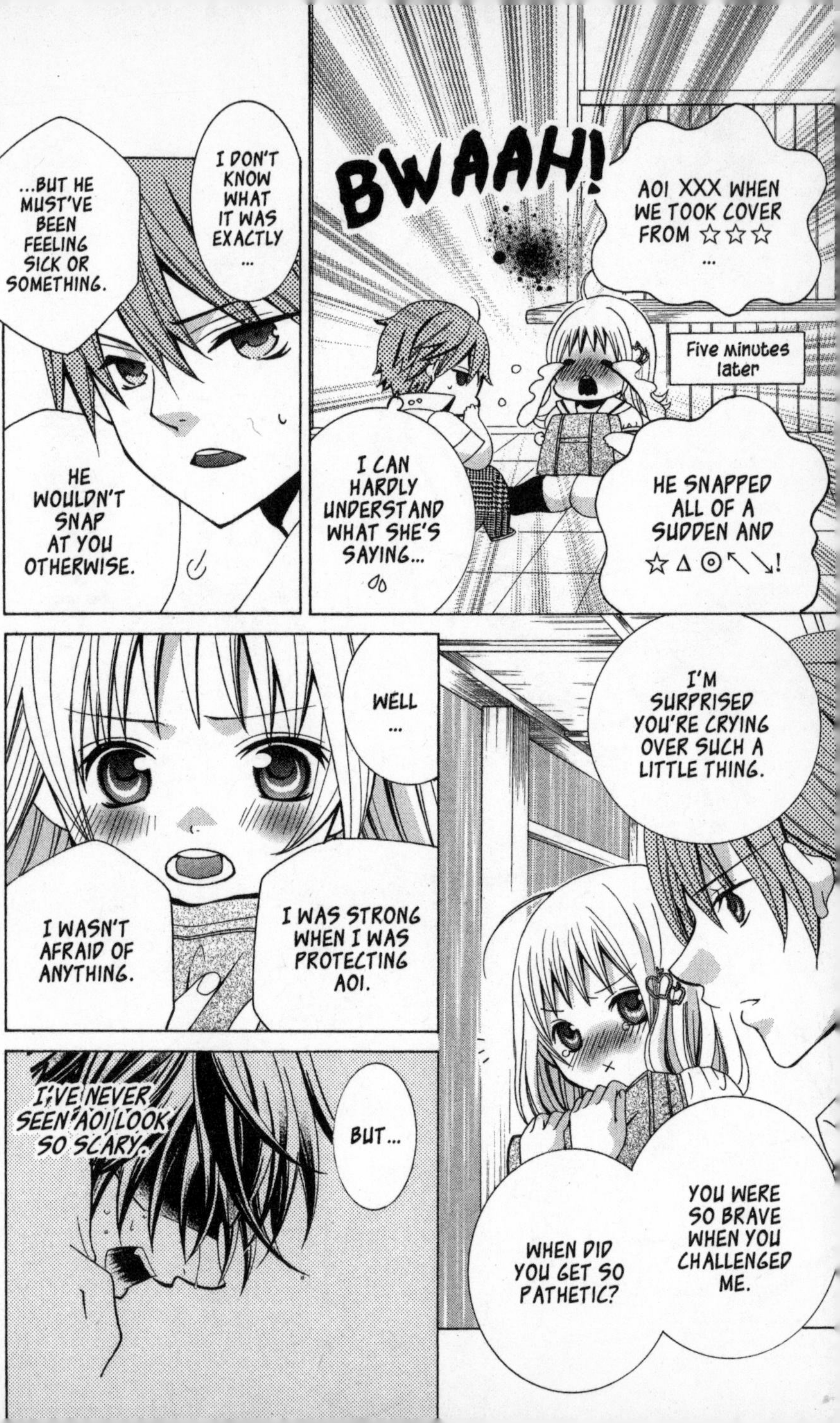
AOI XXX WHEN WE TOOK COVER FROM ☆☆☆ ...
BWAAH!
Five minutes later
HE SNAPPED ALL OF A SUDDEN AND ☆△◎↖↘!
I CAN HARDLY UNDERSTAND WHAT SHE'S SAYING...
I DON'T KNOW WHAT IT WAS EXACTLY ...
...BUT HE MUST'VE BEEN FEELING SICK OR SOMETHING.
HE WOULDN'T SNAP AT YOU OTHERWISE.
I'M SURPRISED YOU'RE CRYING OVER SUCH A LITTLE THING.
YOU WERE SO BRAVE WHEN YOU CHALLENGED ME.
WHEN DID YOU GET SO PATHETIC?
WELL ...
I WAS STRONG WHEN I WAS PROTECTING AOI.
I WASN'T AFRAID OF ANYTHING.
BUT...
I'VE NEVER SEEN AOI LOOK SO SCARY.

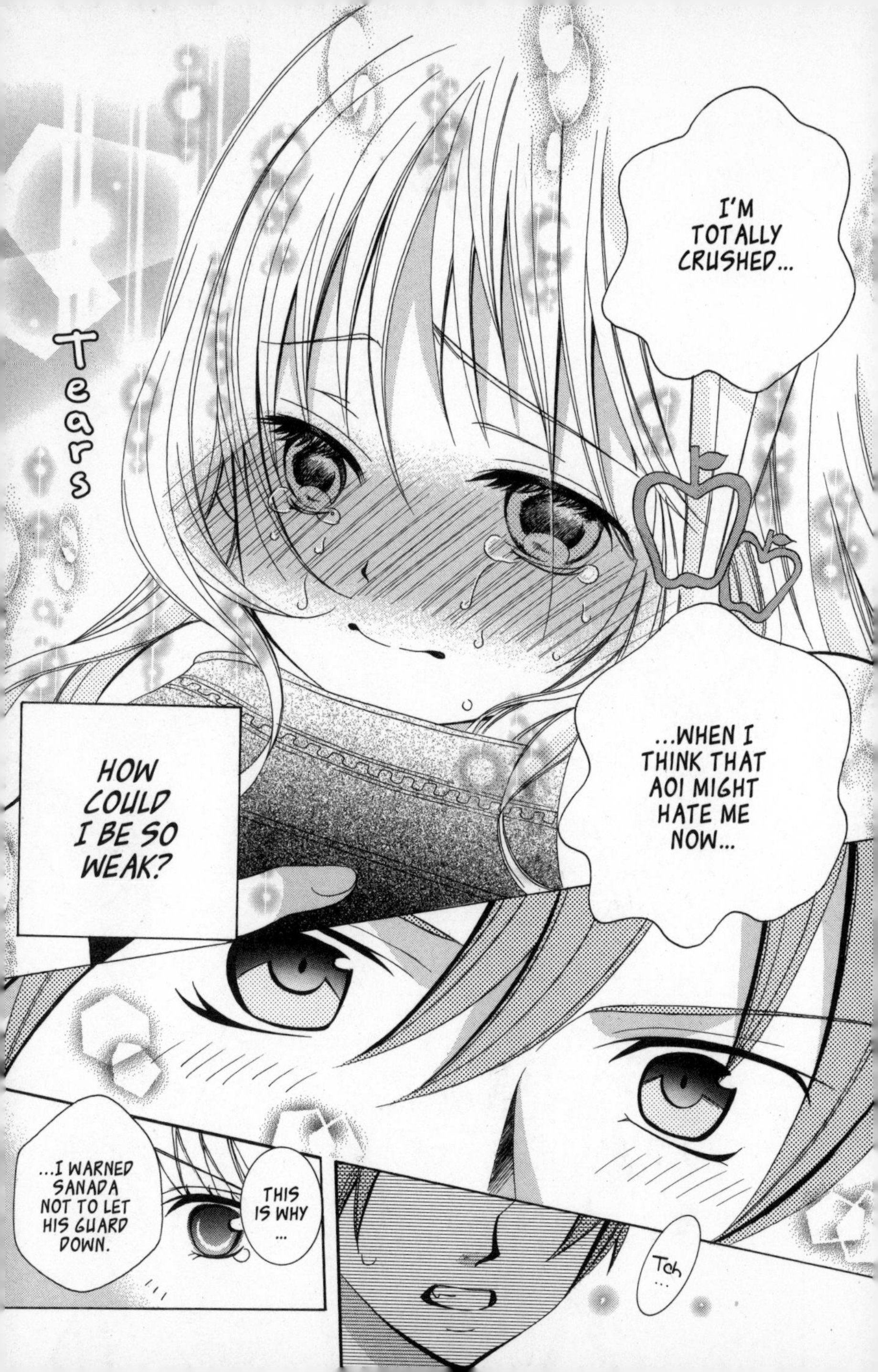

I'M TOTALLY CRUSHED...
Tears
...WHEN I THINK THAT AOI MIGHT HATE ME NOW...
HOW COULD I BE SO WEAK?
Tch...
THIS IS WHY ...
...I WARNED SANADA NOT TO LET HIS GUARD DOWN.

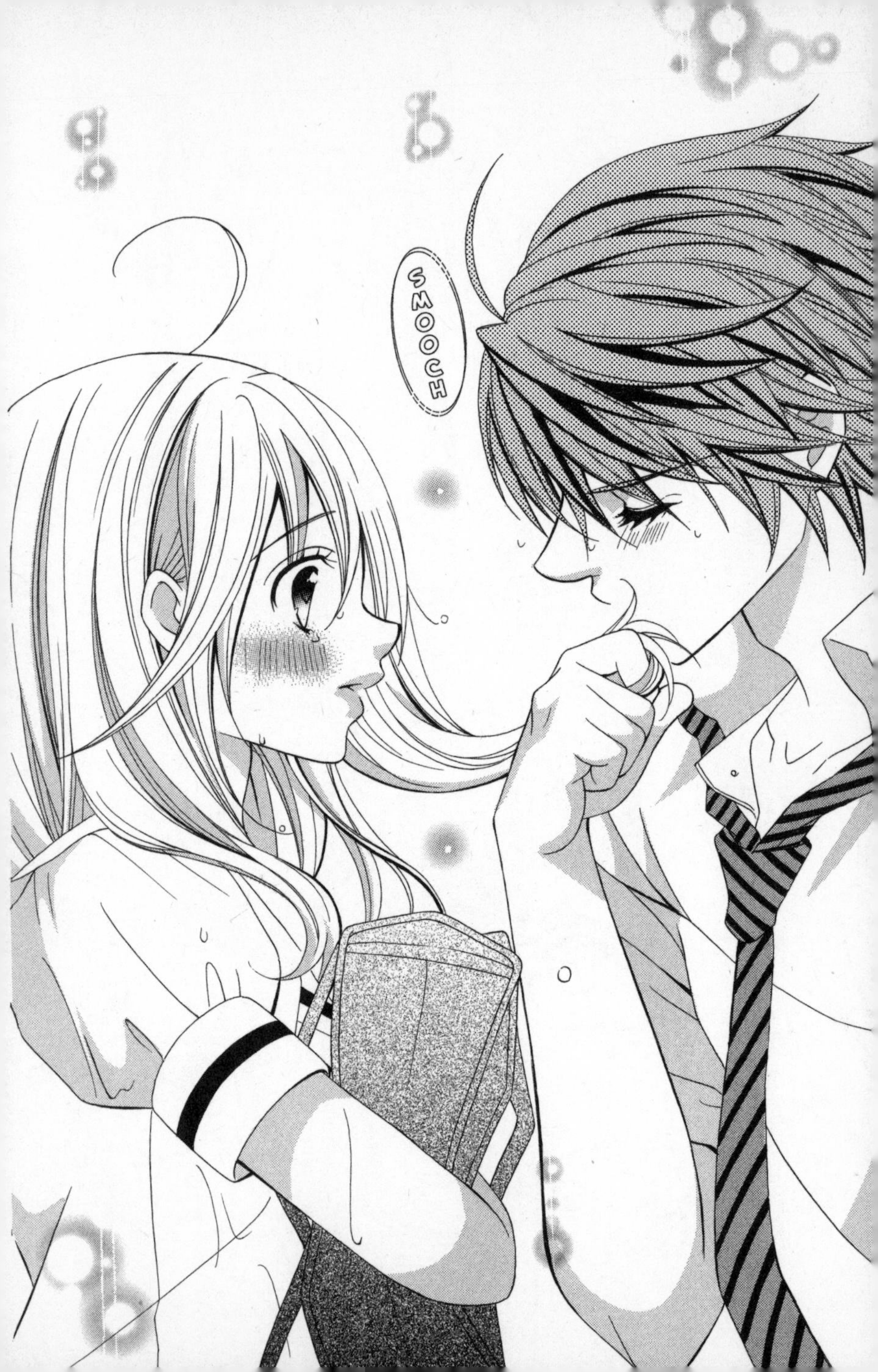
SMOOCH

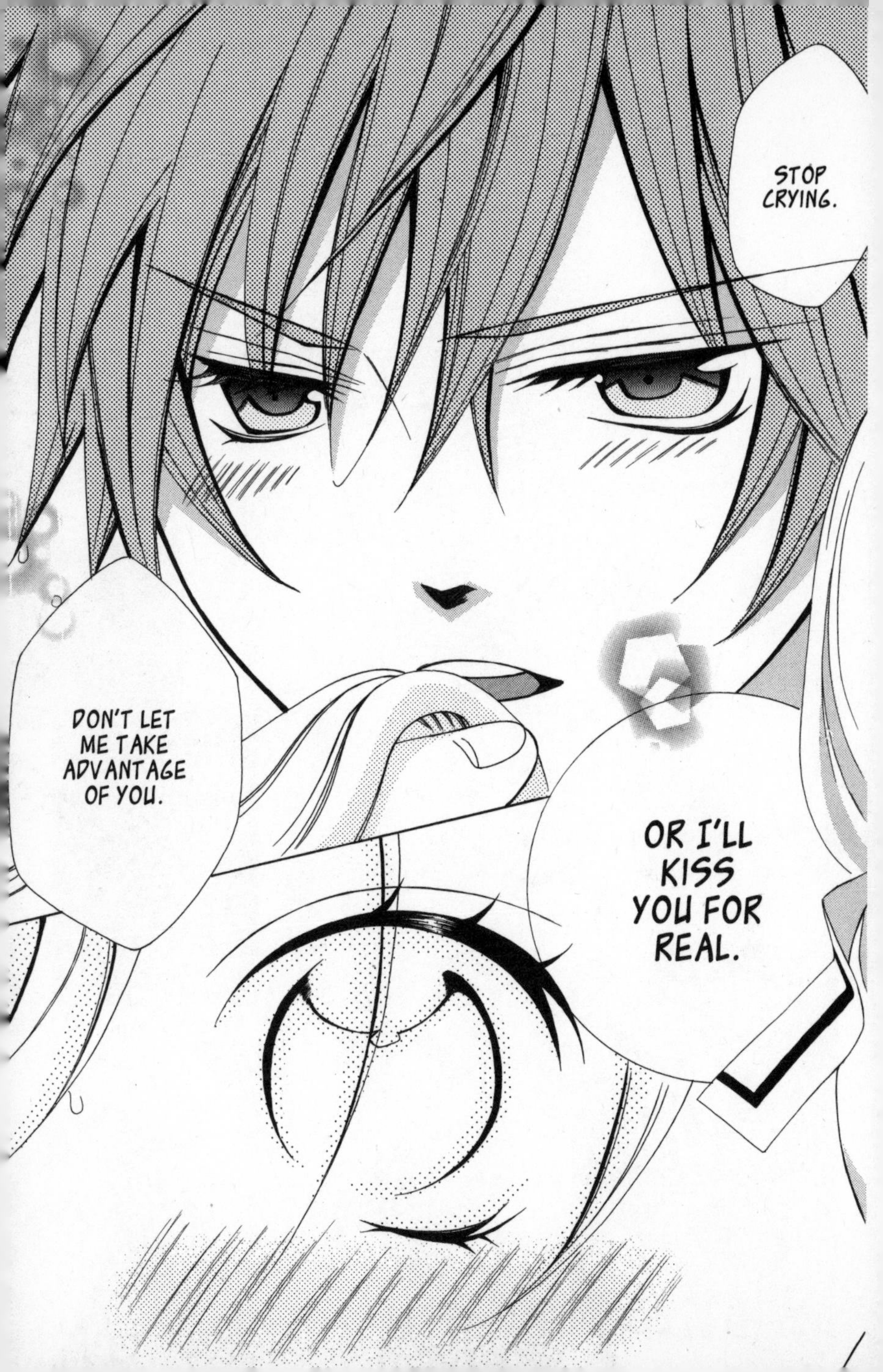
STOP CRYING.
OR I'LL KISS YOU FOR REAL.
DON'T LET ME TAKE ADVANTAGE OF YOU.

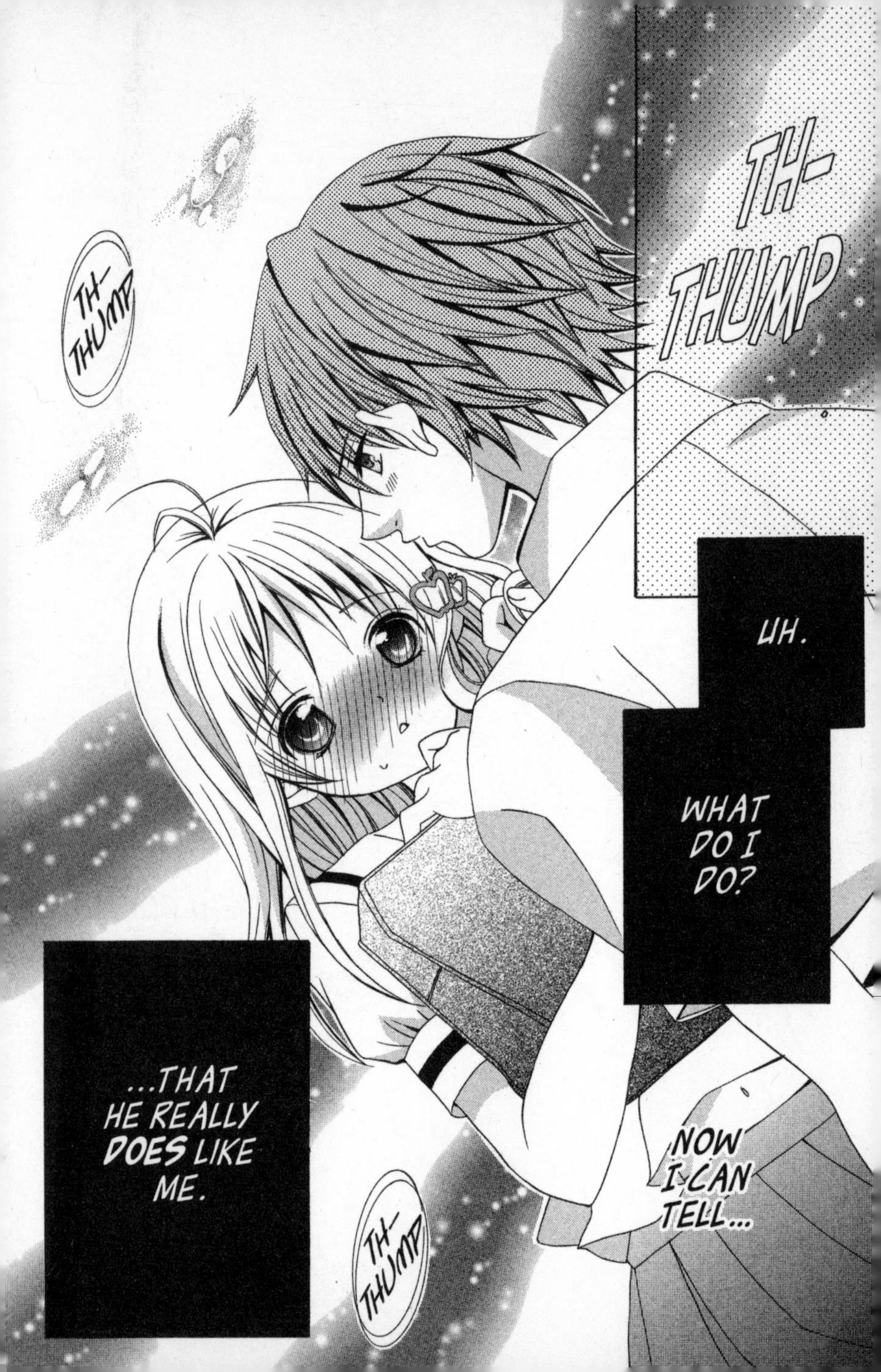
TH-THUMP
UH.
WHAT DO I DO?
TH-THUMP
NOW I CAN TELL...
...THAT HE REALLY DOES LIKE ME.
TH-THUMP

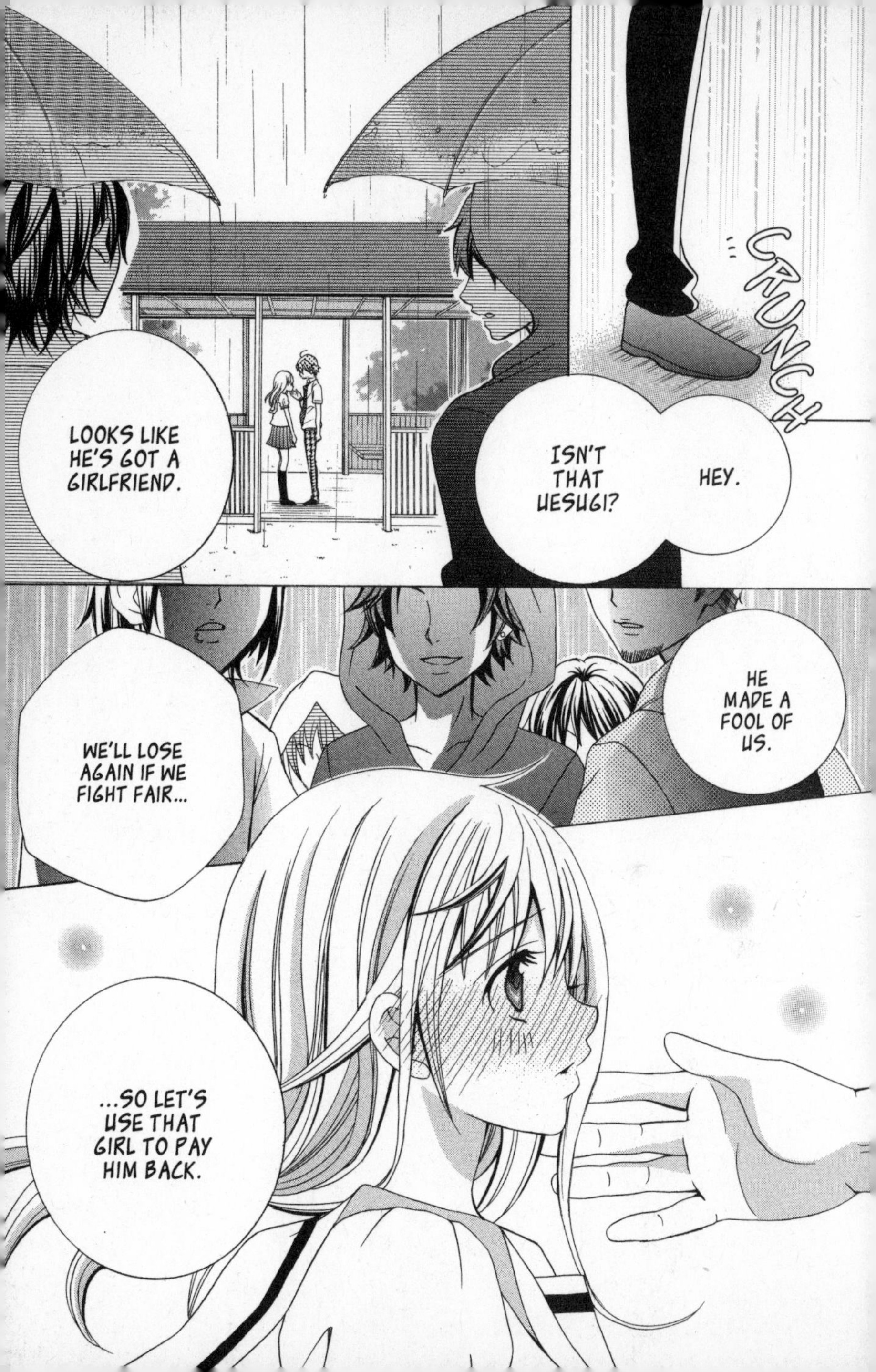
CRUNCH
HEY.
ISN'T THAT UESUGI?
LOOKS LIKE HE'S GOT A GIRLFRIEND.
HE MADE A FOOL OF US.
WE'LL LOSE AGAIN IF WE FIGHT FAIR...
...SO LET'S USE THAT GIRL TO PAY HIM BACK.

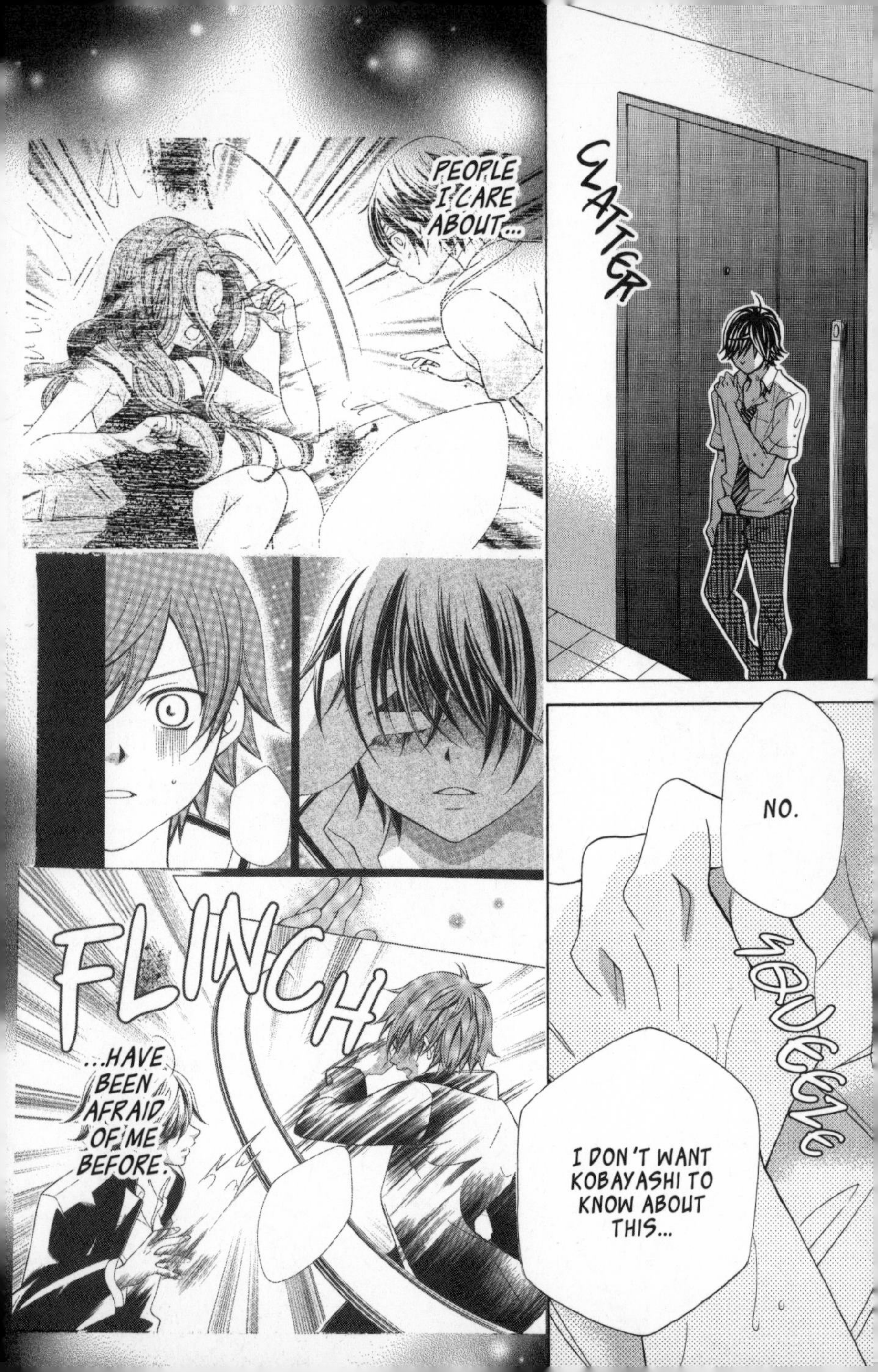
CLATTER
NO.
SQUEEZE
I DON'T WANT KOBAYASHI TO KNOW ABOUT THIS...
PEOPLE I CARE ABOUT...
FLINCH
...HAVE BEEN AFRAID OF ME BEFORE.

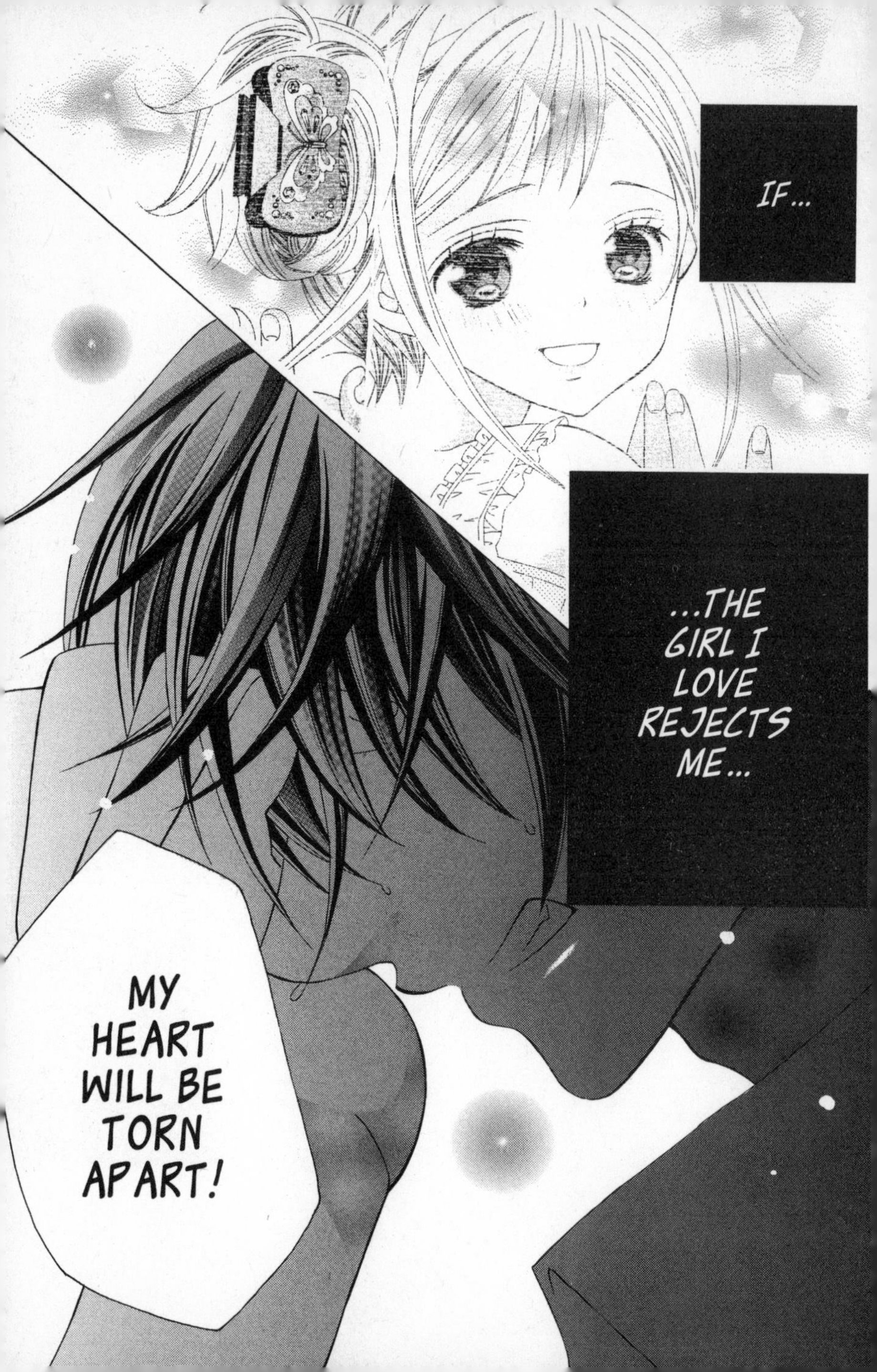
IF...
...THE GIRL I LOVE REJECTS ME...
MY HEART WILL BE TORN APART!

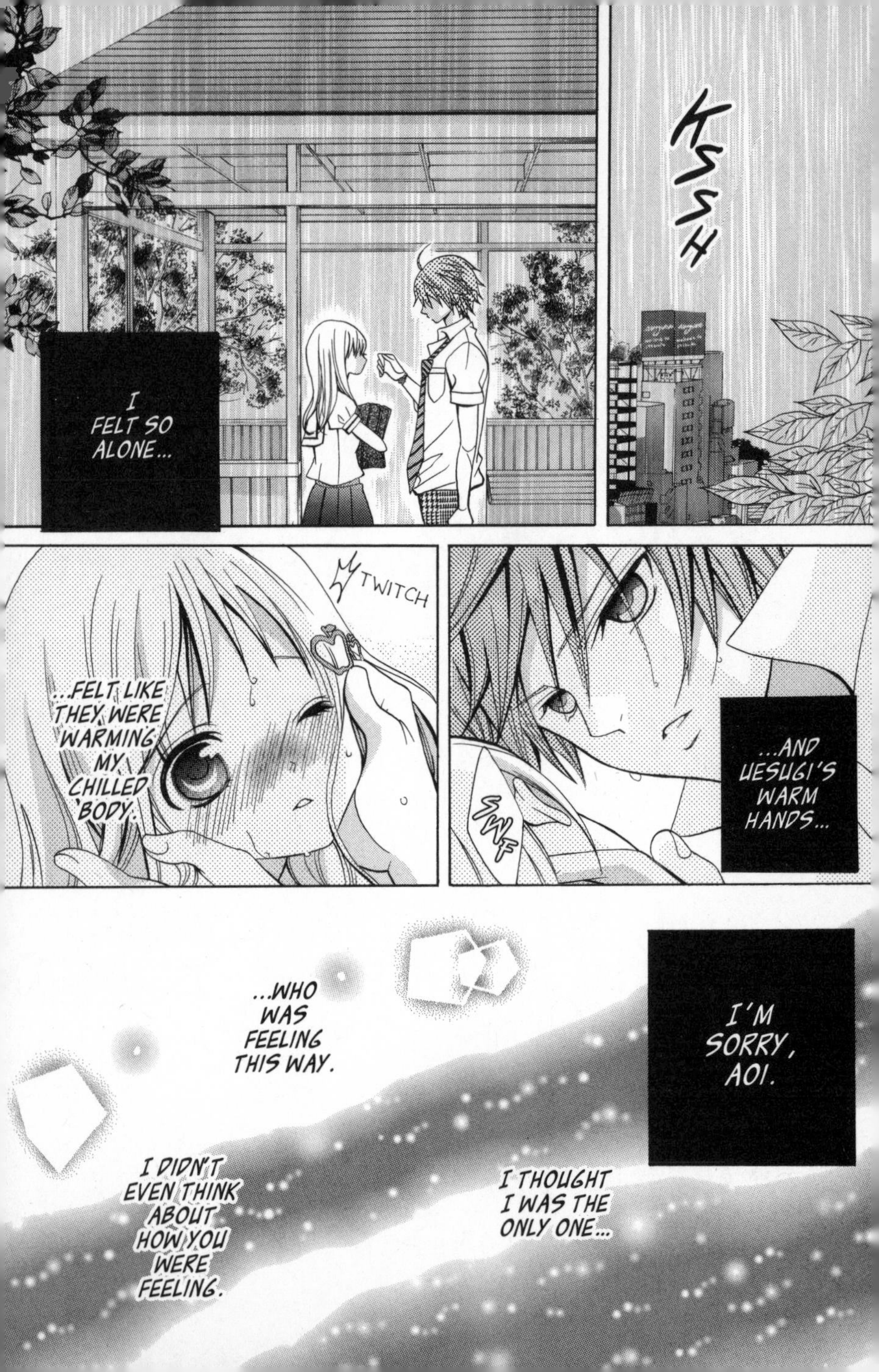
KSSH
I FELT SO ALONE...
...AND UESUGI'S WARM HANDS...
SWF
TWITCH
...FELT LIKE THEY WERE WARMING MY CHILLED BODY.
I'M SORRY, AOI.
I THOUGHT I WAS THE ONLY ONE...
...WHO WAS FEELING THIS WAY.
I DIDN'T EVEN THINK ABOUT HOW YOU WERE FEELING.

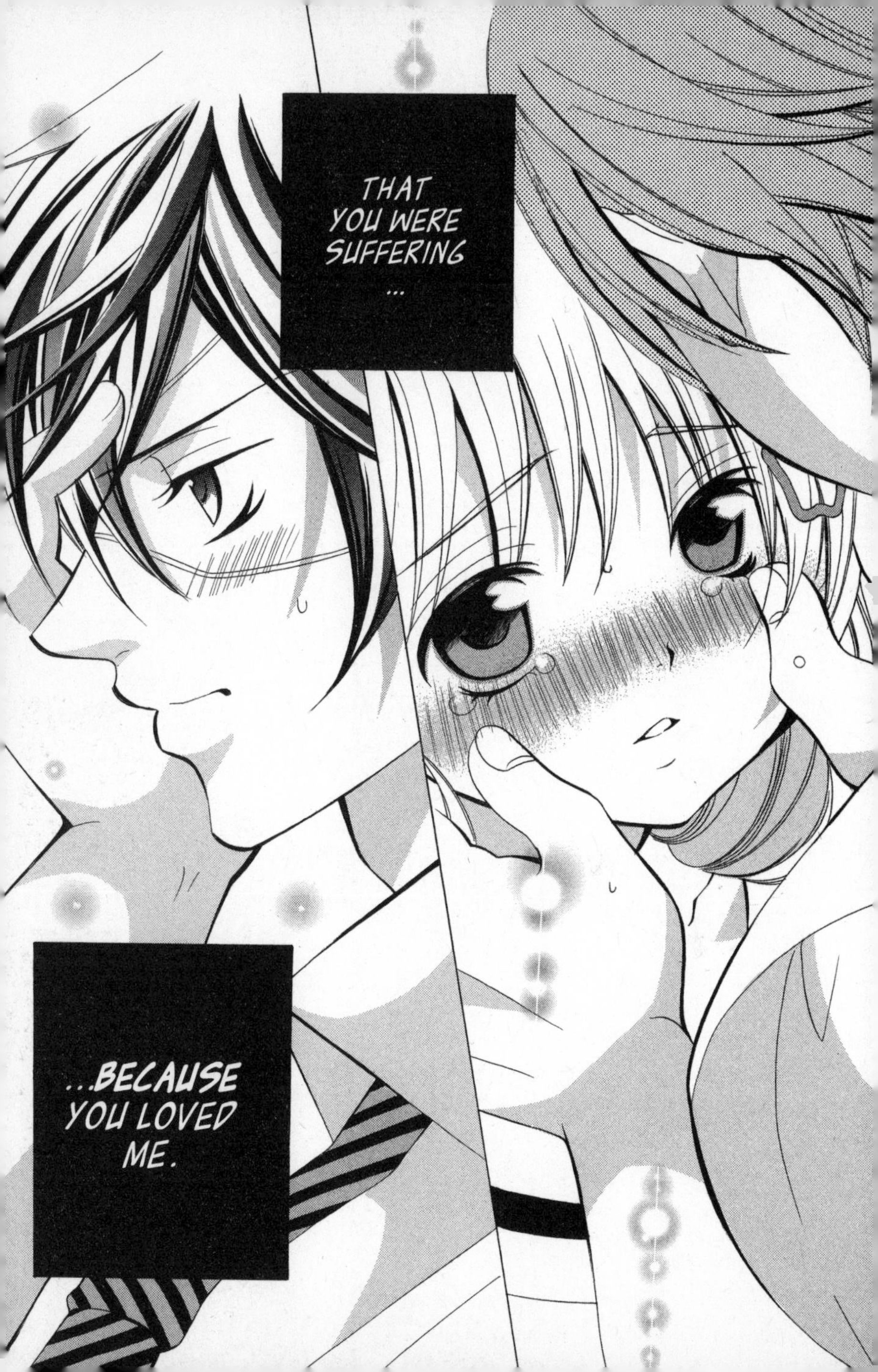
THAT YOU WERE SUFFERING ...
...BECAUSE YOU LOVED ME.

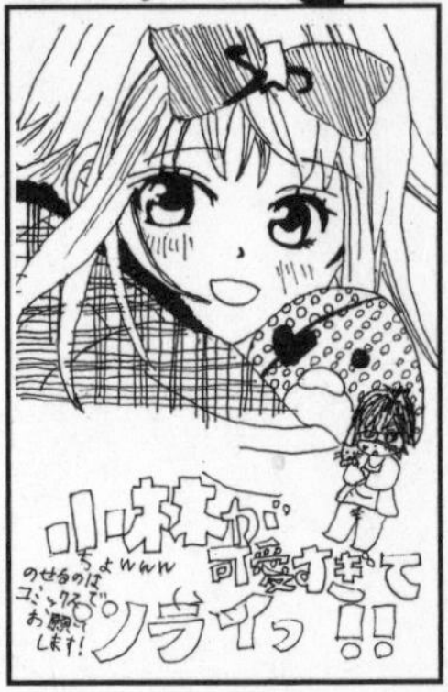

→
Umika Ouchi (Tokyo)
Ed.: Aoi's heart flutters watching the cute Mego. ♥

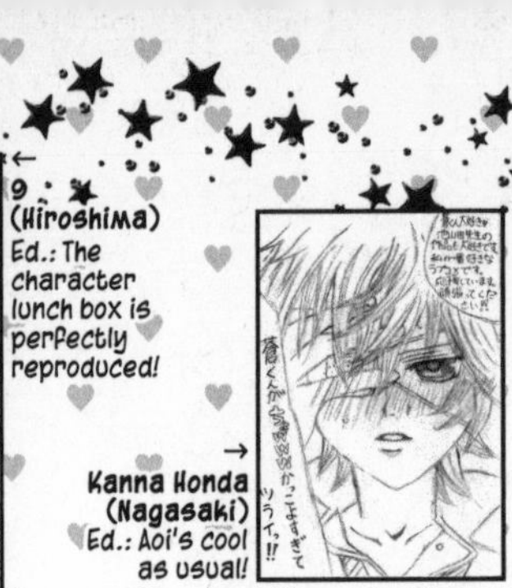

→
Kanna Honda (Nagasaki)
Ed.: Aoi's cool as usual!

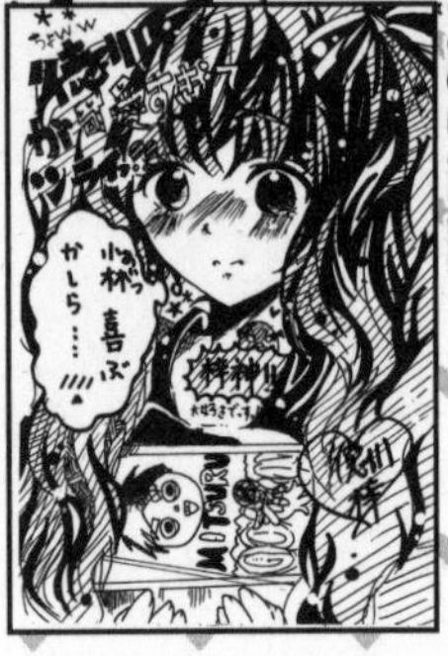

←
9 (Hiroshima)
Ed.: The character lunch box is perfectly reproduced!

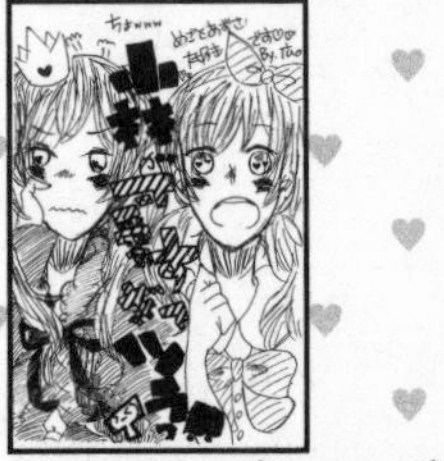

↑ **Yuuna Takagi (Yamaguchi)**
Ed.: They've got hearts in their eyes! Who're they watching?

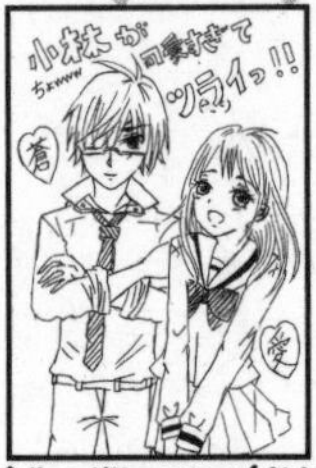

↑ **Nao Kitamura (Shiga)**
Ed.: The distance between them will soon be zero feet. ♥

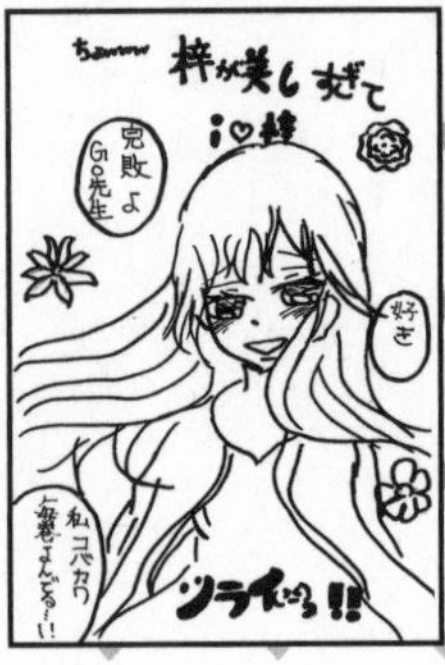

←
Haruka Rachi (Okayama)
Ed.: The very popular scene in volume 8!

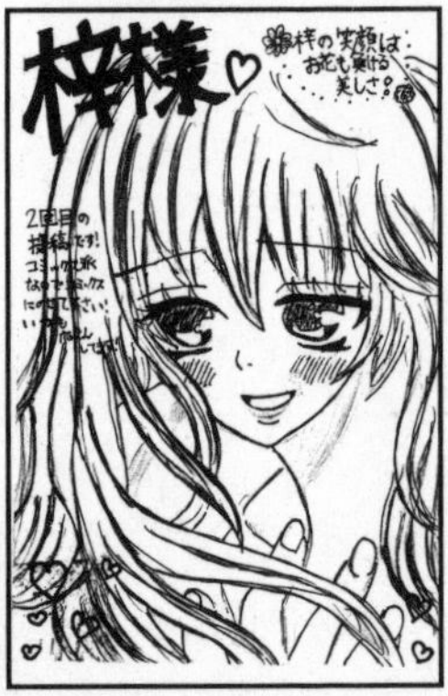

→
Haruka Tanno (Yamagata)
Ed.: You're beautiful... Azusa. ♥

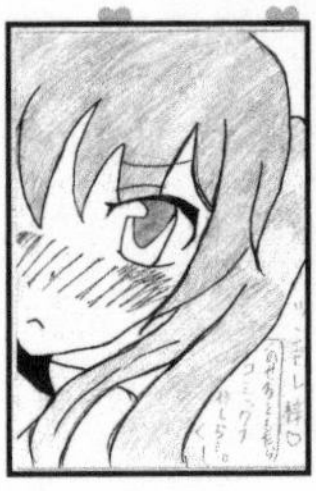

←
Ryouka Kashino (Saitama)
Ed.: The tsundere Azusa is very cute too!!

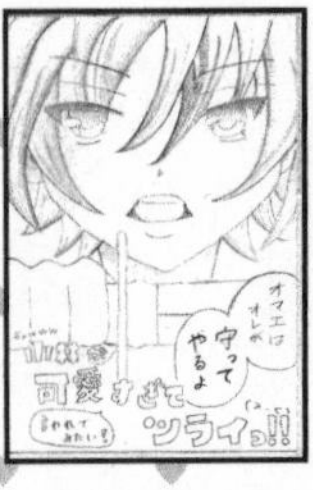

←
I Love So Cute! ☆ (Ishikawa)
Ed.: I want someone to say this to me...

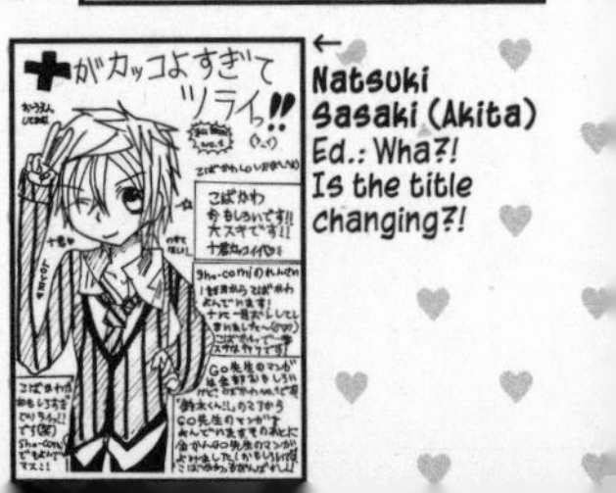

←
Natsuki Sasaki (Akita)
Ed.: Wha?! Is the title changing?!

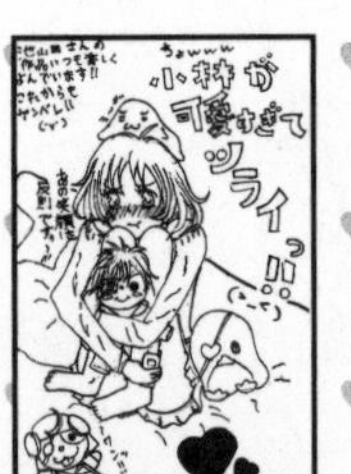

↑ **Rio Hashida (Nagasaki)**
Ed.: I wanna squeeze the tiny Mego!

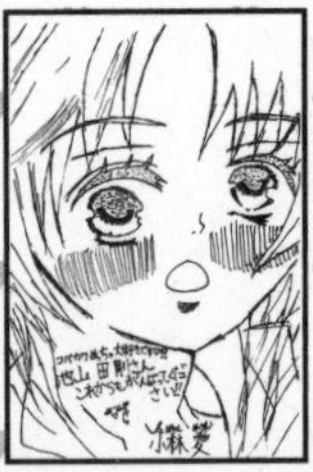

←
"Tereru Megumu" (Kagoshima)
Ed.: Blushing Mego is super cute. ♥

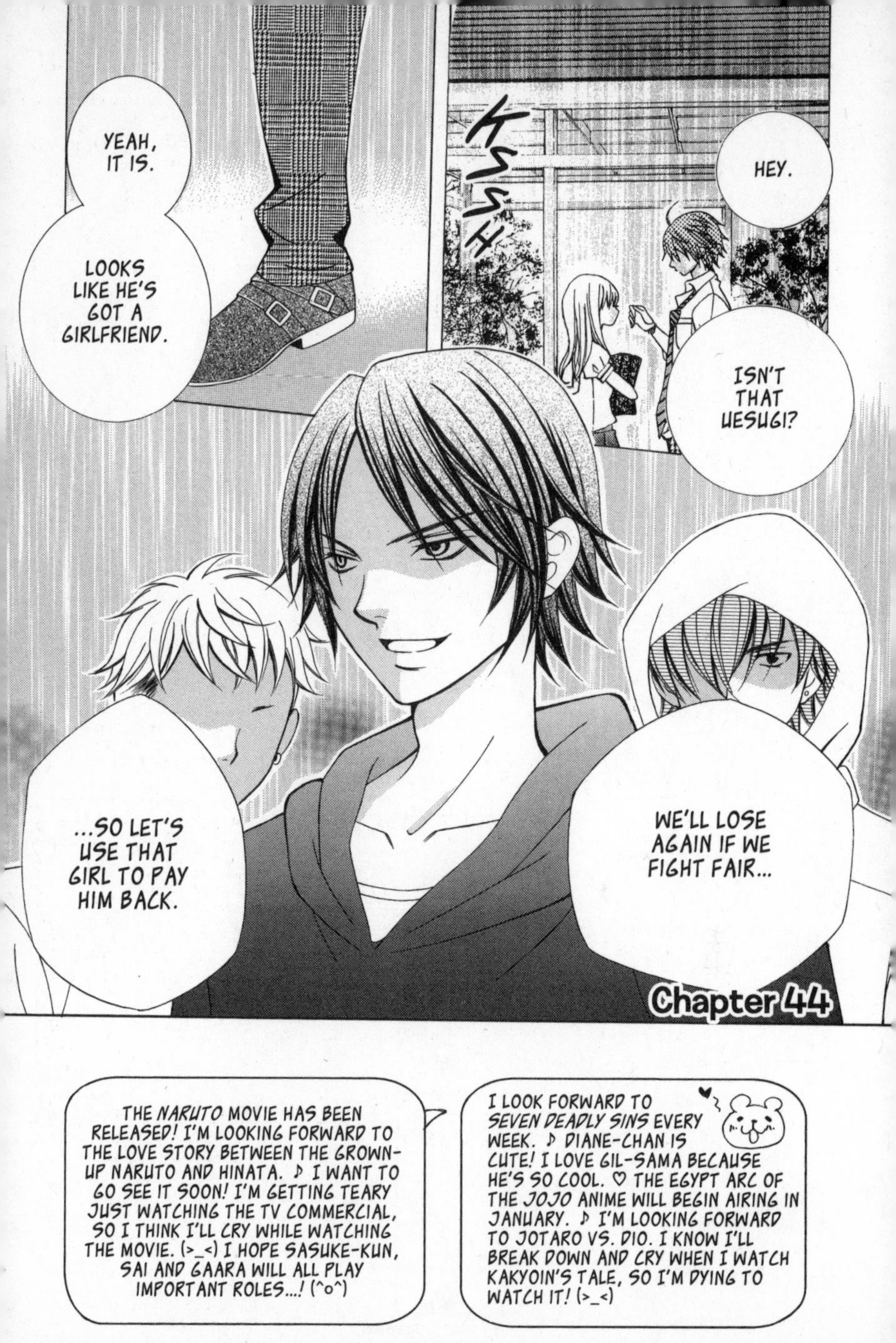
KSSH
HEY.
ISN'T THAT UESUGI?
YEAH, IT IS.
LOOKS LIKE HE'S GOT A GIRLFRIEND.
WE'LL LOSE AGAIN IF WE FIGHT FAIR...
...SO LET'S USE THAT GIRL TO PAY HIM BACK.
Chapter 44

THE *NARUTO* MOVIE HAS BEEN RELEASED! I'M LOOKING FORWARD TO THE LOVE STORY BETWEEN THE GROWN-UP NARUTO AND HINATA. ♪ I WANT TO GO SEE IT SOON! I'M GETTING TEARY JUST WATCHING THE TV COMMERCIAL, SO I THINK I'LL CRY WHILE WATCHING THE MOVIE. (>_<) I HOPE SASUKE-KUN, SAI AND GAARA WILL ALL PLAY IMPORTANT ROLES...! (^o^)

I LOOK FORWARD TO *SEVEN DEADLY SINS* EVERY WEEK. ♪ DIANE-CHAN IS CUTE! I LOVE GIL-SAMA BECAUSE HE'S SO COOL. ♡ THE EGYPT ARC OF THE *JOJO* ANIME WILL BEGIN AIRING IN JANUARY. ♪ I'M LOOKING FORWARD TO JOTARO VS. DIO. I KNOW I'LL BREAK DOWN AND CRY WHEN I WATCH KAKYOIN'S TALE, SO I'M DYING TO WATCH IT! (>_<)

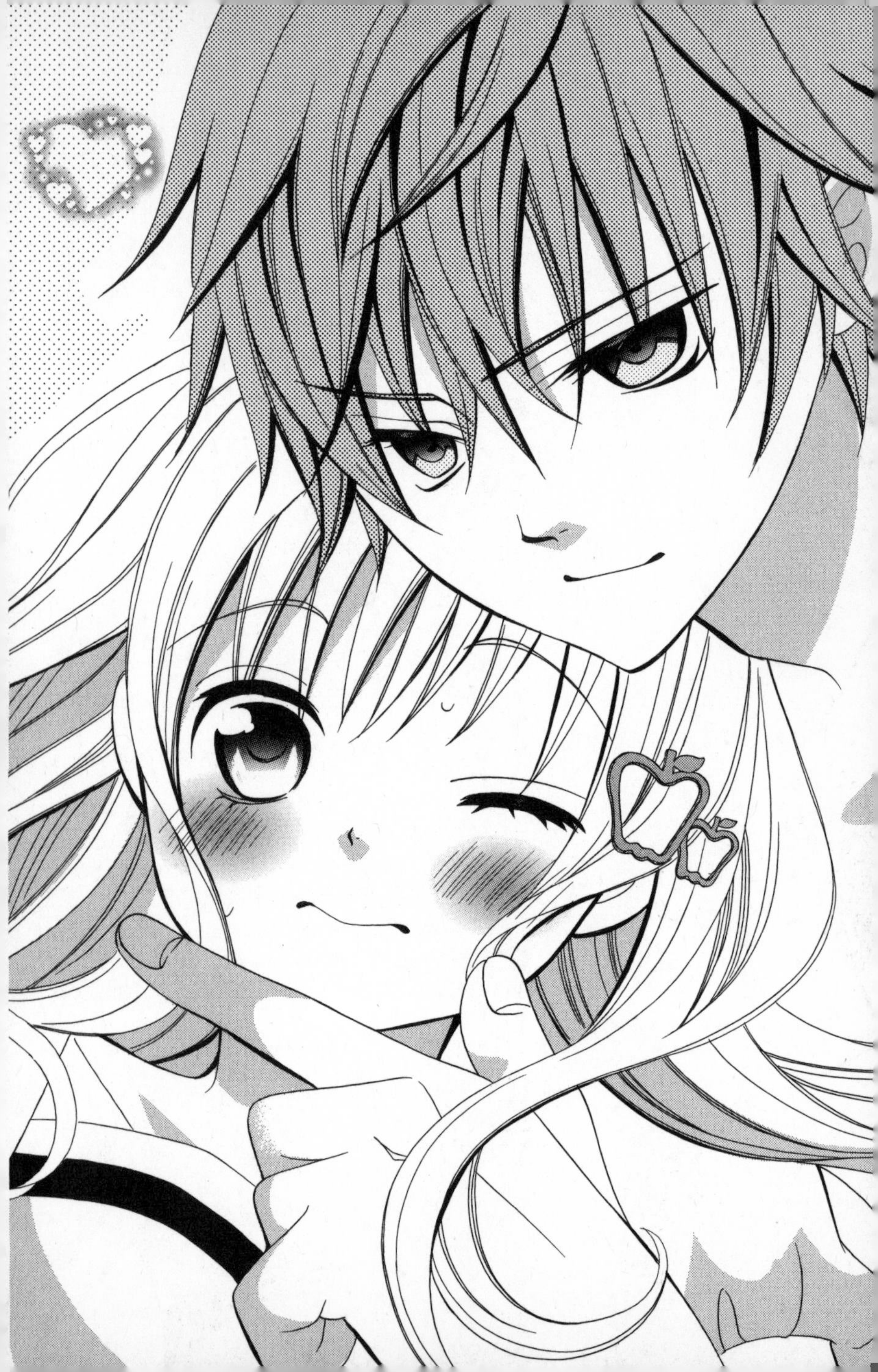

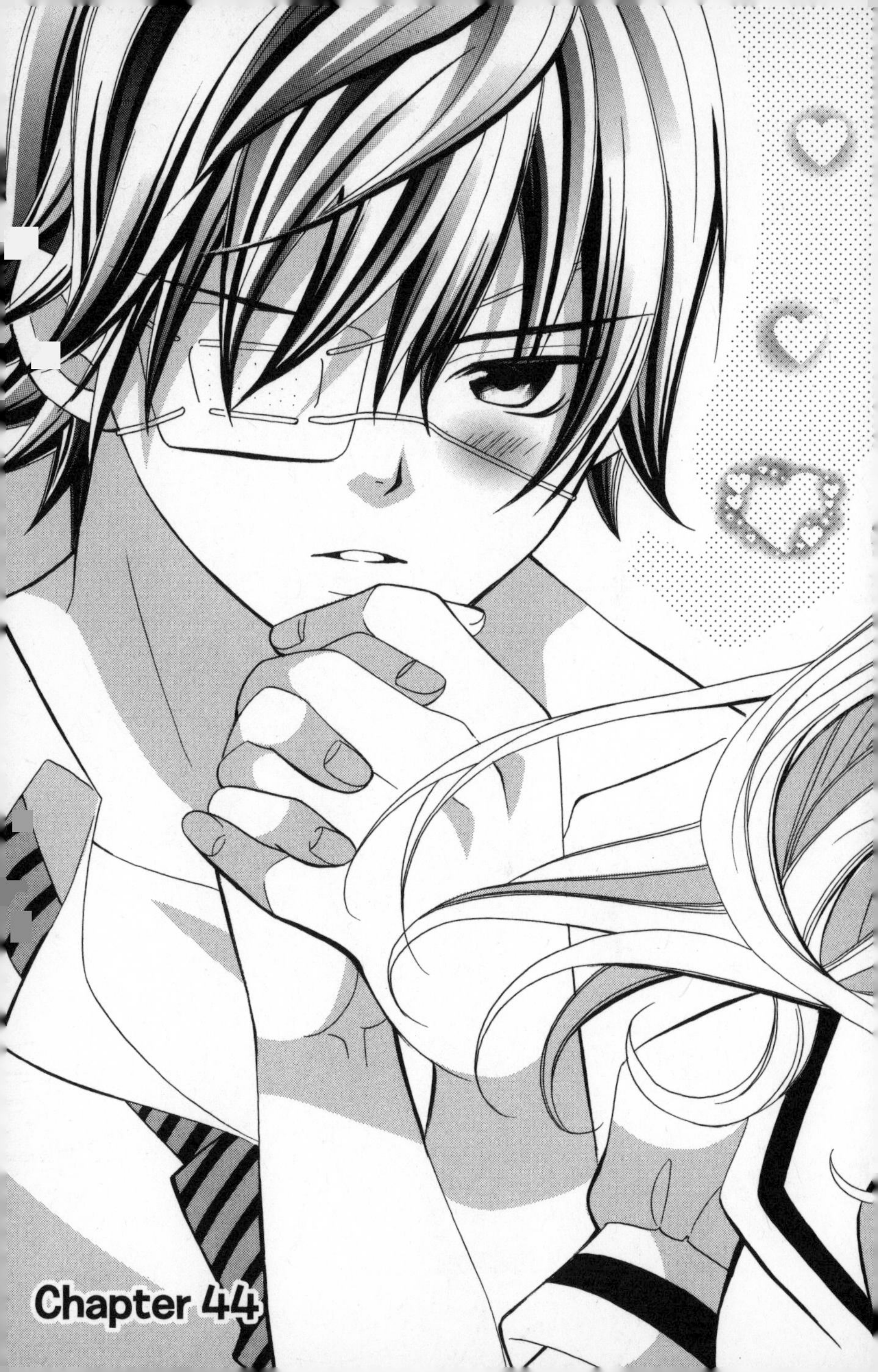
Chapter 44

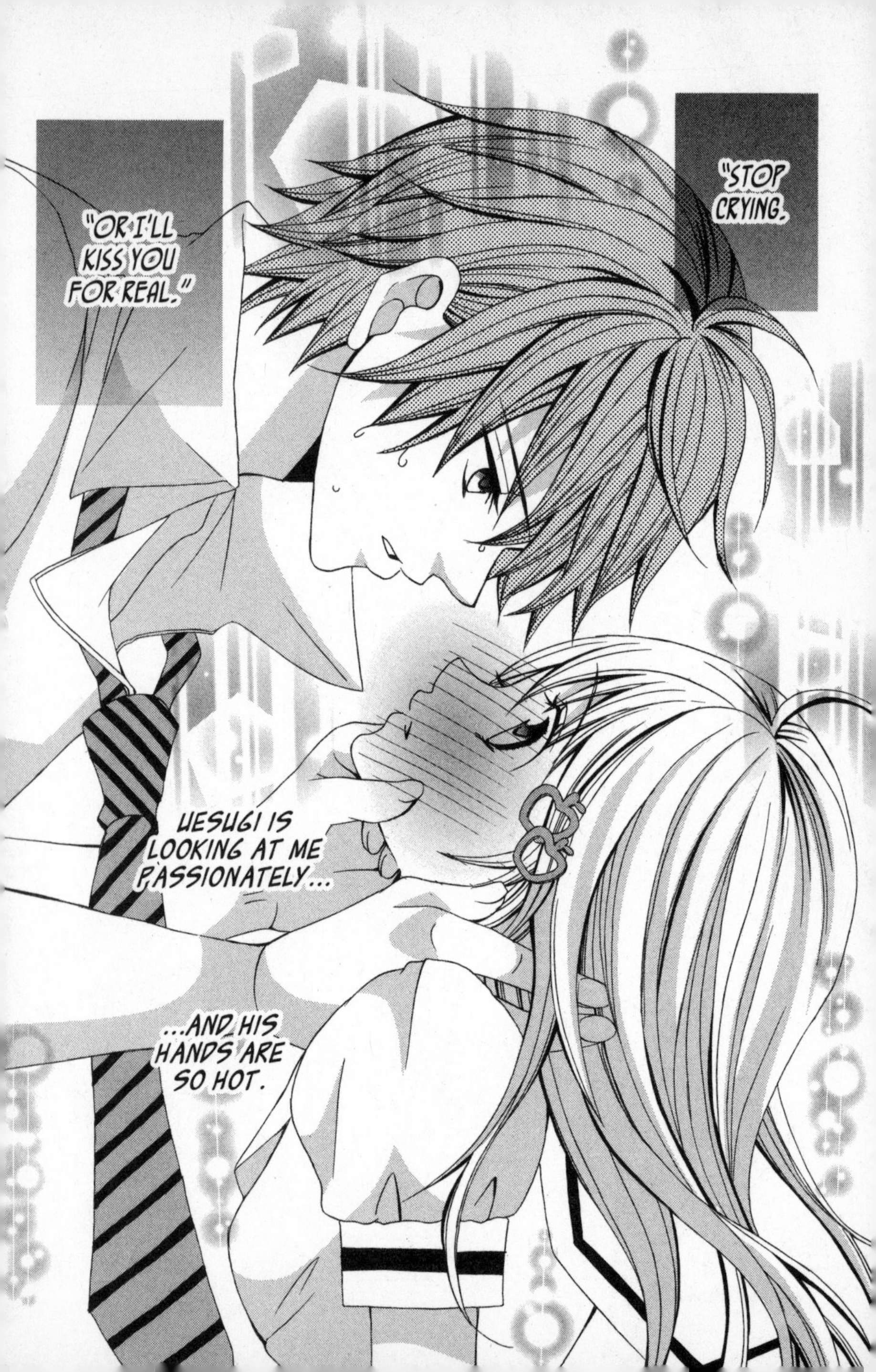
"STOP CRYING.
"OR I'LL KISS YOU FOR REAL."
UESUGI IS LOOKING AT ME PASSIONATELY...
...AND HIS HANDS ARE SO HOT.

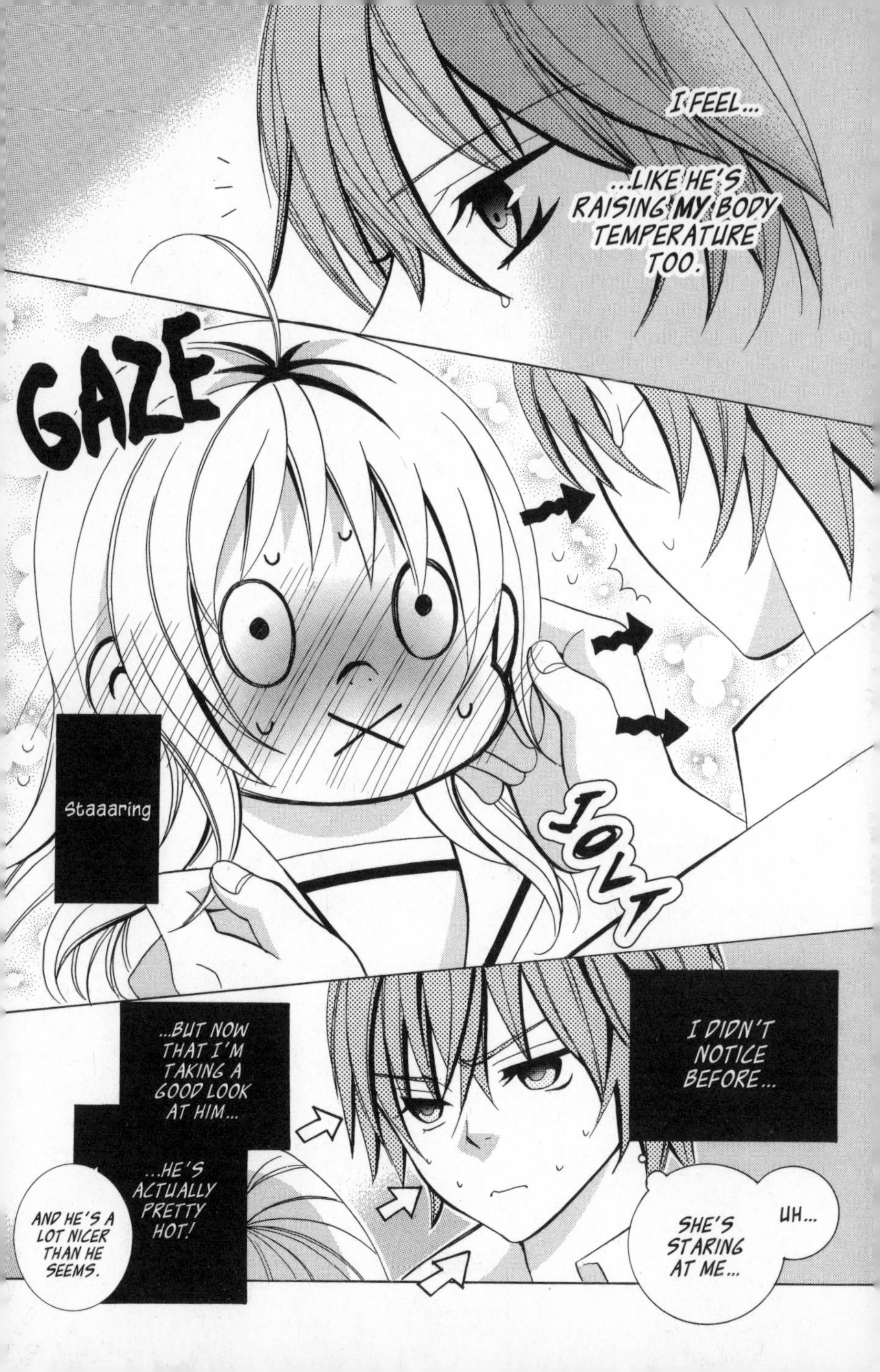
I FEEL...
...LIKE HE'S RAISING MY BODY TEMPERATURE TOO.
GAZE
JOLT
Staaaring
I DIDN'T NOTICE BEFORE...
UH...
SHE'S STARING AT ME...
...BUT NOW THAT I'M TAKING A GOOD LOOK AT HIM...
...HE'S ACTUALLY PRETTY HOT!
AND HE'S A LOT NICER THAN HE SEEMS.

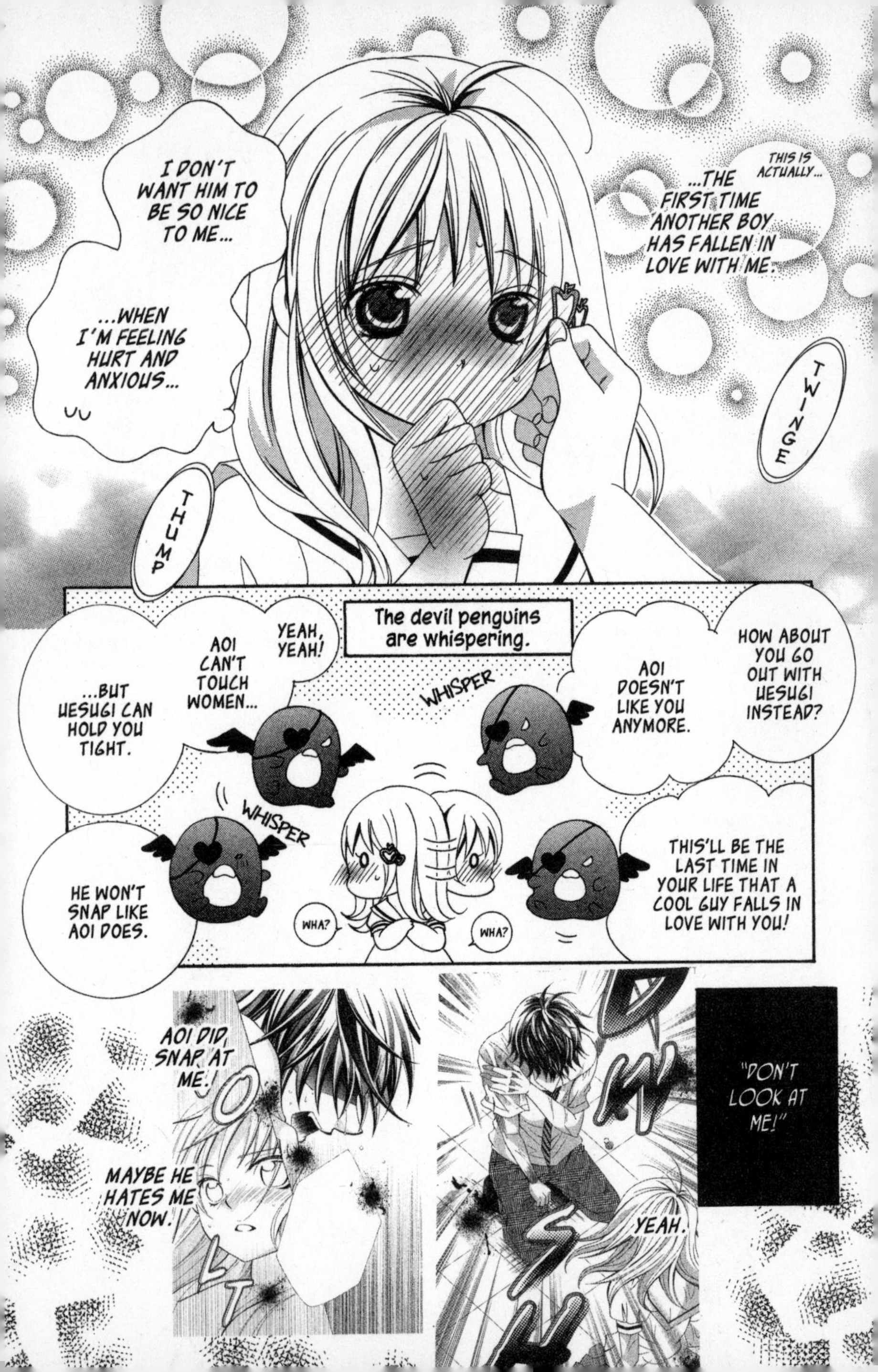
THIS IS ACTUALLY...
...THE FIRST TIME ANOTHER BOY HAS FALLEN IN LOVE WITH ME.
TWINGE
I DON'T WANT HIM TO BE SO NICE TO ME...
...WHEN I'M FEELING HURT AND ANXIOUS...
THUMP
The devil penguins are whispering.
HOW ABOUT YOU GO OUT WITH UESUGI INSTEAD?
AOI DOESN'T LIKE YOU ANYMORE.
WHISPER
YEAH, YEAH!
AOI CAN'T TOUCH WOMEN...
...BUT UESUGI CAN HOLD YOU TIGHT.
THIS'LL BE THE LAST TIME IN YOUR LIFE THAT A COOL GUY FALLS IN LOVE WITH YOU!
WHA?
WHA?
WHISPER
HE WON'T SNAP LIKE AOI DOES.
"DON'T LOOK AT ME!"
YEAH.
AOI DID SNAP AT ME.
MAYBE HE HATES ME NOW.

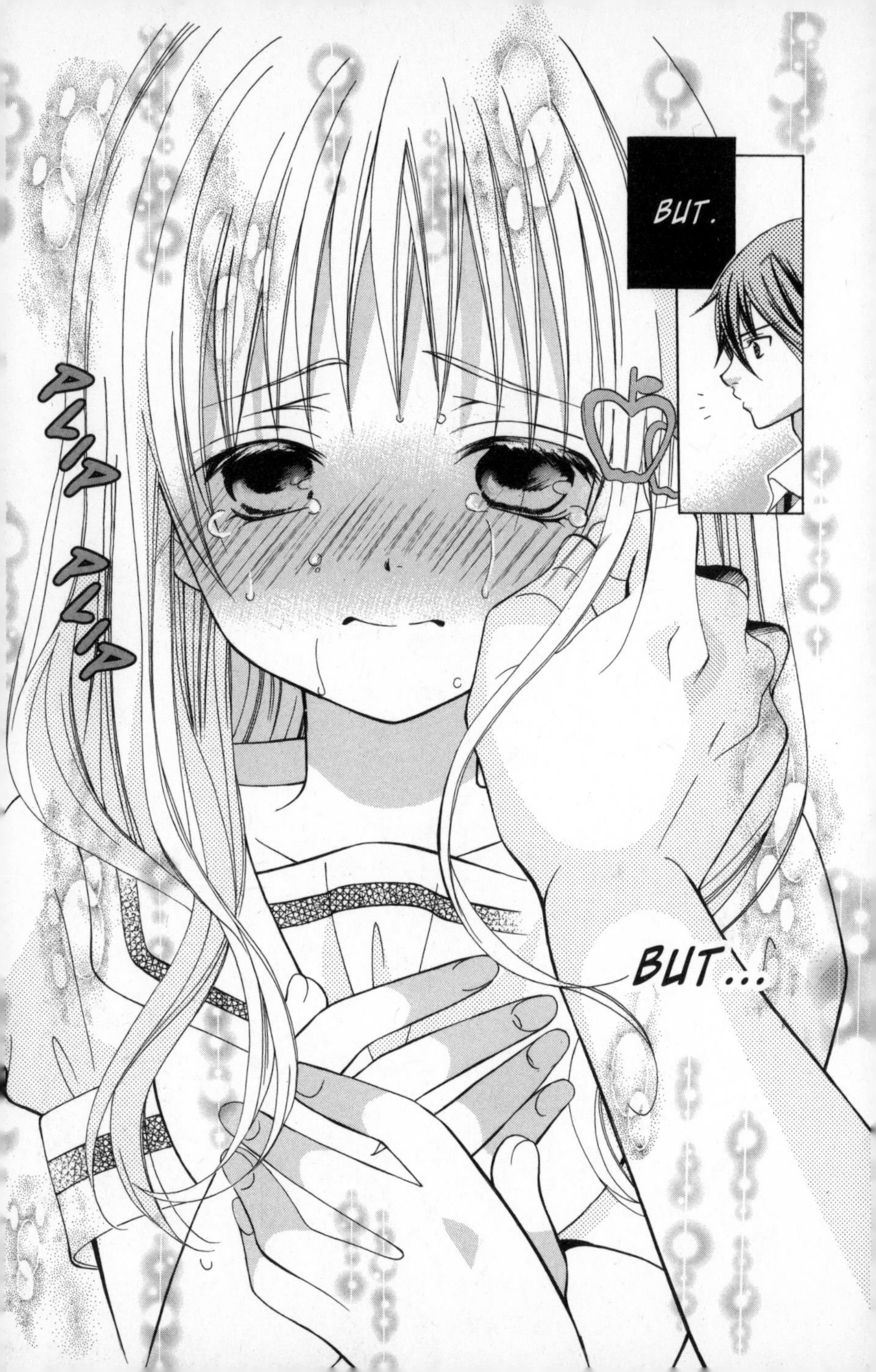
BUT.
PLIP PLIP PLIP
BUT...

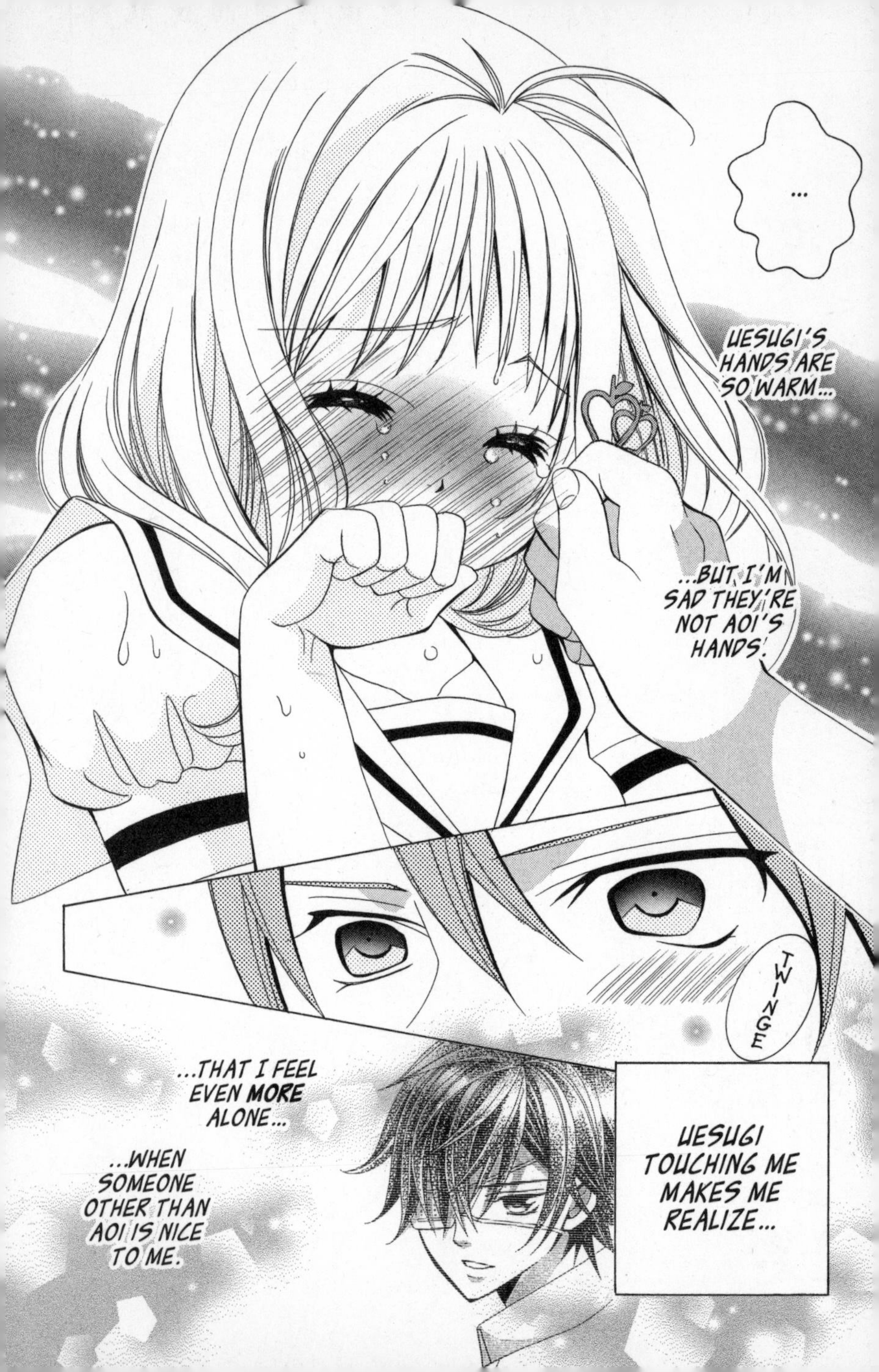
...
UESUGI'S HANDS ARE SO WARM...
...BUT I'M SAD THEY'RE NOT AOI'S HANDS.
TWINGE
UESUGI TOUCHING ME MAKES ME REALIZE...
...THAT I FEEL EVEN MORE ALONE...
...WHEN SOMEONE OTHER THAN AOI IS NICE TO ME.

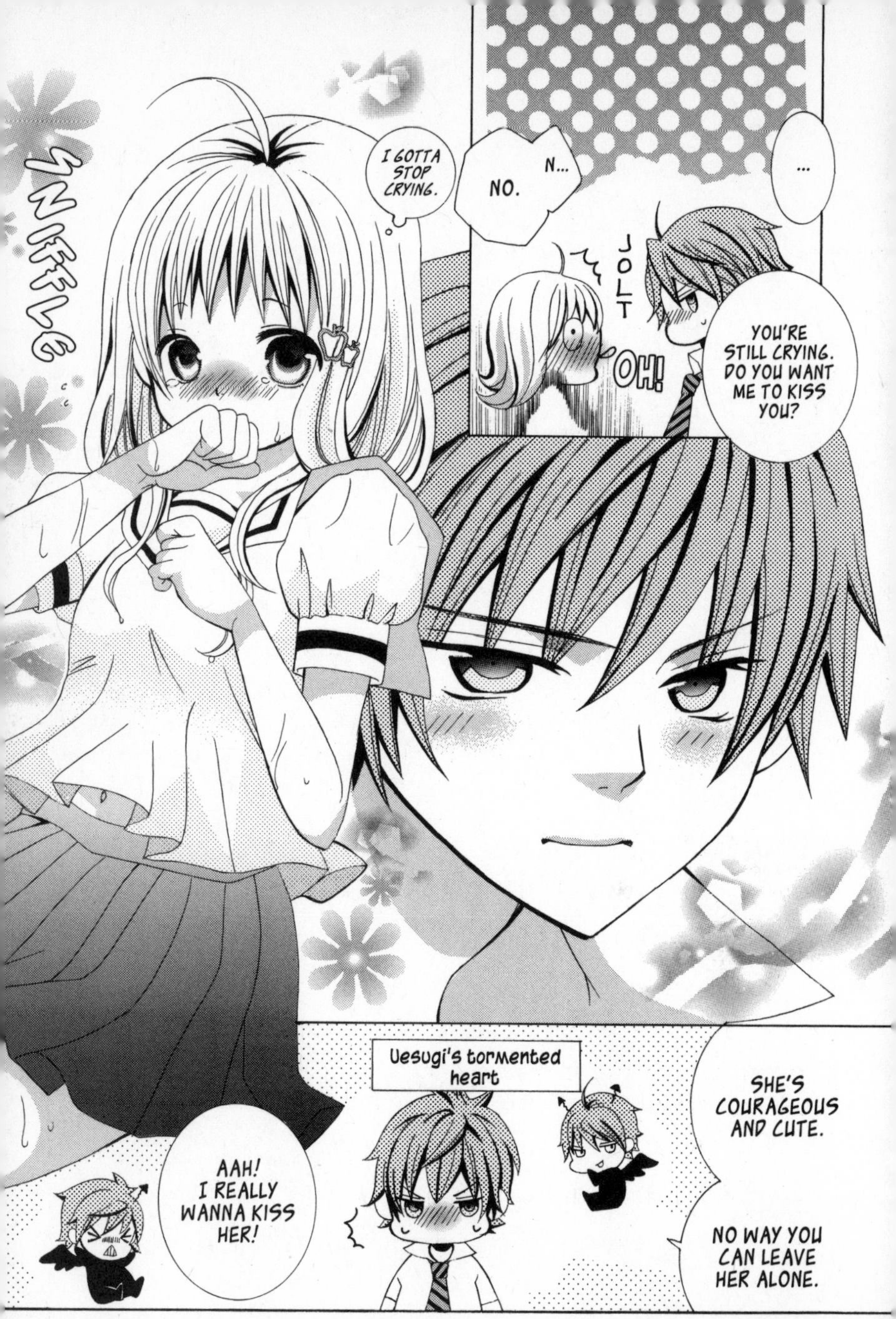
...
YOU'RE STILL CRYING. DO YOU WANT ME TO KISS YOU?
JOLT
OH!
N... NO.
I GOTTA STOP CRYING.
SNIFFLE
Uesugi's tormented heart
SHE'S COURAGEOUS AND CUTE.
NO WAY YOU CAN LEAVE HER ALONE.
AAH! I REALLY WANNA KISS HER!

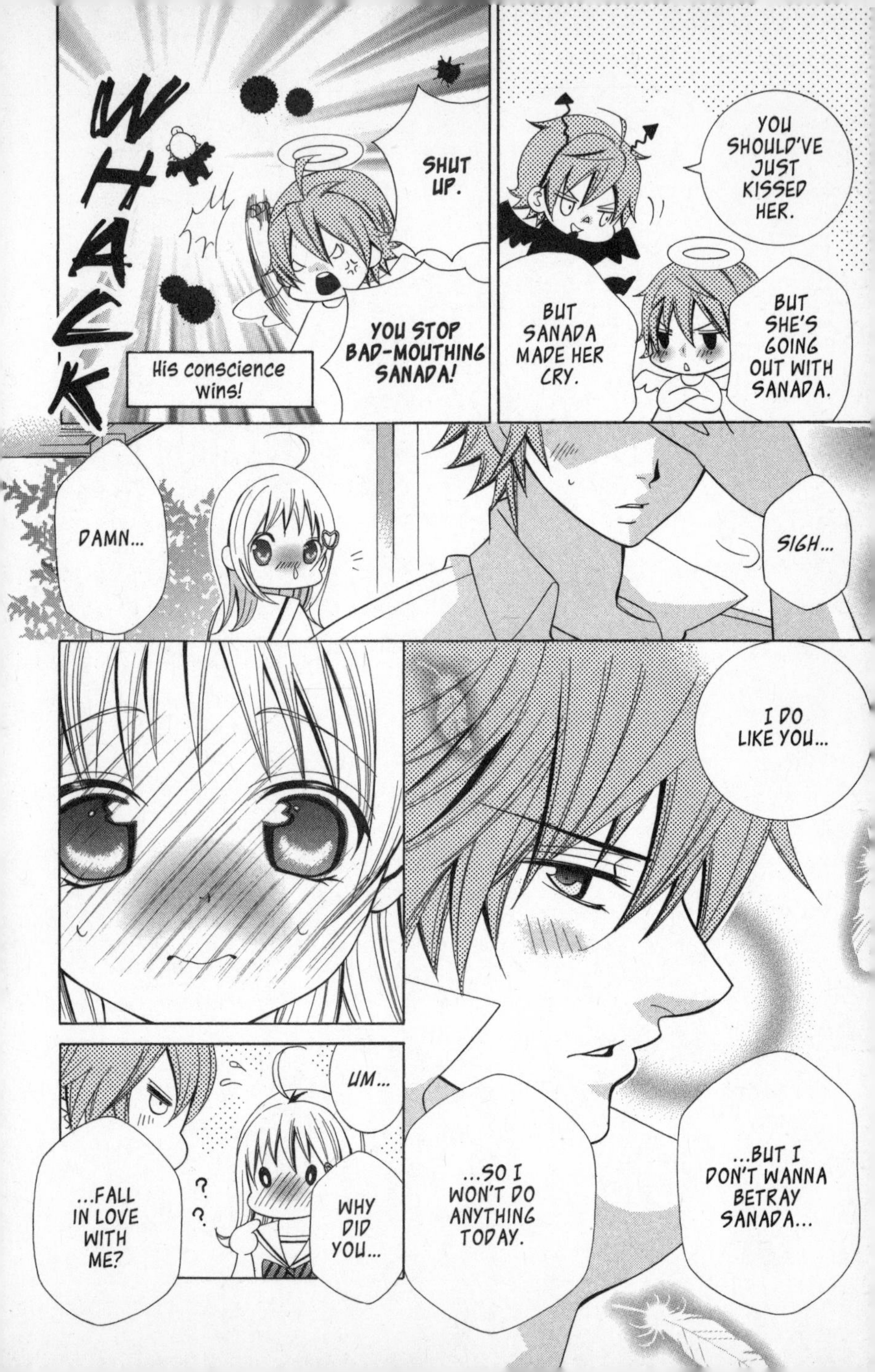
YOU SHOULD'VE JUST KISSED HER.
BUT SHE'S GOING OUT WITH SANADA.
BUT SANADA MADE HER CRY.
SHUT UP.
YOU STOP BAD-MOUTHING SANADA!
WHACK
His conscience wins!
SIGH...
DAMN...
I DO LIKE YOU...
...BUT I DON'T WANNA BETRAY SANADA...
...SO I WON'T DO ANYTHING TODAY.
UM...
WHY DID YOU...
...FALL IN LOVE WITH ME?

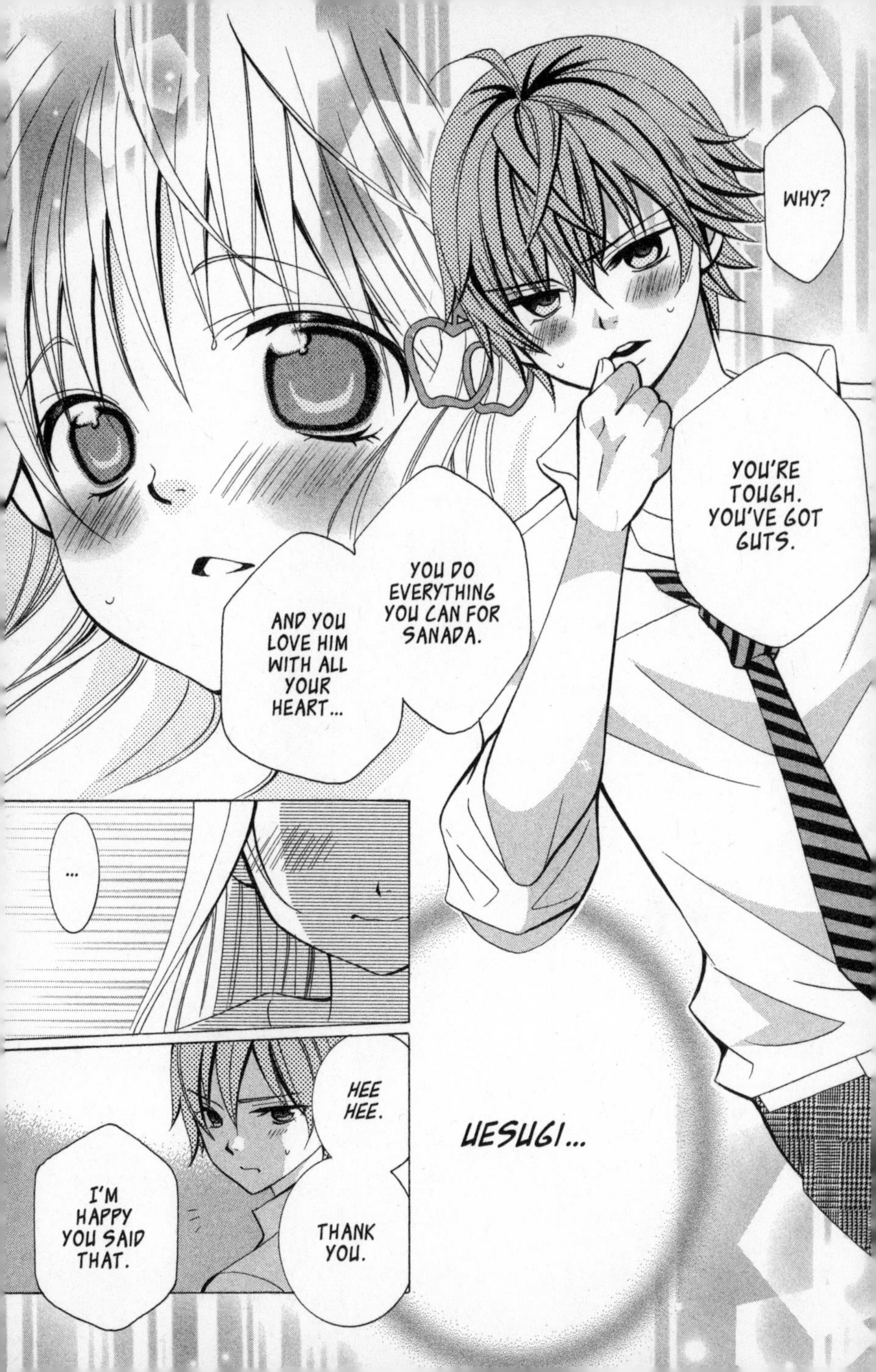
WHY?
YOU'RE TOUGH. YOU'VE GOT GUTS.
YOU DO EVERYTHING YOU CAN FOR SANADA.
AND YOU LOVE HIM WITH ALL YOUR HEART...
UESUGI...
...
HEE HEE.
THANK YOU.
I'M HAPPY YOU SAID THAT.

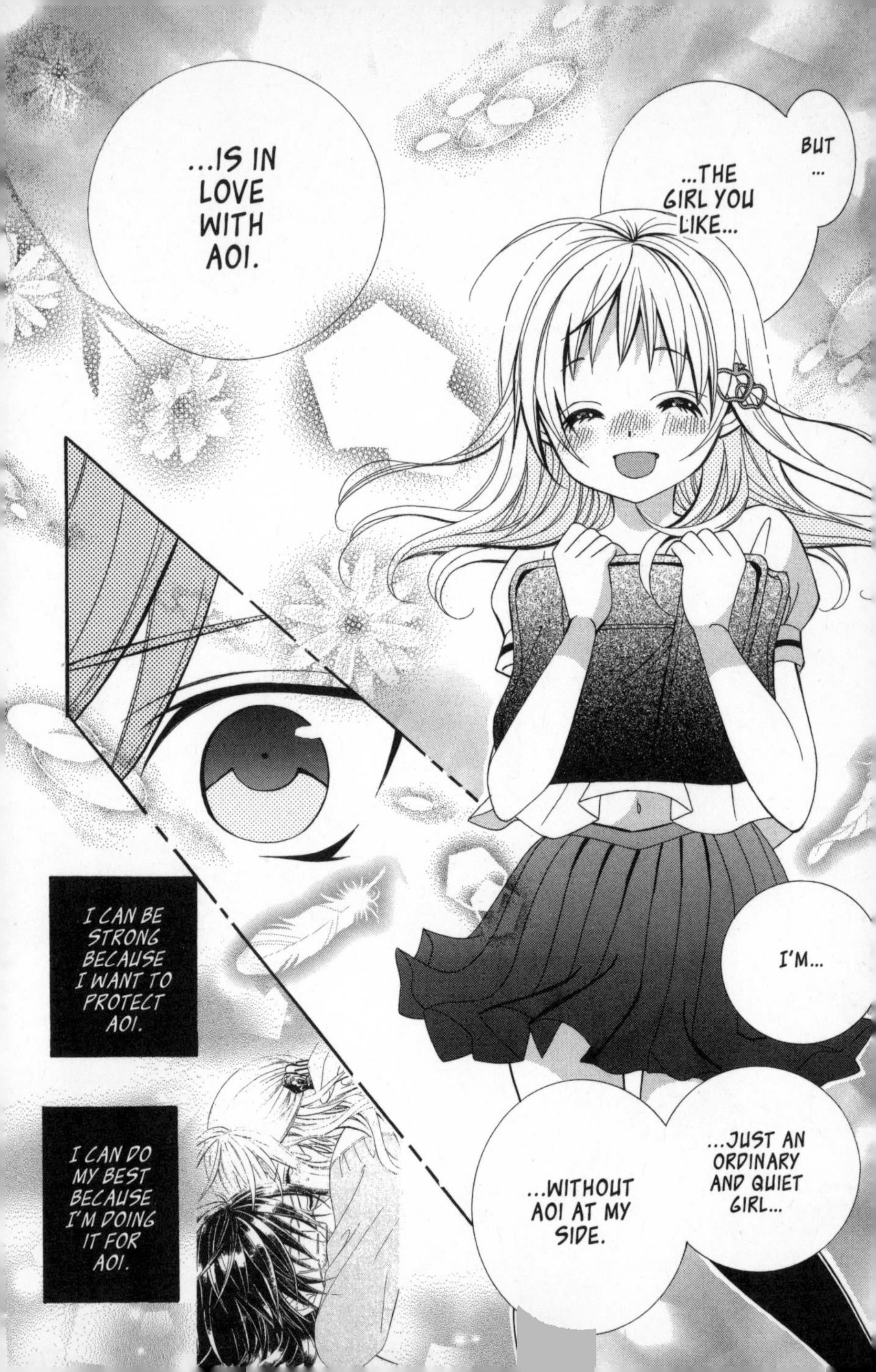
BUT ...
...THE GIRL YOU LIKE...
...IS IN LOVE WITH AOI.
I'M...
...JUST AN ORDINARY AND QUIET GIRL...
...WITHOUT AOI AT MY SIDE.
I CAN BE STRONG BECAUSE I WANT TO PROTECT AOI.
I CAN DO MY BEST BECAUSE I'M DOING IT FOR AOI.

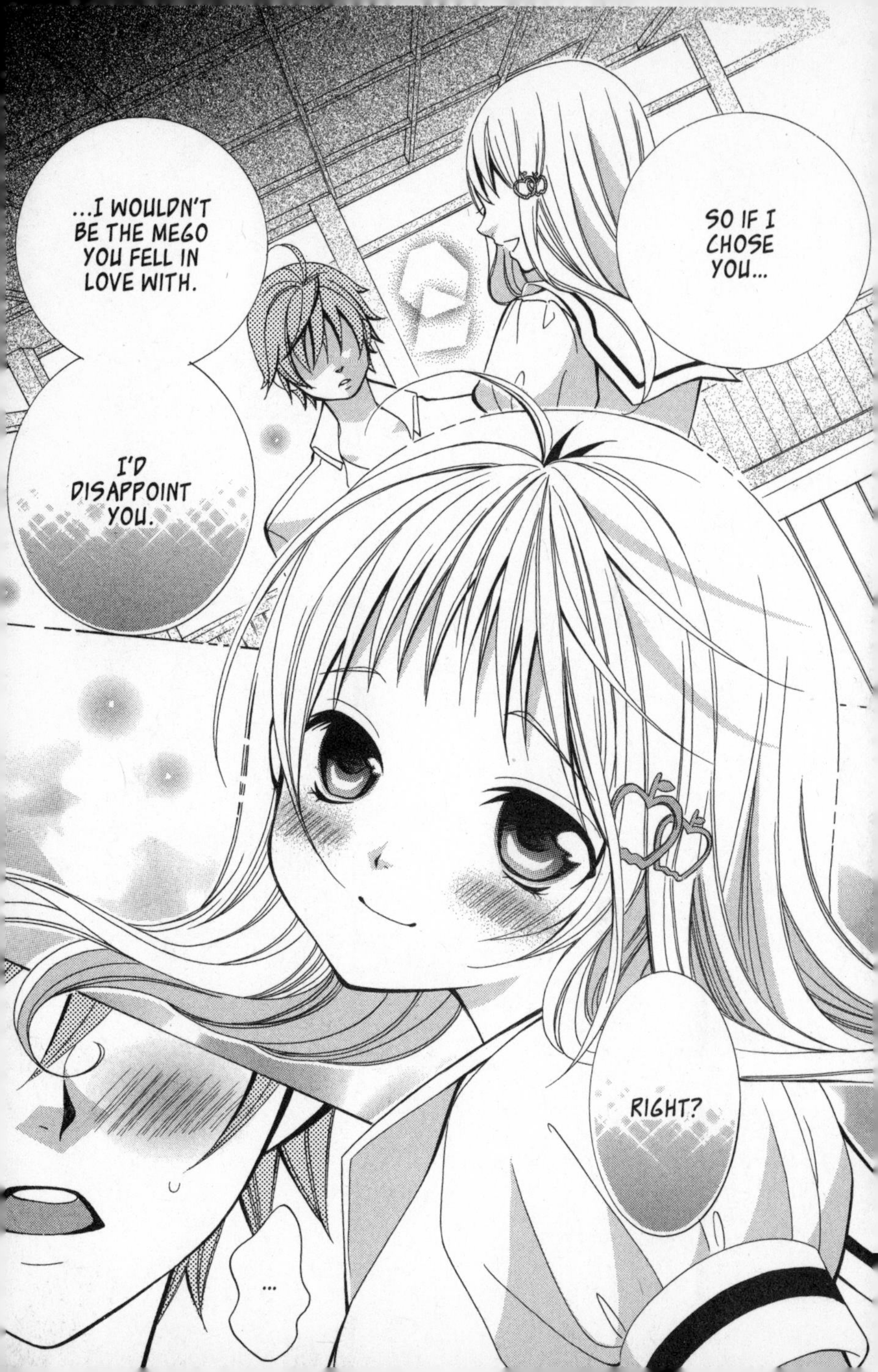
SO IF I CHOSE YOU...
...I WOULDN'T BE THE MEGO YOU FELL IN LOVE WITH.
I'D DISAPPOINT YOU.
RIGHT?
...

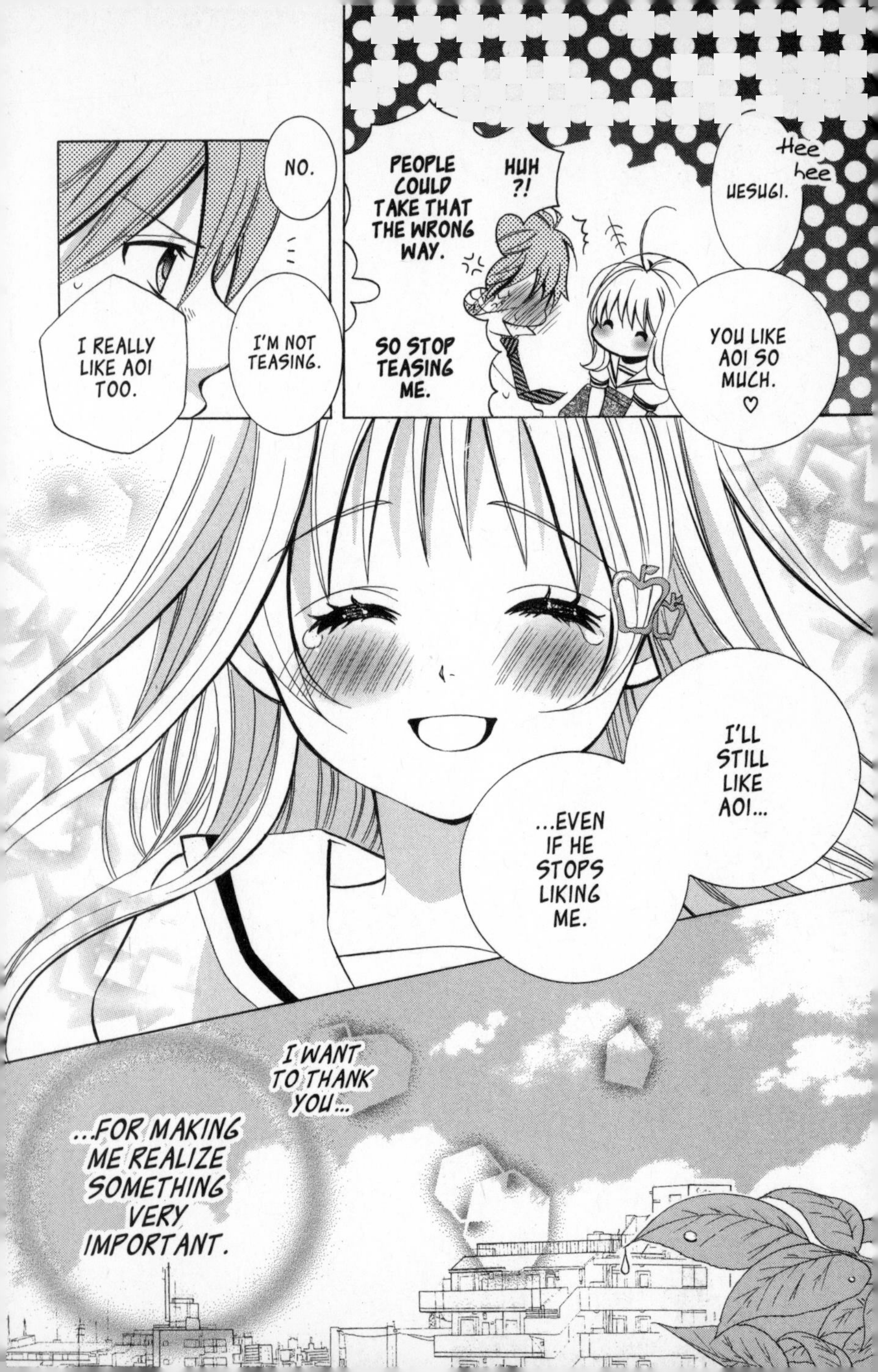
Hee hee
UESUGI.
YOU LIKE AOI SO MUCH. ♡
HUH ?!
PEOPLE COULD TAKE THAT THE WRONG WAY.
SO STOP TEASING ME.
NO.
I'M NOT TEASING.
I REALLY LIKE AOI TOO.
I'LL STILL LIKE AOI...
...EVEN IF HE STOPS LIKING ME.
I WANT TO THANK YOU...
...FOR MAKING ME REALIZE SOMETHING VERY IMPORTANT.

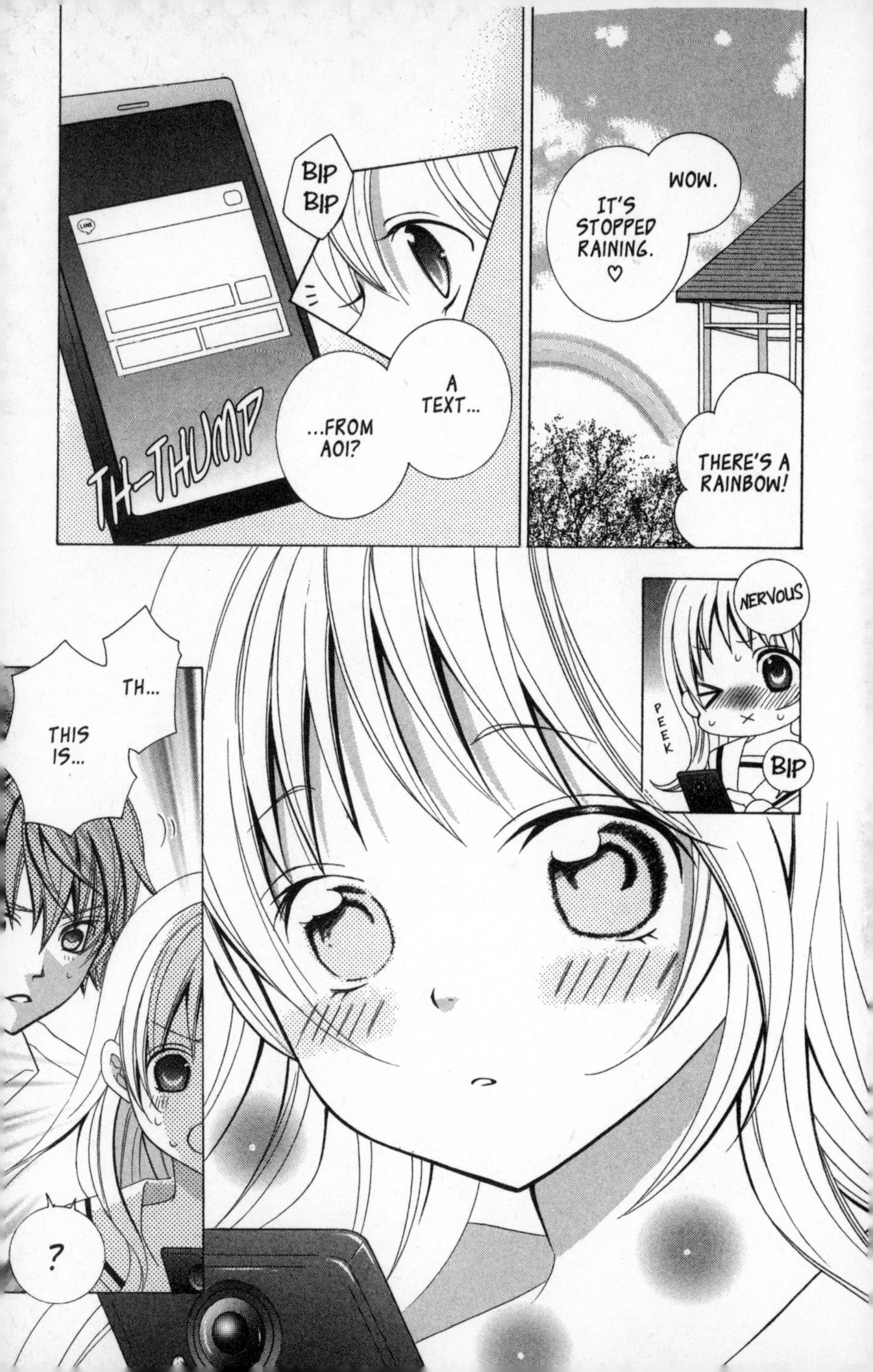
WOW. IT'S STOPPED RAINING. ♡
THERE'S A RAINBOW!
BIP BIP
A TEXT... ...FROM AOI?
TH-THUMP
NERVOUS
PEEK
BIP
TH... THIS IS...
?

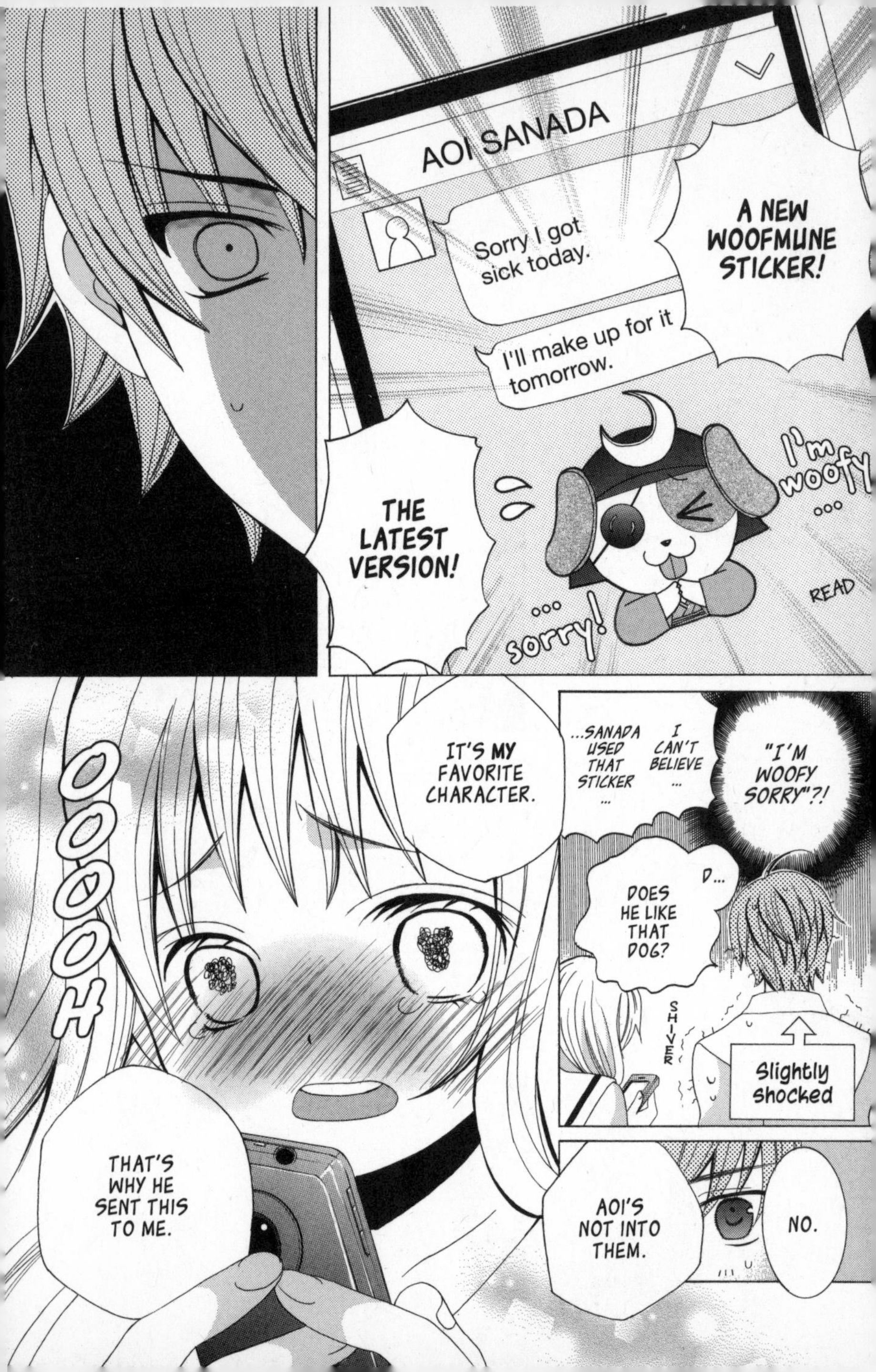
AOI SANADA
Sorry I got sick today.
I'll make up for it tomorrow.
A NEW WOOFMUNE STICKER!
I'm woofy ... ... sorry!
READ
THE LATEST VERSION!
"I'M WOOFY SORRY"?!
I CAN'T BELIEVE ...
...SANADA USED THAT STICKER ...
D... DOES HE LIKE THAT DOG?
SHIVER
Slightly shocked
NO.
AOI'S NOT INTO THEM.
OOOOH
IT'S MY FAVORITE CHARACTER.
THAT'S WHY HE SENT THIS TO ME.

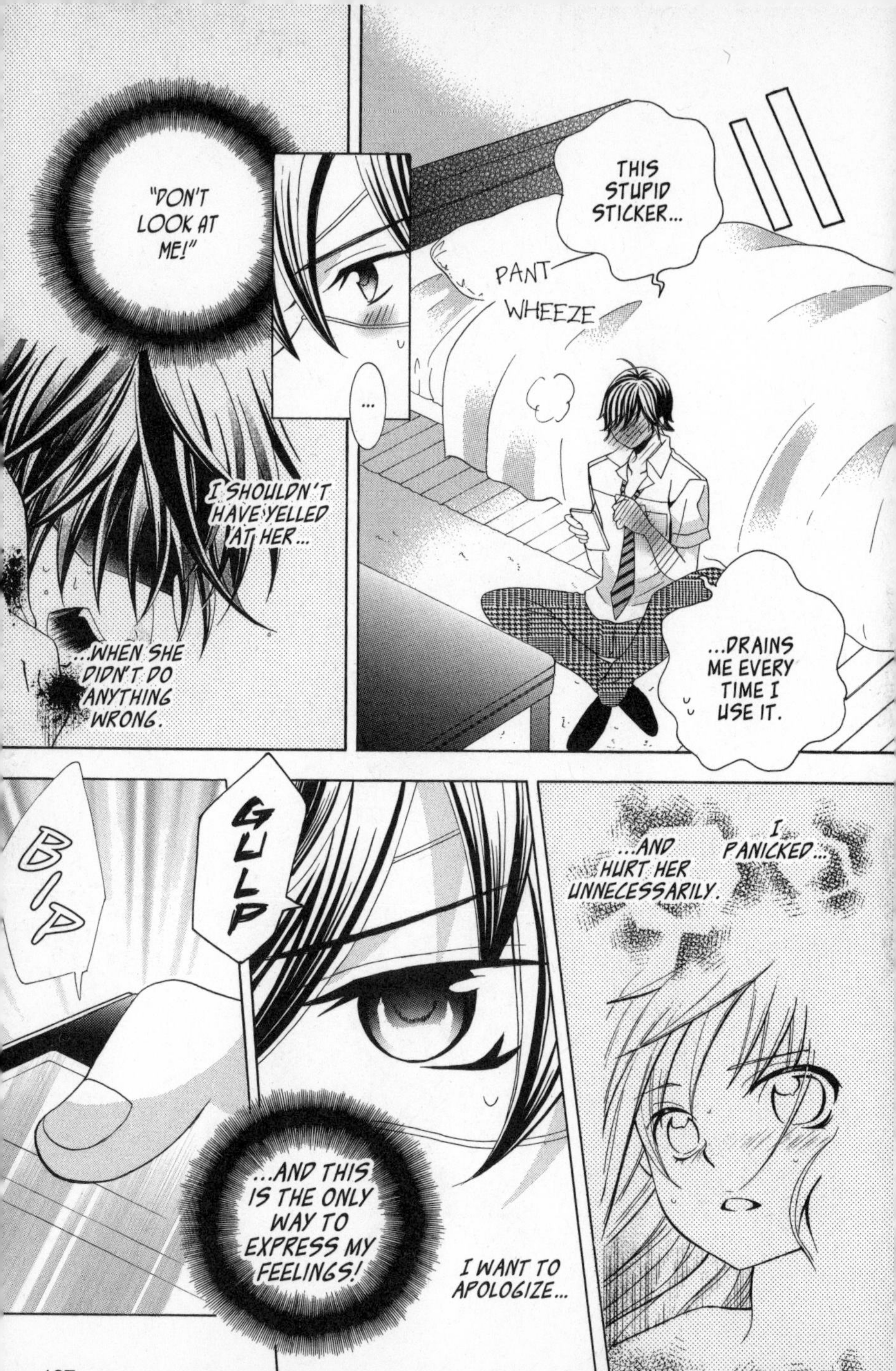
THIS STUPID STICKER...
PANT
WHEEZE
...DRAINS ME EVERY TIME I USE IT.
...
"DON'T LOOK AT ME!"
I SHOULDN'T HAVE YELLED AT HER...
...WHEN SHE DIDN'T DO ANYTHING WRONG.
I PANICKED...
...AND HURT HER UNNECESSARILY.
GULP
I WANT TO APOLOGIZE...
...AND THIS IS THE ONLY WAY TO EXPRESS MY FEELINGS!
BIP

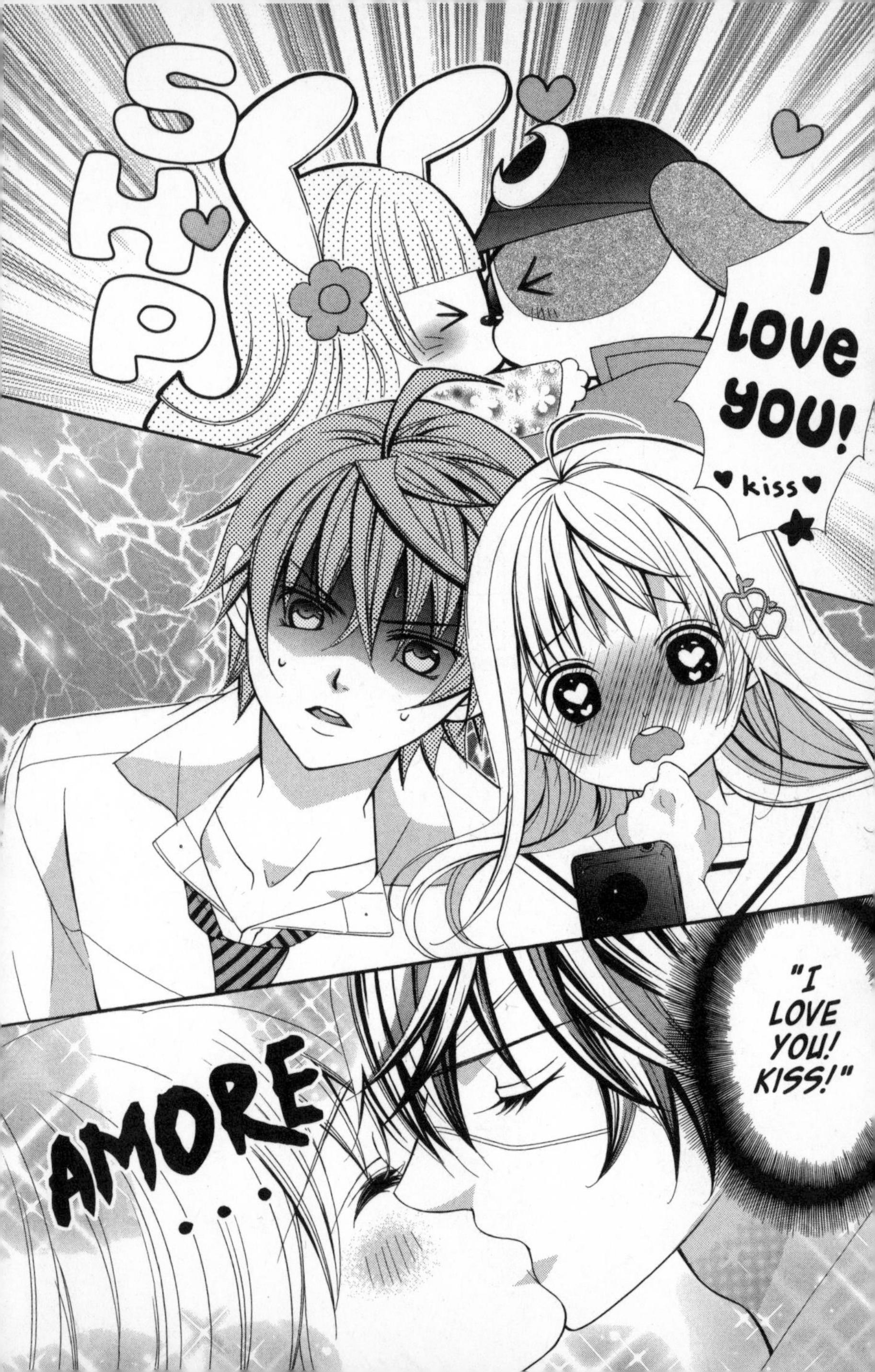
I love you!
♥kiss♥
SHP
"I LOVE YOU! KISS!"
AMORE...

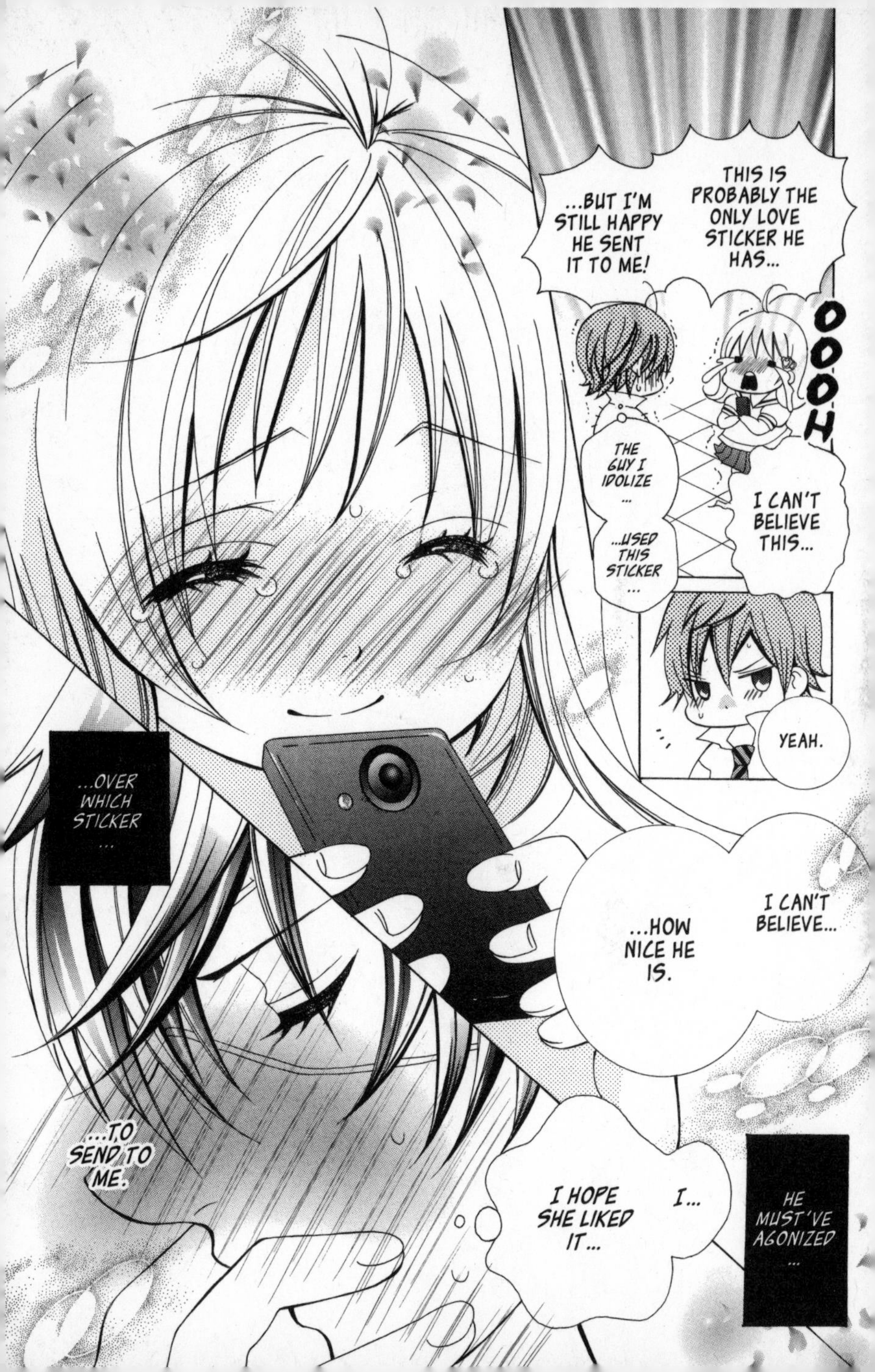
THIS IS PROBABLY THE ONLY LOVE STICKER HE HAS...
...BUT I'M STILL HAPPY HE SENT IT TO ME!
OOOH
I CAN'T BELIEVE THIS...
THE GUY I IDOLIZE...
...USED THIS STICKER...
YEAH.
I CAN'T BELIEVE...
...HOW NICE HE IS.
HE MUST'VE AGONIZED...
I...
I HOPE SHE LIKED IT...
...OVER WHICH STICKER...
...TO SEND TO ME.

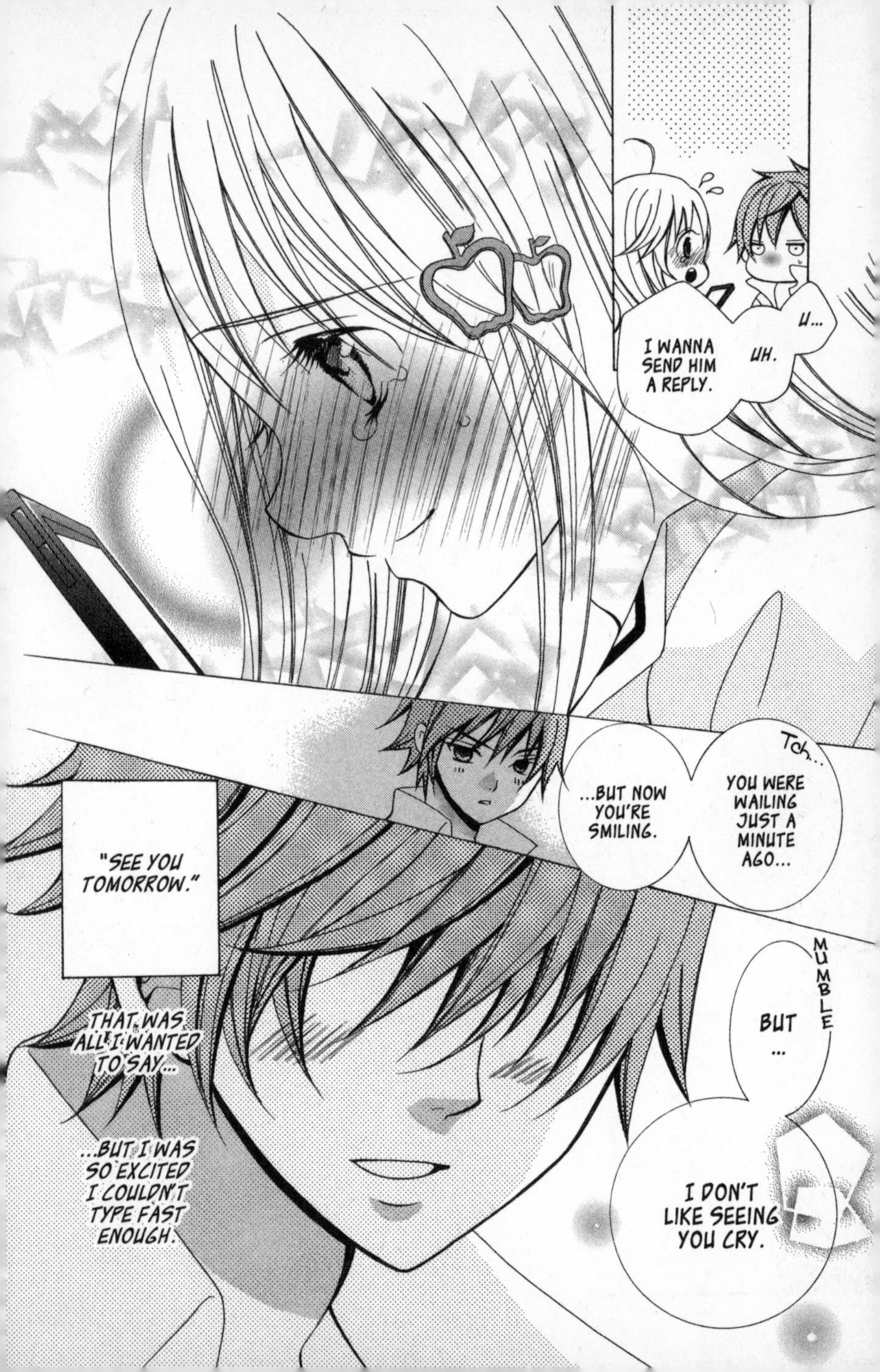
U...
UH.
I WANNA SEND HIM A REPLY.
Tch...
YOU WERE WAILING JUST A MINUTE AGO...
...BUT NOW YOU'RE SMILING.
"SEE YOU TOMORROW."
MUMBLE
BUT ...
I DON'T LIKE SEEING YOU CRY.
THAT WAS ALL I WANTED TO SAY...
...BUT I WAS SO EXCITED I COULDN'T TYPE FAST ENOUGH.

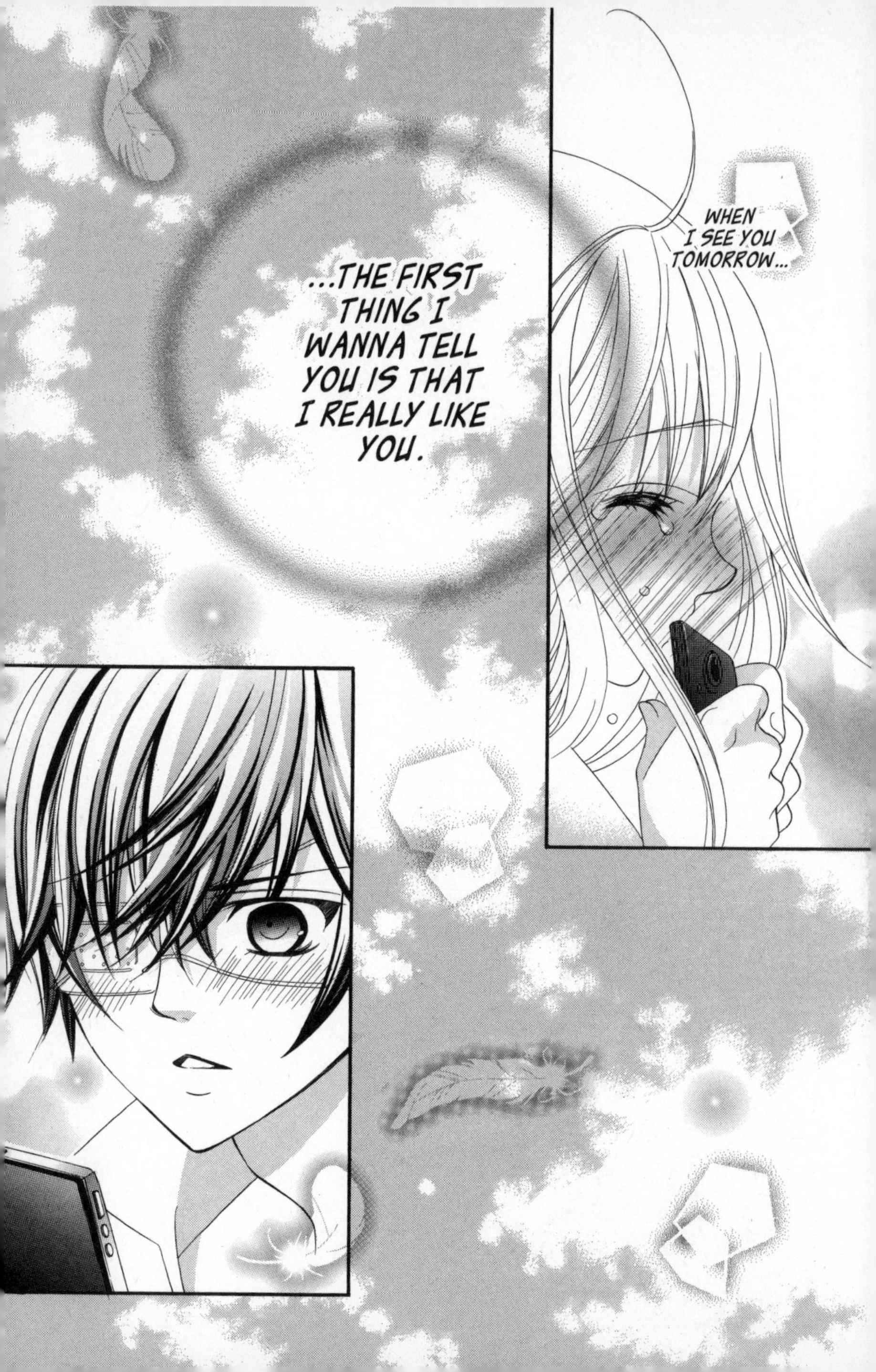
WHEN I SEE YOU TOMORROW...
...THE FIRST THING I WANNA TELL YOU IS THAT I REALLY LIKE YOU.

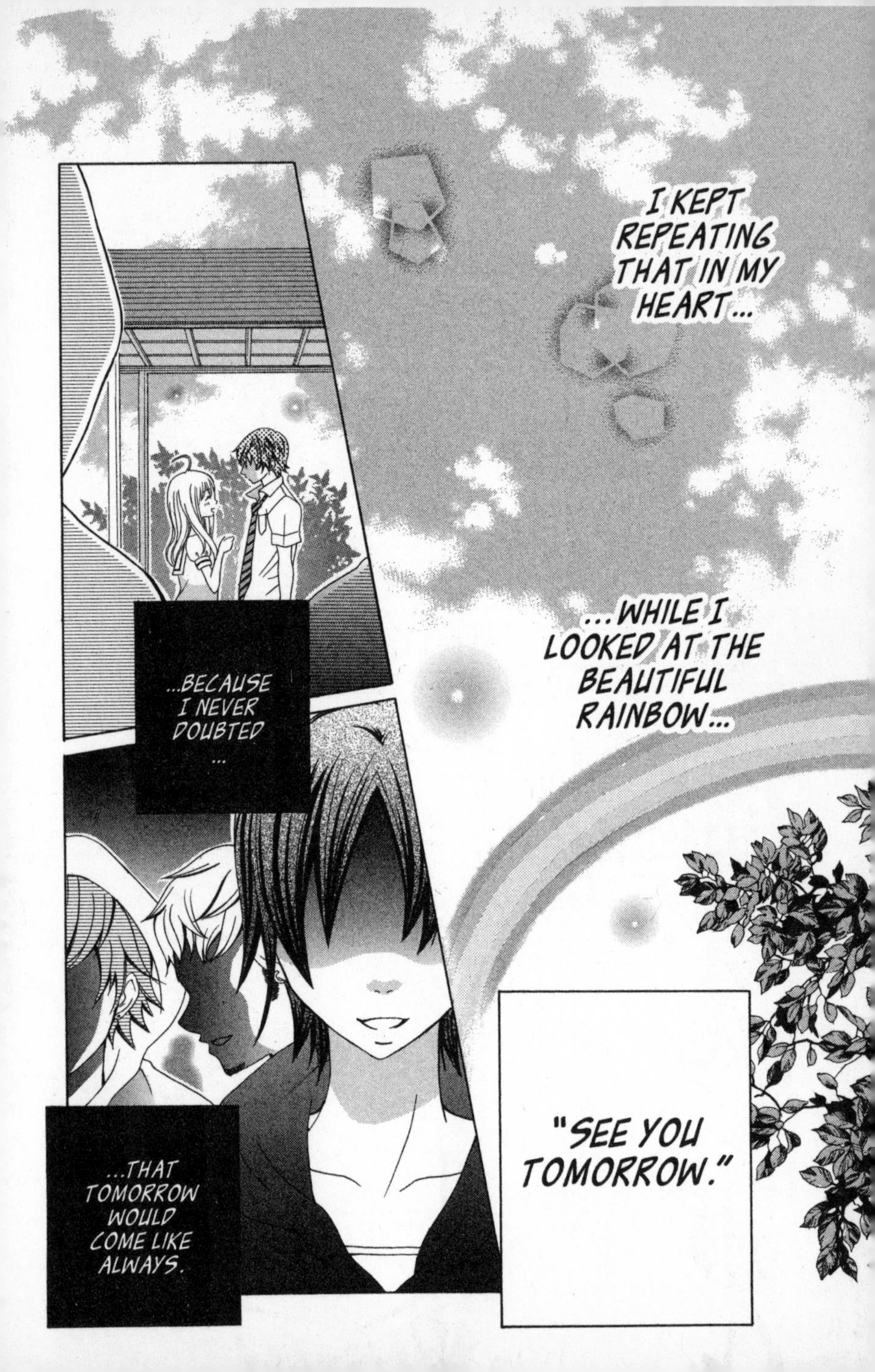
I KEPT REPEATING THAT IN MY HEART...
...WHILE I LOOKED AT THE BEAUTIFUL RAINBOW...
"SEE YOU TOMORROW."
...BECAUSE I NEVER DOUBTED ...
...THAT TOMORROW WOULD COME LIKE ALWAYS.

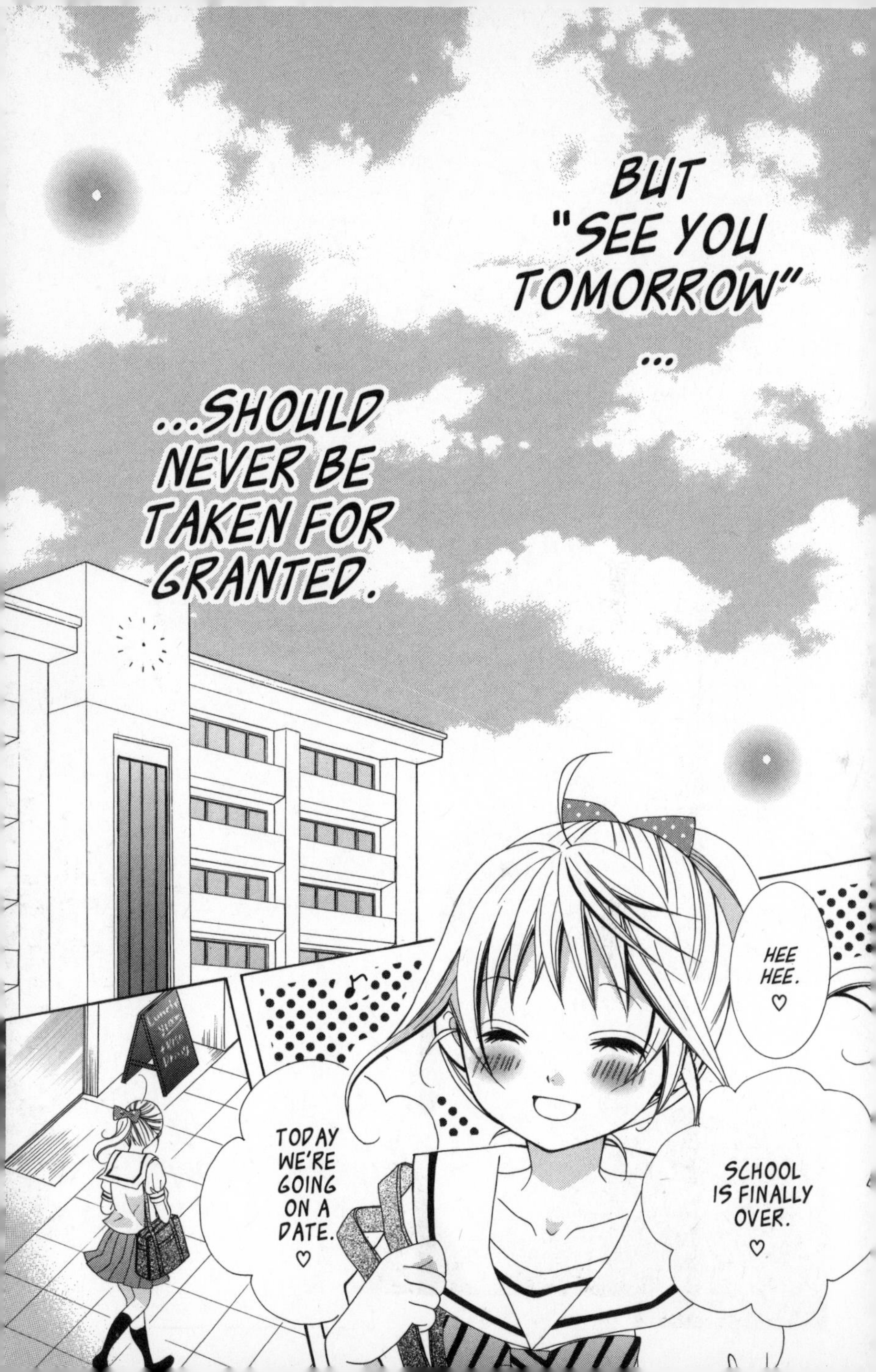
BUT "SEE YOU TOMORROW"...
...SHOULD NEVER BE TAKEN FOR GRANTED.
HEE HEE. ♡
SCHOOL IS FINALLY OVER. ♡
TODAY WE'RE GOING ON A DATE. ♡

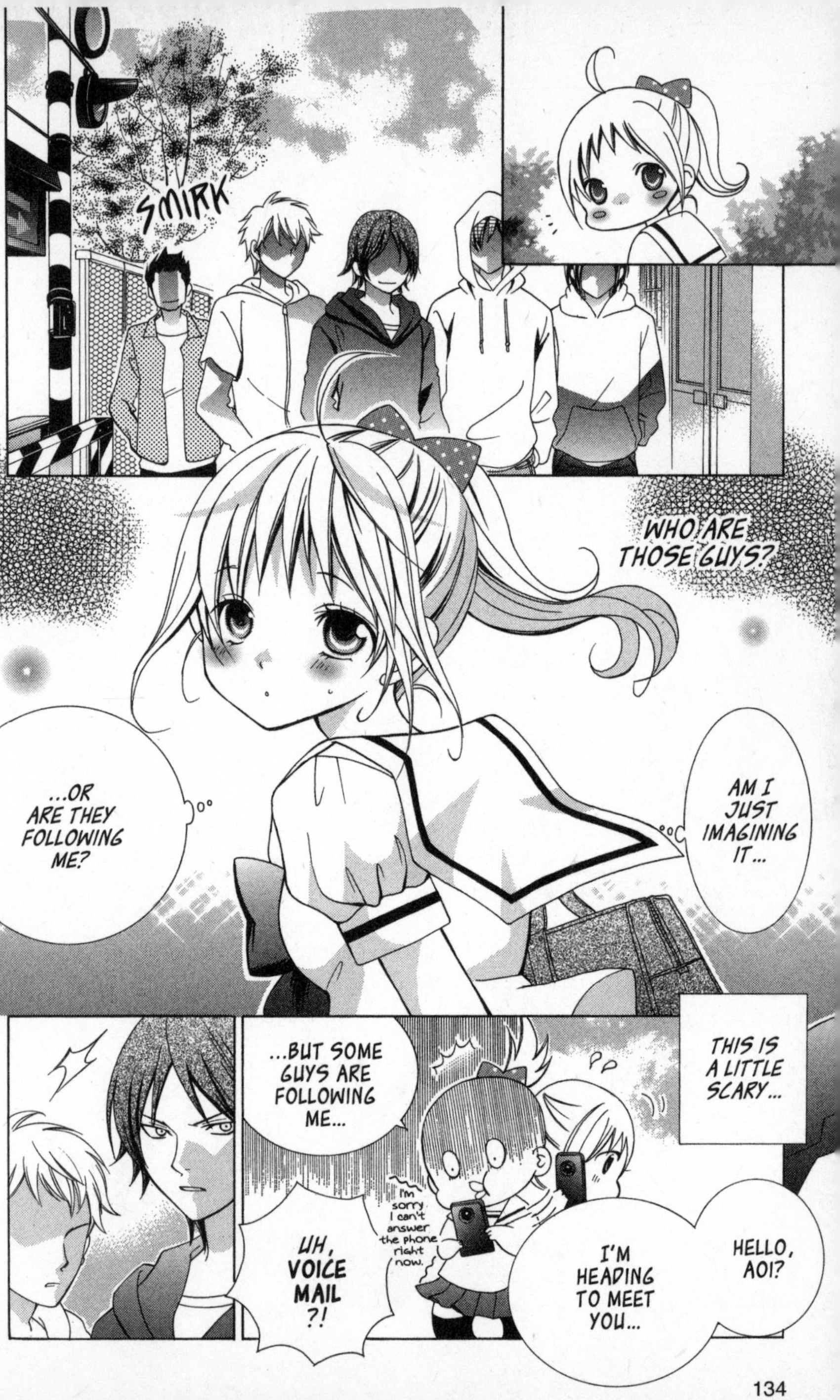
SMIRK
WHO ARE THOSE GUYS?
AM I JUST IMAGINING IT...
...OR ARE THEY FOLLOWING ME?
THIS IS A LITTLE SCARY...
HELLO, AOI?
I'M HEADING TO MEET YOU...
...BUT SOME GUYS ARE FOLLOWING ME...
I'm sorry. I can't answer the phone right now.
UH, VOICE MAIL?!

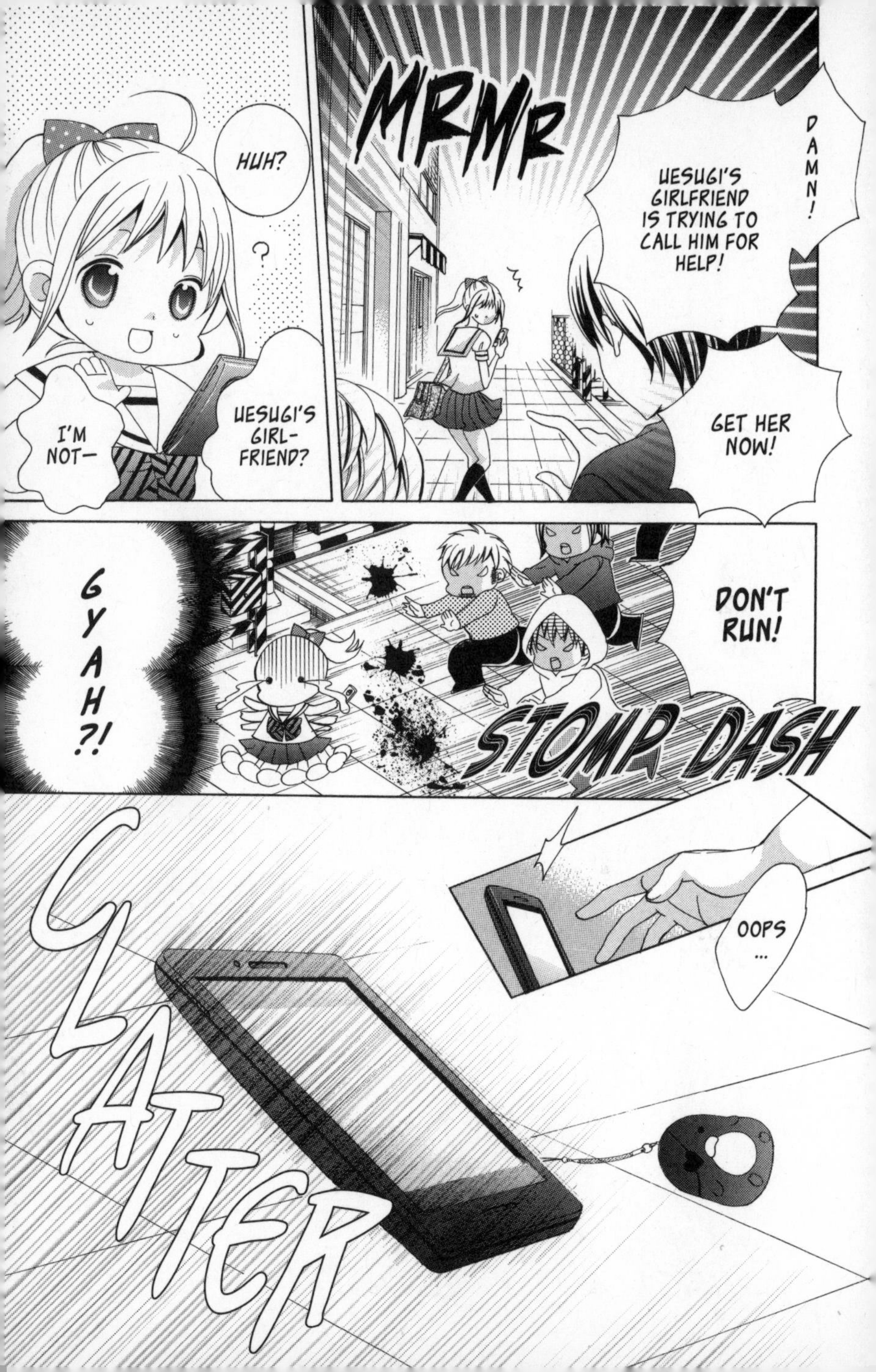
MRMR
DAMN!
UESUGI'S GIRLFRIEND IS TRYING TO CALL HIM FOR HELP!
GET HER NOW!
HUH?
?
UESUGI'S GIRL-FRIEND?
I'M NOT—
DON'T RUN!
STOMP DASH
GYAH?!
OOPS ...
CLATTER

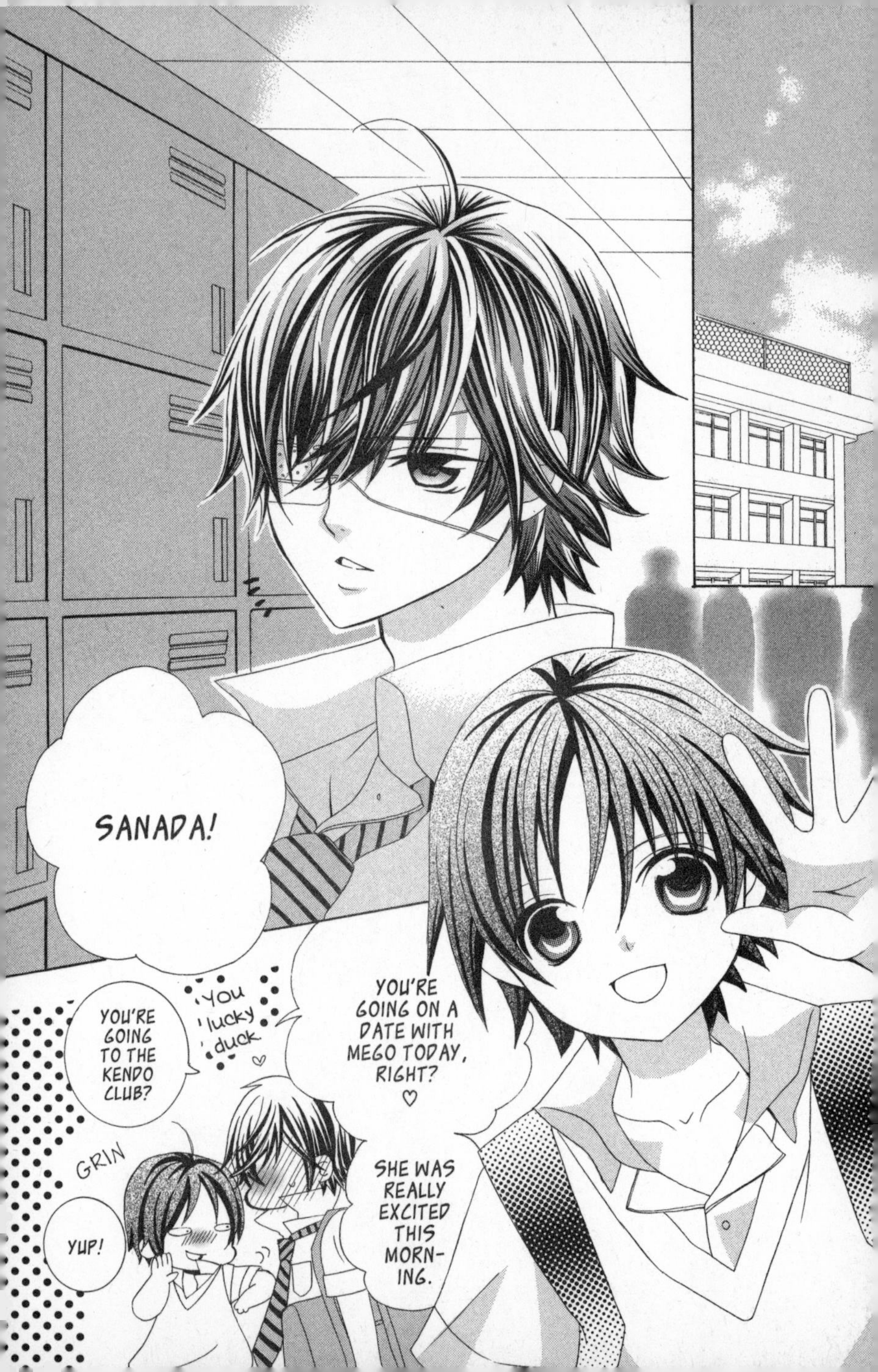
SANADA!
YOU'RE GOING ON A DATE WITH MEGO TODAY, RIGHT? ♡
SHE WAS REALLY EXCITED THIS MORN-ING.
You lucky duck. ♡
YOU'RE GOING TO THE KENDO CLUB?
GRIN
YUP!

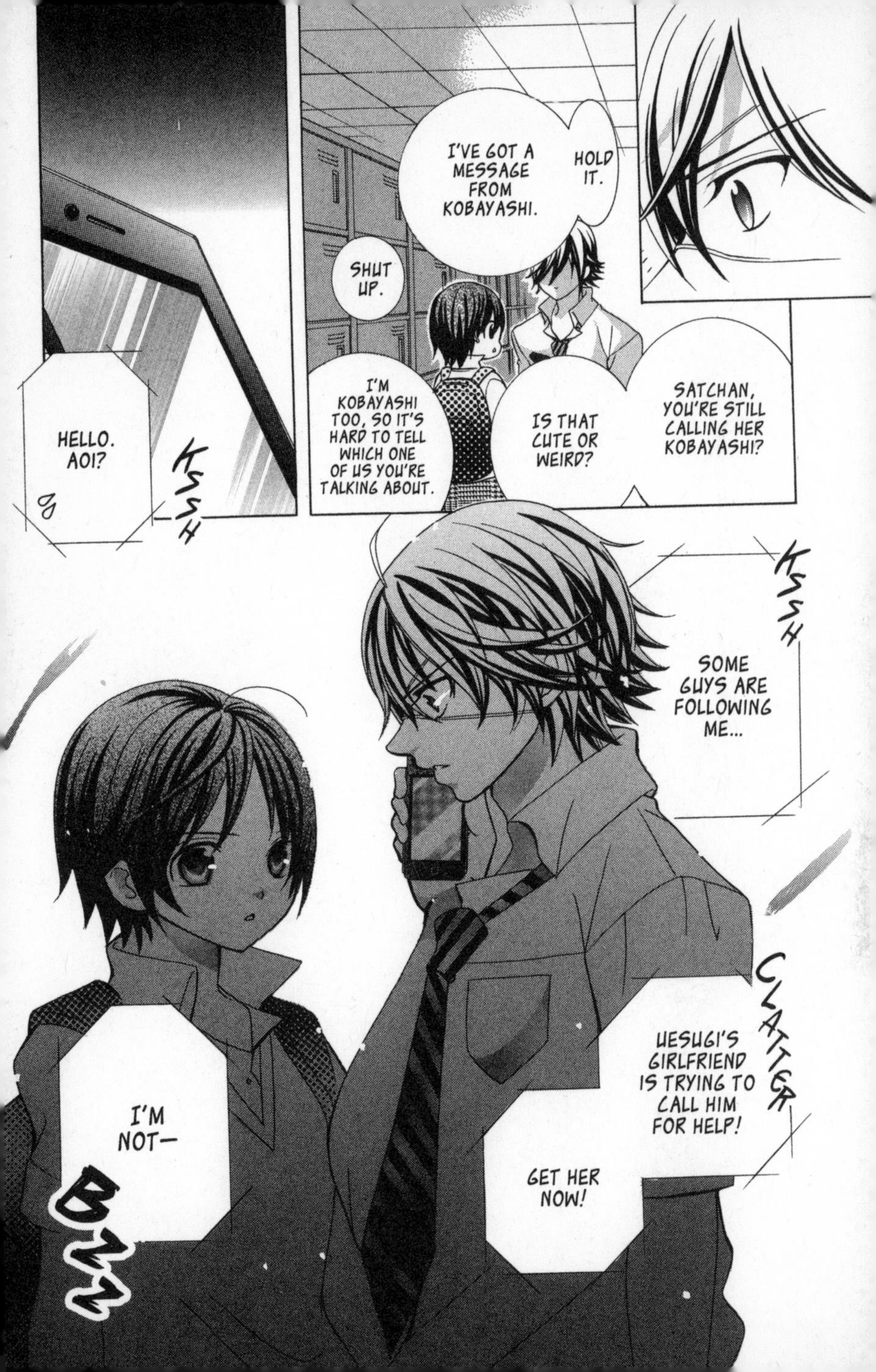
I'VE GOT A MESSAGE FROM KOBAYASHI.
HOLD IT.
SHUT UP.
SATCHAN, YOU'RE STILL CALLING HER KOBAYASHI?
IS THAT CUTE OR WEIRD?
I'M KOBAYASHI TOO, SO IT'S HARD TO TELL WHICH ONE OF US YOU'RE TALKING ABOUT.
KSSH
HELLO. AOI?
KSSH
SOME GUYS ARE FOLLOWING ME...
CLATTER
UESUGI'S GIRLFRIEND IS TRYING TO CALL HIM FOR HELP!
GET HER NOW!
I'M NOT—
BZZ

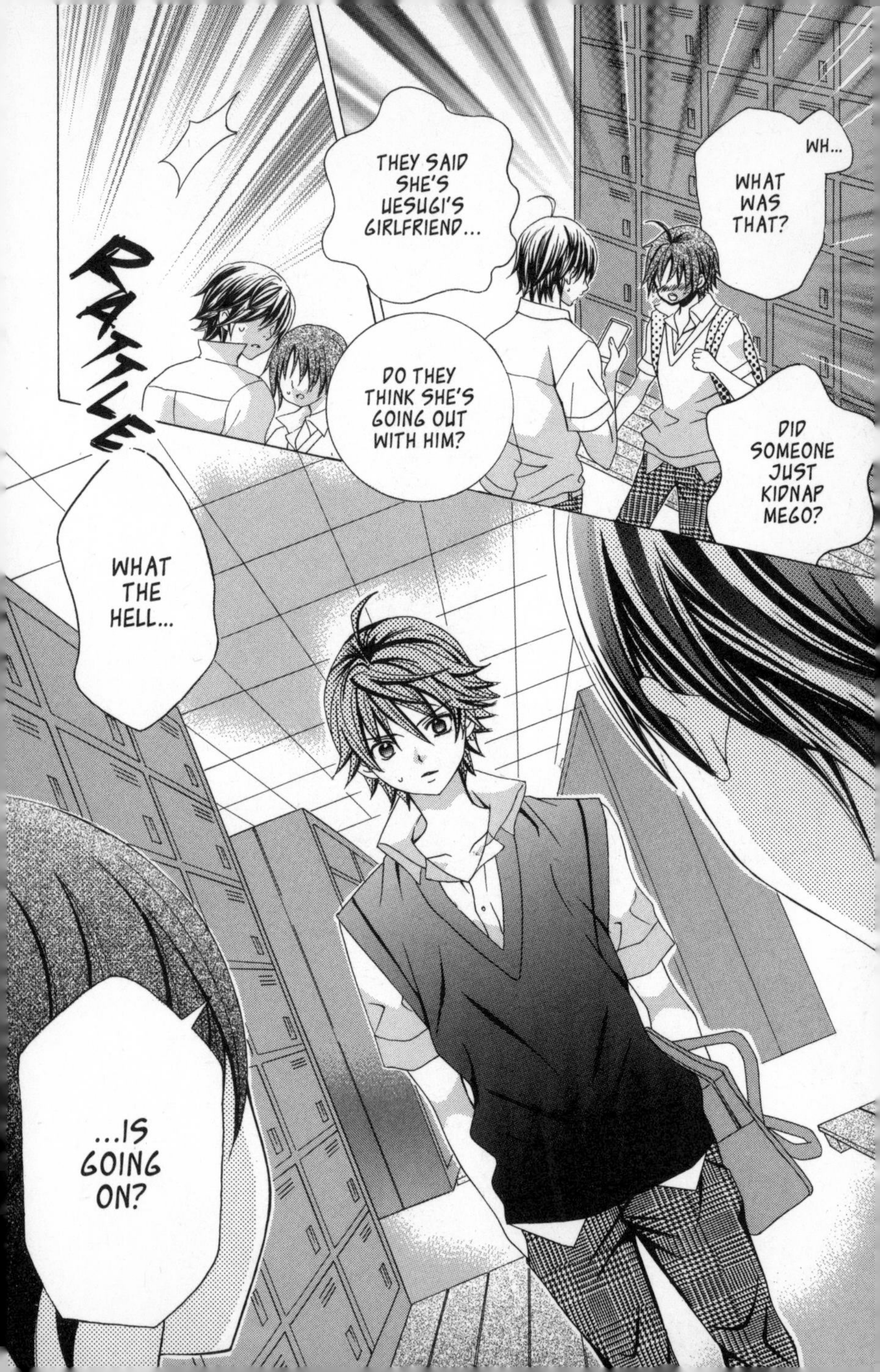
WH...
WHAT WAS THAT?
THEY SAID SHE'S UESUGI'S GIRLFRIEND...
DID SOMEONE JUST KIDNAP MEGO?
DO THEY THINK SHE'S GOING OUT WITH HIM?
RATTLE
WHAT THE HELL...
...IS GOING ON?

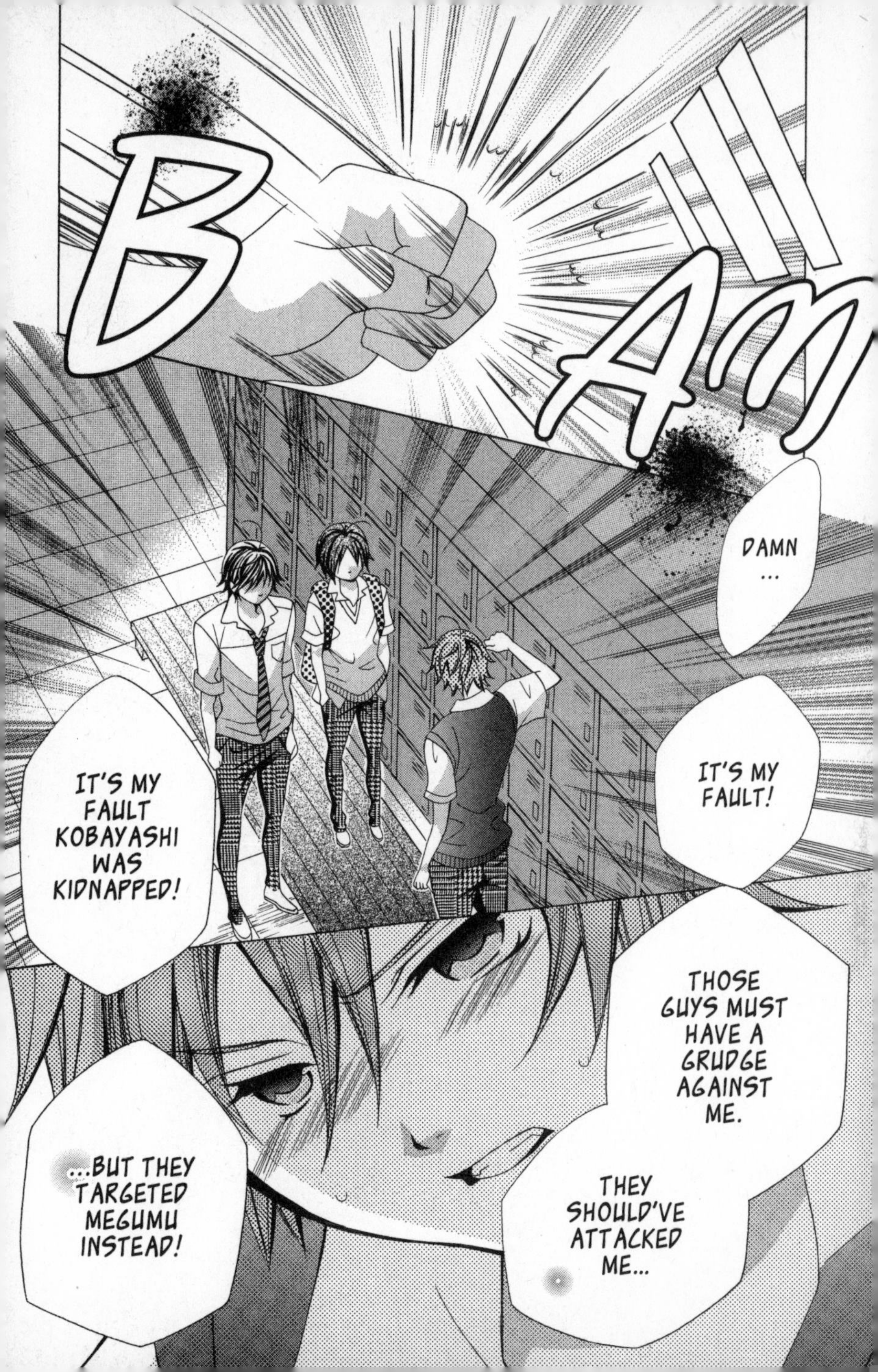
BAM
DAMN...
IT'S MY FAULT!
IT'S MY FAULT KOBAYASHI WAS KIDNAPPED!
THOSE GUYS MUST HAVE A GRUDGE AGAINST ME.
THEY SHOULD'VE ATTACKED ME...
...BUT THEY TARGETED MEGUMU INSTEAD!

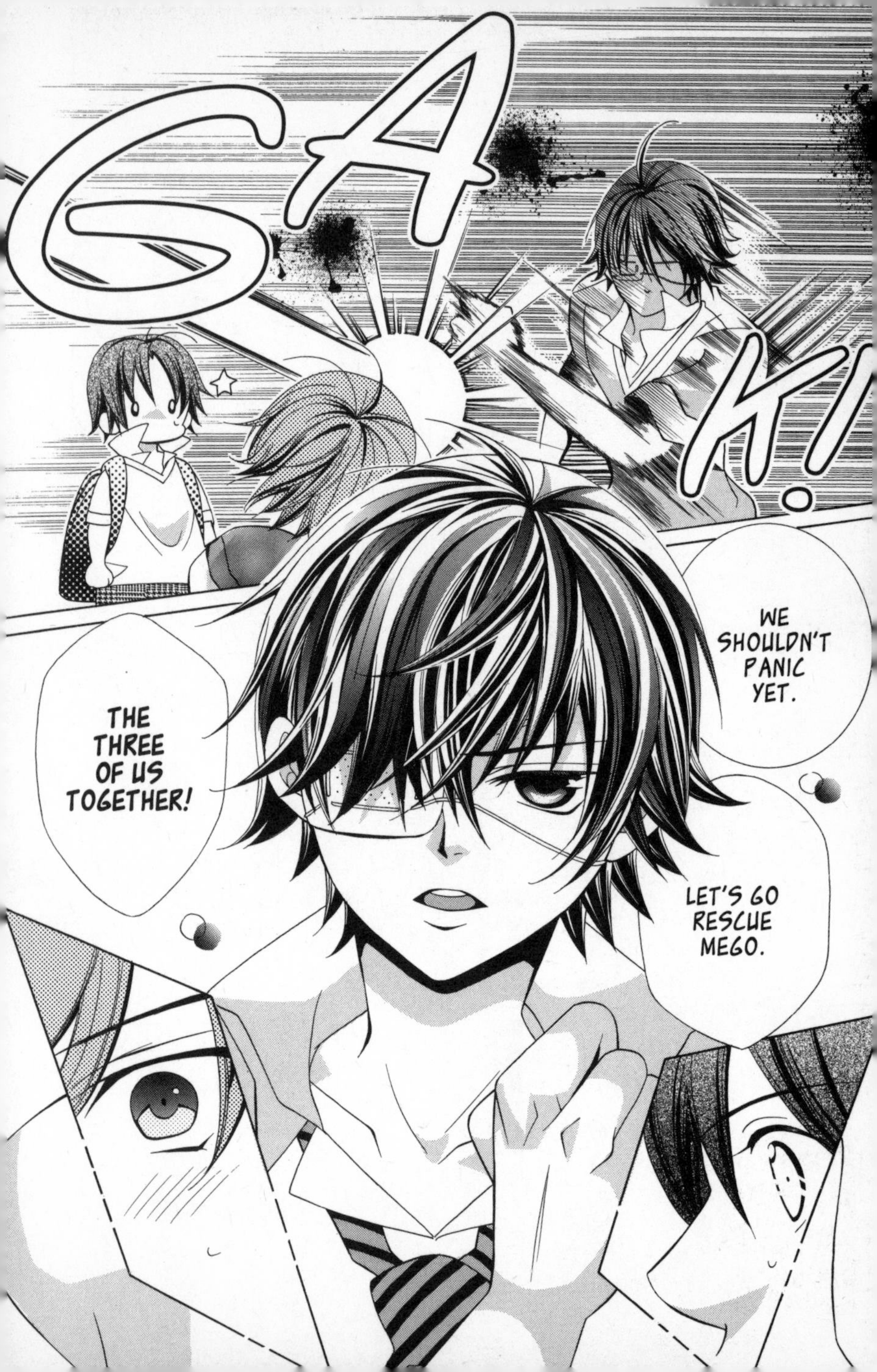
SAKI!
WE SHOULDN'T PANIC YET.
LET'S GO RESCUE MEGO.
THE THREE OF US TOGETHER!

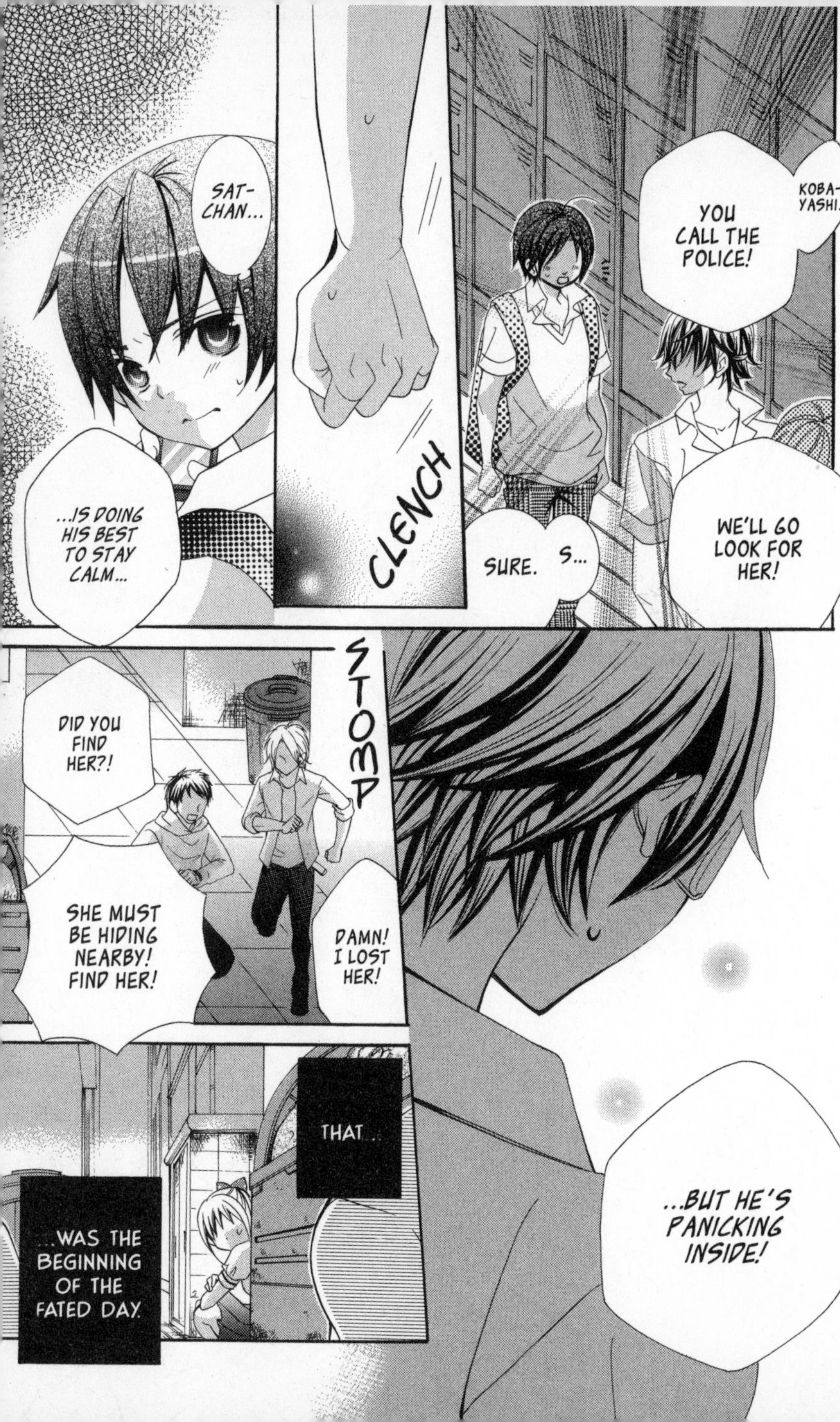
KOBA-YASHI.
YOU CALL THE POLICE!
WE'LL GO LOOK FOR HER!
S...
SURE.
CLENCH
SAT-CHAN...
...IS DOING HIS BEST TO STAY CALM...
...BUT HE'S PANICKING INSIDE!
STOMP
DID YOU FIND HER?!
DAMN! I LOST HER!
SHE MUST BE HIDING NEARBY! FIND HER!
THAT...
...WAS THE BEGINNING OF THE FATED DAY.

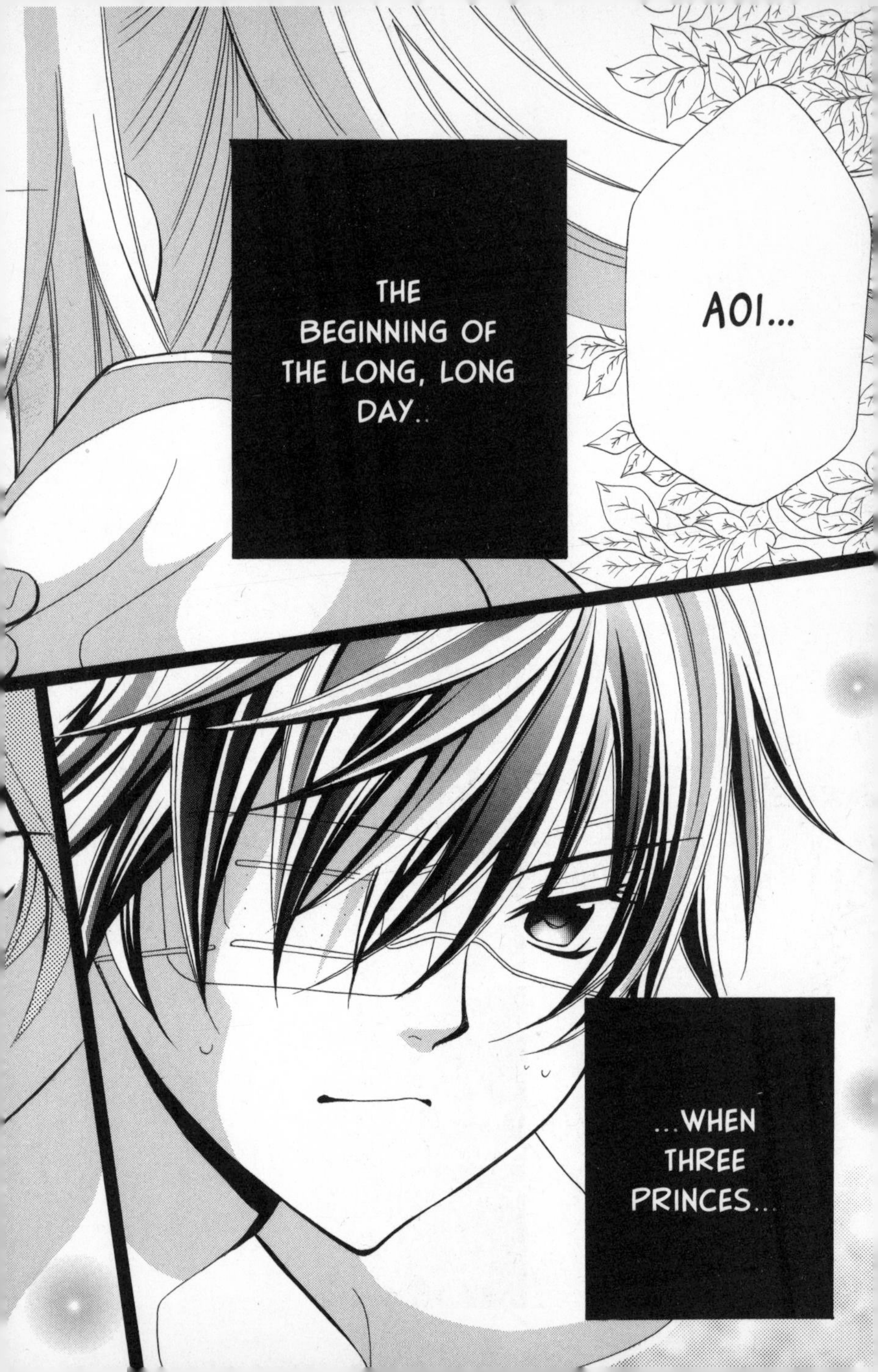
AOI...
THE BEGINNING OF THE LONG, LONG DAY..
...WHEN THREE PRINCES...

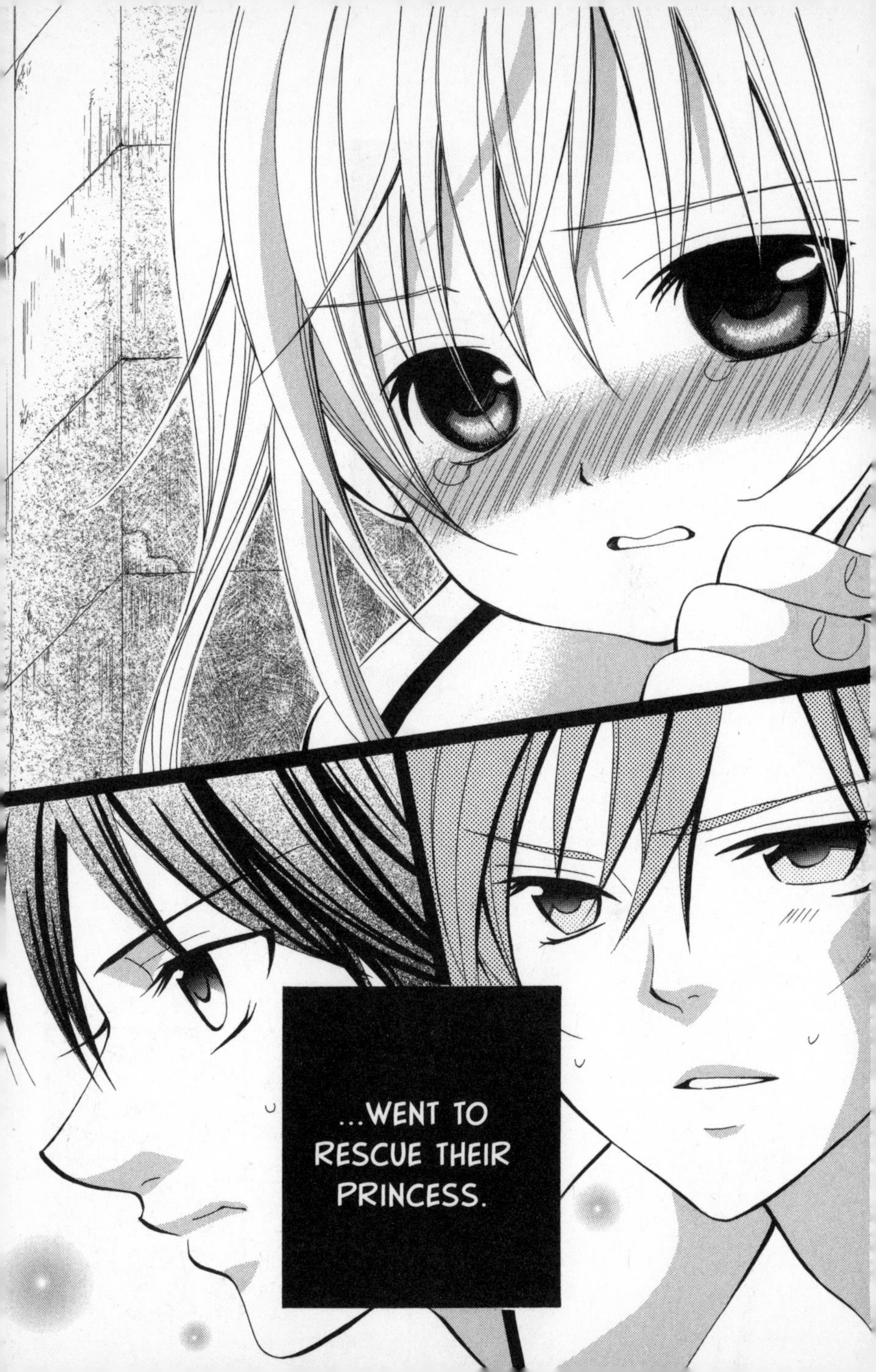
...WENT TO
RESCUE THEIR
PRINCESS.

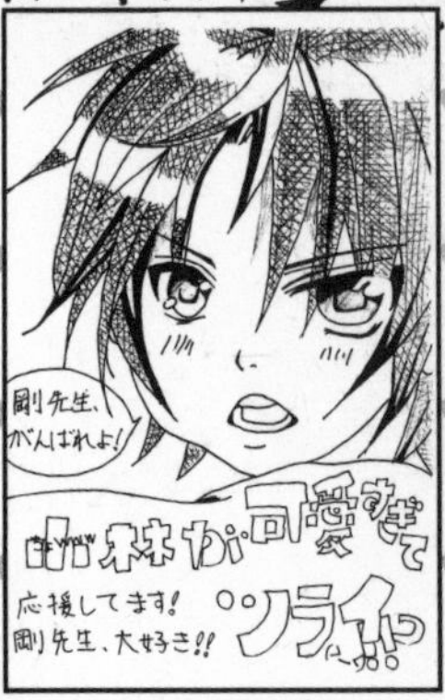

剛先生、がんばれよ!
小林が可愛すぎてツライっ!!
応援してます!
剛先生、大好き!!

→ Mei Arai (Osaka)
Ed.: Mitsuru's cheering makes you feel good!!

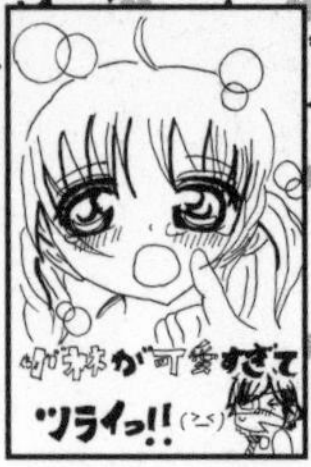

小林が可愛すぎてツライっ!!

← Satokucchi (Tokyo)
Ed.: The pure Mego makes me smile.

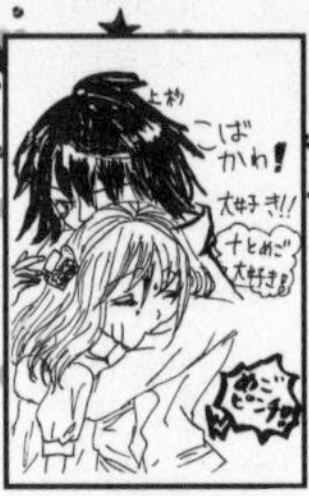

こばかわ!
大好き!!

← Moka (Wakayama)
Ed.: Aoi, come rescue Mego, quick!!

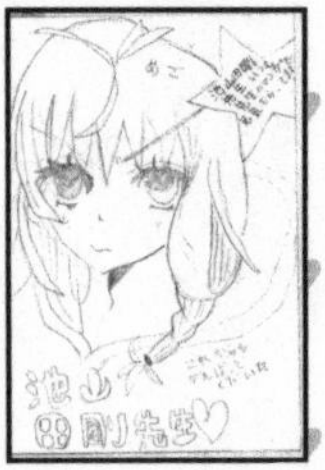

→ Utano ☆ (Osaka)
Ed.: Mego, a-are you mad?

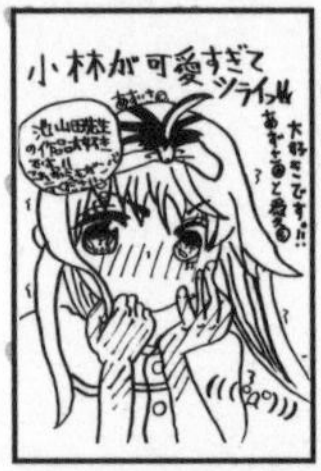

小林が可愛すぎてツライっ!!

← Soko Yamada (Osaka)
Ed.: Azusa is 100 percent *dere* here!!

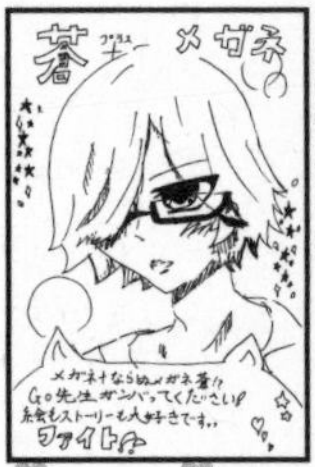

← Riho Kakutomo (Kagawa)
Ed.: Aoi looks cool in glasses!

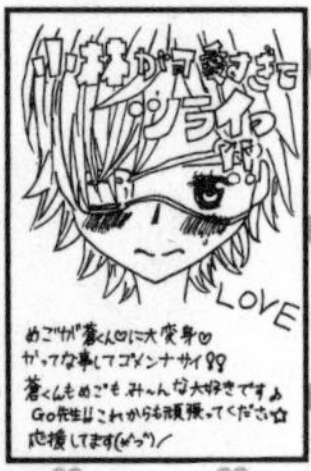

小林が可愛すぎてツライっ!!
LOVE

→ Yuumi Tanaka (Aichi)
Ed.: Here's Mego wearing an eye patch!

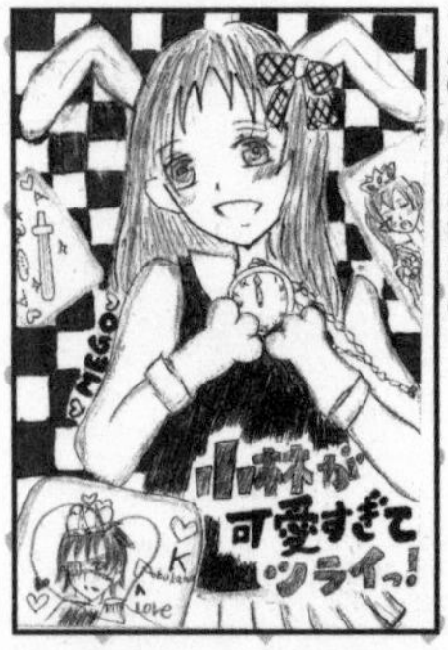

小林が可愛すぎてツライっ!

← Aoi Mukou (Hyogo)
Ed.: A white rabbit cosplay! Rabbit ears look great on her!!

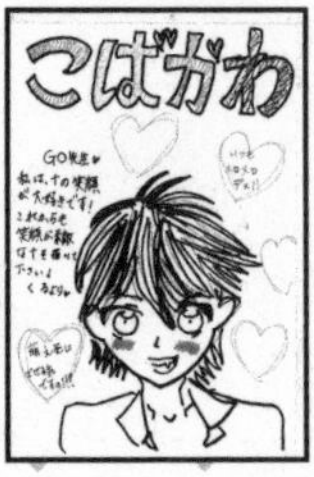

こばかわ

→ Kuru (Mie)
Ed.: I'm gonna die looking at Mitsuru's smile. ♥

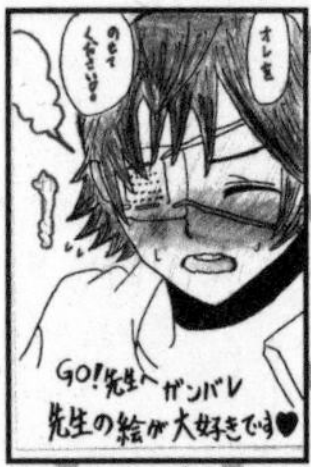

GO!先生へ ガンバレ
先生の絵が大好きです♥

↑ Yuichigo (Okayama)
Ed.: I'm gonna die looking at this blushing Aoi. ♥

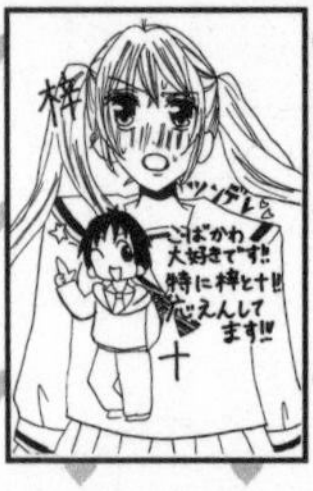

こばかわ大好きです!!
特に梓と十!!
おうえんしてます!!

← Junko Ito (Aichi)
Ed.: The word *tsundere* exists for Azusa!

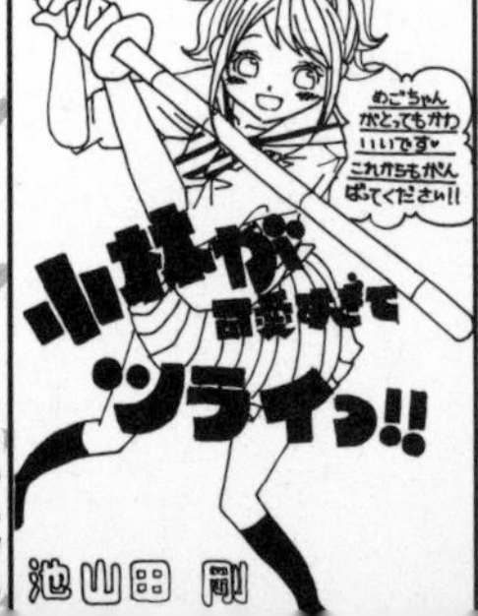

小林が可愛すぎてツライっ!!
池山田 剛

→ Yuumi Minoda (Chiba)
Ed.: Mego's playing kendo?! She looks

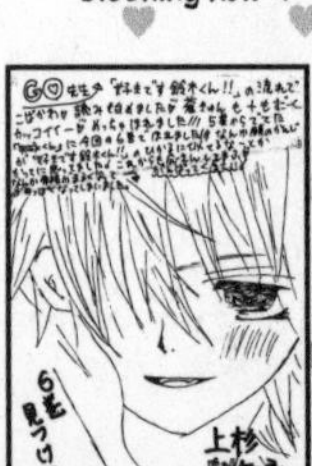

← Honoka Nakamura (Hokkaido)
Ed.: People are drawing lots of Uesugi!!

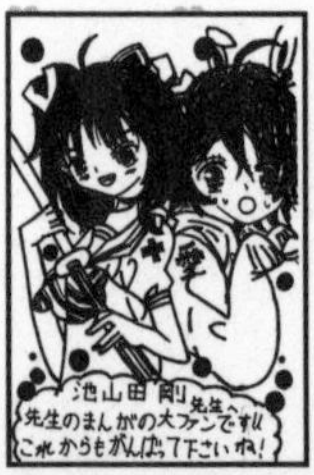

先生のまんがの大ファンです!!

← Kii-chan (Hyogo)
Ed.: The twins gotta pose like this!

Chapter 45

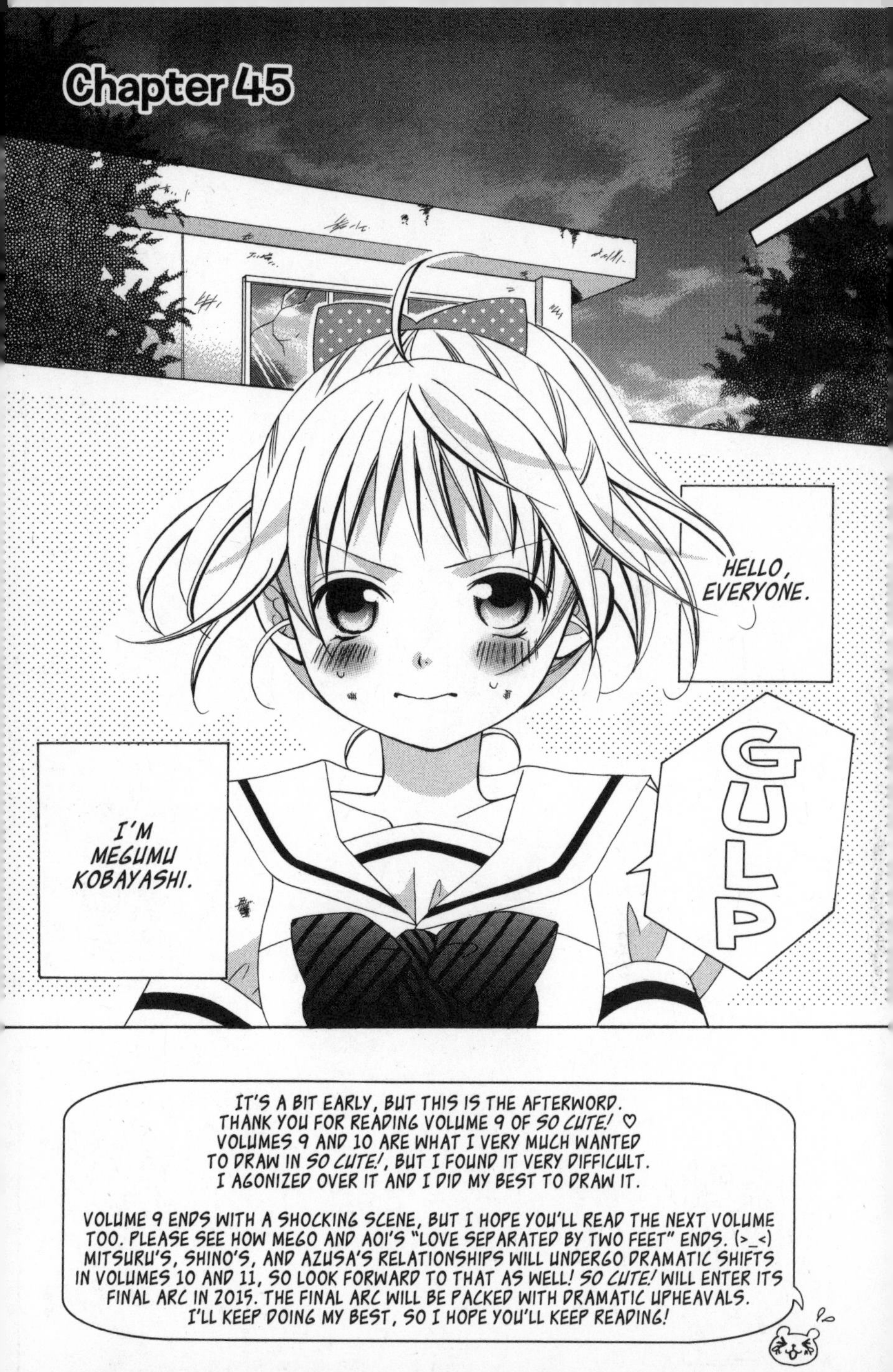
HELLO, EVERYONE.
GULP
I'M MEGUMU KOBAYASHI.

IT'S A BIT EARLY, BUT THIS IS THE AFTERWORD. THANK YOU FOR READING VOLUME 9 OF *SO CUTE!* ♡ VOLUMES 9 AND 10 ARE WHAT I VERY MUCH WANTED TO DRAW IN *SO CUTE!*, BUT I FOUND IT VERY DIFFICULT. I AGONIZED OVER IT AND I DID MY BEST TO DRAW IT.

VOLUME 9 ENDS WITH A SHOCKING SCENE, BUT I HOPE YOU'LL READ THE NEXT VOLUME TOO. PLEASE SEE HOW MEGO AND AOI'S "LOVE SEPARATED BY TWO FEET" ENDS. (>_<) MITSURU'S, SHINO'S, AND AZUSA'S RELATIONSHIPS WILL UNDERGO DRAMATIC SHIFTS IN VOLUMES 10 AND 11, SO LOOK FORWARD TO THAT AS WELL! *SO CUTE!* WILL ENTER ITS FINAL ARC IN 2015. THE FINAL ARC WILL BE PACKED WITH DRAMATIC UPHEAVALS. I'LL KEEP DOING MY BEST, SO I HOPE YOU'LL KEEP READING!

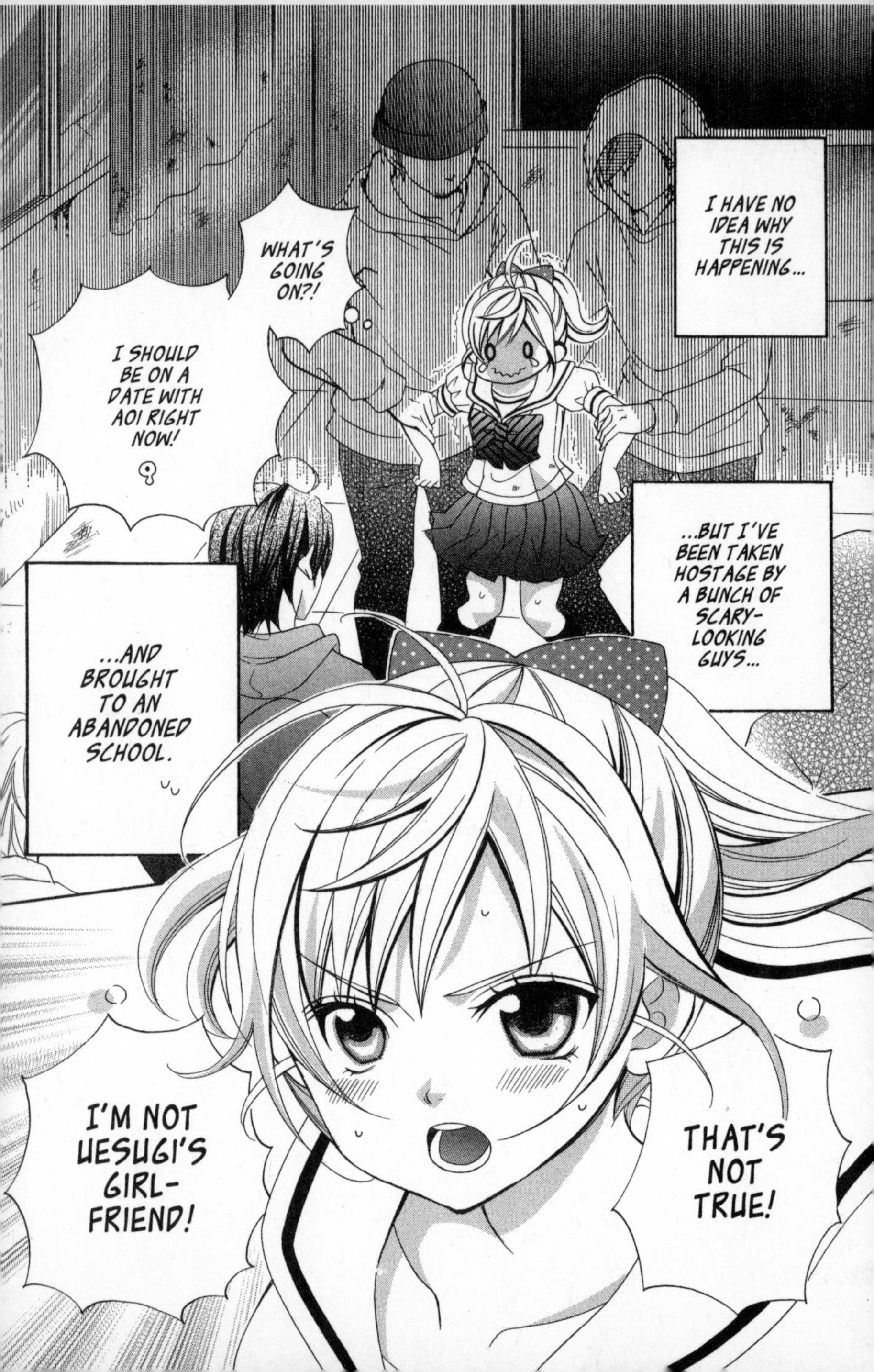
I HAVE NO IDEA WHY THIS IS HAPPENING...
WHAT'S GOING ON?!
I SHOULD BE ON A DATE WITH AOI RIGHT NOW!
...BUT I'VE BEEN TAKEN HOSTAGE BY A BUNCH OF SCARY-LOOKING GUYS...
...AND BROUGHT TO AN ABANDONED SCHOOL.
THAT'S NOT TRUE!
I'M NOT UESUGI'S GIRL-FRIEND!

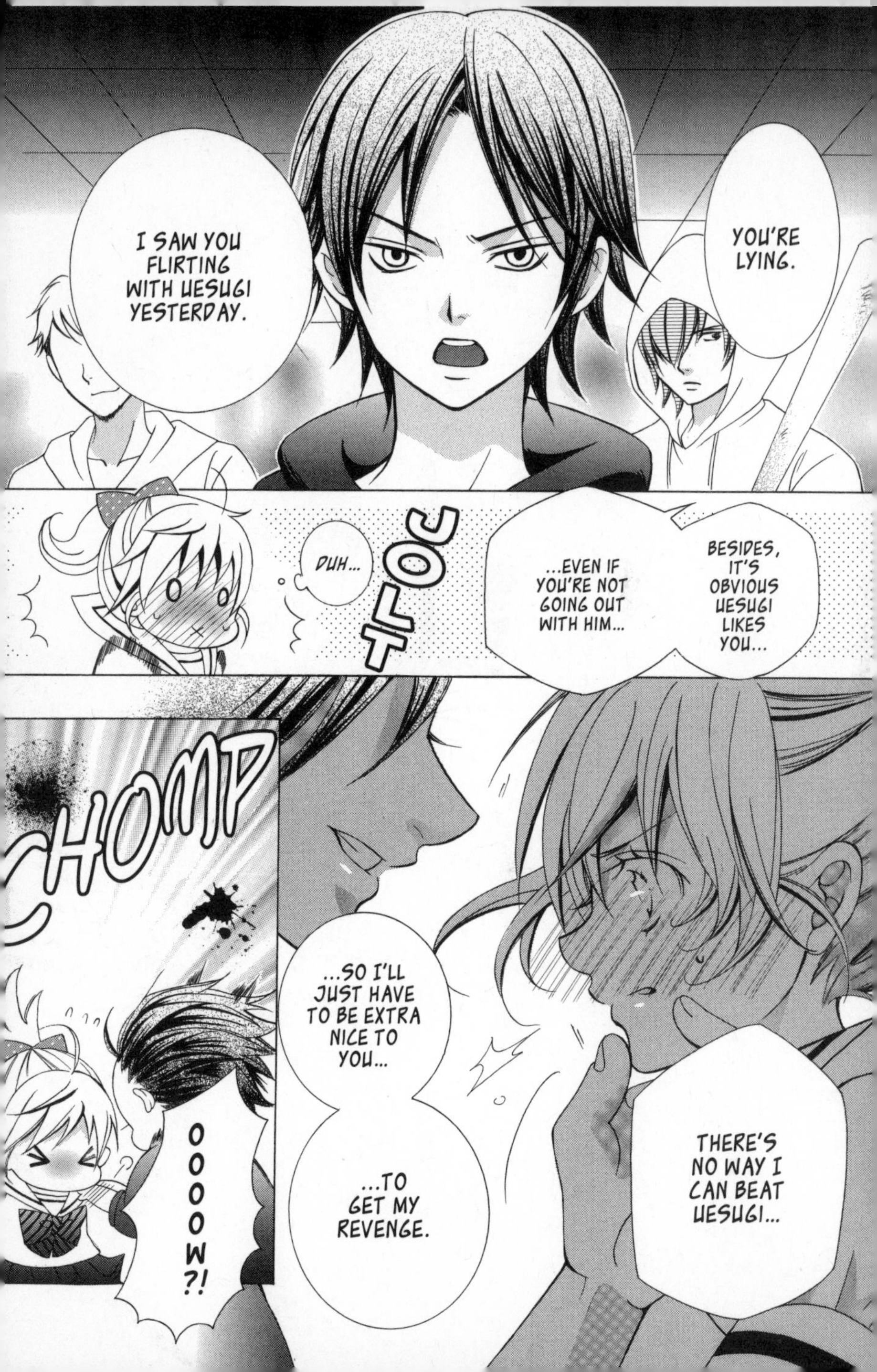
YOU'RE LYING.
I SAW YOU FLIRTING WITH UESUGI YESTERDAY.
BESIDES, IT'S OBVIOUS UESUGI LIKES YOU...
...EVEN IF YOU'RE NOT GOING OUT WITH HIM...
JOLT
DUH...
THERE'S NO WAY I CAN BEAT UESUGI...
...SO I'LL JUST HAVE TO BE EXTRA NICE TO YOU...
...TO GET MY REVENGE.
CHOMP
OOOOOW?!

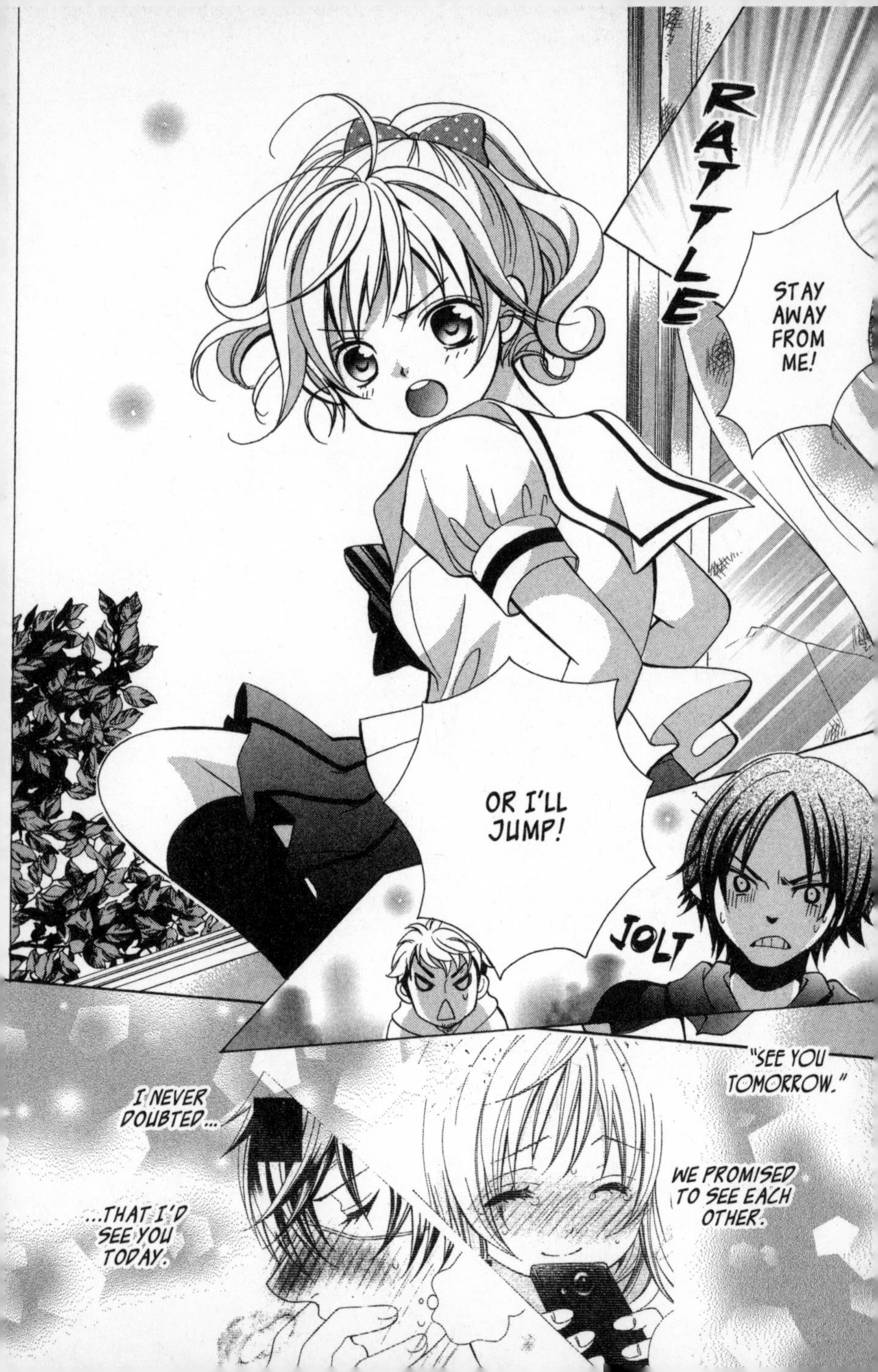
RATTLE
STAY AWAY FROM ME!
OR I'LL JUMP!
JOLT
"SEE YOU TOMORROW."
WE PROMISED TO SEE EACH OTHER.
I NEVER DOUBTED...
...THAT I'D SEE YOU TODAY.

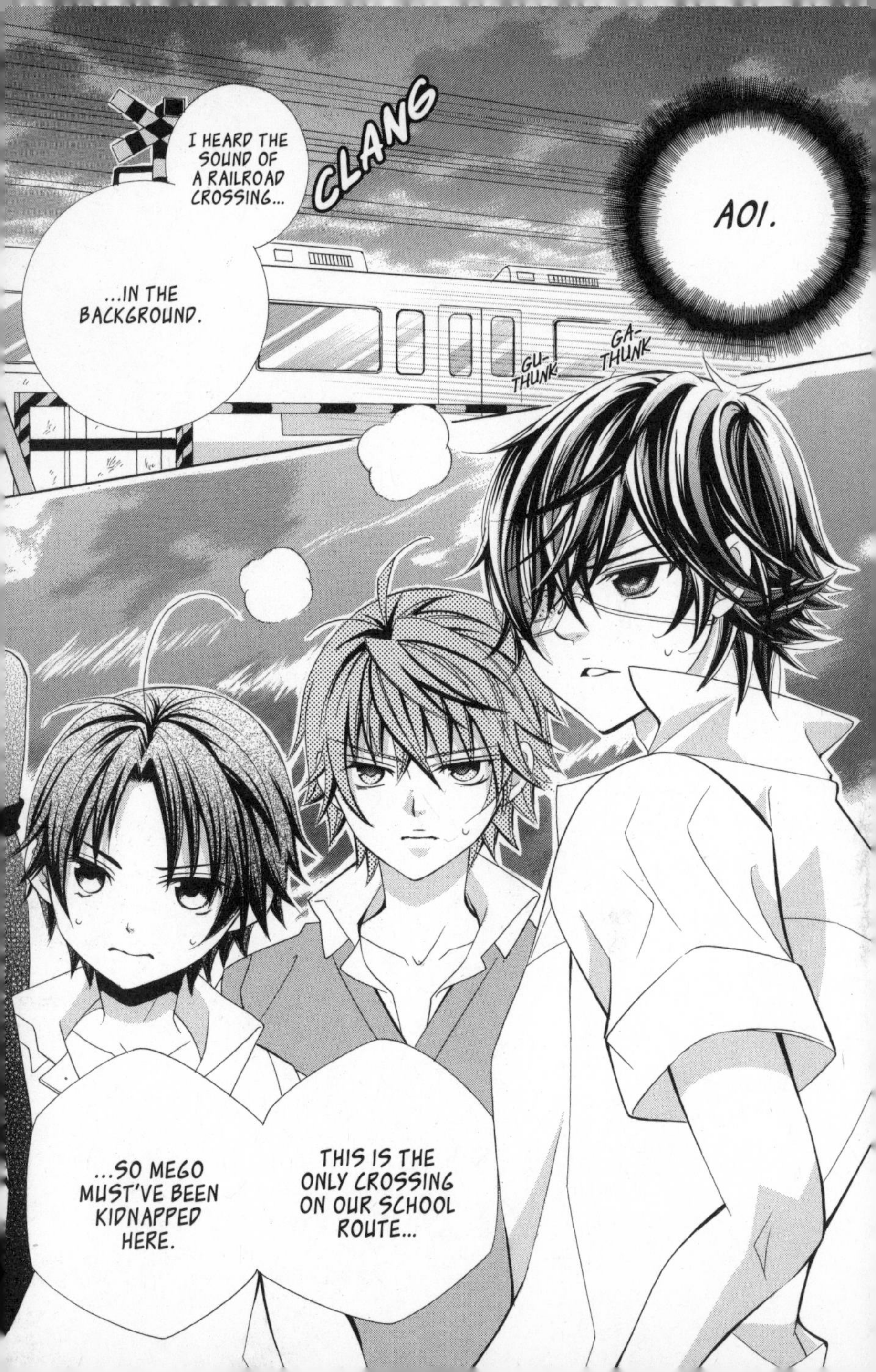
AOI.
CLANG
I HEARD THE SOUND OF A RAILROAD CROSSING...
...IN THE BACKGROUND.
GA-THUNK
GU-THUNK
THIS IS THE ONLY CROSSING ON OUR SCHOOL ROUTE...
...SO MEGO MUST'VE BEEN KIDNAPPED HERE.

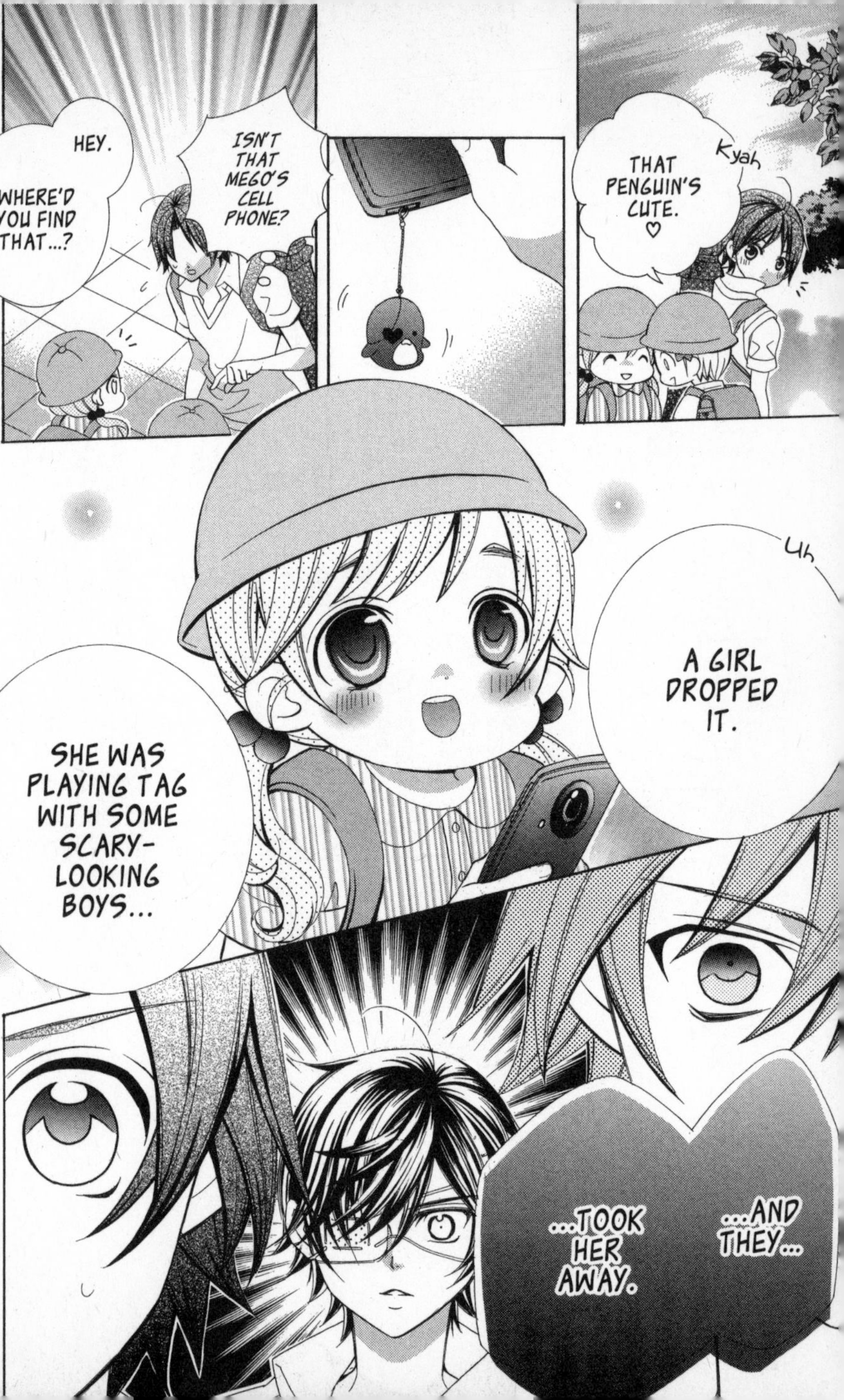
Kyah
THAT PENGUIN'S CUTE. ♡
ISN'T THAT MEGO'S CELL PHONE?
HEY.
WHERE'D YOU FIND THAT...?
Uh
A GIRL DROPPED IT.
SHE WAS PLAYING TAG WITH SOME SCARY-LOOKING BOYS...
...AND THEY...
...TOOK HER AWAY.

SPECIAL THANKS

Yuka Ito-sama,
Rieko Hirai-sama,
Kayoko Takahashi-sama,
Kawasaki-sama,
Nagisa Sato Sensei.

Rei Nanase Sensei,
Arisu Fujishiro Sensei,
Mumi Mimura Sensei,
Masayo Nagata-sama,
Naochan-sama,
Asuka Sakura Sensei
and many others.

Bookstore Dan Kinshicho Branch, Kinokuniya Shinjuku Branch, LIBRO Ikebukuro Branch, Kinokuniya Hankyu 32-Bangai Branch.

Sendai Hachimonjiya Bookstore, Books HOSHINO Kintetsu Pass'e Branch, Asahiya Tennnoji MiO Branch, Kurashiki Kikuya Bookstore.

Salesperson:
Mizusawa-sama

Previous salesperson:
Honma-sama

Previous editor:
Nakata-sama

Current editor:
Shoji-sama

I also sincerely express my gratitude to everyone who picked up this volume.

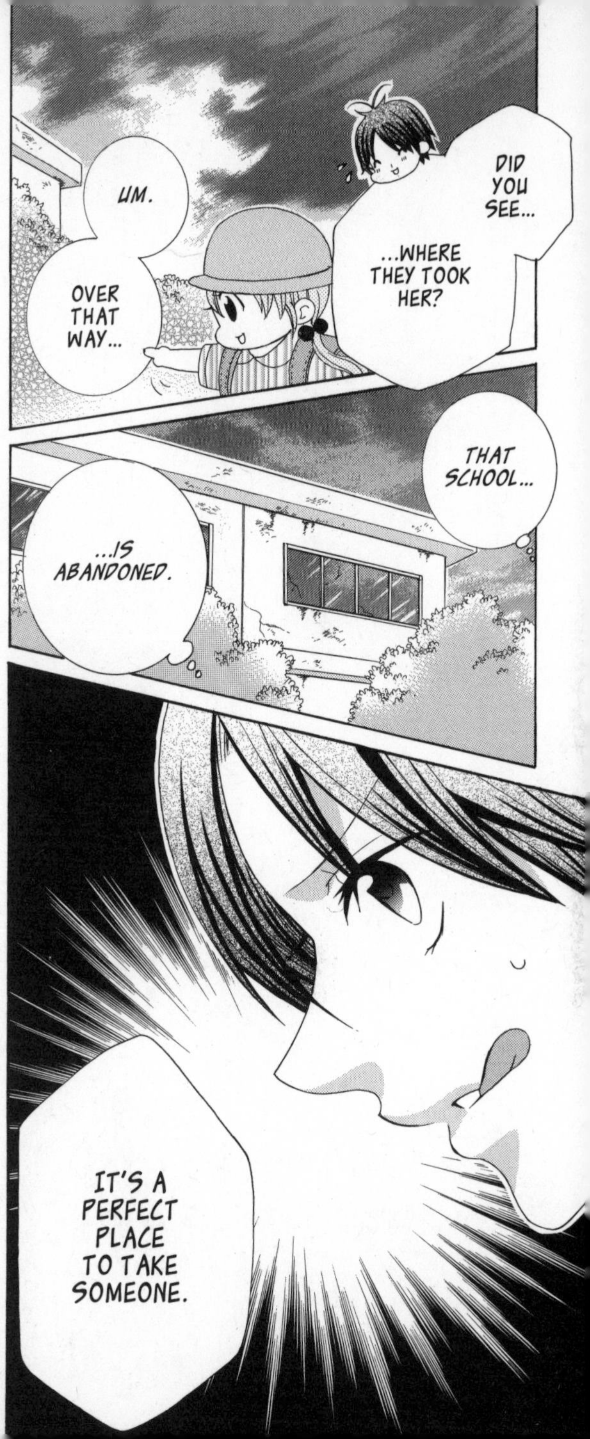
DID YOU SEE...
...WHERE THEY TOOK HER?
UM.
OVER THAT WAY...
THAT SCHOOL...
...IS ABANDONED.
IT'S A PERFECT PLACE TO TAKE SOMEONE.

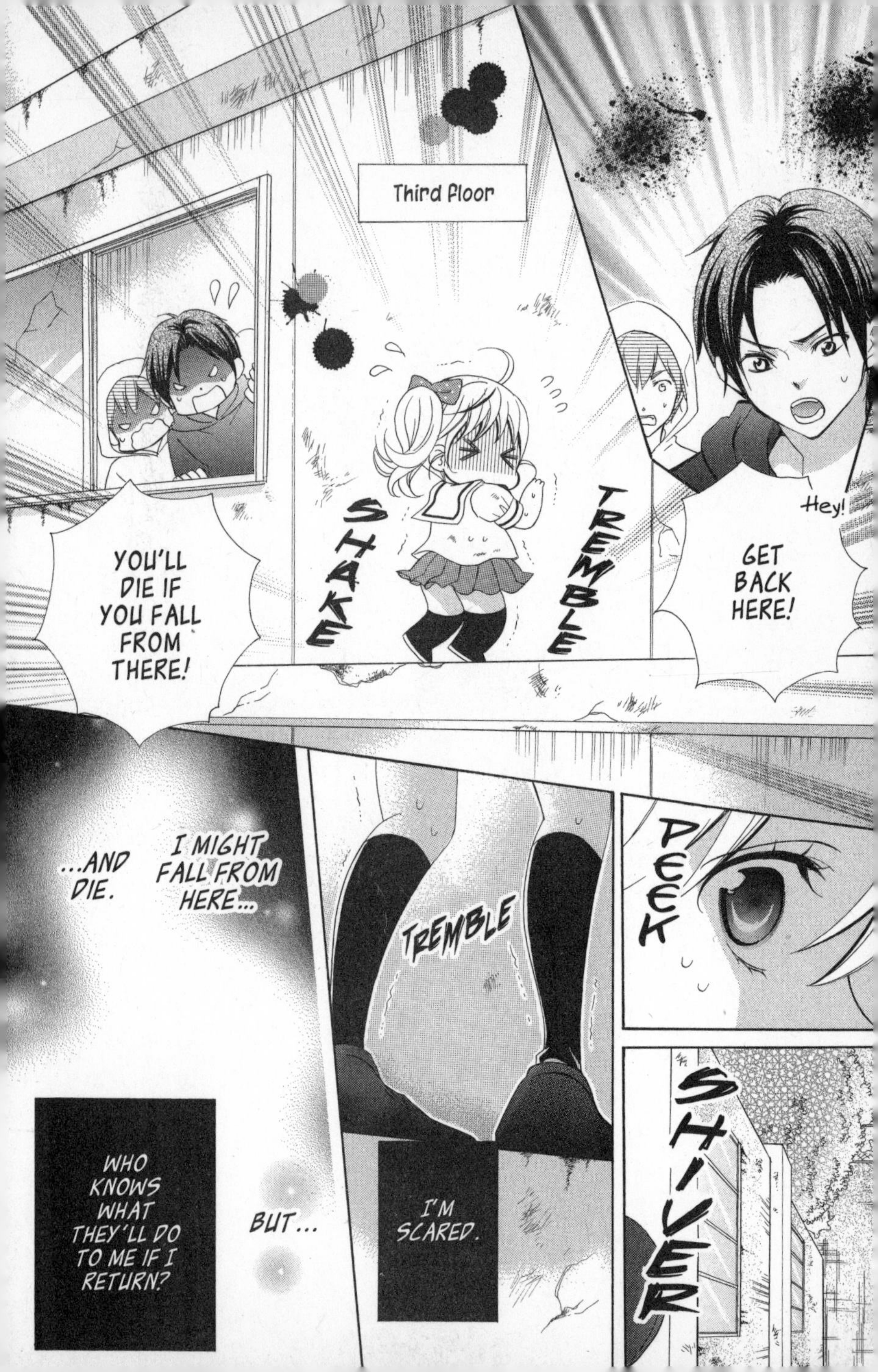
Hey!
GET BACK HERE!
Third floor
TREMBLE
SHAKE
YOU'LL DIE IF YOU FALL FROM THERE!
PEEK
SHIVER
TREMBLE
I'M SCARED.
I MIGHT FALL FROM HERE...
...AND DIE.
BUT...
WHO KNOWS WHAT THEY'LL DO TO ME IF I RETURN?

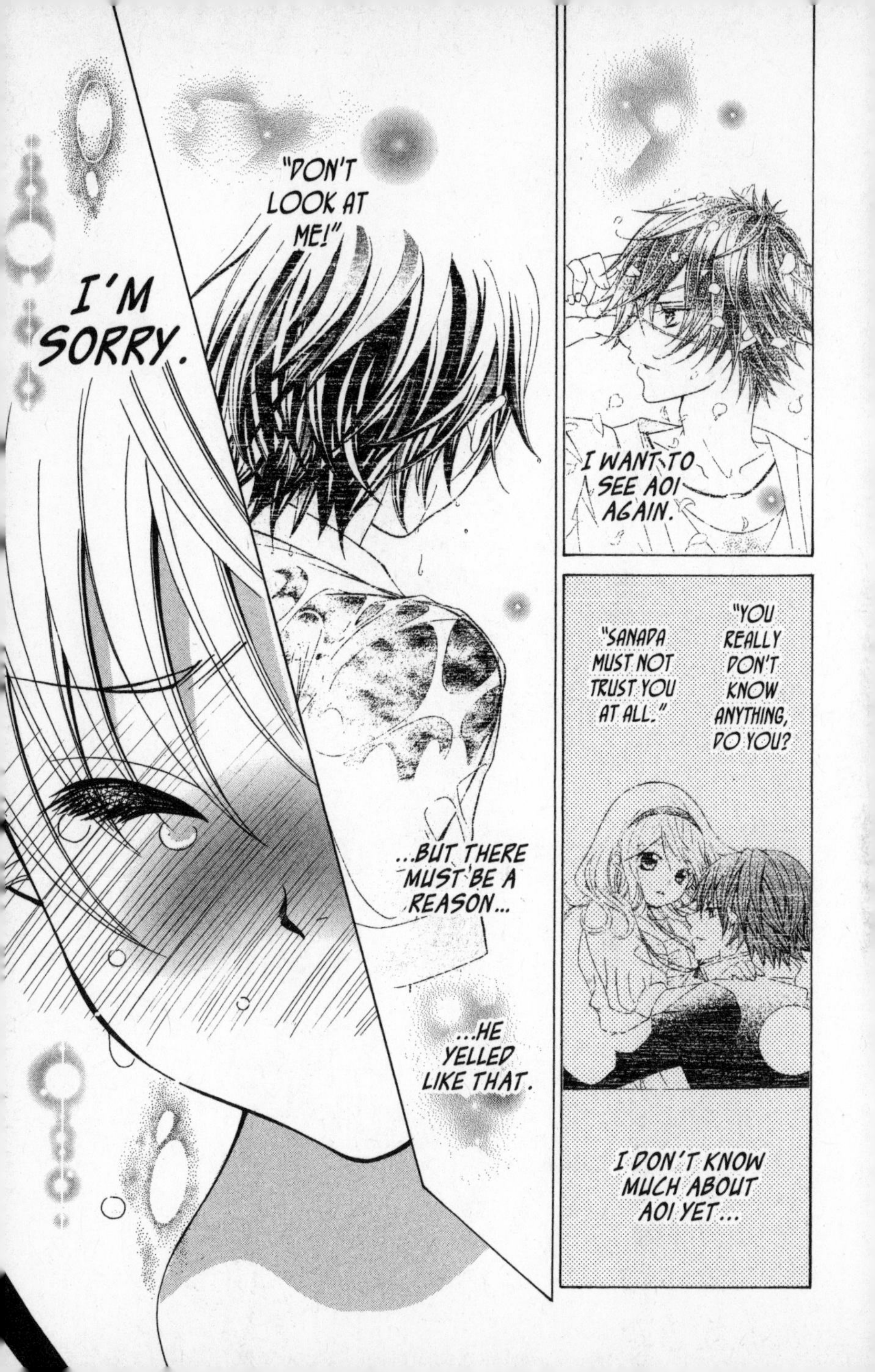
I WANT TO SEE AOI AGAIN.
"YOU REALLY DON'T KNOW ANYTHING, DO YOU?
"SANADA MUST NOT TRUST YOU AT ALL."
I DON'T KNOW MUCH ABOUT AOI YET...
"DON'T LOOK AT ME!"
I'M SORRY.
...BUT THERE MUST BE A REASON...
...HE YELLED LIKE THAT.

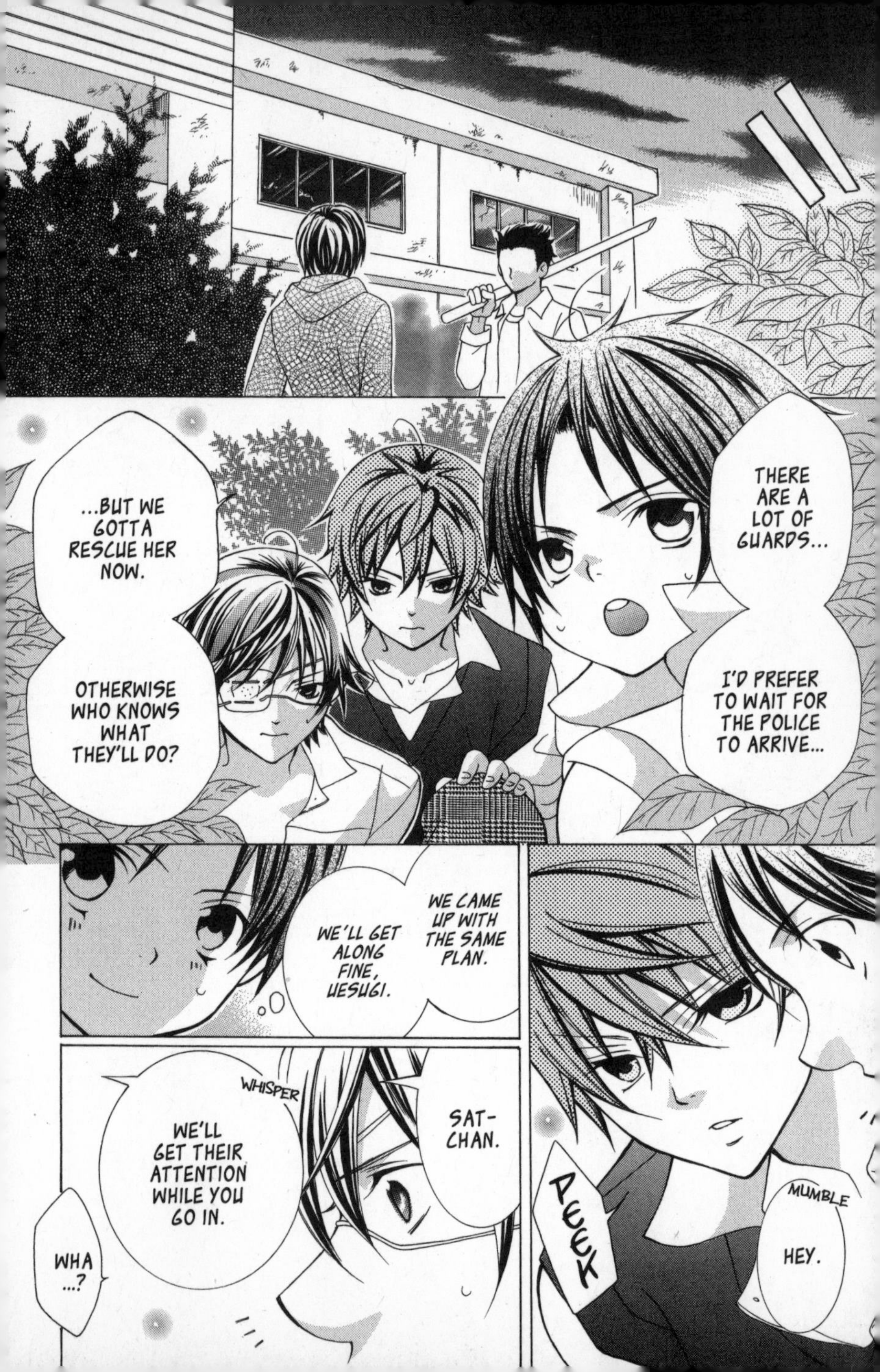
THERE ARE A LOT OF GUARDS...
I'D PREFER TO WAIT FOR THE POLICE TO ARRIVE...
...BUT WE GOTTA RESCUE HER NOW.
OTHERWISE WHO KNOWS WHAT THEY'LL DO?
PEEK
MUMBLE
HEY.
WE CAME UP WITH THE SAME PLAN.
WE'LL GET ALONG FINE, UESUGI.
SAT-CHAN.
WHISPER
WE'LL GET THEIR ATTENTION WHILE YOU GO IN.
WHA ...?

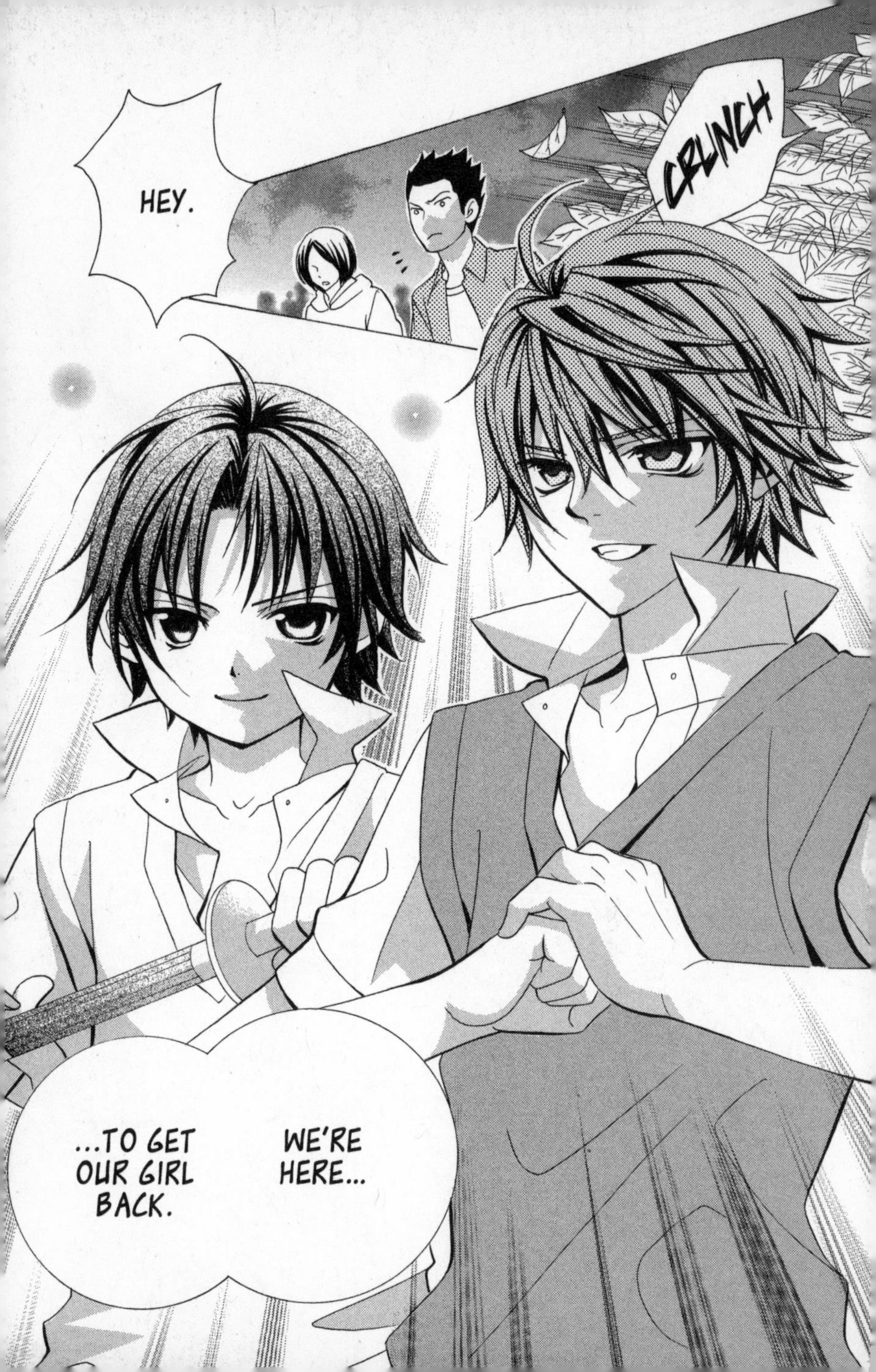
CRUNCH
HEY.
WE'RE HERE...
...TO GET OUR GIRL BACK.

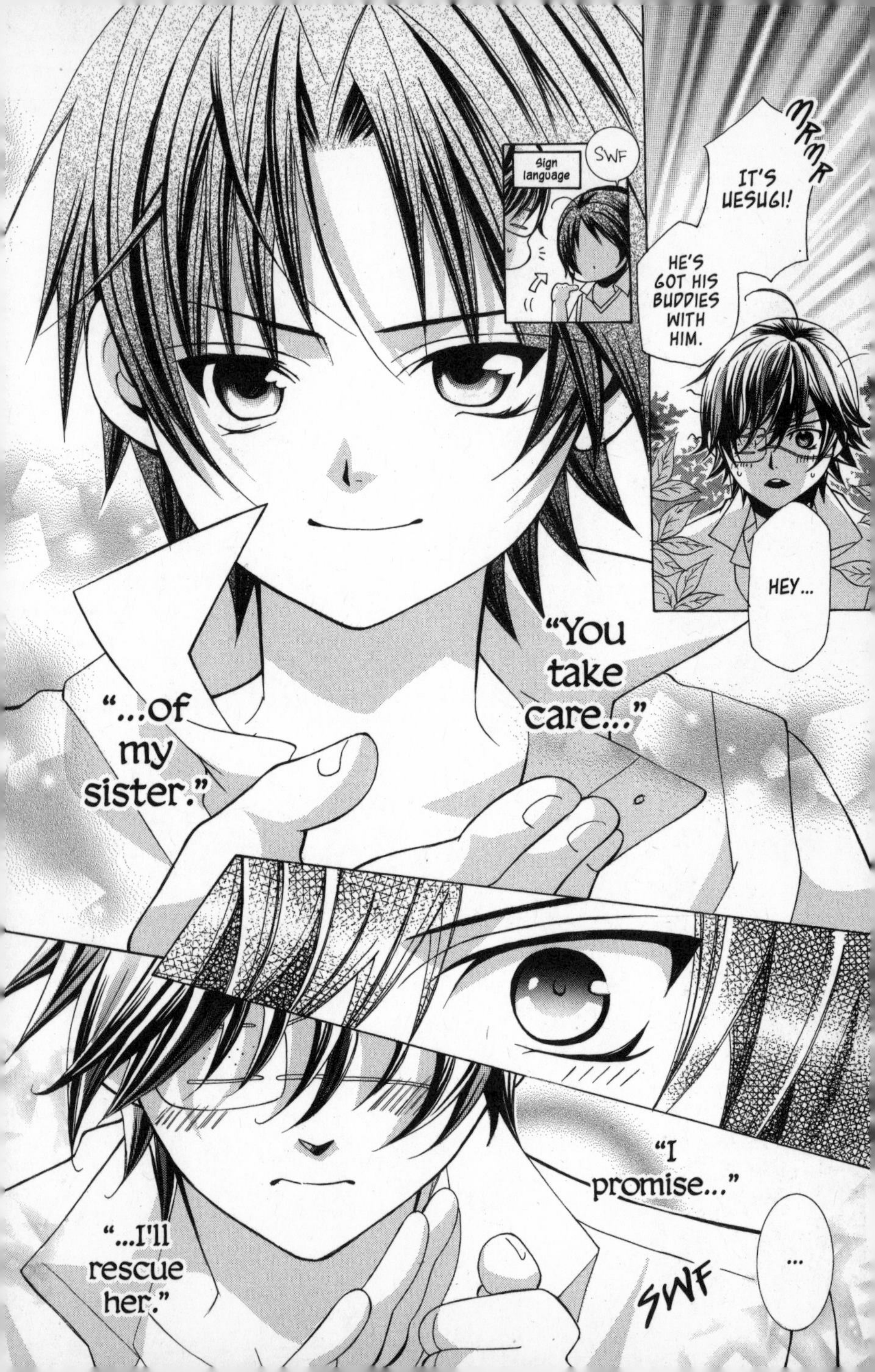
MRMR
IT'S UESUGI!
HE'S GOT HIS BUDDIES WITH HIM.
HEY...
SWF
Sign language
"You take care..."
"...of my sister."
...
SWF
"I promise..."
"...I'll rescue her."

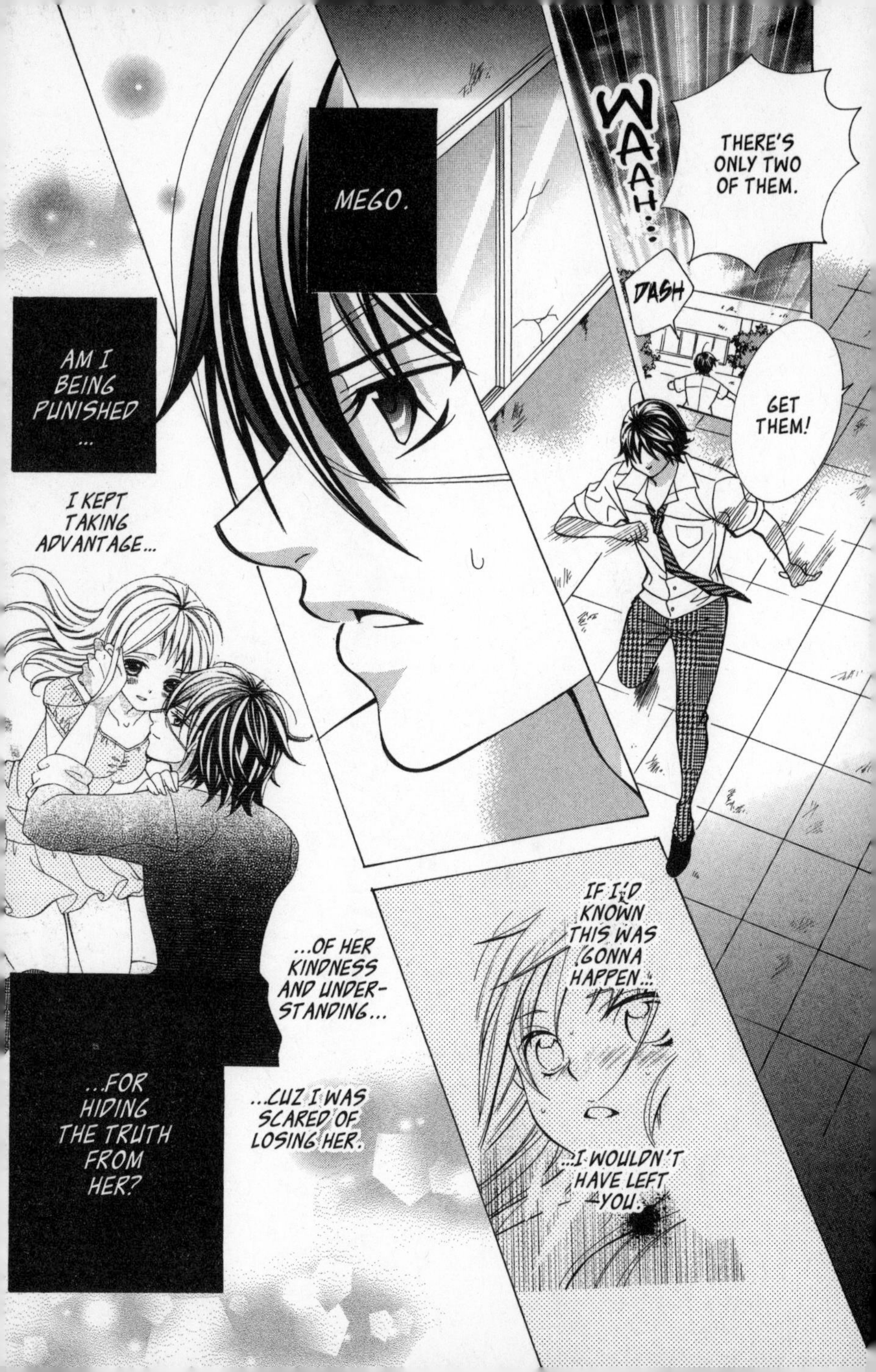
WAAH...
THERE'S ONLY TWO OF THEM.
DASH
GET THEM!
MEGO.
IF I'D KNOWN THIS WAS GONNA HAPPEN...
...I WOULDN'T HAVE LEFT YOU.
AM I BEING PUNISHED ...
I KEPT TAKING ADVANTAGE...
...OF HER KINDNESS AND UNDER-STANDING...
...CUZ I WAS SCARED OF LOSING HER.
...FOR HIDING THE TRUTH FROM HER?

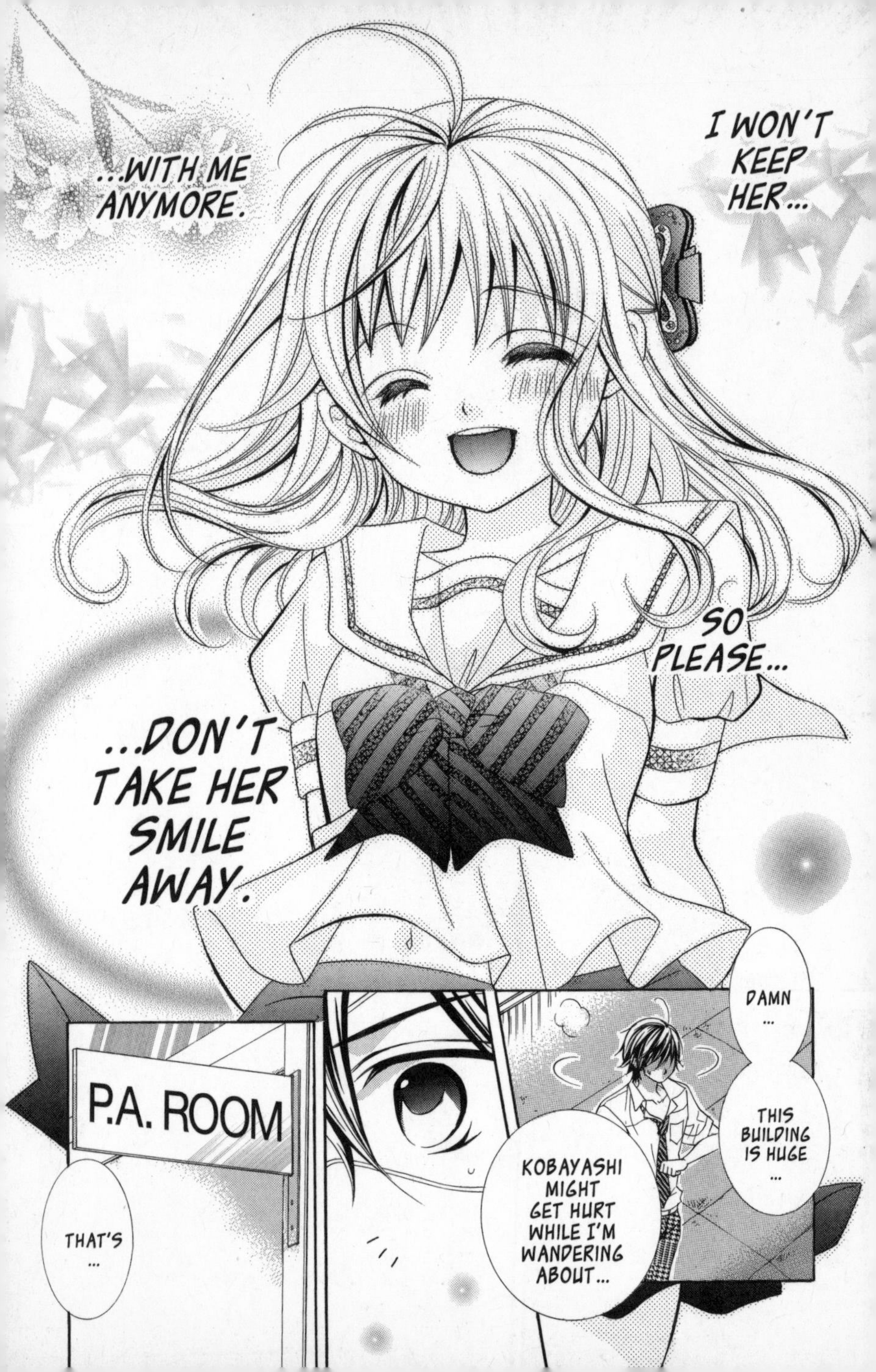
I WON'T KEEP HER...
...WITH ME ANYMORE.
SO PLEASE...
...DON'T TAKE HER SMILE AWAY.
DAMN...
THIS BUILDING IS HUGE...
KOBAYASHI MIGHT GET HURT WHILE I'M WANDERING ABOUT...
P.A. ROOM
THAT'S...

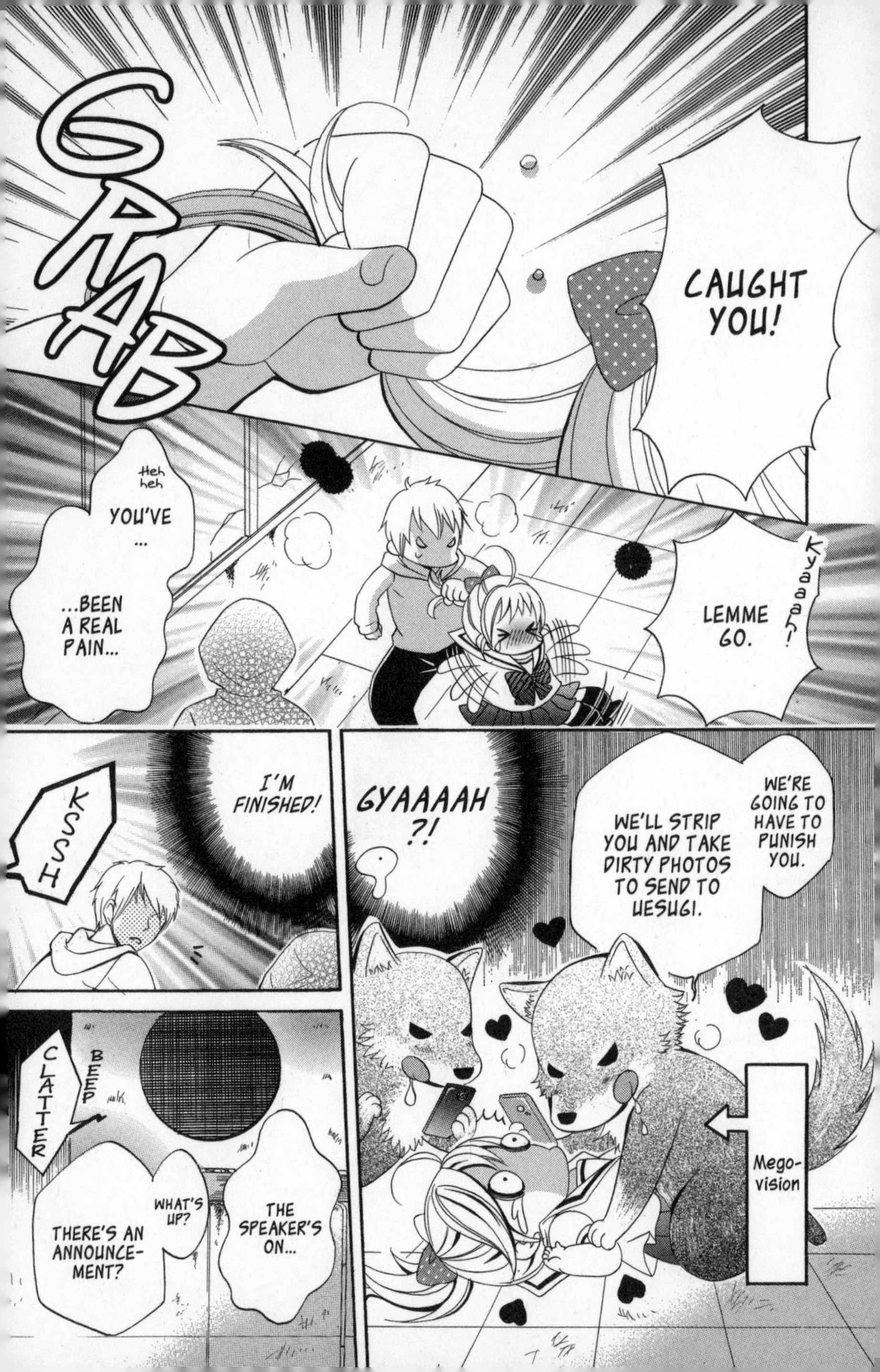
GRAB
CAUGHT YOU!
Kyaaaah!
LEMME GO.
Heh heh
YOU'VE ...
...BEEN A REAL PAIN...
WE'RE GOING TO HAVE TO PUNISH YOU.
WE'LL STRIP YOU AND TAKE DIRTY PHOTOS TO SEND TO UESUGI.
GYAAAAH ?!
Mego-vision
I'M FINISHED!
KSSH
BEEP
CLATTER
THE SPEAKER'S ON...
WHAT'S UP?
THERE'S AN ANNOUNCEMENT?

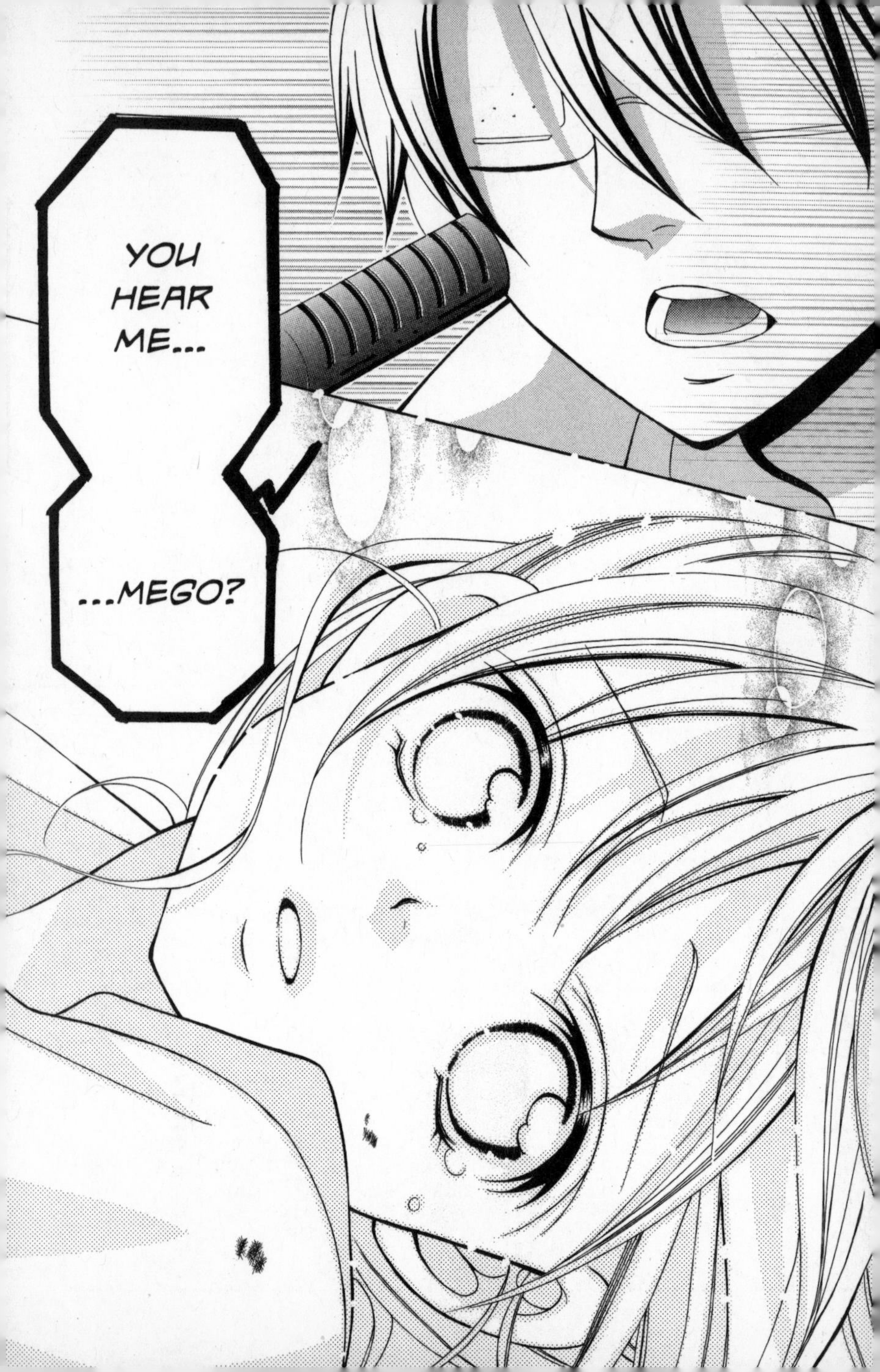
YOU HEAR ME...
...MEGO?

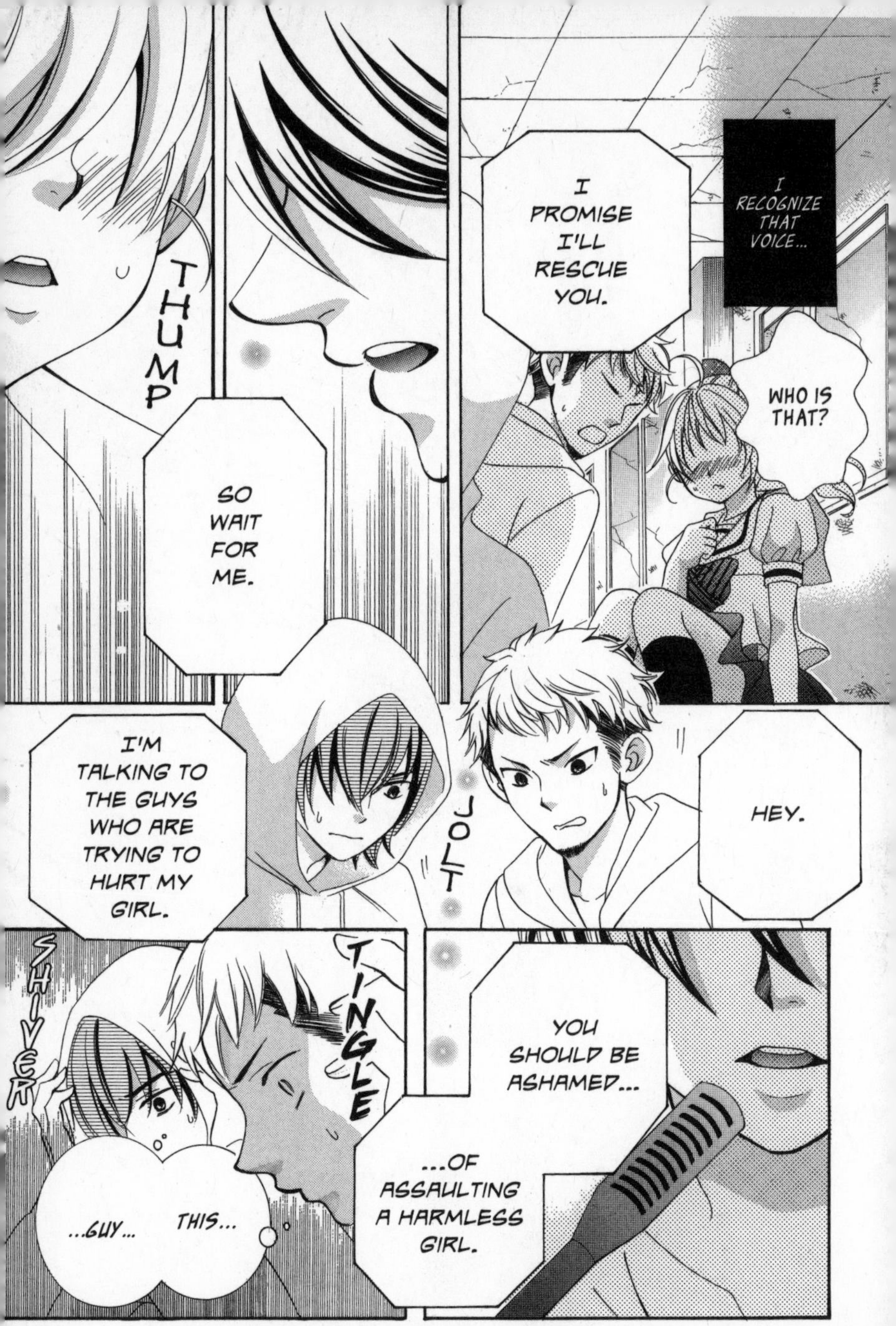
I RECOGNIZE THAT VOICE...
I PROMISE I'LL RESCUE YOU.
WHO IS THAT?
SO WAIT FOR ME.
THUMP
HEY.
JOLT
I'M TALKING TO THE GUYS WHO ARE TRYING TO HURT MY GIRL.
YOU SHOULD BE ASHAMED...
...OF ASSAULTING A HARMLESS GIRL.
TINGLE
THIS...
...GUY...
SHIVER

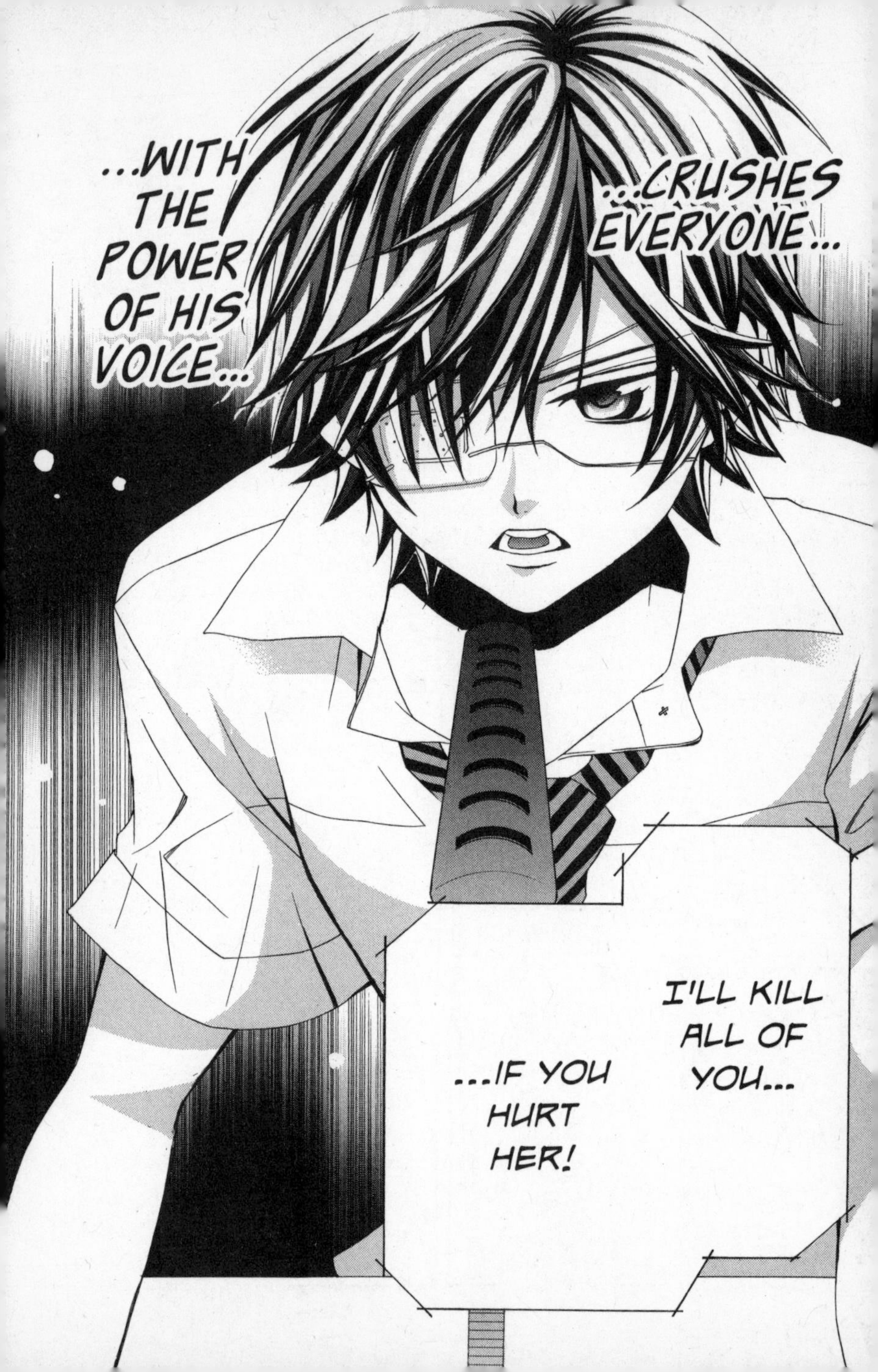
...CRUSHES EVERYONE...
...WITH THE POWER OF HIS VOICE...
I'LL KILL ALL OF YOU...
...IF YOU HURT HER!

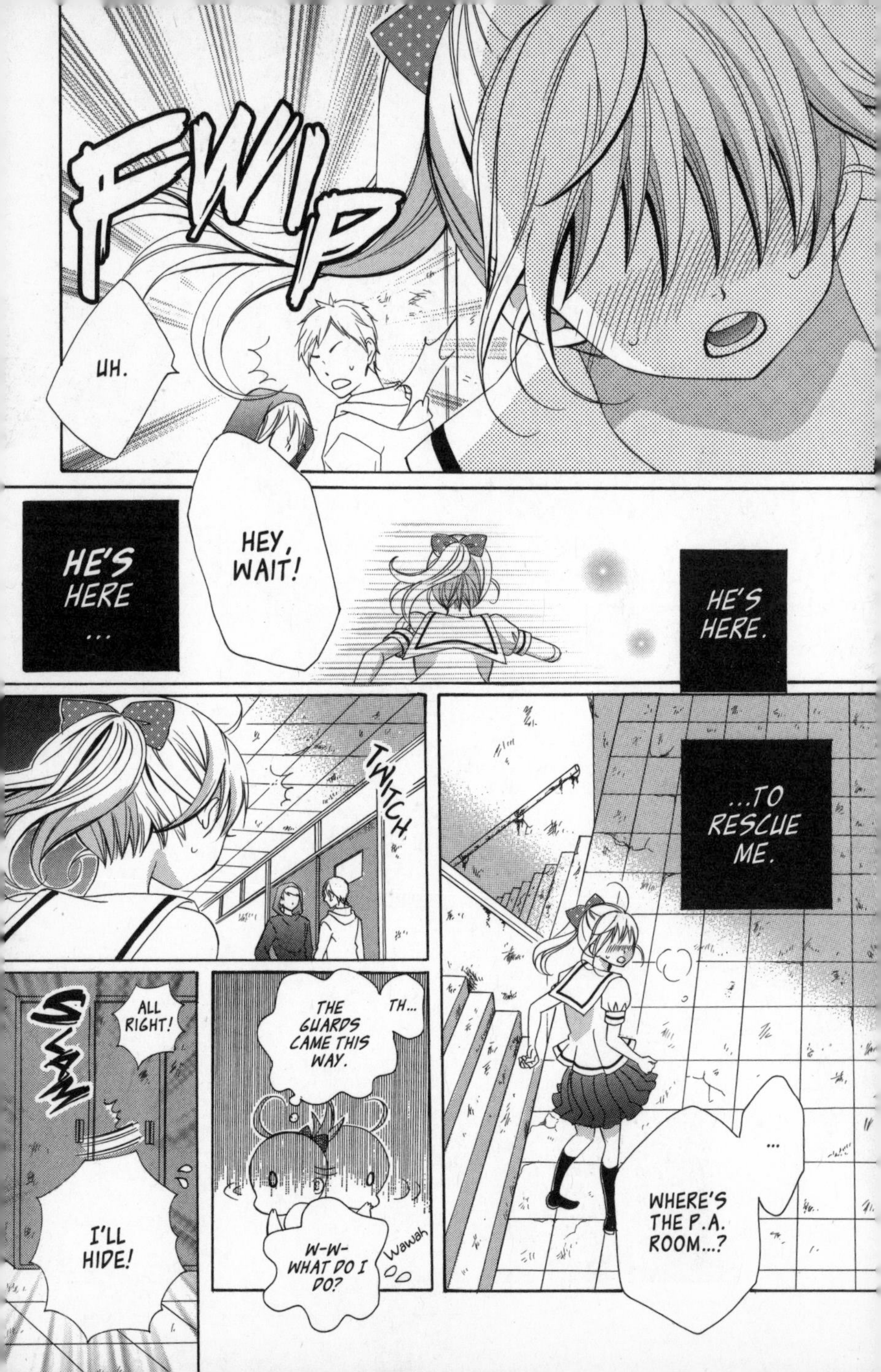
FWIP
UH.
HE'S HERE.
HEY, WAIT!
HE'S HERE ...
...TO RESCUE ME.
...
WHERE'S THE P.A. ROOM...?
TWITCH
TH...
THE GUARDS CAME THIS WAY.
W-W-WHAT DO I DO?
Wawah
ALL RIGHT!
SLAM
I'LL HIDE!

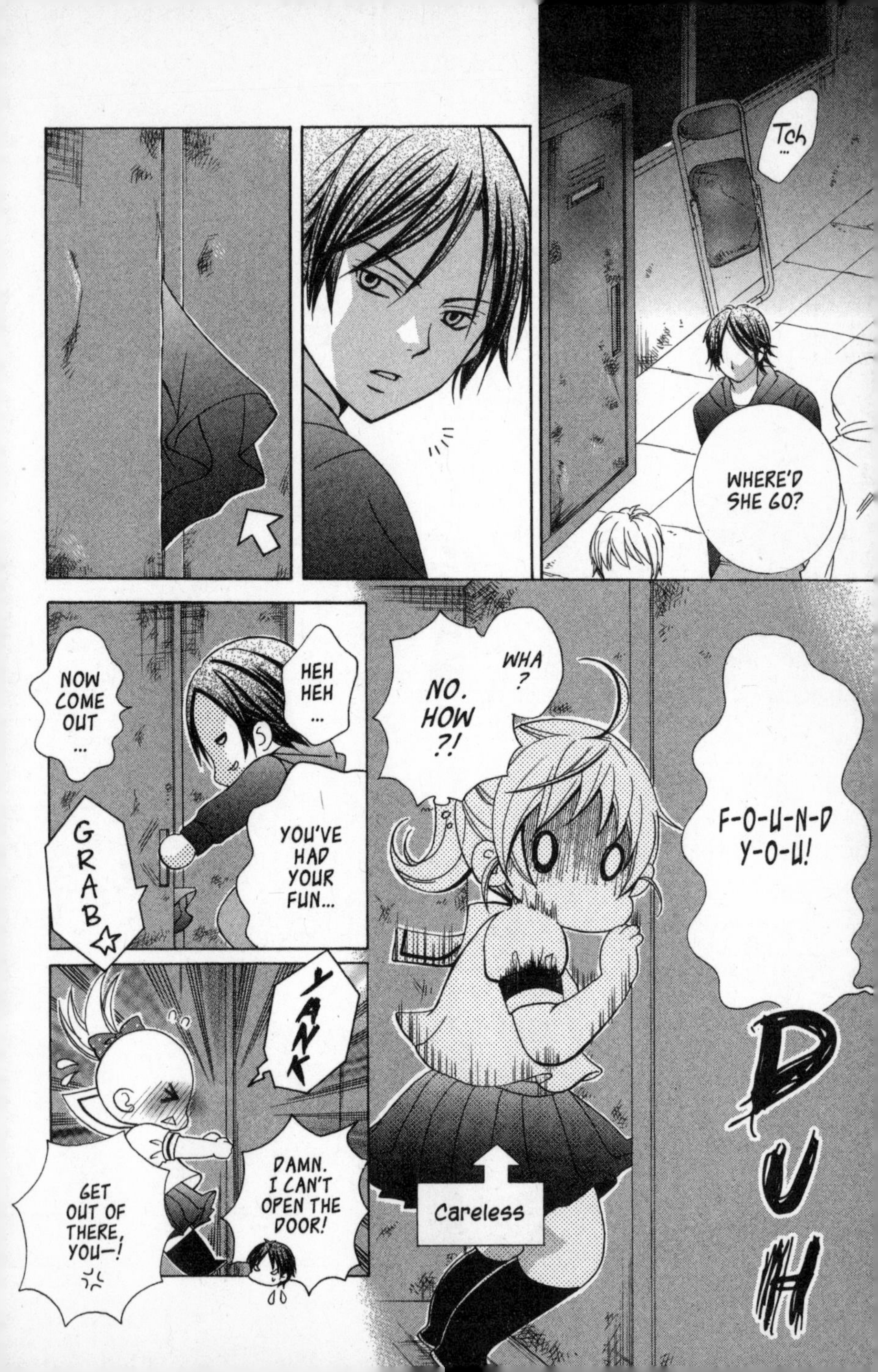
Tch ...
WHERE'D SHE GO?
F-O-U-N-D Y-O-U!
DUH
WHA ?
NO. HOW ?!
Careless
HEH HEH ...
NOW COME OUT ...
YOU'VE HAD YOUR FUN...
GRAB☆
YANK
DAMN. I CAN'T OPEN THE DOOR!
GET OUT OF THERE, YOU—!

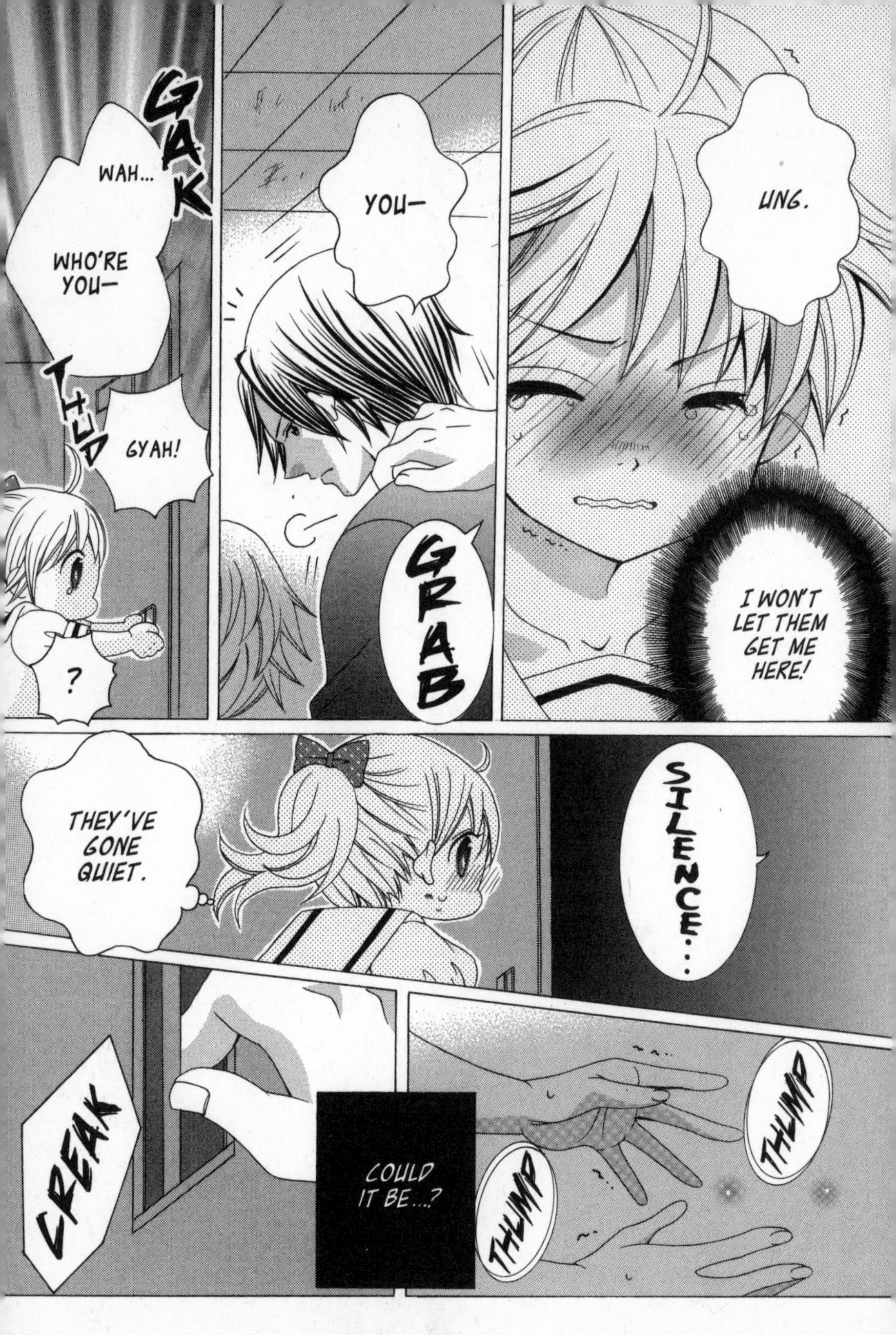
UNG.
I WON'T LET THEM GET ME HERE!
YOU—
GRAB
GAK
WAH...
WHO'RE YOU—
THUD
GYAH!
?
SILENCE...
THEY'VE GONE QUIET.
THUMP
THUMP
COULD IT BE...?
CREAK

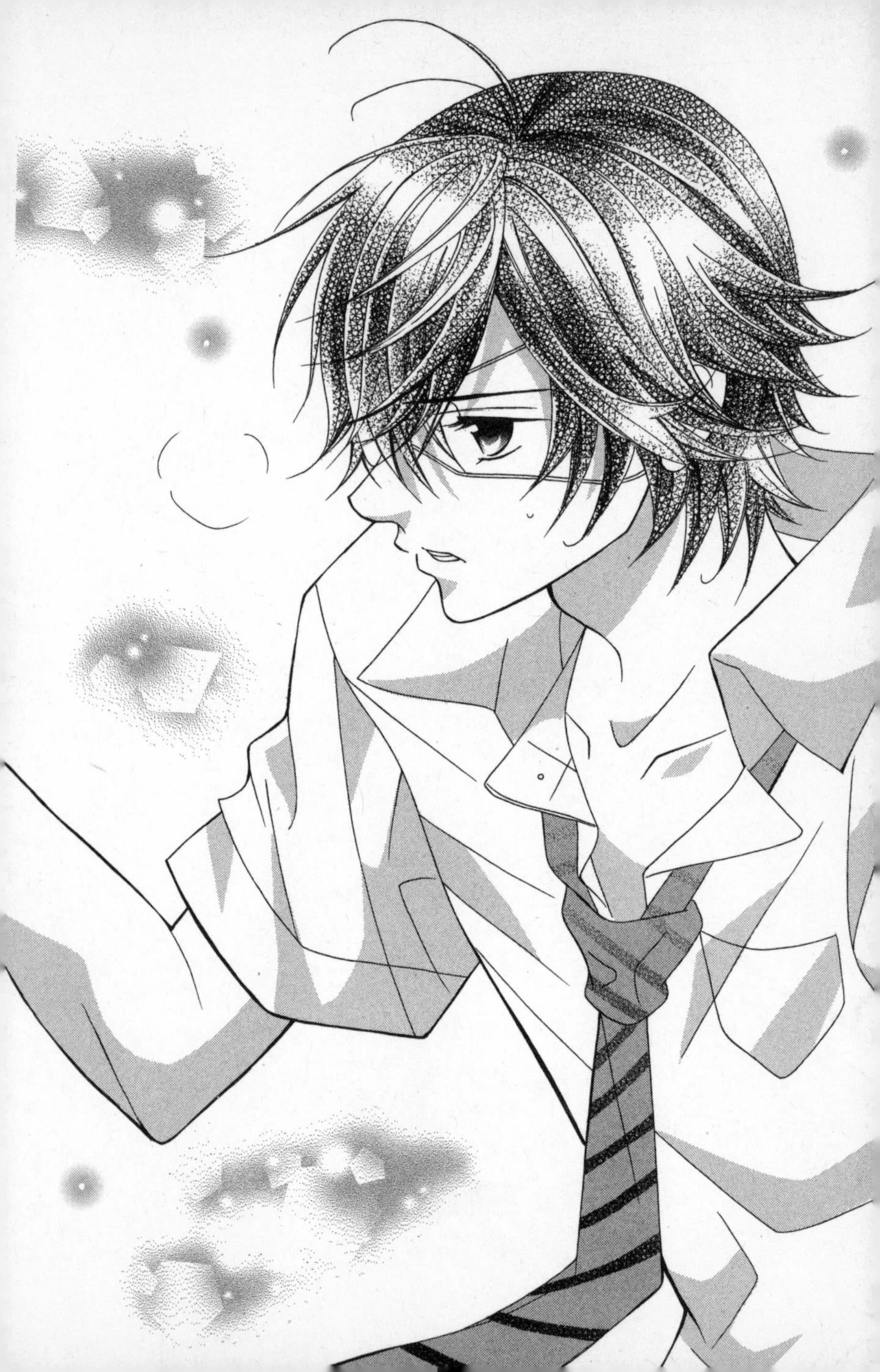

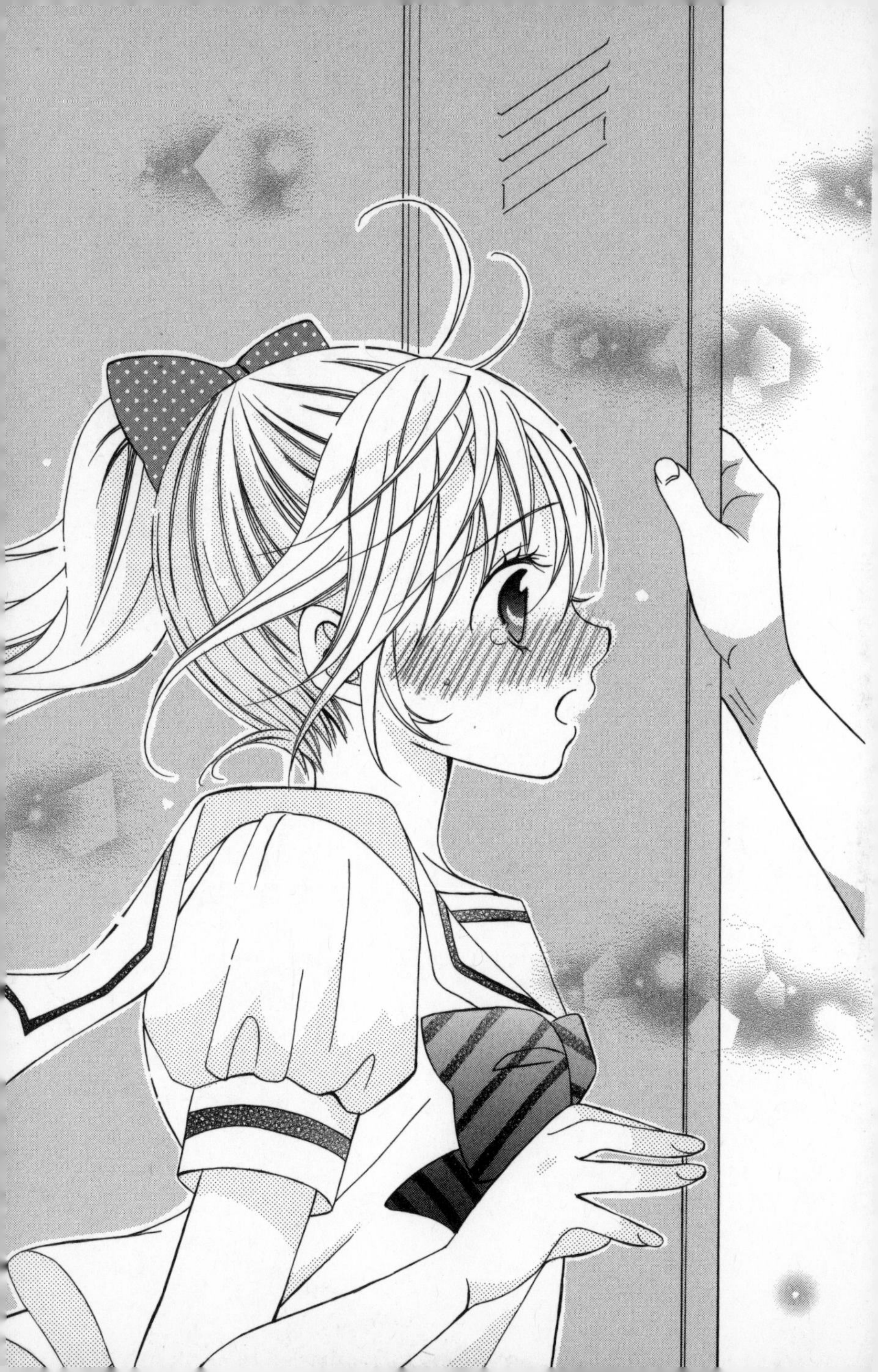

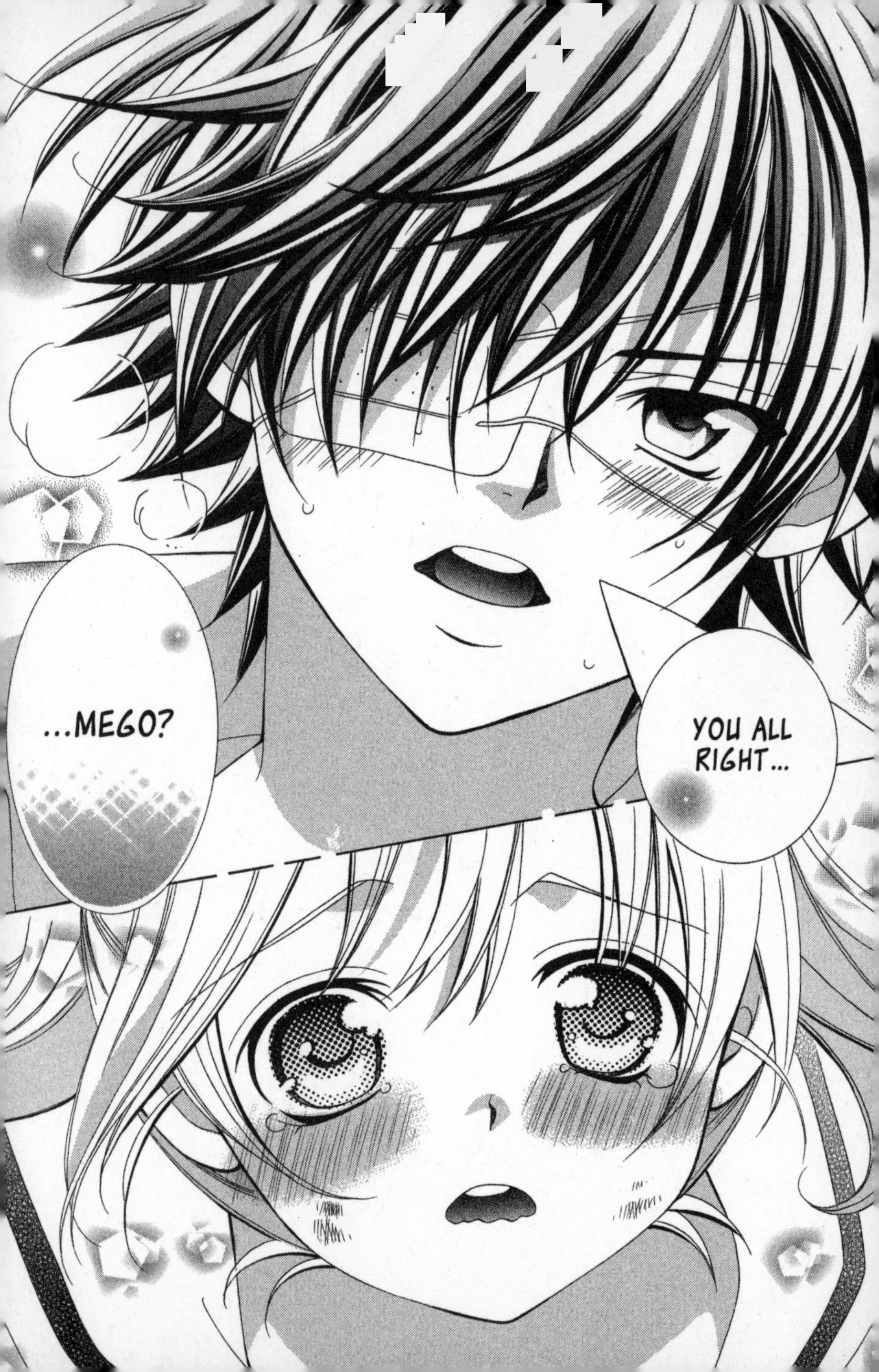
YOU ALL RIGHT...
...MEGO?

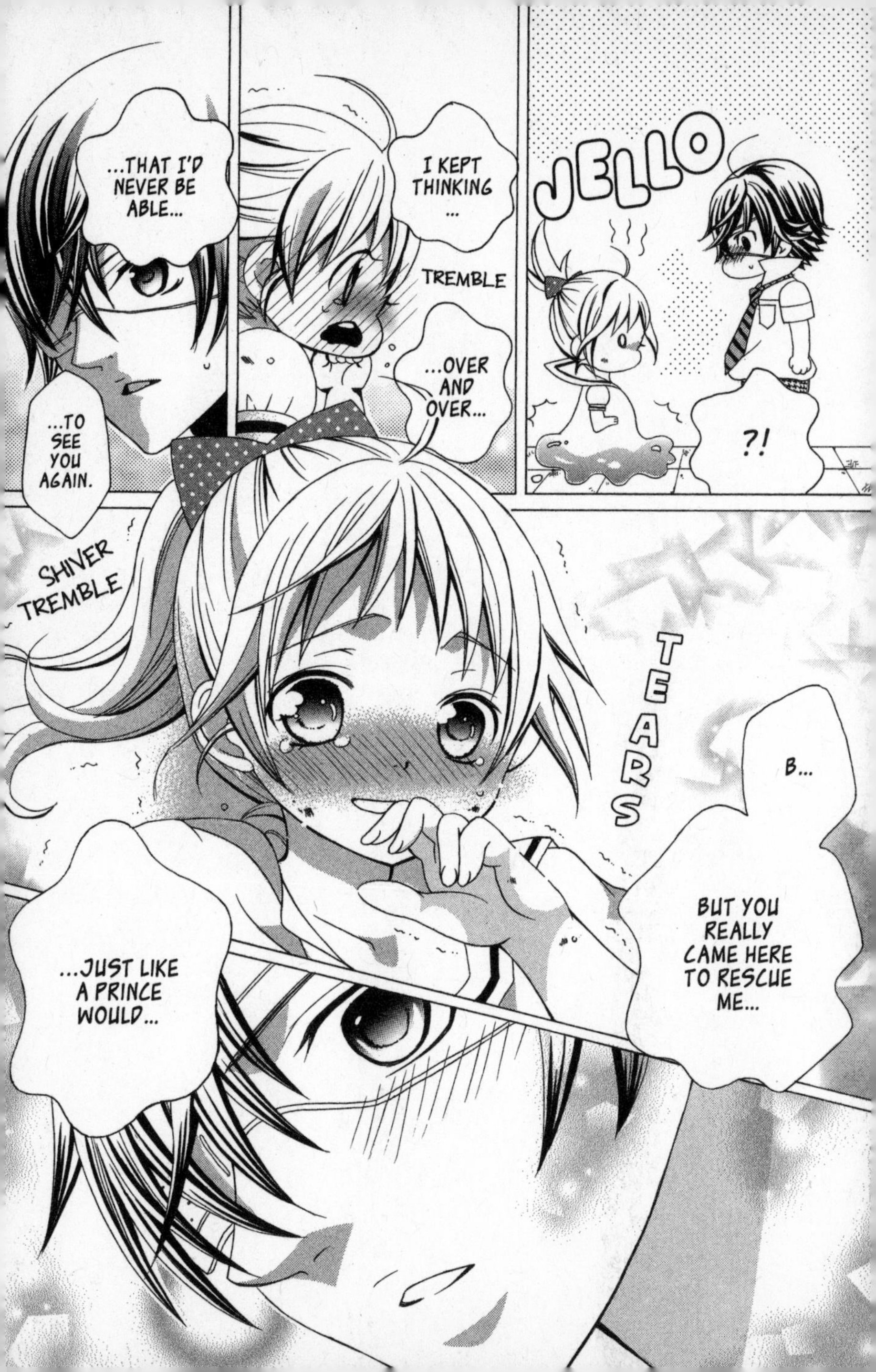
JELLO
?!
I KEPT THINKING ...
TREMBLE
...OVER AND OVER...
...THAT I'D NEVER BE ABLE...
...TO SEE YOU AGAIN.
B...
BUT YOU REALLY CAME HERE TO RESCUE ME...
TEARS
SHIVER TREMBLE
...JUST LIKE A PRINCE WOULD...

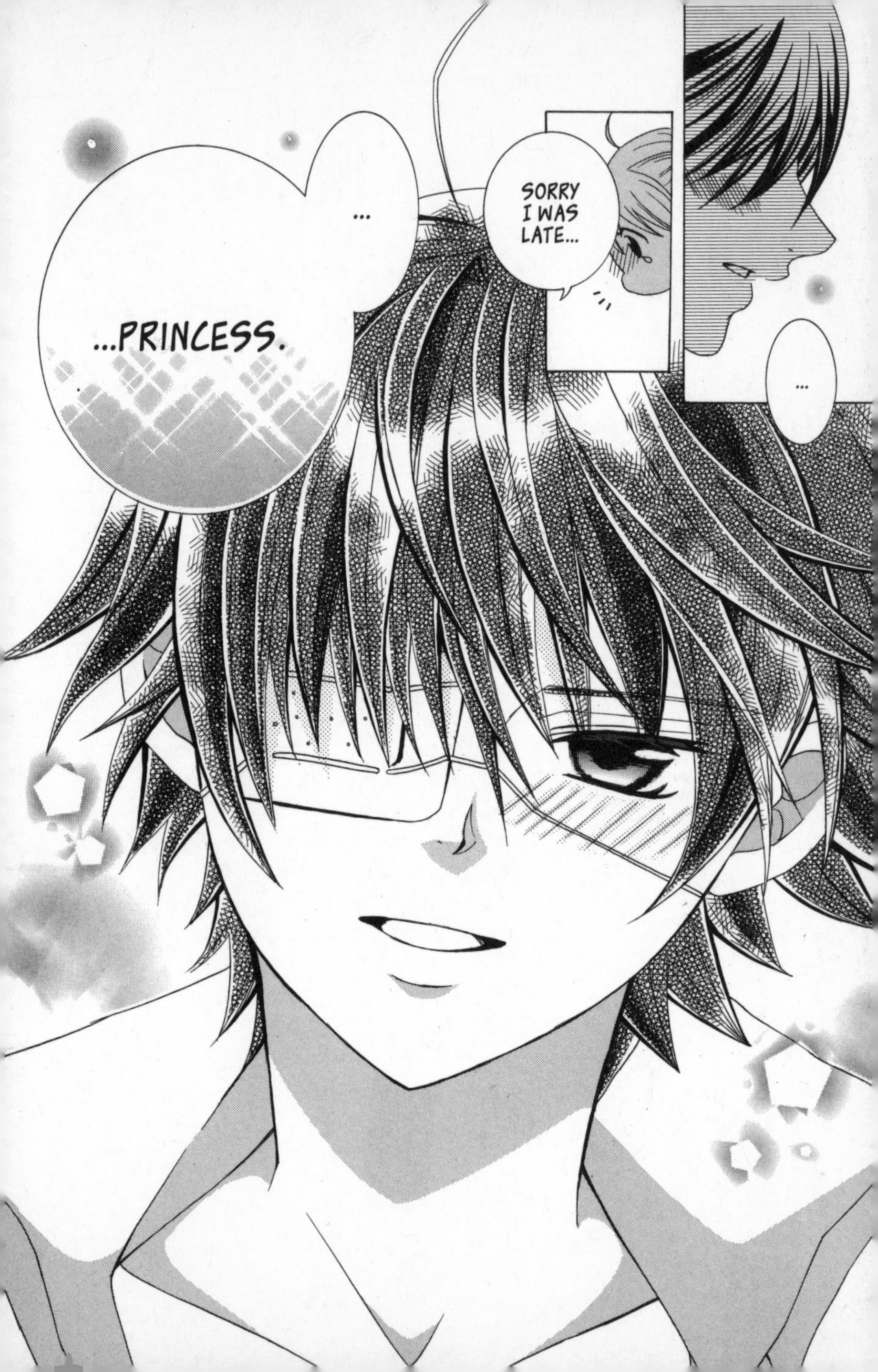
...
SORRY I WAS LATE...
...
...PRINCESS.

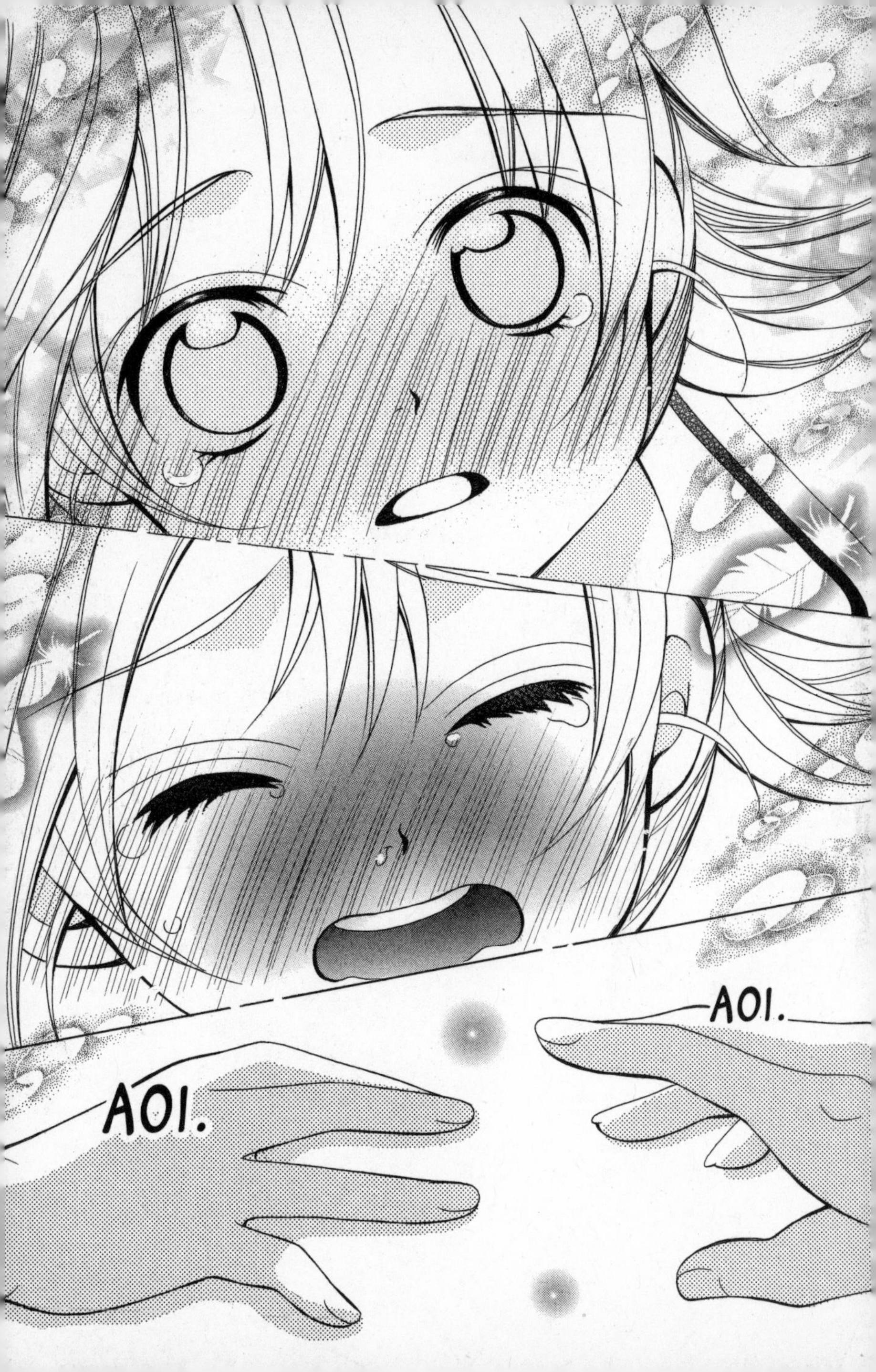
AOI.
AOI.

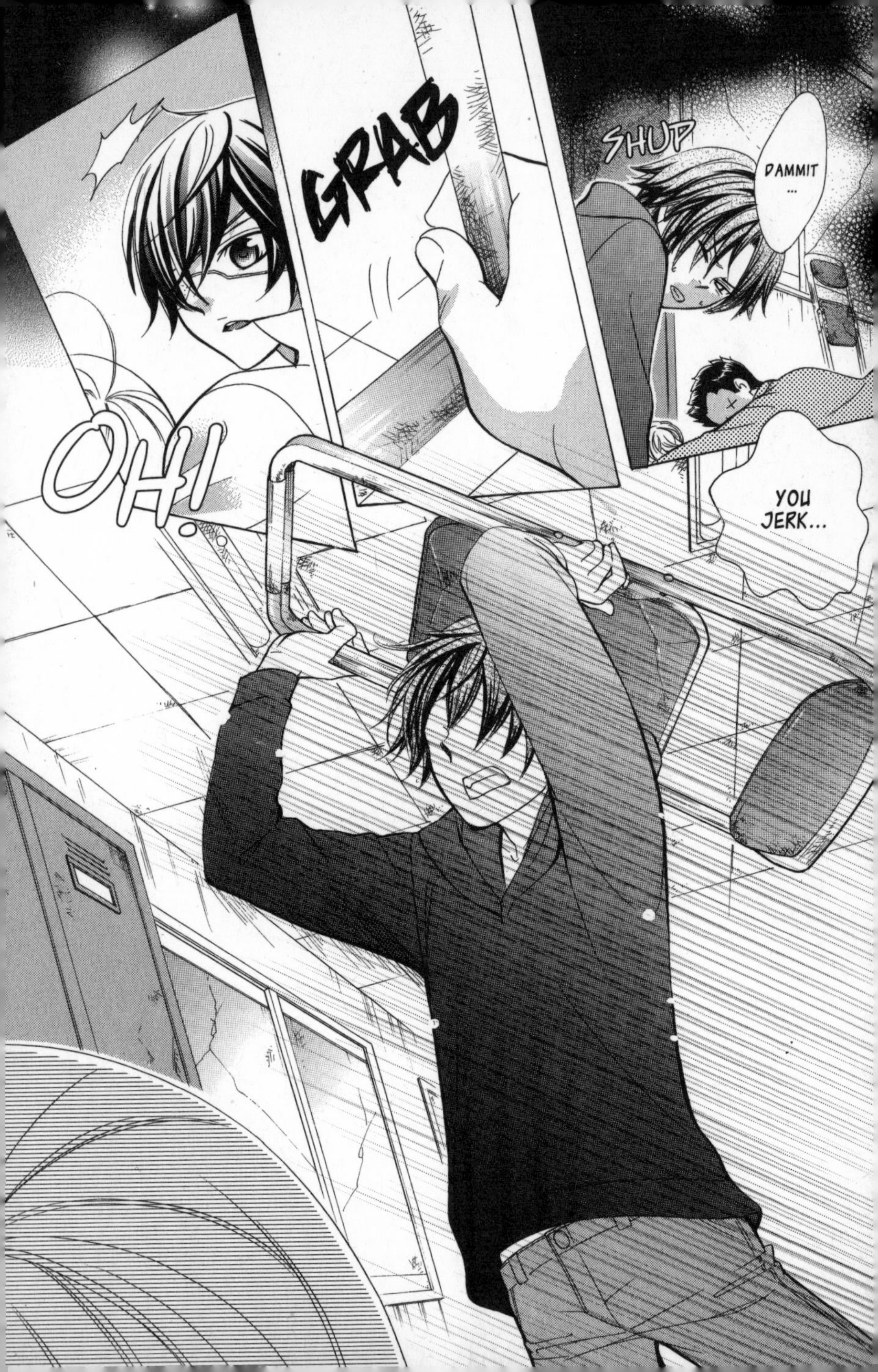
SHUP
DAMMIT ...
YOU JERK...
GRAB
OH!

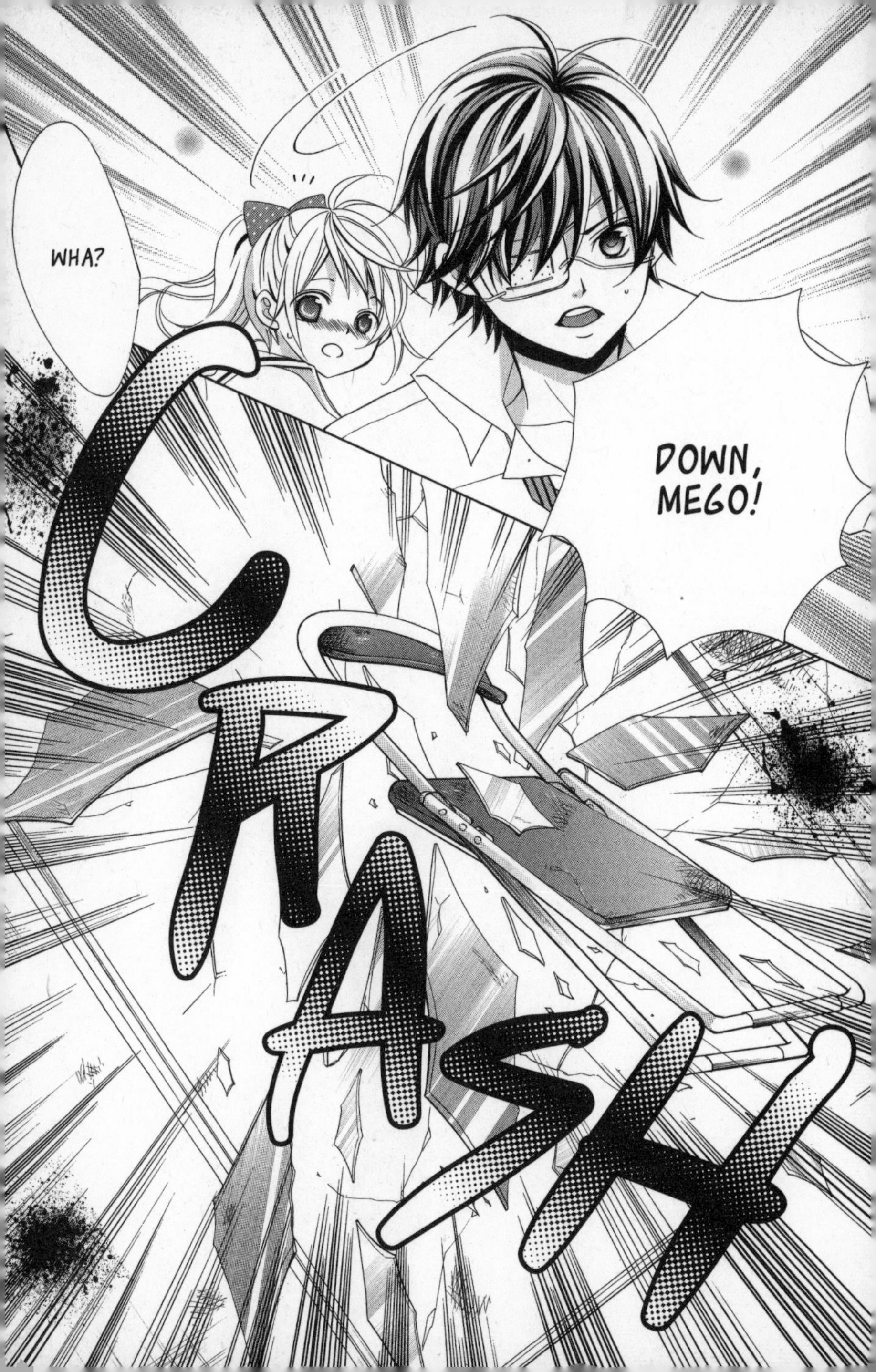
DOWN, MEGO!
WHA?
CRASH

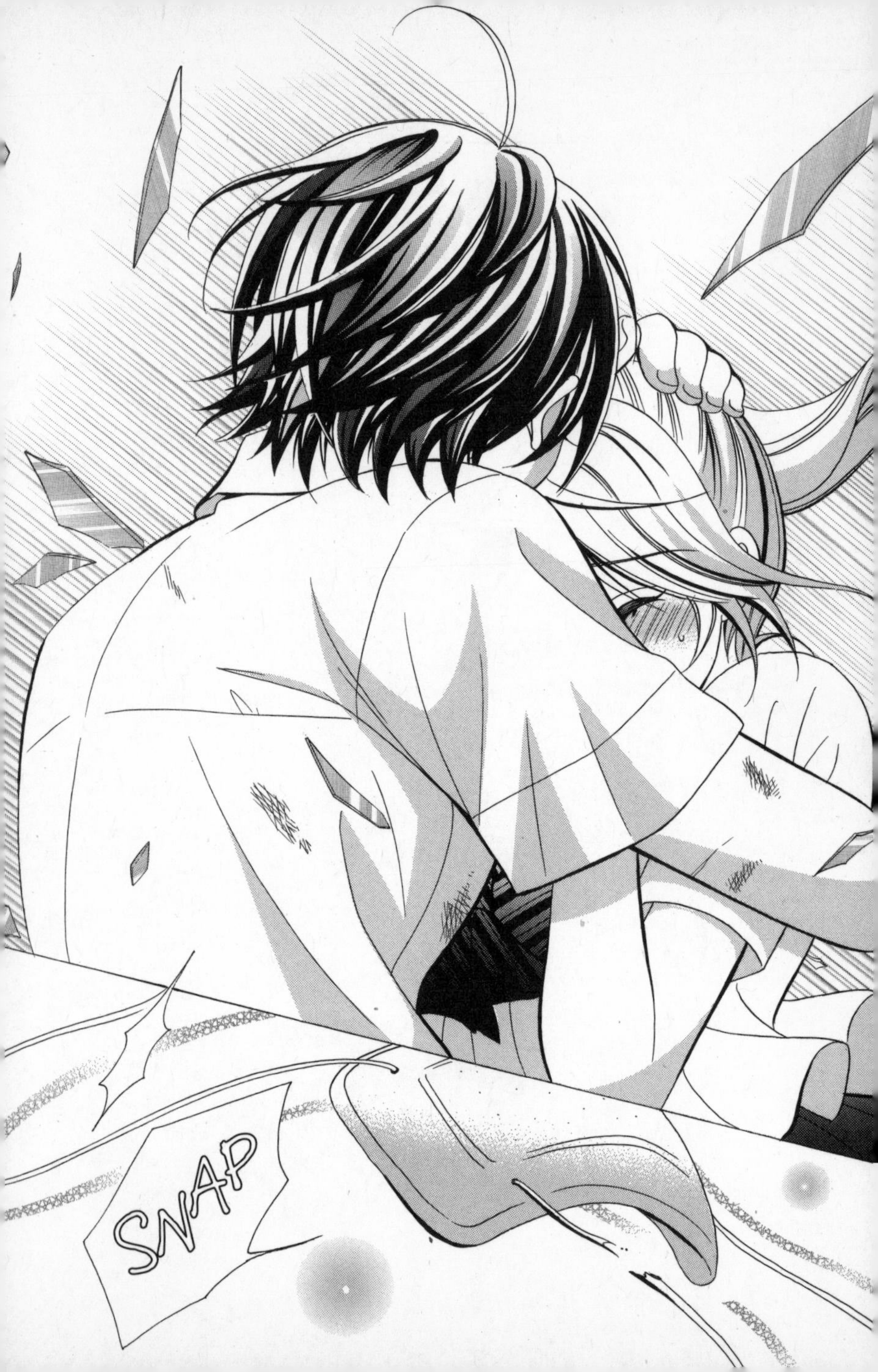
SNAP

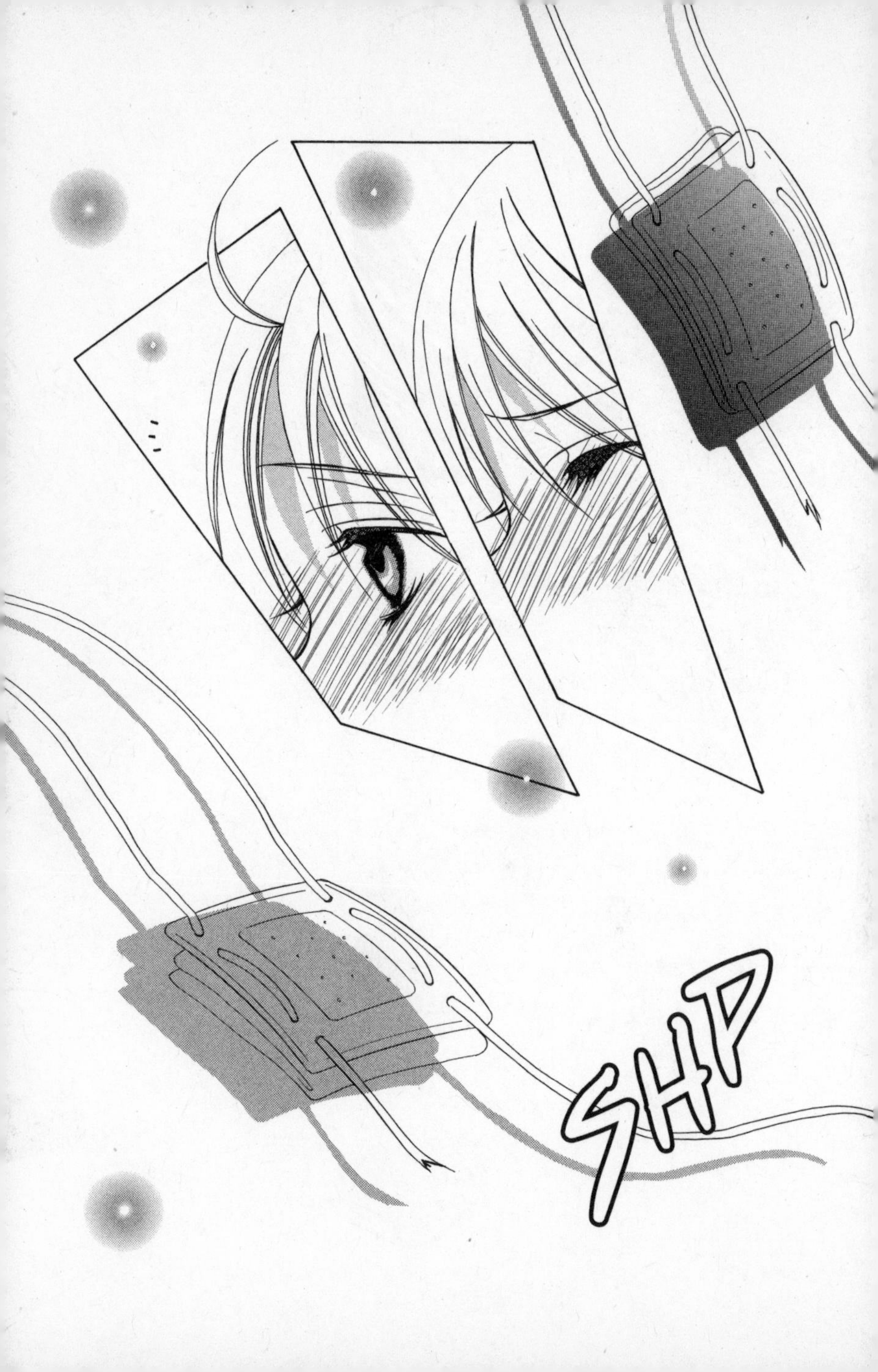
SHP

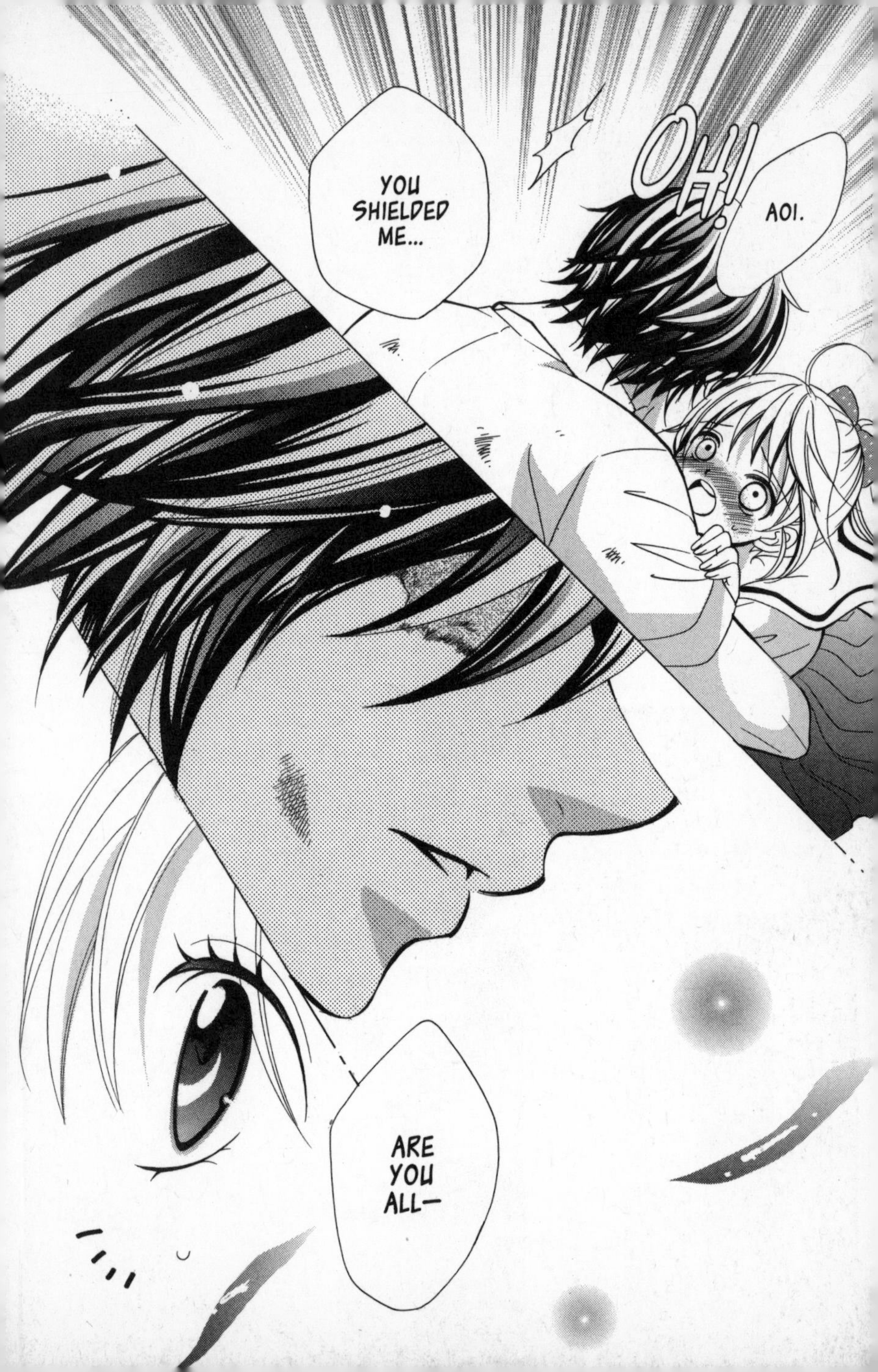
OH!
AOI.
YOU SHIELDED ME...
ARE YOU ALL—

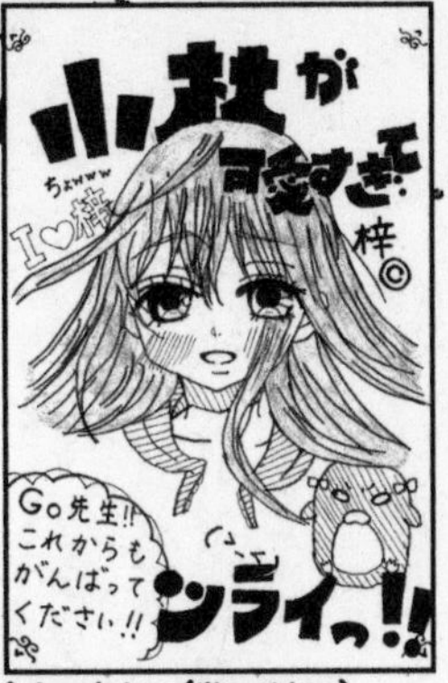
小林が可愛すぎ
梓©
Go先生!! これからもがんばってください!!
ツライっ!!
↑ Sue Arima (Hiroshima)
Ed.: Azusa = beautiful! Azusa penguin = cute!

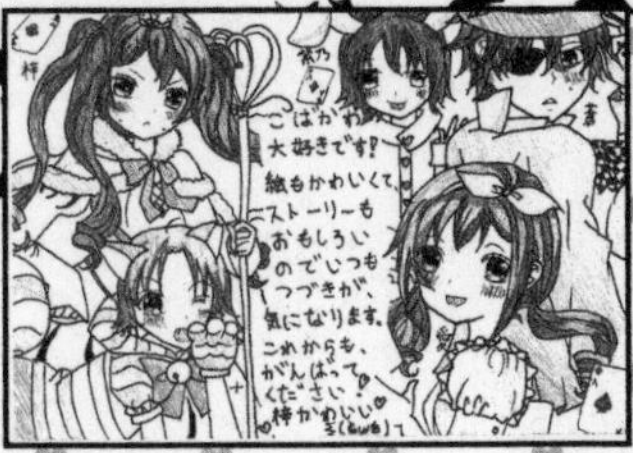
こばかわ大好きです! 絵もかわいくて、ストーリーもおもしろいのでいつもつづきが、気になります。これからも、がんばってください。
梓かわいい
← Mikan (Kyoto)
Ed.: The main characters are all here! Gorgeous!

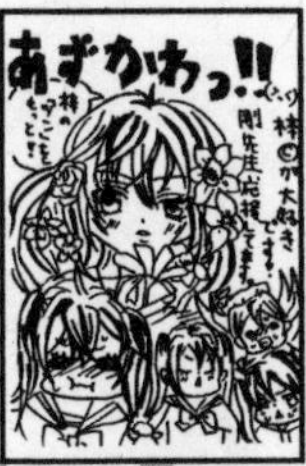
あずかわっ!!
→ Makurrari (Tokyo)
Ed: Is Azusa tsun-tsun-tsun-dere?

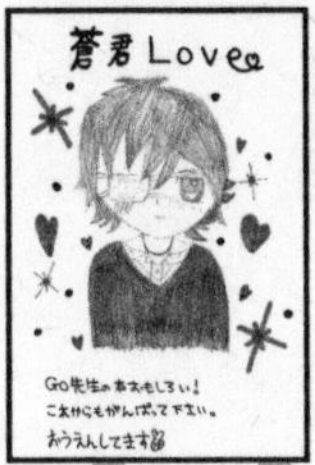
蒼君Love
Go先生のおもしろい! これからもがんばってください。おうえんしてます
← Coco (Niigata)
Ed.: I love Aoi's smile!

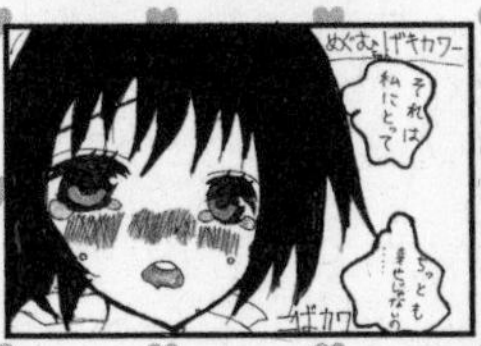
← Ruka Miyazaki (Oita)
Ed.: Mego... don't you cry. (>_<)

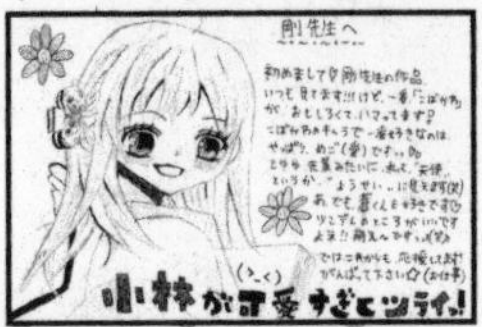
剛先生へ
小林が可愛すぎてツライ!
↑ Makaron ☆ (Hokkaido)
Ed.: Angel Mego... ♥
(I wanna get married.)

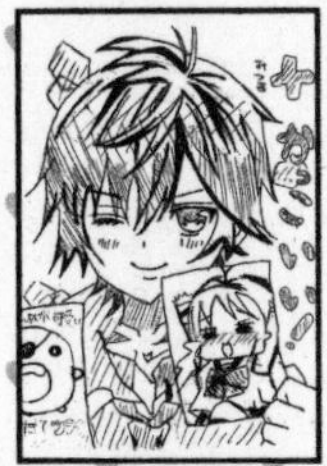
↑ Konoka Nishikawa (Chiba)
Ed.: Mitsuru has become a fine young man.

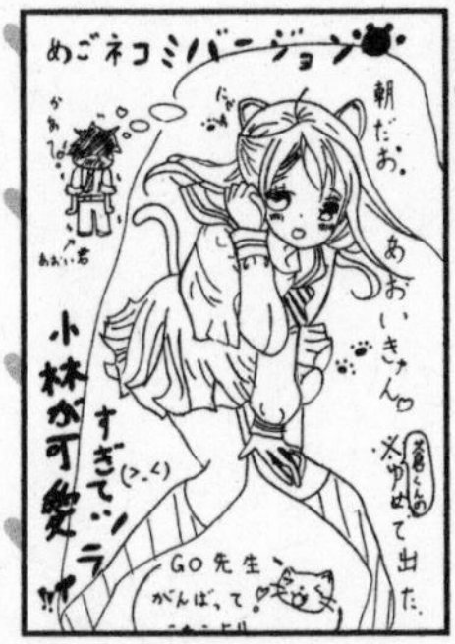
めごネコミバージョン
小林が可愛すぎてツラ
Go先生 がんばって
← Koneko (Kagawa)
Ed.: Aoi, you had a good dream. ♥

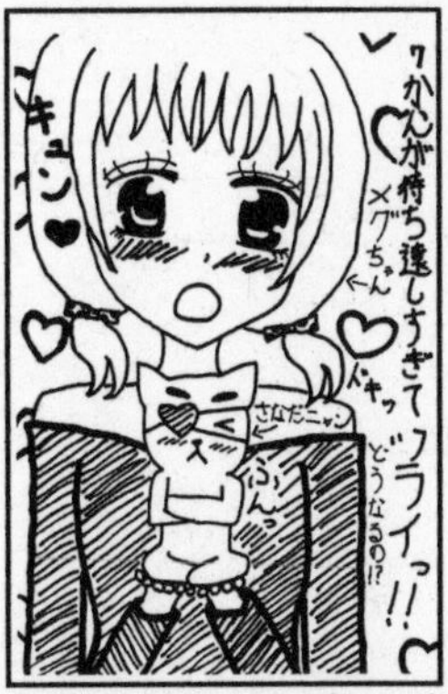
キュン
メグちゃん
ドキッ
さなだニャン
ツライっ!!
どうなるの!?
↑ Mayuge Watanabe (Iwate)
Ed.: Did Sanada Cat steal the show? (><)

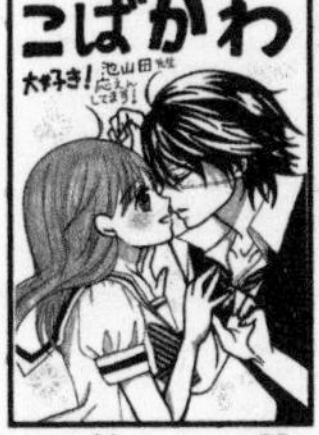
こばかわ
大好き!
← Mayuka Takahashi (Saitama)
Ed.: The two are so in love. ♥

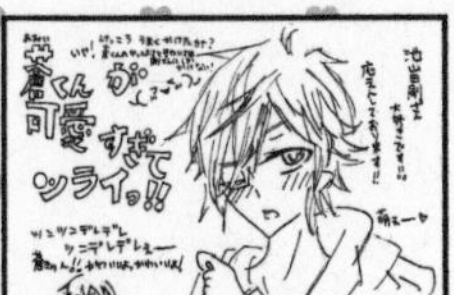
蒼くんが可愛すぎてツライっ!!
↑ Alfoo! (Shizuoka)
Ed.: A cool and cute Aoi!

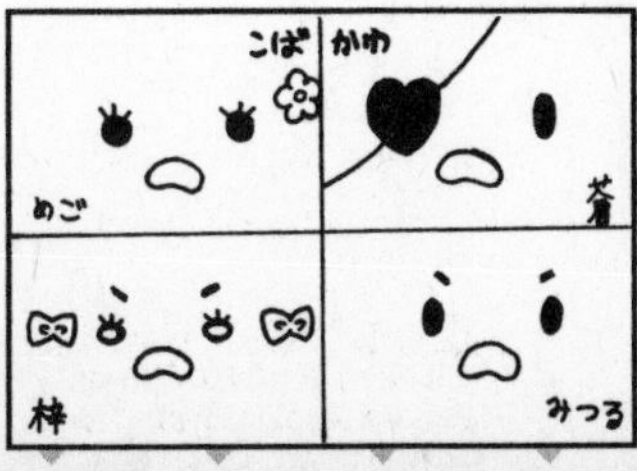
こばかわ
めご
蒼
梓
みつる
← Aoi Otake (Aichi)
Ed.: The four penguins! They're so cute!!

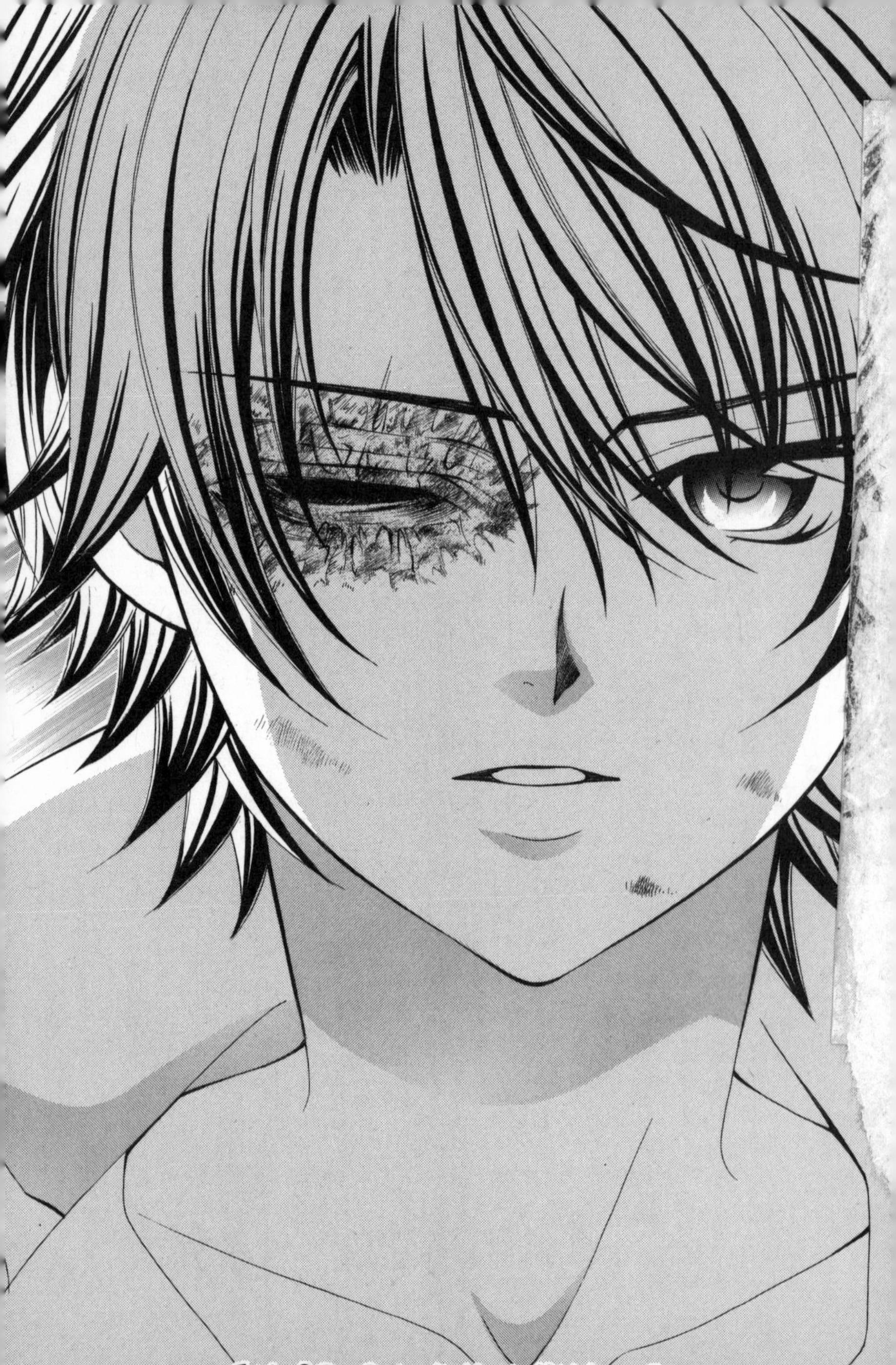

End of *So Cute It Hurts!!* Volume 9

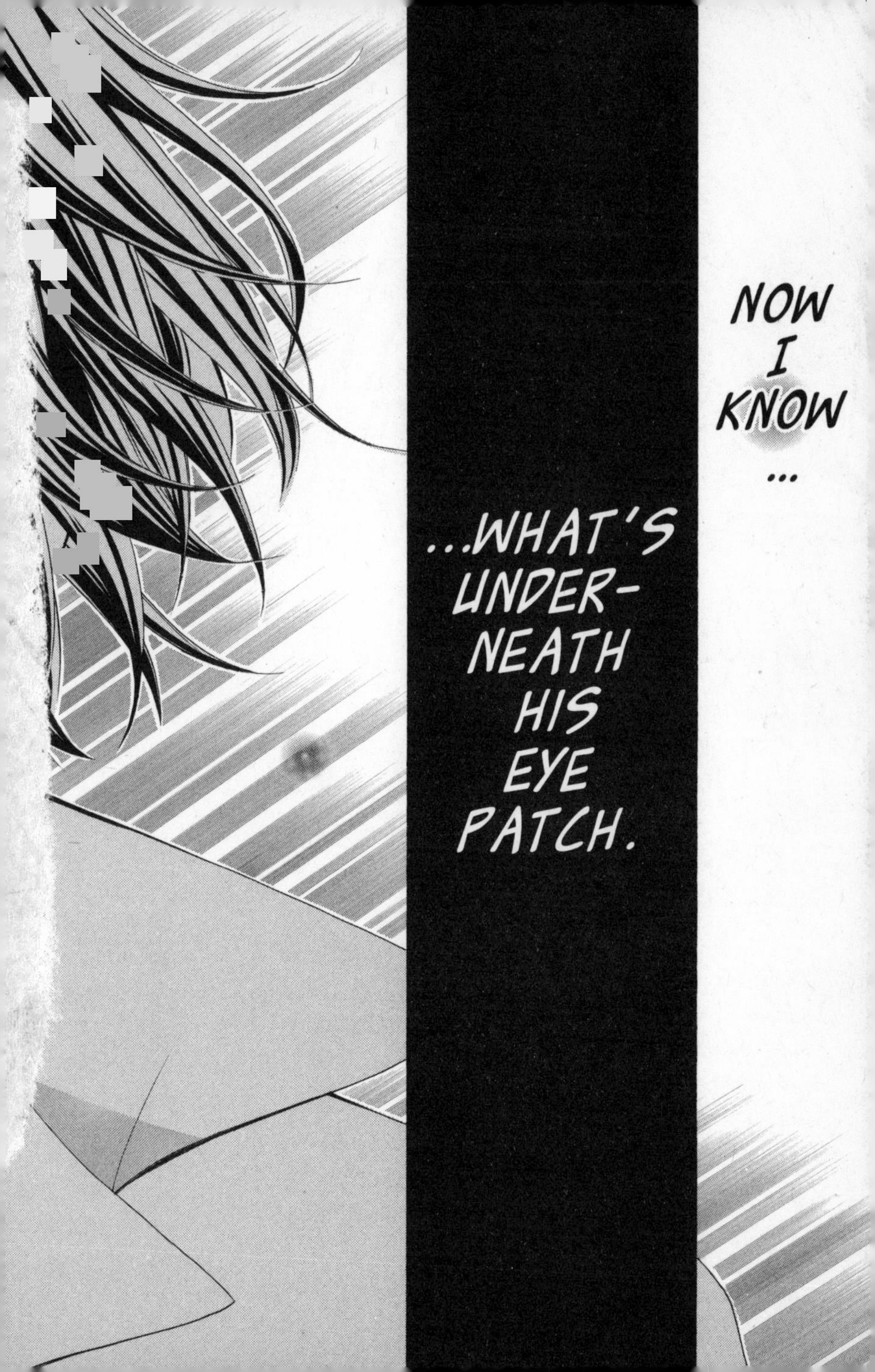
NOW I KNOW...
...WHAT'S UNDER-NEATH HIS EYE PATCH.

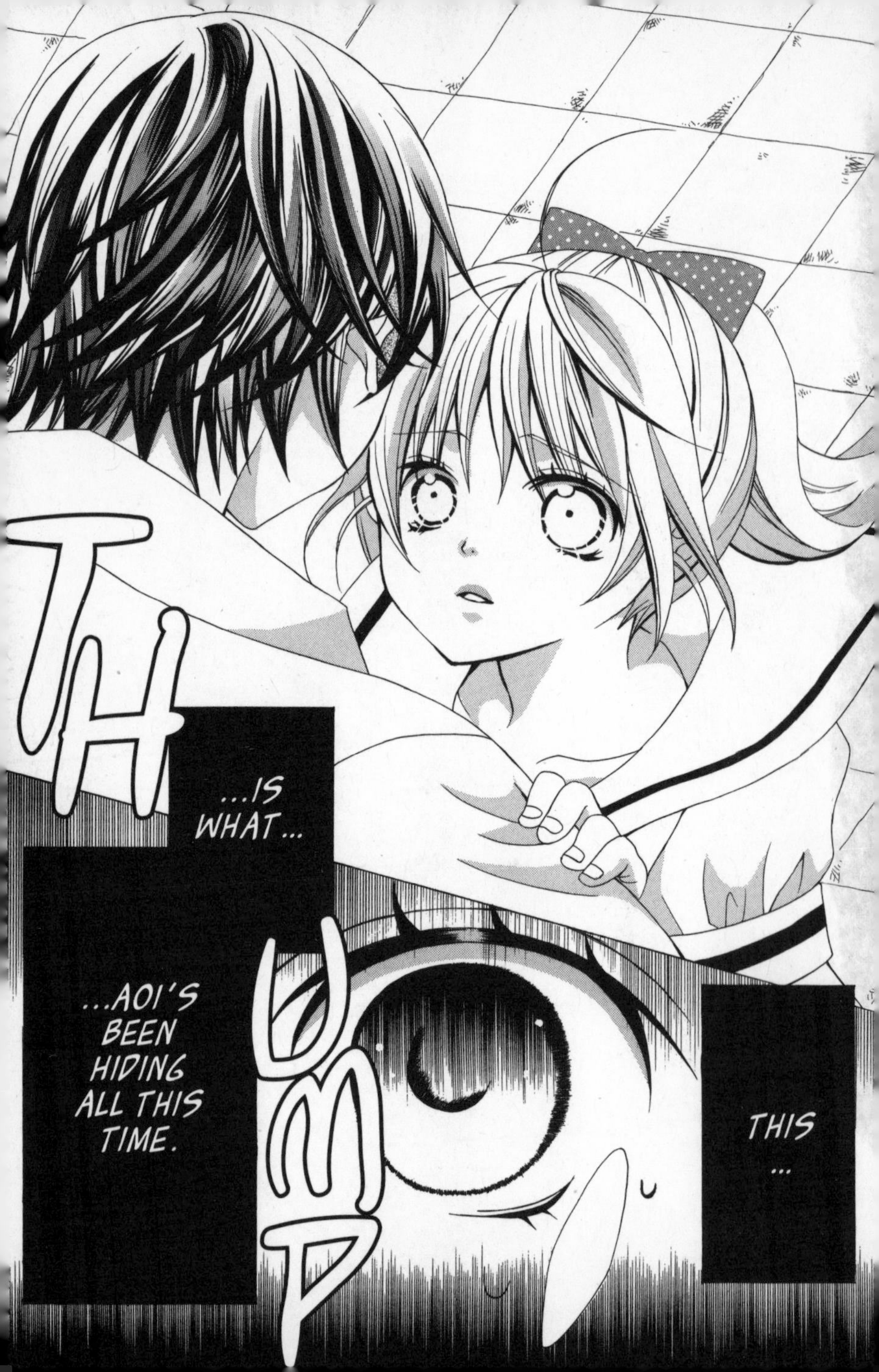
THIS...
...IS WHAT...
...AOI'S BEEN HIDING ALL THIS TIME.
THUMP

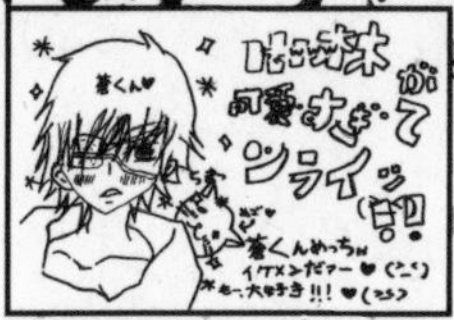

↑ Anna Hashizume (Shizuoka)
Ed.: The cat Mego likes Aoi too!

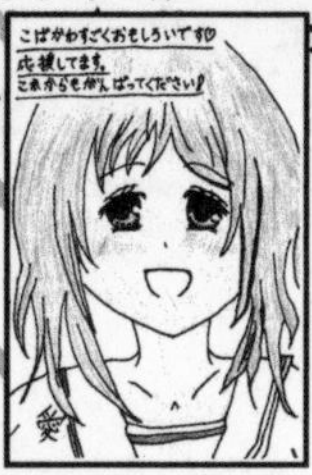

Saho Umeki ☆ (Osaka)
Ed.: Mego was born to make people smile!

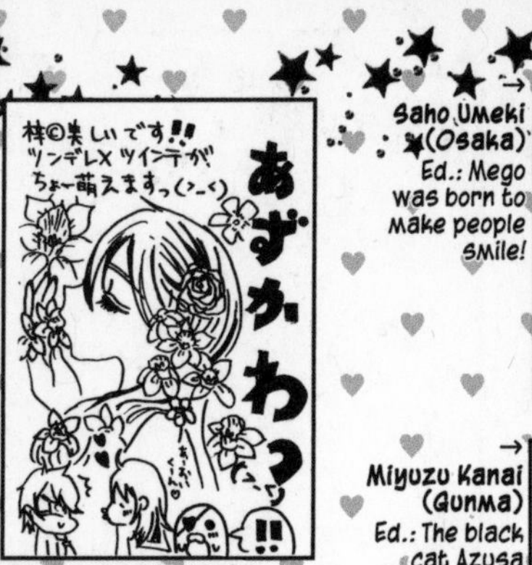

↑ Makurrori (Tokyo)
Ed.: Tsundere x Twin tail = Mega impact!!

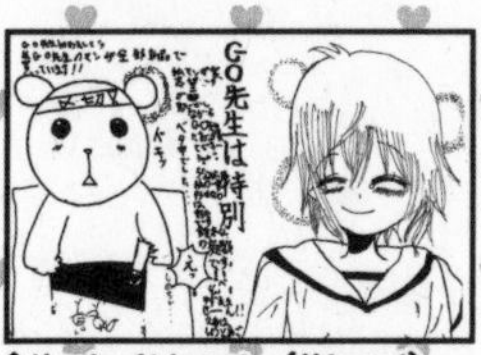

↑ Karin Shinzato (Miyagi)
Ed.: GO-chan, good job inking!

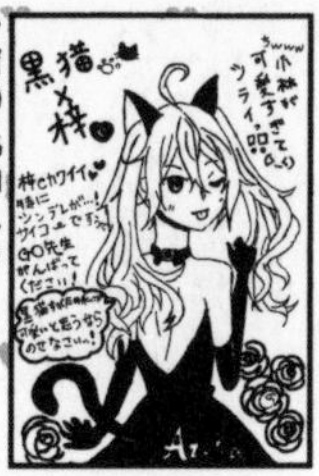

Miyuzu Kanai (Gunma)
Ed.: The black cat Azusa is sexy. ♥

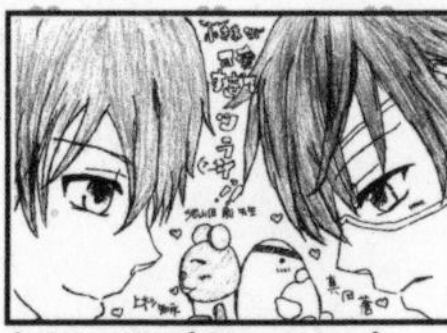

↑ Mika Kia (Kagoshima)
Ed.: The hottest pair right now!

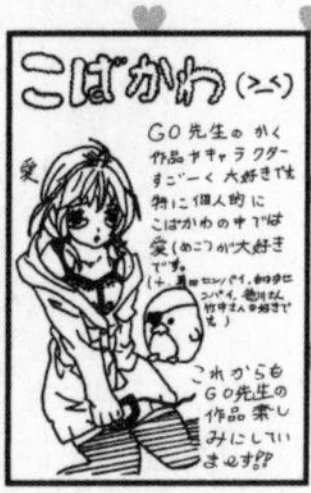

Ayami Ozaki (Kagawa)
Ed.: Mego and penguin. They're too cute. ♥

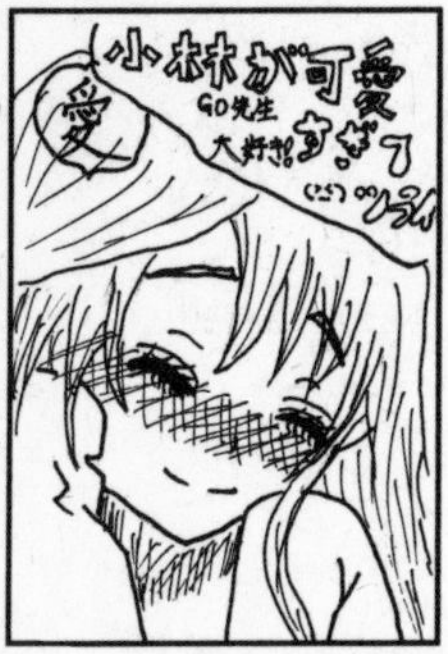

Saya Kuriyama (Gifu)
Ed.: Mego's smile makes you happy...

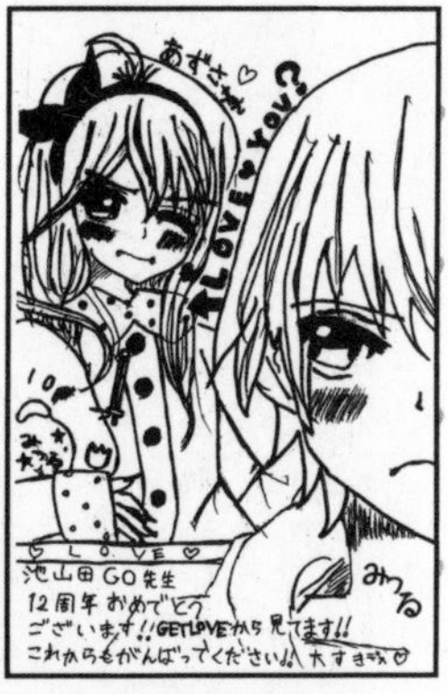

Haa-chan (Okayama)
Ed.: These two will soon realize they like each other...?

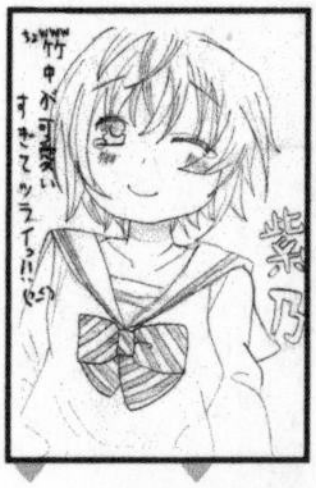

Runa Ikeda (Okinawa)
Ed.: Yeah, we wanna see Shino appear more often.

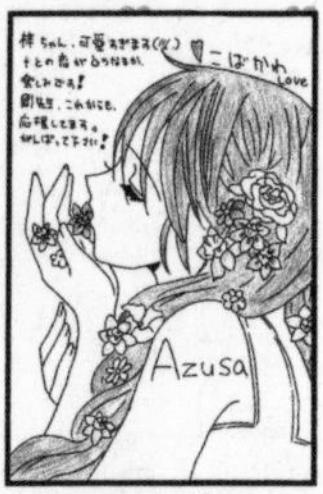

↑ Kanoneko (Okayama)
Ed.: This Azusa looks way too beautiful!

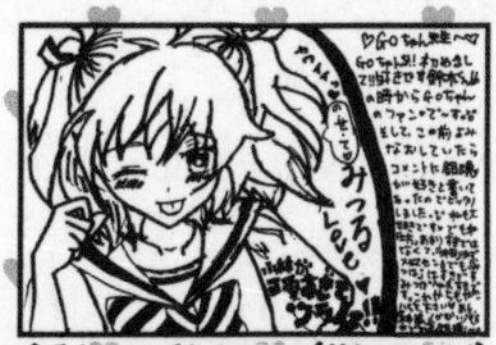

↑ I Love Gintama (Miyazaki)
Ed.: Mitsuru's "my bad" isn't fair!

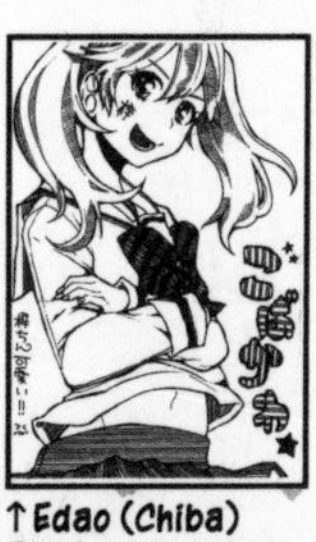

↑ Edao (Chiba)
Ed.: A peek at her belly got me!

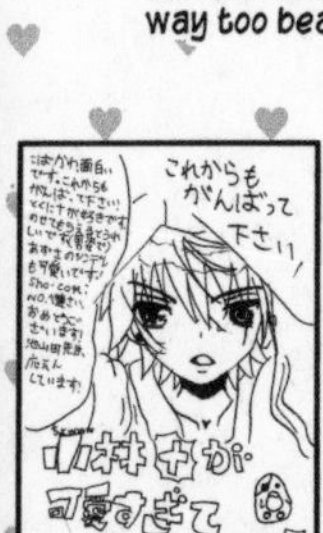

GO-chan ☆ LOVE (Kanagawa)
Ed.: Readers always like Mitsuru!

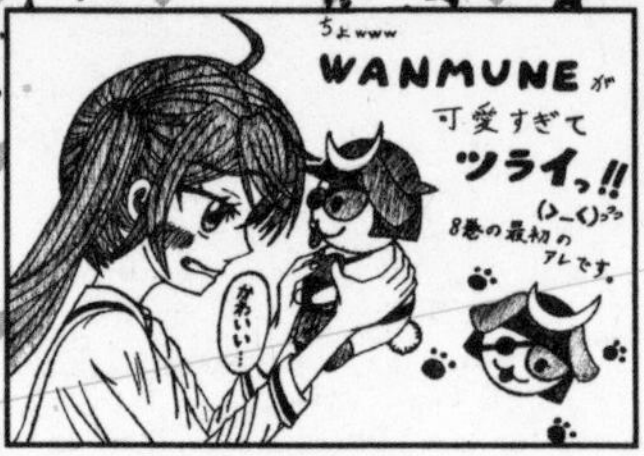
WANMUNE が
可愛すぎて
ツライっ!!
8巻の最初のアレです。
かわいい…

← Asakurakamo (Saitama)
Ed.: Thanks for the plushie!

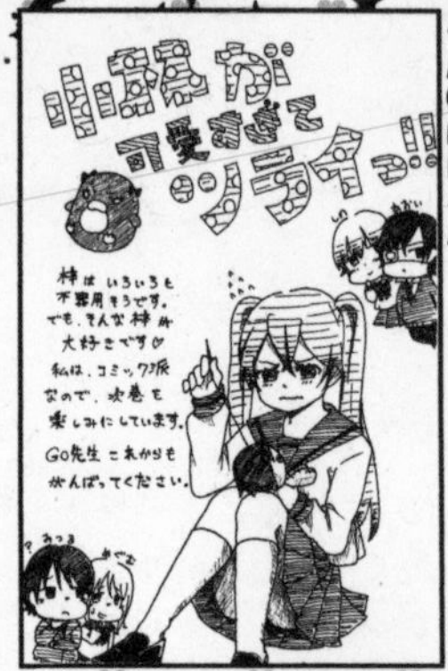
梓はいろいろも不器用そうです。でも、そんな梓が大好きです♡
私は、コミック派なので、次巻を楽しみにしています。
Go先生これからもがんばってください。

← Miisa (Hokkaido)
Ed.: Don't you love the awkward Azusa?

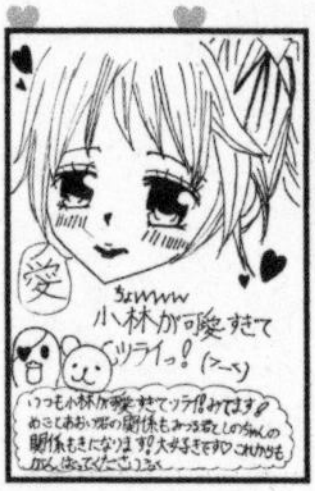

← Sumiren Yamamoto (Hyogo)
Ed.: Mego's so cute it hurts!! (><)

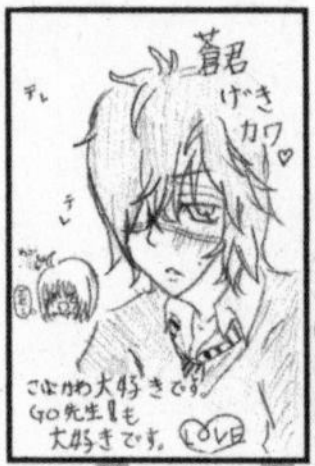
蒼君
げきカワ
こばかわ大好きです。
GO先生も大好きです。
LOVE

← Satomi Sato (Miyagi)
Ed.: My heart flutters at this cute Aoi. ♥

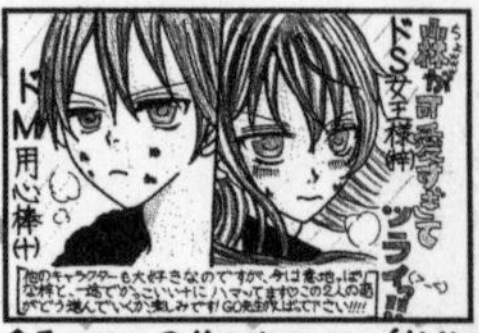

↑ Fuwa x 2 Mashumaro (Akita)
Ed.: Mighty Azusa and Mitsuru the masochist...

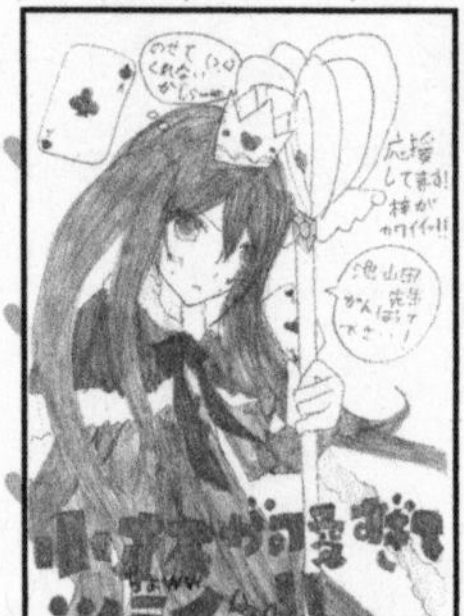

← Rikapon (Osaka)
Ed.: Azusa is queen!!

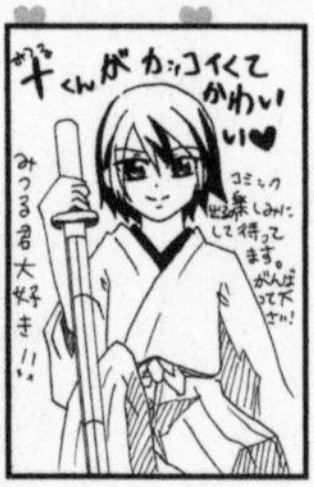
十くんがカッコイくてかわいい♥
みつる君大好き!!
コミック楽しみにして待ってます。がんばって下さい!

→ Yoshie Suzuki (Shizuoka)
Ed.: He looks great in his kendo uniform!

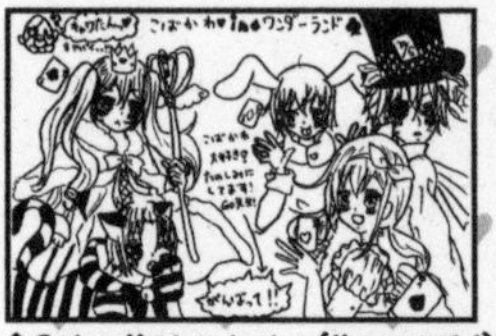

↑ Ruka Matsukata (Nagasaki)
Ed.: Their cosplay looks great!

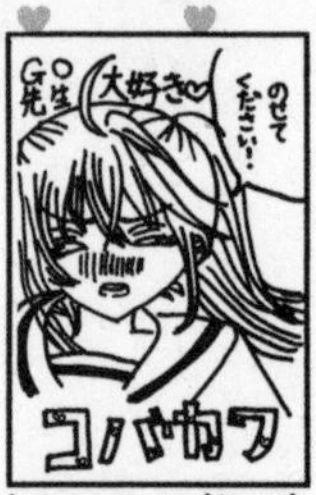
GO先生
大好き
のせてください!
コバカワ

↑ Sahorin ♪ (Aichi)
Ed.: I love the way she's blushing. ♥

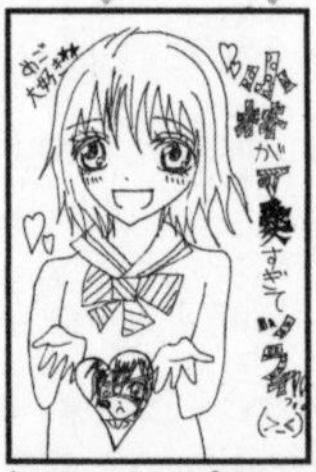

↑ Miyu Kyan (Osaka)
Ed.: Mego's heart is filled with Aoi. ♥

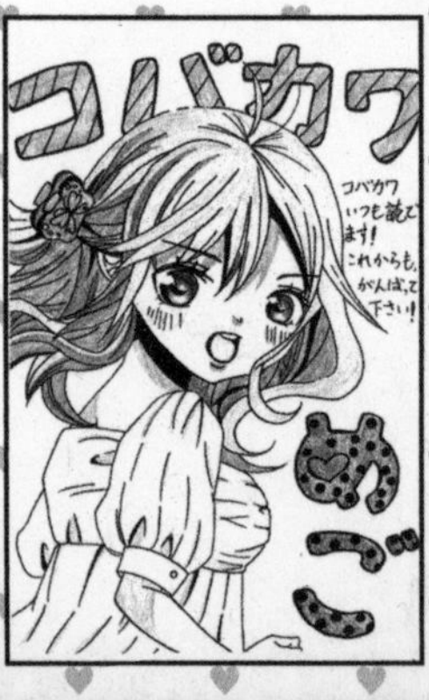
コバカワ
コバカワいつも読んでます!
これからも、がんばって下さい!
めご

→ Mei Ozawa (Saitama)
Ed.: Mego is strong and beautiful!!

Send your fan mail to:

Go Ikeyamada
c/o Shojo Beat
VIZ Media, LLC
P.O. Box 77010
San Francisco, CA 94107

AUTHOR BIO

I drew the above illustration for the cover of *Sho-Comi* issue 15, 2014. I was surprised and moved that I got to draw eight magazine covers in 2014...! (*ToT) I'm also grateful I could draw so many color title pages! The cover illustration for the next volume is something I've wanted to draw for a long time. The critical moment is coming up soon in the story. I put all my soul into drawing the color illustration and the story itself, so I hope you read it!

Go Ikeyamada is a Gemini from Miyagi Prefecture whose hobbies include taking naps and watching movies. Her debut manga *Get Love!!* appeared in *Shojo Comic* in 2002, and her current work *So Cute It Hurts!!* (*Kobayashi ga Kawai Suguite Tsurai!!*) is being published by VIZ Media.

SO CUTE IT HURTS!!
Volume 9

Shojo Beat Edition

STORY AND ART BY
GO IKEYAMADA

English Translation & Adaptation/Tomo Kimura
Touch-Up Art & Lettering/Joanna Estep
Design/Izumi Evers
Editor/Pancha Diaz

KOBAYASHI GA KAWAISUGITE TSURAI!! Vol.9
by Go IKEYAMADA
© 2012 Go IKEYAMADA
All rights reserved.
Original Japanese edition published by SHOGAKUKAN.
English translation rights in the United States of America, Canada,
United Kingdom and Ireland arranged with SHOGAKUKAN.

The stories, characters and incidents mentioned in
this publication are entirely fictional.

Printed in the U.S.A.

Published by VIZ Media, LLC
P.O. Box 77010
San Francisco, CA 94107

10 9 8 7 6 5 4 3 2 1
First printing, October 2016

www.viz.com   www.shojobeat.com

PARENTAL ADVISORY
SO CUTE IT HURTS!! is rated T for
Teen and is recommended for ages
13 and up.
ratings.viz.com